ALTRUISM

ALTRUISM

Edited by

**Ellen Frankel Paul, Fred D. Miller, Jr.,
and Jeffrey Paul**

CAMBRIDGE
UNIVERSITY PRESS

Published by the Press Syndicate of the University of Cambridge
The Pitt Building, Trumpington Street, Cambridge CB2 1RP, England
40 West 20th Street, New York, NY 10011, USA
10 Stamford Road, Oakleigh, Melbourne, Victoria 3166, Australia

First published 1993

Printed in the United States of America

Library of Congress Cataloging-in-Publication Data applied for

ISBN 0-521-44759-3 paperback

This is a special edition of Volume 10, Number 1 of the
journal *Social Philosophy & Policy*, and is available
as part of a subscription to the journal.

CONTENTS

INTRODUCTION

The term "altruism" was first used by the French philosopher Auguste Comte (1798–1857) to denote a devotion to the interests of others as an action-guiding principle. Altruism was thus opposed to egoism, a devotion to one's own interests. Comte held that "the chief problem of human life [is] the subordination of egoism to altruism."* Earlier philosophers discussed the matter in different terms — "beneficence," "charity," or "compassion" instead of "altruism" — but the proper balance to be struck between an individual's regard for himself and his regard for others has always been a central issue of moral philosophy.

The essays in this volume address this fundamental issue. Some discuss the nature of altruistic feelings and the possibility of altruistic actions. Some dispute Comte's claim that egoism is to be "subordinated" to altruism, arguing that self-interest is compatible with regard for others, and that in some cases one's own needs must be given priority. Other essays look at the relationship between morality and rationality, and attempt to explain what reasons we can have for acting altruistically. Still others consider the extent to which we may properly be forced to serve one another's interests, and examine the role government should play in regulating our interactions.

In the first essay of this collection, "Beneficence and Self-Love: A Kantian Perspective," Thomas E. Hill, Jr., explores Immanuel Kant's views on the possibility of altruism. Many philosophers have attempted to determine whether altruistic actions are possible by observing the relative strength and prevalence of altruistic and egoistic feelings: one extreme view holds that human beings are solely motivated by self-interest, and that genuine altruism is impossible; another holds that sympathy for others is a part of human nature, and that we have a duty to attribute as much importance to the interests of others as we do to our own. But Kant held neither position; he approached the matter differently, believing that for practical purposes we cannot take the strength of our feelings as determining, in ordinary cases, what we can do or what we ought to do. A consideration of the prevalence of different kinds of feelings is essential if our purpose is to predict how people will behave in a given situation, but if we view ourselves as agents engaged in deliberation about what to do, we must take a different perspective. Kant held that when deliberating we must presuppose (absent decisive empirical evidence to the contrary) that we have options and can act as reason requires, even when we are not inclined to do so. The key question then, Hill argues, is not

---

* Auguste Comte, *Auguste Comte and Positivism: The Essential Writings*, ed. Gertrud Lenzer (Chicago: University of Chicago Press, 1983), p. 400.

whether altruistic behavior is possible, but whether there are reasons to act to promote the interests of others, that is, to act beneficently. He concludes by examining Kant's arguments for a general duty of beneficence.

Christine M. Korsgaard's essay is also concerned with the reasons we have for acting in certain ways toward others. Indeed, in "The Reasons We Can Share: An Attack on the Distinction between Agent-Relative and Agent-Neutral Values," Korsgaard argues that the proper subject matter of morality is not what sort of world we should produce (as some utilitarians might claim), but how we should relate to one another. She takes as her starting point Thomas Nagel's work on the nature of reasons and values in *The Possibility of Altruism* and *The View from Nowhere*. In the former, Nagel argued that all reasons and values must be objective, that is, valid for all agents; in the latter, he argued that some are subjective (agent-relative) and others are objective (agent-neutral). Korsgaard examines several kinds of reasons for acting that motivated Nagel to alter his position—reasons which do not seem to be objective. The most important of these are reasons of autonomy, those relating to personal projects or ambitions. Such reasons seem capable of prompting action only on the part of the actor whose project or ambition is involved; others may well be indifferent to his ambition and have no stake in his success or failure. Nagel concluded from this that such reasons are agent-relative, but Korsgaard suggests that they should be considered intersubjective, that is, capable of being understood and shared by others. She argues that viewing reasons and values as intersubjective helps us understand how one person can develop a desire to promote another's projects, and that this process—the process of discovering reasons that can be shared—is an important and often overlooked area of moral theory.

Like Korsgaard, David Schmidtz is concerned with how we come to have reasons for caring about the interests and well-being of others. His "Reasons for Altruism" explores the ways in which people can develop regard for others, and why it is rational for them to do so. Schmidtz begins with the limiting case of someone who is purely self-regarding, who cares about no one's welfare but his own. Could such a person discover reasons for acting altruistically, for pursuing goals that are not self-regarding? On the standard model of rationality—the instrumental model—goals are viewed as given, that is, not subject to rational criticism. But the fact remains that we do evaluate our goals; we care about whether the things we choose to do are worth doing. In turn, the choices we make affect the development of our character. Schmidtz argues that concern for our own health, survival, and growth can lead us to cultivate concern for others. It can lead us to make commitments to behaving altruistically, and to follow through on those commitments, even when that means acting in ways that run against our pure self-interest. Developing these kinds of commitments, Schmidtz concludes, is part of what makes our lives worth living.

Robert Sugden takes up the critique of the instrumental model of rationality in his "Thinking as a Team: Towards an Explanation of Nonselfish Behavior." He agrees with Schmidtz that the instrumental model is incapable of giving an adequate account of altruistic behavior. Noting that economists usually explain such behavior by retaining the assumption of instrumental rationality but assuming individuals to have altruistic preferences, Sugden explores an alternative explanation offered by theories of cooperation, in which each individual acts on the rule that, if followed by all, would yield the most-preferred outcome. He examines a class of problems in which the participants must coordinate their actions in order to achieve an outcome that would be best for all. In each problem, it seems intuitively obvious that rational individuals would choose a certain action, but Sugden shows that their choice could not be justified within the conventional theory of rationality. He goes on to argue that the proper choice could be justified within a theory of cooperation in which individuals "think as a team."

The essays of Schmidtz and Sugden cast doubt on the assumption that there is a strict dichotomy between altruistic and self-interested behavior. In her contribution to this volume, Neera Kapur Badhwar challenges this assumption directly. "Altruism Versus Self-Interest: Sometimes a False Dichotomy" develops the idea that there is a kind of moral excellence which is both a form of deep altruism and a form of self-interest. Like Schmidtz, Badhwar believes that self-interest includes an interest in defining and affirming one's character, in expressing and strengthening the dispositions that help make up one's identity. She also argues that, for some people, such self-affirmation is a necessary and sufficient motivation for acting in a wholeheartedly altruistic manner. To support her claim, Badhwar considers the example of rescuers of Jews in Nazi Europe during the Second World War. Recent research into the motives of these rescuers suggests that they acted as they did without expecting rewards of any kind and with a full understanding of the risks involved. They acted spontaneously, and many believed that their actions were not out of the ordinary. The research suggests that the rescuers' conception of themselves as part of a "common humanity" caused them to identify others' interests with their own, and led them to believe that they had no choice but to act as they did. Badhwar argues that in lending assistance to Jews, the rescuers were acting to affirm their own identities as parts of a community. She concludes that an interest in such self-affirmation can have moral worth even if the dispositions it affirms are primarily self-interested, and that in the absence of the right kind and degree of self-interest, altruism would fail to be a virtue.

The activities of the rescuers exemplify a particularly demanding form of altruism, one that involves great risk and sacrifice on behalf of strangers. In "Cosmopolitan Altruism," William A. Galston explores the nature of this kind of activity, distinguishing it from other forms of altruism in

terms of the scope of the actors' concern for others, the kinds of risks they
are willing to take, their motivations, and the ways in which they evaluate their own actions. Like Badhwar, Galston questions whether altruism is always and unconditionally a virtue. He argues that the kind of
altruistic activity undertaken by the rescuers—cosmopolitan altruism—
does not necessarily represent moral progress over forms of conduct governed by more personal, individualistic ties. He notes that in aiding Jews,
the rescuers frequently put both themselves and their families at risk (often without their family members' consent). Moreover, the kind of sin-
gle-mindedness and independence that made it possible for the rescuers
to act as they did often left them indifferent to postwar efforts to honor
them and unable to understand or relate to those who wished to commend their activities. These facts lead Galston to question whether the
widening of moral sympathy to encompass endangered strangers is always worth the significant moral costs which it entails.

The theme of altruism's moral costs is picked up in Jean Hampton's
contribution to this volume, "Selflessness and the Loss of Self." Hampton notes that philosophers who commend altruism usually assume that
someone who neglects his own welfare in order to promote that of another is a virtuous and praiseworthy figure. Yet she argues that not all
self-sacrifice is worthy of praise, and that not all such sacrifice really
benefits those whom it is intended to benefit. Rejecting the conception of
morality as purely other-regarding, Hampton sets out to examine its self-
regarding component. She maintains that a proper conception of morality would recognize that agents must respect themselves as valuable
human beings, and that they must have a sense of what they require to
flourish, both as human beings and as particular persons. On this view,
"selfless" acts which satisfy the needs of others while neglecting the actor's own needs are considered morally bad, while "selfish" acts that
demonstrate the actor's proper self-respect are considered morally good.
It is this self-regarding aspect of morality that enables us to develop our
own interests and projects, and to lead rich and fulfilling lives. The most
challenging task of a moral theory is to help us strike a balance between
the weight we give to our own interests and the weight we give to those
of others. A theory that directs us to give too much to others is as deficient as one that directs us to give too little.

While Hampton considers what we ought to be willing to do for others, Roderick T. Long considers what we may legitimately be forced to do
for them. In "Abortion, Abandonment, and Positive Rights: The Limits
of Compulsory Altruism," Long uses the case of a mother's obligations
to her unborn or newborn child to explore the extent of positive rights—
rights that justify forcing some individuals to take positive action for the
sake of others (as opposed to negative rights that require refraining from
certain kinds of action). Many people believe that abortion is permissible
while abandoning a newborn infant is not; yet many also believe that kill-

ing someone is far more serious than letting him die. These two judgments seem incompatible: for abortion seems to be an active killing, while abandonment seems to be a case of refraining from action, a letting-die. To resolve the apparent incompatibility, Long presents a model of rights expressed in terms of individual boundaries, where performing an action which involves using someone as a means to the ends of others is taken to be a crossing of his boundary. Long goes on to distinguish permissible boundary-crossings from impermissible ones, arguing that the crucial distinction lies between crossings that are required to repel someone else from one's own boundary and those that are not. He concludes that abortion is justified on the ground that it involves repelling the fetus from the mother's boundary, while abandonment has no such justification. His broader conclusion is that there are some positive rights (the newborn's right to be cared for and not abandoned is one), but that such rights are always derived from prior negative rights.

Positive rights and compulsory altruism are also the subject of Douglas J. Den Uyl's contribution to this collection, "The Right to Welfare and the Virtue of Charity." Den Uyl questions the compatibility of a duty to provide for the welfare needs of others with a conception of charitable giving as a virtue. The difficulty lies in the fact that the *duty* is considered a matter of justice—it can be enforced by the state—while the *virtue* of charity must be undertaken voluntarily. Den Uyl examines the history of views of charity, focusing on the treatment of the virtue in the writings of Thomas Aquinas, and the relationship between charity and classical-liberal political orders in the writings of Adam Smith. A crucial part of Den Uyl's project is to distinguish an early view of ethics as a tool of self-realization (a view inherited by Aquinas and Smith from Aristotle) and a more modern view of ethics based on adherence to duty, where one's duties are usually aimed at helping others. The virtue of charity is a carry-over from the earlier approach and implies a concern with the character of the giver of aid, while the right to welfare is a product of the modern approach and implies a focus on the needs of the recipients. Den Uyl argues that the theoretical framework needed to defend the virtue contrasts in many ways with the framework needed to defend the right, and that if we value the virtue of charity we may find that a classical-liberal political order can accommodate it far more readily than a socialist or welfare-statist model can.

The final essay in this volume, Tyler Cowen's "Altruism and the Argument from Offsetting Transfers," offers another view of the right to welfare. Some economists have argued that welfare programs are doomed to be ineffective because private individuals will adjust their own charitable gifts to offset any attempts by government to redistribute wealth. On this view, for example, government budget deficits would not constitute a genuine burden on future generations, since parents could offset the effects of such deficits by increasing gifts to their children, that is, by transferring the gains realized through deficit spending in the present to those who have to pay for that spending through higher taxes in the future. This argument relies, Cowen notes, on the assumption that people have at least some altruistic preferences and that they act rationally to fulfill them. But it also assumes that they have sufficient knowledge of the effects of government programs, and of the things they need to do to counteract those effects. Moreover, the argument neglects to take into account the fact that each individual is linked through chains of altruistic feelings to many others, and thus that there is an immense problem of coordination to be solved as each individual attempts to anticipate what the others will do. Cowen concludes that the preferences of private individuals for a particular distribution of wealth are far less effective than might be thought at offsetting the outcomes of government programs.

These ten essays offer a variety of views on the kinds of obligations we have toward others. It is hoped that they can provide valuable contributions to the debate over the centrality of altruism to morality, and over the nature and value of altruistic feelings and actions.

ACKNOWLEDGMENTS

This volume could not have been produced without the help of a number of individuals at the Social Philosophy and Policy Center, Bowling Green State University. Among them are Mary Dilsaver, Terrie Weaver, Jennifer Lange, and Maureen Kelley.

The editors would like to extend special thanks to Executive Manager Kory Swanson, for offering invaluable administrative support; to Publication Specialist Tamara Sharp, for attending to innumerable day-to-day details of the book's preparation; and to Managing Editor Harry Dolan, for providing dedicated assistance throughout the editorial and production process.

CONTRIBUTORS

Thomas E. Hill, Jr., is Professor of Philosophy at the University of North Carolina at Chapel Hill, where he has taught since 1984. He previously taught for sixteen years at the University of California, Los Angeles, and more briefly at Pomona College, Johns Hopkins University, and (on a visiting appointment) at Stanford University. He is the author of *Dignity and Practical Reason in Kant's Moral Theory* (Cornell University Press, 1992) and *Autonomy and Self-Respect* (Cambridge University Press, 1991), which are collections of essays on Kant's ethics and various moral problems.

Christine M. Korsgaard is Professor of Philosophy at Harvard University, where she received her Ph.D. in 1981. She has taught at Yale, the University of California, and the University of Chicago. Her published essays concern the ethical theories of Kant, Aristotle, and Hume, and contemporary discussions of the relationship between ethics and practical reason. Her current research projects include the development of a Kantian account of personal relationships and an investigation into the ways in which moral philosophers have attempted to establish the normativity of ethics.

David Schmidtz is Associate Professor of Philosophy at Yale University. He is the author of *The Limits of Government: An Essay on the Public Goods Argument* (Westview Press, 1991). His essay in this volume is part of a larger project on the subject of rational choice and moral motivation.

Robert Sugden is Professor of Economics at the University of East Anglia, England. Born in 1949, he trained at the Universities of York and Wales, and has taught at the Universities of York and Newcastle upon Tyne. He has done research on welfare economics, social choice, the evolution of social conventions, choice under uncertainty, and experimental economics. Currently, he is particularly concerned with the role of rationality assumptions in economics. His most recent book is *The Economics of Rights, Co-operation, and Welfare* (Basil Blackwell, 1986).

Neera Kapur Badhwar is Assistant Professor of Philosophy at the University of Oklahoma. She received her Ph.D. from the University of Toronto in 1986, and was a Killam Postdoctoral Fellow at Dalhousie University in 1986–87. She has published articles in *American Philosophical Quarterly*, *Philosophy and Phenomenological Research*, *Journal of Political Philosophy*, *Ethics*, *Dialogue*, and *Logos*, and has an anthology on the philosophical dimensions of friendship forthcoming from Cornell University Press.

William A. Galston is Professor at the School of Public Affairs, University of Maryland at College Park, and Senior Research Scholar at the Institute for Philosophy and Public Policy. He is the author of four books and numerous articles in political philosophy, American politics, and public policy. His most recent book is *Liberal Purposes: Goods, Virtues, and Diversity in the Liberal State* (Cambridge University Press, 1991).

Jean Hampton is Professor of Philosophy at the University of Arizona, and is the author of *Hobbes and the Social Contract Tradition* (Cambridge University Press, 1986) and (with Jeffrie Murphy) *Forgiveness and Mercy* (Cambridge University Press, 1988). She has published many articles in moral, political, and legal theory, especially in the areas of contractarian moral theory, history of political theory, retributive justice, and liberalism. She has been a fellow of the American Council of Learned Societies, has held a summer grant from the National Endowment for the Humanities, and is the recent recipient of a fellowship from the Pew Charitable Trusts.

Roderick T. Long is Assistant Professor of Philosophy at the University of North Carolina at Chapel Hill. He has recently completed a book on the free will problem in Aristotle.

Douglas J. Den Uyl is Professor of Philosophy, Chair of the Philosophy Department, and Director of the Masters of Arts in Liberal Studies program at Bellarmine College. He has authored numerous articles and books in the areas of social/political theory and ethics, including *Power, State, and Freedom: An Interpretation of Spinoza's Political Thought* (Van Gorcum, 1983); *The Virtue of Prudence* (Peter Lang, 1991); and (with Douglas B. Rasmussen) *Liberty and Nature: An Aristotelian Defense of Liberal Order* (Open Court, 1991).

Tyler Cowen is Associate Professor of Economics at George Mason University, and has edited *The Theory of Market Failure: A Critical Examination* (George Mason University Press, 1988). He has published in the areas of public-goods theory, public choice, welfare economics, social discounting of utility, rational-choice ethics, population economics, and the economics of self-control. He is currently working on a book, *Explorations in the New Monetary Economics*, with coauthor Randall Kroszner.

BENEFICENCE AND SELF-LOVE:
A KANTIAN PERSPECTIVE*

By Thomas E. Hill, Jr.

I. Questions, Assumptions, and Preview

What, if anything, are we morally required to do on behalf of others besides respecting their rights? And why is such regard for others a reasonable moral requirement? These two questions have long been major concerns of ethical theory, but the answers that philosophers give tend to vary with their beliefs about human nature. More specifically, their answers typically depend on the position they take on a third question: To what extent, if any, is it *possible* for us to act altruistically?[1]

Theories that provide related answers to these three questions can differ radically. At one extreme, for example, is an egoist position often attributed to Hobbes.[2] This denies the possibility of genuine altruism and

---

* I want to thank all those who made helpful comments on an earlier version of this essay, especially Jean Hampton, Christine Korsgaard, Geoffrey Sayre McCord, Ellen Frankel Paul, Andrews Reath, and Michael Zimmerman.

[1] The familiar idea of *altruism* is notoriously hard to pin down, and philosophical definitions can vary as widely as those of the contrasting term, *egoism*. I do not want to limit my general discussion by insisting on a specific definition, but roughly I mean by "altruistic acts" those done to benefit others and not motivated by self-interest. They are done "for the sake of others" from motives such as sympathy, respect, group loyalty, or moral duty. The idea of "self-interest," unfortunately, is almost as slippery as the ideas of "egoism" and "altruism," but when more than a common-sense understanding is needed, I favor the characterization suggested by Gregory S. Kavka in his account of "Narrow Egoism." That is, acts motivated by self-interest have as their ultimate end "personal benefits," as best identified by a list of examples. Kavka's list includes "pleasure, [avoidance of] pain, wealth, security, liberty, glory, possession of particular objects, fame, health, longevity, status, self-respect, self-development, self-assertion, reputation, honor, and affection." Gregory S. Kavka, *Hobbesian Moral and Political Theory* (Princeton: Princeton University Press, 1986), p. 42. Here I set aside, as nonaltruistic, acts done *both* for others and for oneself, even though for some purposes these might be called "altruistic" in another sense. Also, importantly, I do not assume, as some do, that acts done for the sake of others are done out of compassionate or sympathetic *feelings* towards others, for I want to count among altruistic acts those done to benefit others because one believes that helping others on such occasions is what one morally should do. In such cases, on the Kantian view, the aim or *end* one seeks is others' welfare and nothing further, but the motivating *principle* is to act as one believes morally right, and the accompanying *feeling* may be respect for moral principle rather than compassion. It should be noted further that altruistic acts, as understood here, need not be motivated by *general benevolence* (i.e., a concern for the welfare of human or sentient beings in general) rather than concern to help particular individuals.

[2] The view in question is a combination of psychological egoism and ethical egoism, as these terms are generally understood. Whether Thomas Hobbes actually was an unqualified egoist in these senses is a matter of controversy, which turns partly on the exact defi-

---

1

argues that reason and morality can only require us to look out for others to the extent that doing so will serve our own long-term self-interest. Others, like Hume, suppose that sympathy for others is a basic feature of human nature; and, on this assumption, some even argue (beyond Hume) that our moral duty is to count each other person's happiness as having the same weight in our decision making as our own. Theories at both extremes tend to draw conclusions about how we should treat others from initial beliefs about how we are naturally inclined to feel about them. There are, of course, many intermediate positions, with subtle variations, between these extremes.

In my discussion I describe some main features of one of these less extreme positions — what I call "a Kantian perspective" — on my initial three questions, though I focus primarily on the third issue (the *possibility* of altruistic conduct). In labeling the position "Kantian" I mean only to acknowledge respectfully that the position in question has roots in Kant's ethical theory, not to raise historical and interpretative questions about Kant's texts. My main purpose is to put the ideas in question on the table for consideration, not to do textual exegesis.

My project is limited in another way as well. I want to consider our questions about altruism as they might arise for us when we take up a practical, deliberative, and conscientious point of view.[3] We want answers appropriate for sincere deliberation about what we can do, what we should do, and why. From this perspective our questions are not idle speculative ones, for we want not merely to understand the world but to change it in some ways — or at least to act responsibly in it. In addition, I want to assume that the practical task before us is not primarily how to persuade and motivate others to do what we believe they should. Rather, the task is first and foremost to determine how we ourselves should act.

---

nitions of relevant senses of "egoism" and partly on the interpretation of familiar passages. It is clear that Hobbes acknowledged that we sometimes act from *apparently* altruistic motives, for example, "pity" and "compassion," but his definitions can be read as efforts to reinterpret such terms in a way compatible with psychological egoism and its denial of *genuine*, i.e., actual, altruism. For finer distinctions and varying views on Hobbes, see, for example, the following: C. D. Broad, *Five Types of Ethical Theory* (London: Routledge & Kegan Paul, 1930), p. 54; Richard B. Brandt, *Ethical Theory* (Englewood Cliffs, N.J.: Prentice-Hall, 1959), ch. 14, especially pp. 370–71; William K. Frankena, *Ethics*, 2nd ed. (Englewood Cliffs, N.J.: Prentice-Hall, 1973), ch. 2, especially p. 15; James Rachels, *The Elements of Moral Philosophy* (New York: Random House, 1986), chs. 5 and 6; Jean Hampton, *Hobbes and the Social Contract Tradition* (Cambridge: Cambridge University Press, 1986), ch. 1, especially pp. 19–24; and Gregory S. Kavka, *Hobbesian Moral and Political Theory*, ch. 2, especially pp. 44–51.

[3] As I intend these terms, we take a "practical, deliberative" point of view when we think seriously about reasons for and against policies or courses of action, and this perspective is also "conscientious" when our background assumption, and indeed our point, in deliberating is that we intend to do what is morally right. Conscientious people, of course, may have different views about what is morally right, but they have in common a commitment to act on their best judgment about this. Here I assume only that *in taking up the conscientious perspective* we seek what is right with the intent to do it, not that we are all moral saints, *always* perfectly free from weakness of will, negligence, and perversity.

Given these assumptions, as deliberators we ask what we should do because we mean to do what we should. We seek good reasons for acting, not merely for predicting or explaining how people do behave. Nevertheless, what we learn from psychology is potentially important, for in trying to decide what *to do*, we must set aside any alleged "oughts" that we *know* we *cannot* fulfill. When deliberating as conscientious persons, we are not entertaining or responding to the doubts of moral skeptics who ask, "Are moral judgments *objective?*" — "Are obligations *real?*" Nor are we trying to answer amoralists who pose the challenge, "Show me why I should *care* about morality at all."

Thus, for present purposes I am supposing that, like most people who bother to discuss ethical issues, we accept some minimal moral limits to how we may treat others. We are not doubting, for example, that there are some reasonable moral principles against theft, fraud, promise-breaking, murder, rape, and torture. But, realizing that many are inclined to accept such minimal constraints as morally sufficient, we raise further questions. For example, "Isn't it optional whether we give to charity, do favors, and generally give regard to the concerns of others, provided that we fulfill our strict obligations of honesty, promise-keeping, noncoercion, and the like?" Even if we enjoy helping others and know that others like us better when we do, we may still wonder, "Isn't this beyond duty, a matter of preference, 'nice' to do but not wrong to omit? If not, why not?" And, seeing rampant greed and selfishness, we ask, "Is it possible for human beings to be altruistic as, some say, duty requires?"

In sum, we pose our questions about altruism as conscientious agents who accept certain core moral constraints but have questions and disagreements about the nature, grounds, and limits of their moral obligations to act beneficently towards others.[4] This means that our concerns are more specific than those of moral skeptics; but they should not be confused with even more particular questions that individuals may raise in special contexts. For example, suppose a volunteer has worked long and hard for strangers (or even competent adult family members) whose basic needs are provided for, who refuse to avail themselves of ample opportunities, and who show her neither gratitude nor reciprocity. Then to ask, in these circumstances, "Do I have any obligation to help them further?" is not to ask our more general question about the duty of benefi-

---

[4] The point of specifying that we are to address the questions in this essay as conscientious deliberating agents is methodological, not rhetorical. What one can take for granted, what is in doubt, and even what one is looking for can vary with the context of discussion of normative matters. Purposes and working assumptions tend to shift as one moves within contemporary philosophical literature from abstract philosophical arguments about "moral realism," to practical debates on specific moral issues, to general explanatory accounts of moral belief and behavior from a third-person perspective. Ideally, we expect that reasonable conclusions in these different contexts will eventually cohere, but in the meantime it is only good procedure to keep in focus the background aims and assumptions of each particular discussion.

cence but rather to doubt its application to a quite specific, though perhaps all too common, situation. To take another example, suppose that a woman comes to see that she has diminished herself by constantly submitting to male demands that women devote themselves to others, and she wonders, "Is it wrong for me to concentrate my energies on myself now?" Her concern is more specific and contextually focused than my opening questions, which were about our general obligation to help others, rather than about how such an obligation directs us to act in troublesome special contexts.

Kant addresses these questions, more or less from the point of view described above, in several works, but his most sustained discussion of the duty of beneficence is in the second part of *The Metaphysics of Morals*.[5] There Kant takes for granted that his audience has followed him through (or is not now doubting) his earlier attempts to characterize the fundamentals of a moral attitude, to confront doubts about its rational authority, and to establish the principles of justice and respect prior to beneficence. The problem is not to judge how the general duty of beneficence applies to particular cases, but to say in general what it requires and why, while granting that human beings have a limited natural disposition to help others and cannot call up sympathetic feelings at will. The questions are about our duty to others, not about how to get others to do their duty. Kant never doubted that his audience could hear the voice of duty, once clearly expressed, even if he was not an optimist about how regularly they would heed it.

The Kantian position, as I understand it, offers practical alternatives to opposing extremes with regard to the three questions that I posed at the beginning of this essay.

First, what beneficence towards others is morally required? An answer at one extreme is the minimalist idea that helping others (beyond the requirements of justice and contractual obligations) is optional, and at the opposing extreme is the maximalist idea that one must always help others, provided doing so does not diminish the general welfare impartially viewed. The Kantian position is that beneficence is a moral duty, but a wide, imperfect duty of virtue, unenforceable and constrained by prior requirements of justice and respect.

Second, why is beneficence a duty? Some would attempt to answer by reference to the demands of God, social convention, or our compassionate natures; others would appeal to a metaphysical belief in the reality of

---

[5] Immanuel Kant's *The Metaphysics of Morals* is available in translation in two volumes: *The Metaphysical Elements of Justice*, trans. John Ladd (Indianapolis: Bobbs-Merrill, 1965) and *The Metaphysical Principles of Virtue*, trans. James Ellington (Indianapolis: Bobbs-Merrill, 1964). Kant's position on the possibility of altruism is inseparable from his ideas of autonomy and practical freedom, discussed in many of his major works. For commentary and detailed references, see Henry E. Allison, *Kant's Theory of Freedom* (Cambridge: Cambridge University Press, 1990).

intrinsic values, perceived by us but not constituted by their relation to human or divine thoughts and feelings. The Kantian alternative attempts to ground a duty of beneficence in our acknowledgment that, as rational agents, we each value ourselves in a special way and, as conscientious agents, we are committed to evaluative consistency and a constraint to act only in ways that we believe we could defend before others in morally appropriate joint deliberations.[6]

Third, can we act altruistically? Here the extremes are the belief that natural self-regard makes genuine altruistic conduct impossible and the belief that natural sympathy makes it possible and even common. The Kantian position, by contrast, is that, once we see the reasons for doing so, we can guide our conduct by a limited principle of beneficence, no matter how warm or cold our feelings towards others may run. That we can do so, at least in normal circumstances, is not refuted by empirical evidence and is presupposed in our conception of ourselves as moral agents.

My primary focus will be on the Kantian position with regard to the third question, whether or not we are capable of acting altruistically. But since Kant's response on this issue is not complete without reference to his answers to the first two questions, these will be considered (more briefly) in Sections IV and V.

II. Diverse Opinions on the Prevalence of Benevolent Feelings and Their Relevance for Ethics

Beliefs vary about what we *can* do for others, and these beliefs tend to influence in various ways views about what we *should* do for others. Let us review some variations.

1. Some believe that altruistic conduct is impossible, and thus conclude that there is no moral obligation to be altruistic. Moral arguments for ac-

---

[6] Here I paraphrase what Kant expresses in his more specialized terminology and what I explain more fully in the last section of this essay. What I call "conscientious agents" are roughly, in Kant's terms, (*imperfectly*) *rational agents* that acknowledge that they are subject to *duties*, conceived as *categorical imperatives*. This implies a "will," though not an invariably effective disposition, to conform to what one judges (or "knows") to be morally obligatory. Kant held that all (even imperfectly) rational human beings have such a will; and so, though he implied that there are rational requirements that are not duties, he believed that "rational agents" are also "conscientious" (as I use the term here). In saying that (for Kant) conscientious agents are "committed to evaluative consistency," I allude (rather imprecisely) to the standards expressed in the "universal-law" formula of the Categorical Imperative, which is discussed briefly in the last section of this essay. The constraint of defensibility "before others in morally appropriate deliberations" is drawn from the "kingdom of ends" formula, not discussed in this essay. I present a more thorough view of some of these matters in my collection of essays *Dignity and Practical Reason in Kant's Moral Theory* (Ithaca: Cornell University Press, 1992), especially chs. 1, 3, 7, 10, and 11, and in "A Kantian Perspective on Moral Rules," *Philosophical Perspectives*, vol. 6 (1992). See also H. J. Paton, *The Categorical Imperative* (London: Hutchison, 1947); and Onora O'Neill, *Constructions of Reason* (Cambridge: Cambridge University Press, 1989).

cepting other-regarding principles, on this view, must appeal at some
point to self-interest. Hobbes is often thought to be a prime example. By
nature, he held, we always act for the sake of some good for ourselves.
What is called "compassion," he tells us, is really one's "grief for the
calamity of another . . . [that] ariseth from the imagination that a like calamity may befall [oneself],"[7] and the laws of nature that prescribe ac-
commodation and forbid hatred are derivative from the primary law
directing one to further one's own interests.[8]

2. Others hold, less radically, that though concern for others for their
own sake is occasionally possible, due to human nature such other-
regarding concerns can only be rare, unstable, and restricted in scope
(e.g., to family, friends, and associates). If one assumes that altruistic acts
must be motivated by altruistic feelings, then the belief that altruistic feelings are severely limited tends to undermine belief in a general obligation
to act for the sake of others. It seems pointless, and even dangerous, to
expect people to act from selfless regard for others if, because of human
nature, such motives are uncommon, unreliable, and narrowly focused.
Even if one imagined oneself to be the rare exception, having frequent,
strong, and wide-ranging compassion, one could only try to make *oneself*
act from this motive and could not fairly or reasonably prescribe the same
to all. 'Ought' in this context implies 'can', and to regard a principle as
a basic moral principle is to understand it as a standard for everyone. If
an individual lacks and cannot acquire a kind or degree of benevolent
feeling, then that person cannot be under obligation, all things considered, to have such a feeling or to take action that requires this feeling as
a motive. And if *most* people are similarly lacking, then it seems doubtful that having and acting on the motive can be a *basic* moral obligation
even for the few who have the capacity for it.

3. Many who agree that altruistic feelings are in fact rare in our world
may nevertheless believe that this is an ideal motive, within human capacities, and that we are obligated to cultivate it. What our observations
show, they may argue, is that people *do not* (often) act from altruistic feelings, but not that they *cannot*. Various explanations may be given for the
fact that most do not develop and act from their capacity for this ideal motive. The failure may be attributed, for example, to pervasive problems
that, according to some theological and social theories, can eventually be
overcome or transcended: for example, original sin, capitalism, or the use
of inadequate techniques of socialization.

If pressed with the objection that it is foolish and dangerous to expect
people to act on motives that are in fact quite uncommon, idealists may

[7] Thomas Hobbes, *Leviathan*, ed. C. B. MacPherson (Baltimore: Penguin Books, 1951),
part I, ch. 6, p. 126. This passage, as Jean Hampton has reminded me, can be interpreted
in several ways. A reading that assimilated Hobbes's point to Hume's account of sympathy would allow that acts moved by compassion (as Hobbes defines it) could count as altruistic. See the references in note 2 above.
[8] Hobbes, *Leviathan*, part I, chs. 14 and 15.

reply in different ways. Some Christians may say that love for all, even though rare, has a supreme value and that one should have faith that God will prevent or compensate for the disasters that seem predictable when one trusts that people can be more loving than evidence shows them capable of being. Some revolutionary idealists, confronted with the same objection, may reply that indeed we should not count on most people, as currently conditioned, to act from anything less than selfish motives, but after the revolution, they may argue, radically altered social conditions will mold new personalities in which other-regarding motives dominate.

4. Another common view is that compassion and general benevolence are not only possible in rare circumstances but are powerful and pervasive features of human nature. This belief about human psychology can also influence moral views. For example, the belief makes it easier to affirm utilitarianism as a theory of moral obligation, for it sets aside the alleged problem that human beings cannot consciously strive for the greatest happiness for all without ulterior motives. Believing that general benevolence is a powerful natural motive would also make it more reasonable for utilitarians (and others) to believe that we need not and so (given costs) should not resort to state coercion, manipulation, and indoctrination to maintain a decent social order. More radically, the belief that benevolence is natural may be regarded as the *basis* for an altruistic ethics. For example, some philosophers seem to hold that an ethics that prescribes acting for the good of others *follows* from their empirical beliefs that benevolence is a powerful natural motive, and that people tend, when disinterested, to look favorably on acts motivated by benevolence.[9]

III. THEORETICAL AND PRACTICAL PURPOSES, AND THE PROBLEM OF THE POSSIBILITY OF ALTRUISM FOR KANTIANS

Kant's view on the possibility of altruism is an important alternative to the views sketched above, but it is not so much an intermediate position on the same scale as it is the introduction of another way of thinking. Kant does not try to settle the issue by determining the extent to which we naturally have, or can acquire, benevolent or sympathetic feelings. Instead, he invites us to see ourselves as agents, trying to decide what to do, in a setting where human motives are mixed and difficult to discern in most cases. As a deliberating agent, one looks at empirical evidence about one's own inclinations and the motives of others as potentially rel-

---

[9] This view is at least suggested by various philosophers who interpret moral judgments as expressing sentiments of impartial spectators, but my unqualified summary of the position no doubt oversimplifies their views. See, for example, David Hume, *Moral and Political Philosophy*, ed. Henry D. Aiken (New York: Hafner, 1948), especially pp. 175–84 and 249–61. See also selections from Adam Smith and Joseph Butler in *British Moralists*, ed. Selby-Bigge (Indianapolis: Bobbs-Merrill, 1964), pp. 255–336 and 181–254; and Roderick Firth, "Ethics and the Ideal Observer," *Philosophy and Phenomenological Research*, vol. 12 (1952), pp. 317–45.

evant background information, but not as data sufficient by itself to determine which option one should choose. What one can introspect and infer from one's past behavior about one's own current inclinations is not seen as a glimpse at an inner mechanism of wheels and levers from which one can predict what one will do or calculate what one should do. Rather, all this merely sets the factual scene within which one must undertake the deliberative task of deciding reasonably what to do.

To move beyond these metaphors, a distinction needs to be made between two importantly different purposes one can have in thinking about the world, human motives, one's particular situation, and what one can and cannot do. One purpose is to gain theoretical understanding of the phenomena we observe. With this aim we seek to describe, comprehend, explain, and predict human behavior by empirical generalizations conceived as causal laws.[10] The other purpose is to decide reasonably, in practical deliberation, what to do in the factual situation in which one finds oneself. The two sorts of purposes necessarily require somewhat different presuppositions and methodologies. When we deliberate, for example, we presume that we have genuine options, that our reasoning can (and should) direct our decisions, that our decisions typically manifest themselves in our behavior, and that our behavior has some effects on the rest of the world. We presuppose that we can and will act for reasons that we can assess, with some objectivity, as better or worse. We are looking for reasons for choosing to act this way or that, intending to act as reason directs, and this is not the same as seeking to discover the physical or psychological events, conditions, and laws by reference to which an observer might predict and explain the resulting behavior.[11]

A. The theoretical task of empirical explanation

Now, when guided by the first (theoretical) purpose, what are the basic features of human motivation that we can infer from our observations? The details of Kant's view are subject to scholarly controversy, but the main picture is clear enough for present purposes. Human beings have variable impulses and inclinations, as well as steady interests, that stem

[10] Kant maintained that the idea of agent-initiated causation (e.g., I intentionally moved the lever with my hand) is importantly different from the idea of event causation (e.g., the explosion knocked my hand against the lever and/or my hand's movement caused the lever to move). All events, Kant argued, have prior causes sufficient to produce them with necessity, but from a practical point of view, we can and must think of agents as initiating causal sequences without being determined to do so by prior causes. See his *Critique of Pure Reason*, trans. Norman Kemp Smith (London: Macmillan, 1956), especially pp. 464–79; *Groundwork of the Metaphysic of Morals*, trans. H. J. Paton (New York: Harper & Row, 1964), ch. 3, pp. 114–31; and *Critique of Practical Reason*, trans. Lewis White Beck (New York: The Liberal Arts Press, 1956), especially pp. 74–92.

[11] Both the agent's (normative) reasons for choosing and explanatory causes may be referred to as "the reasons why" the agent acted, and this ambiguity can cause confusion. See Stephen Darwall, *Impartial Reason* (Ithaca: Cornell University Press, 1983), pp. 28–29.

from their "sensuous nature." They *find* themselves feeling drawn and repulsed by various things, including other people. They do not acquire these feelings by choice, and they cannot simply choose to be rid of them. Though individuals vary in their particular desires, most have some mixture of self-regarding and other-regarding concerns. The latter, however, tend to be weaker and less reliable. Self-love may in fact underlie all or most of what appears to be altruistic feeling.[12] Everyone, by nature, wants to be happy.[13] Though Kant held that no one has a very definite and coherent idea of what his or her happiness would consist in, he clearly did not suppose that for most of us happiness (in this world) consists in sacrificing our own pleasures, material comfort, and security to satisfy intrinsic desires for others' welfare.[14]

On the Kantian view, then, preference for oneself over others is a strongly felt, pervasive human tendency, perhaps even the ultimate source of our other-regarding affections. Moreover, it seems quite foreign to a Kantian perspective to suppose that human nature is so malleable that we can be molded by social conditions into predominantly other-regarding creatures. Through something analogous to religious conversion, Kant thought, individuals may reorder their principles of action, but this may leave their selfish feelings and tendencies unaltered.[15] General benevolence and sympathy are far too weak and unreliable to maintain a decent social order; for that purpose punishment, even "an eye for an eye," is needed.[16] In fact, Kant suggests, in designing a system of public justice, we should assume no altruistic or even conscientious motivation, but instead should provide incentives sufficient to govern even a group of (prudentially rational) fiends.[17]

Empirically, then, we find some limited (and perhaps mixed) benevolent feelings, but these are too unreliable to encourage hope for widespread altruistic conduct. This is not the whole empirical story, however. We also find feelings that are *called* "respect," "guilt," "sense of obligation," and so on, accompanied by talk of "principles," "reasons," and "duties"; and, oddly enough, we observe that people show tendencies to act correspondingly, even when they show no signs of sympathetic feelings. We find, I suppose, that people do act in ways that benefit others, despite apparent costs to themselves, more often than we would have predicted from our estimate of the prevalence of benevolent feelings. Sometimes we hear people *saying* that feelings of "obligation" and "re-

---

[12] See Kant, *Critique of Practical Reason*, pp. 20–21.

[13] Kant, *Groundwork*, p. 83.

[14] *Ibid.*, pp. 85–86.

[15] Kant, *Religion Within the Limits of Reason Alone*, trans. Theodore M. Greene and Hoyt H. Hudson (New York: Harper & Row, 1960), pp. 40–49.

[16] See Kant, *The Metaphysical Elements of Justice*, pp. 99–106.

[17] See Kant, "Perpetual Peace," trans. H. B. Nisbet, in *Kant's Political Writings*, ed. Hans Reiss (Cambridge: Cambridge University Press, 1970), p. 112.

spect for duty" moved them, but for all we know empirically, such reported feelings may simply be masks for deeply self-interested motives or conditioned responses to early training. Whatever their deep motives, we observe that sometimes people do *behave* in ways that benefit others, responding to the thought that another is in need, even at considerable cost to their apparent interests. Since they do, we infer that they can.

These observations, Kant granted, do not contradict the working assumption, found in most sciences, that there must be a causal explanation for all phenomena, whether we can identify it or not. In fact, he believed that he had proved that the principle "every event has a cause" is necessary to human understanding of the world.[18] Thus, the fact that apparently altruistic behavior is not found to be always preceded by identifiably egoistic feelings, such as desire for personal benefit, does not mean that such behavior has no causes. The practical terms we typically use in making sense of human action (intending, willing, choosing, adopting policies, assessing reasons, accepting responsibility, etc.) are not precisely definable variables that could fit into any exact science, but this fact, again, is supposedly compatible with there being causes of all human behavior.[19] In sum, we must suppose for theoretical purposes that altruistic acts, if any, have causes, but empirically we find that, whatever the causes, human beings do at times benefit others even contrary to perceived personal benefit, with the typical feelings and verbal signs we associate with intentional and principled action.

B. The practical purposes of deliberation

Let us turn now to the second reflective standpoint, which is distinguished by Kant from the theoretical stance just considered. This second standpoint is that of practical deliberation, and its purpose is to answer the normative question "What ought I to do?" From this practical perspective, how does a Kantian view the possibility of altruism?

First it should be noted, and if necessary emphasized, that reasonable practical deliberators must take empirical facts very seriously. They must seek to know the facts of the choice situation they face. They must try to understand the feelings of others and their own dispositions in order to give due weight to each, when appropriate, in assessing what they should do. But as practical deliberators we seek these facts as background information, characterizing the scene within which we must make a choice. For example, finding, by introspection or self-observation over time, that I enjoy playing tennis more than helping out at the homeless shelter (or the reverse) may be a relevant fact to consider as I weigh the reasons for and against scheduling my time in a certain way; but I can-

[18] Kant, *Critique of Pure Reason*, pp. 218–33, 409–15, and 443–49.
[19] Kant, *Groundwork*, pp. 118–29, and *Critique of Practical Reason*, pp. 92–110.

not assume that such facts alone determine the answer to my practical question, because the basic principles of reason and morality do not make what I *ought* to do simply a function of how I feel. Nor is what I ought to do determined simply by how my act will affect the feelings of others, or by whether it maximizes good feeling "for everyone, all considered."

Further, if empirical facts establish that human beings never do and indeed *cannot* act in certain ways, then, knowing this, in deliberation I cannot reasonably treat acting in these ways as an option. Imagine, for example, that I am aware that scientists have discovered, in a series of horrible experiments, that no one can persist in a plan to protect others if tortured to a certain measurable degree. Then, if confronted with the prospect of such torture, I can be sure that I will "crack" just as others have; and knowing that I cannot withstand the torture, I cannot sincerely deliberate about whether to do so, treating this as one of my options.[20] I could, of course, deliberate about whether to *try as long as possible*, and to do so might be a heroic gesture; but if I were *fully* convinced that I cannot succeed in achieving an end (e.g., not giving any information under torture), it would be conceptually impossible for me to deliberate about whether to achieve that end.[21] Similarly, if empirical psychology gives decisive evidence that people do not and cannot always maintain benevolent feelings towards those who grossly abuse them and their children, then, knowing this, I could not deliberately make it a policy to have nothing but love in my heart for everyone, no matter what.

These are merely special instances of the obvious point that, in deliberating about what one ought to do, one *cannot sincerely* consider as an option something one *knows* that one cannot do. Moreover, except in special circumstances, one *cannot reasonably* treat something as an option when available empirical evidence *most strongly indicates* that one cannot do it.[22] For example, since there is ample evidence that human beings cannot run a three-minute mile or hold their breath for an hour, one cannot, unless ignorant, deliberate about whether to do these things; and "trying" is unreasonable. All this seems only common sense.

[20] This is a conceptual point. That is, if a person really knows and is immediately and fully aware that it is impossible for him to do something, then it does not make sense to describe the person as "deliberating." I might stand before a thousand-pound weight mouthing the words "Shall I—or shall I not—lift it?"—but anyone who knows that I know that I cannot lift it will also know that I am joking.

[21] In most actual cases, perhaps, those who face torture do not know for certain that they cannot withstand the degree of torture that they will receive. Even a glimmer of hope that one might succeed, despite weighty but not decisive evidence, might be enough to enable one to "decide" to succeed. One can also self-deceptively "half-believe," contrary to solid evidence and one's own "best judgment," and sometimes, no doubt, doing so has good results. But the main point remains that deliberating about what to do presupposes seeing oneself as having options, and empirical evidence can sometimes show quite decisively that ways we might wish to act are not in fact options.

[22] The special circumstance that might make it reasonable to try to do what seems almost certainly impossible (thereby *treating* it as an option) might be, for example, the fact that nothing else can save one's life or one's friends.

Unfortunately, Kant at times seems to suggest a contrary view, that is, that we must first determine our duty independently of empirical evidence and then simply infer (from 'ought' implies 'can') that we can do it. To proceed this way in general would be foolish, for certain limits to our capacities can be empirically determined and (by 'ought' implies 'can') these limits are also constraints on what we can reasonably judge that we ought to do. If empirical investigation is inconclusive regarding what we can do, leaving room for hope, sometimes there may be special considerations for first thinking, "What should we do if we can?" and then proceeding to make resolutions and plans in the faith that we can act accordingly, despite some counter-evidence. But to proceed from "duty" to "can" in this way makes sense only in special conditions. Even William James, who carried pragmatic faith to an extreme, called for a "will to believe" in possibilities only when empirical evidence did not weigh against them.[23] (Similarly, in the *Critique of Pure Reason* Kant is careful to speculate about agent-initiated causation only after trying to establish that there could be no empirical evidence against believing in it.)[24] Kant's main ideas about practical deliberation, I think, are not incompatible with the common-sense position on these matters. In any case, the "Kantian" perspective I am sketching here will take for granted that common-sense position.

C. The case for doubting that altruism is possible

The relevant question, then, is neither whether our behavior is uncaused nor whether our options for choice are unlimited. Obviously, there is much that we cannot do even if we choose to, and also much that we cannot even choose to do. The question at hand is whether we can, by choice, be altruistic in the ways necessary for there to be a genuine and meaningful duty to be altruistic. Can I reasonably consider it "up to me" in the senses presupposed if I am to make the practical judgment "I ought"? The possible obstacles to believing in my freedom to be altruistic are not special individual circumstances, such as my being penniless, paralyzed, or isolated from others. Nor are the obstacles the (already conceded) general thesis that all behavior has causes, or the (empirically unsupported) particular belief that human beings never behave in ways beneficial to others without perceived personal benefit. The main challenge to the idea that it is "up to us" whether to be altruistic comes from three claims: that what motivates us to act are the feelings we have at the time; that we cannot simply choose what to feel; and that genuine benevolent feelings towards others, if not impossible, are rare, unstable, and

---

[23] William James, *The Will to Believe and Other Essays* (New York: Dover, 1956).
[24] See especially "The Third Antinomy," in Kant's *Critique of Pure Reason*, pp. 409–17, 422–30, and 439–59. Regarding Kant's views on causation, see note 10 above.

directed to our close associates. Thus, allegedly, we will act for the sake of others only if we feel warm towards them; but our warm feelings are severely limited, and whether we feel warm, cool, or hotly antagonistic towards others is not something we control by will.

Simply noting that we can to some extent cultivate dispositions to feel kind towards others does not solve the problem for Kantians. Admittedly, by doing things now we can sometimes affect our feelings in the future, but this process is indirect, difficult, and often ineffective. More importantly, acknowledging an ability to influence one's later feelings indirectly would give one no reason to believe that one can be altruistic now, when (let us suppose) one is feeling rather cool towards others. But it seems odd to suppose that the duty of beneficence, if there is one, would bind us only when we are "in the mood." It seems almost as bizarre to think that, to those feeling cool to others, the duty says merely, "Do what will indirectly *result* in your being in an altruistic mood, so that then your feelings will *cause* you to give proper help to others."

IV. CONDITIONAL KANTIAN ANSWER: THE POSSIBILITY OF REASONABLE BENEFICENCE

Kant, of course, held that we have a duty of beneficence and that we can act as it requires. How then does he respond to the challenge sketched above, that we are moved by our feelings, which are not "up to us" and tend to be nonaltruistic? The reply, I think, has several parts worth considering separately.

1. Since the challenge suggests that we cannot simply choose to be altruistic, the first step is to clarify the relevant idea of "being altruistic." More specifically, in order to consider whether we can be altruistic, as many think duty requires, we need first to define the sort of altruism that we suppose morality demands. For Kant this is the duty of beneficence.[25] This is not a duty to feel warm towards others, but to take action to promote the happiness of others. Strictly, it is a duty to make it one's "maxim" to promote the (morally permissible) ends of others. But the duty is "nonjuridical"; it is not the correlative of *rights* of those we may help, and one cannot be legitimately coerced to comply with the duty.[26] Moreover, the duty is an "imperfect duty" of the "widest" obli-

[25] See Kant, *The Metaphysical Principles of Virtue*, pp. 45–55, 60–61, and 112–27. Kant claims that we do have a duty of beneficence of the sort he describes, but at this point in the essay we should consider it merely a *supposed* duty, because we have not yet considered any reasons for it and are still considering the question whether it is possible for us to do what it prescribes. If we assume now that beneficence is really a duty, then we could *simply infer* that we can conform to it because, in the relevant senses, "ought" implies "can." But obviously that would be too facile a reply to those egoists who (relying on the idea that "cannot" implies "not ought") would argue the reverse, i.e., that we have no duty of beneficence because acting altruistically (they say) is impossible.

[26] These distinctions are discussed at length in Mary Gregor, *Laws of Freedom* (Oxford: Blackwell, 1963); and also in my *Dignity and Practical Reason in Kant's Moral Theory*, ch. 8.

gation. As such, it leaves "playroom" for free action, and does not specify how much, to whom, or when one should be beneficent. What is strictly *wrong* is to reject the principle of beneficence, that is, to refuse to count the ends of others as important in one's deliberations.

On Kant's view, it is only reasonable (as well as an "indirect duty") to pursue one's own happiness, and, contrary to Bentham, what one morally ought to do is not determined by what will maximize happiness overall, counting each person's pleasures and pains (of equal intensity, duration, etc.) as equal on a quantitative scale to each other person's.[27] Promoting the happiness of others is also not the prima facie duty of beneficence as W. D. Ross influentially defined it. There are two important differences.[28] First, Kant held that, though the duty of beneficence allows much room for individual choice about when and how much to help others, one is strictly required to make it one's principle (maxim) to promote the happiness of others.[29] Second, despite this, Kant's imperfect duty of beneficence is more lenient in practice than Ross's prima facie duty of beneficence, for unlike Ross's, Kant's principle does not imply that it is one's actual duty to promote others' happiness on every occasion when one can and other duties are absent.

The importance of these points for the issue at hand is this: by circumscribing *what* altruism requires, Kant makes it more plausible that we can be altruistic as required. What is obligatory is adopting a modest maxim of beneficence and choosing over time to act accordingly. The demands on action are flexible and limited, and there are no demands for warm sentiments. This by itself does not resolve all doubts about the possibility of altruism, however, for some will say that no one *can* act as the duty of beneficence requires unless driven by other-regarding sentiments.

[27] See Jeremy Bentham, *An Introduction to the Principles of Morals and Legislation*, especially chs. 1 and 4. The work is available in many editions, including *A Fragment on Government and An Introduction to the Principles of Morals and Legislation*, ed. Wilfrid Harrison (Oxford: Basil Blackwell, 1960).

[28] See W. D. Ross, *The Right and the Good* (Oxford: Clarendon Press, 1930), pp. 16–47. A prima facie duty, according to Ross, is a feature of an act that would make the act an actual duty (i.e., a duty, all things considered) if there were no conflicting moral considerations. Examples of such features include: that an act fulfills a promise, that it returns a favor, that it promotes someone's happiness, or that it makes reparation for past wrongs.

[29] Kant's view, as I understand it, is that everyone is strictly required to maintain as an effective guiding principle (or maxim): "Promote the happiness of others, counting their (permissible) ends as among your own ends." Like Ross's prima facie duty of beneficence, this principle does not specify exactly how, when, or how much one must do for others. Unlike Ross, however, Kant held that the duty of beneficence cannot be fully satisfied by helping others unless one makes it a principle to do so. (Kant also implies, even beyond this, that one must maintain the principle for moral reasons, not merely for self-interested reasons; but this introduces complications best left aside here.) On Ross's view, *adopting the maxim* as one's personal action-guiding standard is neither a prima facie duty nor an actual duty. For Ross the principle "It is a prima facie duty to promote the happiness of others" is supposed to be a self-evident truth that once recognized tends to motivate, but one can satisfy this principle by doing what makes others happy even if one never makes it a principle to do so.

2. Another background claim important to the Kantian answer is that the empirical evidence, as reviewed above, does not establish that we cannot behave in the ways that the duty of beneficence directs.[30] Observation raises doubts about the depth and frequency of purely altruistic feelings, but it reveals that people do sometimes, and so can, contribute to the good of others, even at some cost to themselves. Whatever their deep motives, which we may never know fully, some apparently adopt the policy of beneficence and act accordingly.

This alone is not sufficient to dismiss relevant doubts about the possibility of altruism, however; for observation merely shows that beneficence is within human capacities, not that you and I, at the time of deliberation and action, can act beneficently. There are many things that are within human capacities in the sense that people can do them when they are in the mood (cry, fall asleep, make love, be creative), but one cannot always simply choose to be in the mood. Experience, one might argue, leaves it unsettled whether at particular moments of choice I can or cannot maintain and follow a maxim to benefit others.

3. There are certain general presuppositions that anyone who is sincerely deliberating must make. Without these we can only predict or "wait and see" what we do, rather than trying to decide reasonably what *to do*. Most obviously we presuppose that we have some *options* before us that we can take and we can refrain from taking. Moreover, when we deliberate we consider *reasons* for choosing to do one thing rather than the other. These can be expressed as propositions that we believe to be true and that upon reflection we count in favor of or against an option: e.g., that eating more now will make me sick, that telling the truth about Jill will anger Harry, or that giving to Oxfam will lessen a child's misery.

Even the feelings we have at the moment, so far as we can recognize them, enter deliberation as possible considerations for or against options.[31] The fact that we have them is potentially relevant information, to be reviewed along with information about how we expect to feel later, how others are affected, and much besides. Of course, we also "experience" our sentiments of the moment as yearnings, leanings, aversions, inclining us for or against options; but, if sincerely deliberating, we do not see the sentiments as pushes and pulls, like vector forces, determining

---

[30] See Section III (A) above.

[31] Unrecognized feelings, of course, cannot enter the deliberation. That is, though sometimes they may unfortunately distort our judgment in ways we are helpless to prevent, the fact that they may be present is irrelevant to the question under deliberation, "What ought I to do?" Learning empirically that unrecognized feelings can skew our judgments gives us reason to be wary and to seek greater self-awareness; and in extreme cases, e.g., where afterthought reveals a pattern, suspecting that my judgment is likely to be skewed may be a reason not to try to deliberate at all. But once an issue is up for deliberation, I must treat facts about how I feel, like all other facts, as data for reasonable decision making, not as controlling forces.

what we will do.[32] When, for example, I feel an urge to abandon a writing project, have a snack, or write an insulting letter, then in reasonable deliberation *the fact that* I have such an urge is a proposition to review in my project to find which option is supported by the best reasons. Only when that is settled can I treat the urge as an aid, or obstacle, in carrying out my plans.

4. A crucial further presupposition of deliberation, on the Kantian view, is that one can act on what one judges to be the best reasons. If one deliberates reasonably one has already excluded from the list of options any action that one has strong reason to believe one cannot do; so addictions and any susceptibility to "irresistible impulses," if empirically substantiated as special incapacities, have already been accounted for. Absent these, deliberative reflection must proceed on the assumption that after reviewing the possible pros and cons, one can act as directed by what one judged to be the best reasons. To do so, after all, is the point of the project of deliberating. The idea is to determine what *to do*, not merely to consider what would be desirable if one were to do it. So only what we believe to be options are on the agenda.

5. Now we can imagine the following objection arising. Suppose you have assessed the background of your problem, estimated the consequences, and identified as well as you can the inclinations you have for and against. Suppose, further, that you have weighed these considerations appropriately, giving due regard (or disregard) to each. Now having a reasonable deliberate decision as to what you ought to do, you must act. Let us grant that in your deliberations it was reasonable to assume that you could act a certain way, e.g., beneficently, but you could not be aware of the very state of mind/desire/preference that you would be in at the moment you set yourself to act. This state consists of impulses and sentiments that may be different from those you identified in deliberation, and this state, rather than your deliberative judgment, may be what finally moves you. If the unidentified feelings actually present at the moment of action are not predominantly warm towards others, then, for all your fine deliberations, you may not act on your reasoned decision to act beneficently. Call this "weakness of will" or whatever, the presumption in deliberation that you can and will follow your final judgment as to what you ought to do may prove false.

To this objection, the Kantian reply might go as follows. First, admittedly we do often observe that people act contrary to their professed judgments as to what they ought to do. Knowing this, even when deliberating I should perhaps acknowledge that it is possible that I will not in fact act on my best judgment. But since the point of deliberation is to find the best reasons in order to act on them, when deliberating I must *intend* to

---

[32] This Kantian (and, I believe, common-sense) view of deliberation contrasts significantly with that of Hobbes. See *Leviathan*, part I, ch. 6, pp. 127–28.

do so and thus anticipate that I will. For purposes of my deliberative task (e.g., trying to decide whether to act beneficently), the *possibility* that I will deviate from my best judgment in the end is simply irrelevant.

Now if I had overwhelming *antecedent* evidence that I *could* not act in a certain way (e.g., beneficently) even if I tried, then *that* would be relevant to my deliberative task (making it reasonable for me to rule out acting beneficently as an option). But, by hypothesis, this is not the situation in question. The objection under consideration hypothesized that momentary inclinations might prevent me from following even my best deliberations, which must have already taken into account the available antecedent evidence as to what I can and cannot do. In sum, lacking powerful empirical evidence that I cannot act beneficently if I judge this best, it still makes sense to continue to deliberate about this. And the mere possibility that unknown conditions will somehow prevent me from behaving as I judge best is irrelevant to my task, for it is not a reason for or against deciding that I ought to do the beneficent thing.

Behind the objection above there seems to lie a picture of human acts and motives that does not fit well with either science or how we conceive of ourselves. The model seems to be this: inner impulses mechanically cause the behavior that immediately follows. Terms from our practical vocabulary (desiring, liking, feeling inclined, etc.) are transported into quasi-scientific explanations, even though what they refer to is not measurable and often is not even identifiable before the behavior it is said to cause. Also, the model does not fit our normative conception of ourselves as agents in typical cases. Except in extraordinary cases, for example, we do not count momentary contrary sentiments as excusing us from acting as we judge we ought. Imagine: "I knew that I should meet you at noon as I promised, but I couldn't because I felt an urge for a pizza." Or: "I thought I should donate but, just as I was about to, a sudden feeling of greed made me refuse."

Thinking practically, we suppose that in most cases our feelings incline but do not coerce, that they are potentially relevant data for decision making and not forces that bypass deliberative processes, and that weakness of will is often just *willing weakly* rather than *lacking willpower*.[33] These ideas, in any case, are the presuppositions of the Kantian perspective that I am trying to characterize.

6. Another assumption of the Kantian perspective is that our inclinations in deliberation are not necessarily good reasons to act. What reason prescribes is not simply a function of how one feels at the time of deci-

---

[33] This distinction, admittedly controversial, is discussed at length in "Weakness of Will and Character," in my collection of essays *Autonomy and Self-Respect* (Cambridge: Cambridge University Press, 1991), p. 9. Roughly, the idea is that what we call "weakness of will" is often not a disability beyond the agent's control (*lack of willpower*) but rather the agent's pattern, for which he or she may be responsible, of making half-hearted efforts, breaking and fudging resolutions, and not following through on projects and commitments (*willing weakly*).

sion (or even of anticipated satisfactions over time). That we desire, or feel a preference, for doing something is not *necessarily* any reason to do it; though, of course, we naturally count it as a reason in the absence of countervailing considerations. What facts are good reasons in favor of a project is something that must be determined by reflecting under rational procedural constraints, not something fixed in advance by nature or anyone's authority.[34]

Since we presuppose that we can act on the best reasons and that our feelings at the moment do not always correspond to what we judge good reasons, we are committed to the idea that we can do what we consider reasonable, whether or not this conflicts with what we feel inclined to do. The upshot is this: we can now see that Kantian deliberation presupposes that we *can* act beneficently, independently of how we are feeling towards others, *if we acknowledge good reasons for doing so*. We can act on our best reasons, and these are not a function of how warm or cold we feel towards others but are rather something to be worked out in an appropriate sort of reflection. Thus, the historical debate about how common, pure, and stable altruistic feelings are becomes irrelevant from the Kantian perspective, for on this view the practical issue about the possibility of altruism does not turn on what *sentiments* we have but rather on whether we can find adequate *reasons*, on reflection, for adopting at least the modest maxim of beneficence. We must now turn, at least briefly, to this final issue.

V. Is Beneficence a Reasonable Requirement?

From a deliberative perspective, then, we must suppose that we can act beneficently if there is adequate reason to do so. For Kantians addressing doubts about the possibility of altruism, therefore, the remaining question is whether the alleged duty of beneficence is really a requirement of reason. This is a large topic, but for now a few comments must suffice.

First, we have already noted a number of points that tell us something about what the Kantian argument for beneficence must be like. For example, since having an inclination or sentiment does not necessarily give one a reason to act, we could not simply infer a duty of beneficence from sentiments of benevolence, even if these were universal and felt by all impartial spectators. Because the duty is supposed to stand regardless of variations in the warmth of our feelings towards others, the reason for acknowledging the duty must not vary with such feelings. An enlightened concern for one's own interest would meet this criterion, supposing

[34] The ideas expressed here, as well as some in the preceding three sections, are part of what Kant seems to have meant in claiming that it is necessary in conceiving ourselves as moral agents to take ourselves to have *autonomy* of the will. For further discussion, see my *Dignity and Practical Reason in Kant's Moral Theory*, ch. 5; my *Autonomy and Self-Respect*, ch. 12; and Henry Allison, *Kant's Theory of Freedom*, ch. 5.

(with Joseph Butler and others) that beneficence coincides with self-interest. But Kantians cannot rely on an argument from enlightened self-interest, for the duty of beneficence is supposed to be a categorical imperative, binding us independently of our interests. Appeals to the authority of tradition, community values, and God's commands will not serve the purpose, for the reasons the Kantian seeks are ones that any reasonable, conscientious agent will acknowledge, if thinking deeply and clearly. Thus, many of the traditional arguments for helping others are ruled out at the start.

Kant addresses the problem in several places. In the *Groundwork*, the final example to illustrate two formulations of the Categorical Imperative is a case where a person who is well-off considers refusing to help others who are "struggling under great hardships."[35] Here the problem whether to help is narrower, and perhaps easier to handle, than some other cases that could fall under the imperfect duty to promote the happiness of others. A principle of "mutual aid" might suffice: that is, a principle prescribing that one help those in need if the cost to oneself is little. (Compare the more general characterization of the duty of beneficence: make it one's principle to promote the permissible ends of others.) Even in *The Metaphysics of Morals* Kant's arguments are focused on cases where one can help someone in need (as opposed, say, to "doing favors" for the well-off). To simplify, then, let us also concentrate, for now, on the imperfect duty of beneficence only as it applies to cases of needy recipients and comfortable givers.

Kant argues for a duty of beneficence not only from the universal-law formula of the Categorical Imperative, but also from the formula of humanity as an end in itself.[36] An even more persuasive case might be made, I suspect, from a reconstructed formula of the kingdom of ends.[37] But here I will discuss only arguments that appeal to the universal-law formula. There are variations even in these arguments, but some main points remain the same. Here is one version.[38]

---

[35] Kant, *Groundwork*, pp. 90 and 98.

[36] *Ibid.*

[37] Kant presents this formula in his *Groundwork*, pp. 100–102 and 105–7, and my efforts to reconstruct it are cited in note 6 above.

[38] Some other versions are the following:

> Every morally practical relation of men to one another is a relation of them in the representation of pure reason, i.e., of free actions according to maxims which are suitable for universal legislation and which thus cannot be selfish. I want every other person to have benevolence for me; I should therefore be benevolent to every other person. (Kant, *The Metaphysical Principles of Virtue*, p. 115).

> It is a duty of every man to be beneficent, i.e., to be helpful to men in need according to one's means, for the sake of their happiness and without hoping for anything thereby.
> For every man who finds himself in need wishes that he might be helped by others. But if he should make known his maxim of not wanting to give assistance in turn to others in their need — if he should make such a maxim a universal permissive law —

That beneficence is a duty results from the fact that since our self-love cannot be separated from our need to be loved by others (to obtain help from them in case of need), we therefore make ourselves an end for others; and this maxim can never be obligatory except by qualifying as a universal law and, consequently, through a will to make others our ends. Hence the happiness of others is an end which is at the same time a duty.[39]

The argument here appeals to certain ideas that appear in virtually all versions: (i) the fact that we have a special self-regard (self-love, concern for our happiness, valuing our humanity as an "end in itself"); (ii) the fact that, as human beings, we have needs that only others can meet (their assistance, their love); and (iii) a general moral assumption that we should consider what we are proposing to do from a broader perspective, looking beyond the immediate case and our own projects towards what would be reasonable "universal laws." This moral assumption, of course, is what Kant tried to express in several formulations of the Categorical Imperative.

There are different ways to reconstruct the Kantian rationale for beneficence, depending on how one construes the famous universal-law formula of the Categorical Imperative.[40] The details are controversial, but some points seem clear enough.

For example, though the rationale begins with the fact that we love ourselves and need the love and help of others, the point is not that it actually pays to be beneficent. The point is not simply that if you scratch others' backs, then they *will* in fact scratch yours. That, of course, is not always true: sometimes no one helps the helpers. More importantly, what is to be justified is a moral duty, i.e., a categorical imperative, and this prescribes what one ought to do, whether it serves one's interests or not. Even if helping others is not the best strategy to obtain help when

---

then everyone would likewise refuse him assistance when he was in need, or at least everyone would be entitled to refuse. Thus the selfish maxim conflicts with itself when it is made a universal law, i.e., it is contrary to duty.

Consequently, the altruistic maxim of beneficence towards those in need is a universal duty of men; this is so because they are to be regarded as fellow men, i.e., as needy rational beings, united by nature in one dwelling place for mutual aid. (*Ibid.*, p. 117)

[39] Kant, *The Metaphysical Principles of Virtue*, p. 52.
[40] For some of the many interpretations, see the following: Christine Korsgaard, "Kant's Formula of Universal Law," *Pacific Philosophical Quarterly*, vol. 66 (1985), pp. 24–47; Onora O'Neill, *Constructions of Reason* (Cambridge: Cambridge University Press, 1989), pp. 81–104; Onora (O'Neill) Nell, *Acting on Principle* (New York: Columbia University Press, 1975); Nelson T. Potter and Mark Timmons, eds., *Morality and Universality: Essays on Ethical Universalizability* (Dordrecht: Reidel, 1985); M. G. Singer, *Generalization in Ethics* (New York: Alfred A. Knopf, 1961), pp. 217–99; and Barbara Herman, "Mutual Aid and Respect for Persons," *Ethics*, vol. 94 (1984), pp. 577–602.

we need it, Kant holds that we cannot reasonably refuse all help to others.

It is also clear that the initial assumptions are not special claims about individual circumstances but rather quite general features of the human condition, namely, that we are the sort of creatures who have self-love and need the love and help of others. The degree to which individuals have self-love and need help varies, but that may not matter since the principle to be justified does not specify any particular amount that one is required to help others. Self-love, having happiness as an end, and wanting things that may require the assistance of others are features of us as human beings with feelings, but the concerns in question are not rare and unstable, as (in Kant's opinion) altruistic feelings are. Moreover, self-love obviously gives us steady reasons for acting, even though our particular moods may vary. Indeed, our concern for happiness, at least when not in conflict with moral demands, gives us reasons that typically override the reasons provided by particular desires and aims.

One common way of reconstructing the Kantian argument, drawing particularly from the *Groundwork*, runs as follows.[41] It is wrong to act on maxims that one cannot will as universal law. A person who repeatedly refused to help others in need, failing to adopt even an indefinite policy of promoting the ends of others, would be acting on the maxim: "I'll never help others, even when their need is great and the cost to me is little." As "universal law," this would be: "Everyone will [or may] never help others, even when their need is great and the cost of helping is little." As a reasonably prudent person, aware that everyone is liable to fall into need, you "could not will" such a law. To do so would conflict with your "will" to pursue happiness prudently. Hence it is wrong for you to act on your maxim to refuse to help others. The only way to avoid this is to make it a policy to help others sometimes. If something is the only way to avoid doing wrong, then it is a duty. Hence it is your duty to adopt the policy to help others sometimes.

Now, there seems to be something right about this; but when we try to construe it as a rigorous argument, all sorts of problems arise. Most obviously, we need criteria for how to specify a maxim, more information about what enables one to will or not will a universal law, and some account of why the universal-law formula of the Categorical Imperative is a morally necessary assumption. Kant's critics and sympathizers have played with these problems for many years, but I remain doubtful that they can ever be resolved sufficiently to justify using the universal-law formula as a rigorous moral decision procedure — or even as a loose and partial action-guide *operating independently of other moral judgments*. But there are some other ways of thinking of the Kantian rationale for beneficence. These are obviously not rigorous proofs that helping others is ra-

---

[41] Kant, *Groundwork*, ch. 2, pp. 90–91.

tional. Rather, to twist a phrase of Daniel Dennett's they are "conscience pumps."[42]

In one version of the argument for beneficence, Kant says that we "make ourselves an end for others." This suggests a consideration that is true for virtually everyone. Though we no doubt have a current desire that we be helped in the future if we should become needy, this is not all. We also have accepted and asked for help in the past; we are willingly dependent on others' help now; and, if honest, we should admit that we intend to ask for and count on help from others later. That is, we in fact *will* the help of others in past activities, current dependencies, and future plans. In effect, we ask others to give some consideration to our ends when they set their own plans and goals.

The moral question, then, is this: Can we conscientiously ask and expect others to limit their own pursuit of self-interest to help us if we are unwilling to reciprocate? The minimal moral assumption here is that we cannot demand sacrifices from others when we are unwilling to sacrifice for anyone, unless we could cite special facts that might justify this. Sometimes, of course, there will be morally relevant differences between my situation and theirs, but one could not honestly and realistically claim that such differences justify my not helping as a rule. It is logically possible, but practically absurd, to judge that there are relevant differences in every case between others' helping and my helping.

This familiar line of thought does not pretend to be a rigorous deduction, and it frankly calls for morally informed judgment as well as honest thinking and realistic assessment of the facts. Nonetheless, it uses the main ideas that Kant appeals to in his arguments, and for those who take our initial perspective of reasonable, minimally conscientious agents, it may be enough for practical purposes.

A few may object on the grounds that they sincerely try to avoid accepting help from anyone. They declare a policy of "rugged individualism," swim or sink, every dog for himself, show no pity and ask for none. Let us imagine that their record gives evidence of their sincerity: for example, they have often risked ruin and death by refusing to accept aid from others. Now to appeal to them to acknowledge that they have in fact "made themselves an end for others" seems insufficient.

This suggests a possible way of extending the Kantian rationale. The idea that we *will* the help of others, making ourselves an end for them, need not be construed as our making actual demands for others' help (though most of us do). What we "will," in Kantian theory, is not identical with what we wish, or even ask for. Often it refers to our deep commitments based on what we count as good reasons, considerations that survive critical rational reflection. So we might construe the idea that we

---

[42] Dennett's phrase is "intuition pumps." See Daniel Dennett, *Elbow Room* (Cambridge: MIT Press, 1984), p. 12.

will the help of others, not as saying that we actually demand it, but rather as claiming that, if we reflect deeply, we will realize that it only makes sense for others to help us when we are in dire need. In effect, the question is: "Given the facts, don't you really think that there are good and sufficient reasons for you to ask for help when you need it and to expect others to give it sometimes?"

The point of the question would not be to prove that one should be beneficent. The aim would be simply to focus attention on the case closest to our hearts, so we can see more clearly that we are committed to a judgment that presupposes a duty of beneficence. Thinking first of your desperately needing help may serve to pump the conscientious judgment "They should help me." But to say they "should," that it is only reasonable for them to help, calls for a general principle to support it. In saying, as reasonable and minimally conscientious persons, "They should help," we are not just saying that it serves my self-interest — or theirs. We have implicitly moved to a level of reflection where we critically review policies of helping and refusing to help in general, or as "universal laws." Here, presumably, most will find that they cannot conscientiously approve of the "no help" policy. The "argument" cannot force them or prove that they must, but it turns moral reflection in the right direction.

These brief and loose remarks are not meant to endorse the idea that we strictly perceive or "intuit" what is right, even though I repeatedly use the metaphor of "seeing." In Kantian ethics, what is right specifically is the product of rational reflection of an appropriate kind. At times we can "see" without lengthy discussion what is implied by our deepest rational commitments, but this calls for confirmation in thorough discussion. Compare an employer's "intuition" that his employee is a thief: it may be useful, even reliable, but it is no substitute for evidence. Thus, when I claim that we "see" that the principle of beneficence is reasonable when we deliberate from a minimally conscientious Kantian perspective, I must acknowledge the need for a deeper, more thorough account of the moral point of view and of why, from this standpoint, beneficence is reasonable. To do this more thorough job in a Kantian theory, we need to give more weight to the later versions of the Categorical Imperative, give up thinking of these formulas as direct action-guides for specific cases, and be willing to trim, refurbish, and repair the grand old edifice that Kant himself constructed. And, unless we can find ways to illuminate them, we may need to abandon some of the darker rooms.

Philosophy, The University of North Carolina at Chapel Hill

THE REASONS WE CAN SHARE:
AN ATTACK ON THE DISTINCTION BETWEEN
AGENT-RELATIVE AND AGENT-NEUTRAL VALUES*

By Christine M. Korsgaard

To later generations, much of the moral philosophy of the twentieth century will look like a struggle to *escape* from utilitarianism. We seem to succeed in disproving one utilitarian doctrine, only to find ourselves caught in the grip of another. I believe that this is because a basic feature of the consequentialist outlook still pervades and distorts our thinking: the view that the business of morality is to *bring something about*. Too often, the rest of us have pitched our protests as if we were merely objecting to the utilitarian account of *what* the moral agent ought to bring about or *how* he ought to do it. Deontological considerations have been characterized as "side constraints," as if they were essentially restrictions on ways to realize ends.[1] More importantly, moral philosophers have persistently assumed that the primal scene of morality is a scene in which someone does something *to* or *for* someone else. This is the same mistake that children make about another primal scene. The primal scene of morality, I will argue, is not one in which I do something to you or you do something to me, but one in which we do something together. The sub-

* This essay leaves me with many debts. It is the result of a number of years of teaching Thomas Nagel's books, and I owe a great deal to my students for many helpful comments and pressing challenges. In the fall of 1990, when I was developing my own responses to Nagel in class, I benefited especially from comments by Andrew Livernois and David Sussman; over the course of the last few years, my ideas on these topics have been shaped by conversations with Scott Kim. Arthur Kuflik read drafts of the material at two different stages and commented usefully and extensively both times. I received helpful written comments on an earlier draft from many people, among them James Dreier, Barbara Herman, Andrews Reath, and Amélie Rorty; and benefited from conversations with Catherine Elgin, Patricia Greenspan, Michael Hardimon, and Samuel Scheffler. A discussion with Thomas Scanlon and the members of his seminar on value theory in the spring of 1992 provided me with many useful suggestions and clarifications. And I am sure I have been influenced by Stephen Darwall, who makes many of the same points I do in this essay in part III of his book *Impartial Reason* (Ithaca: Cornell University Press, 1983). But my greatest debt here is of course to Thomas Nagel, whose ideas I have found endlessly fertile even when I have disagreed. I thank all of these people.

[1] The term is used by Robert Nozick in *Anarchy, State, and Utopia* (New York: Basic Books, 1974). I should emphasize that it is the *term* that I am criticizing here. Nozick's account of side constraints anticipates some of what I will say in this essay about deontological reasons: in particular, that they are based on the Kantian notion that people must not be treated as means (*ibid.*, p. 30), and that they will seem puzzling only to someone who assumes that "a moral concern can function only as a moral goal" (p. 28).

ject matter of morality is not what we should bring about, but how we should relate to one another. If only Rawls has succeeded in escaping utilitarianism, it is because only Rawls has fully grasped this point. His primal scene, the original position, is one in which a group of people must make a decision together. Their task is to find the reasons they can share.[2]

In this essay, I bring these thoughts to bear on a question which has received attention in recent moral philosophy. In contemporary jargon, the question is whether reasons and values should be understood to be agent-relative or agent-neutral, or whether reasons and values of both kinds exist. In slightly older terms, the question is whether reasons and values are subjective, existing only in relation to individuals, or objective, there for everyone. I begin by explaining the distinction in more detail, and then examine two kinds of examples which have been used to support the claim that values of both kinds must exist. By explicating the structure of the values in these examples, I hope to show that employing the distinction between agent-relative and agent-neutral is not the best way to account for their normative force. Values are neither subjective nor objective, but rather are *intersubjective*. They supervene on the structure of personal relations.[3]

I. AGENT-RELATIVE AND AGENT-NEUTRAL VALUES

In what I have said so far, I have assumed an equivalence or at least a direct correspondence between values and practical reasons: to say that there is a practical reason for something is to say that the thing is good, and vice versa. In this I follow Thomas Nagel, whose work will be the focus of what I have to say (*VFN*, p. 139).[4] Although assuming this equivalence gives us a variety of ways to characterize the distinction in question, it still turns out to be a delicate matter to do so.

According to Nagel, a subjective or agent-relative reason is a reason only for a particular agent to promote something; an objective reason is

---

[2] John Rawls, *A Theory of Justice* (Cambridge: Harvard University Press, 1971). See especially pp. 139–42.

[3] This formulation may give rise to the misapprehension that I do not think that there can be duties to the self, or that questions of value cannot arise for the self. What I actually think is that the relations between stages of a self have many of the same features as the relations between separate persons; if stages of the self are to lay each other under normative demands, they too owe each other reasons they can share. But, for reasons indicated in Section IV of this essay, it follows that the self cannot have a reason it *could* not, in principle, share with others. This gives the question of the reasons we can share with others a certain priority, and that is the focus of this essay. Duties to the self do not get an adequate treatment here.

[4] In this essay, references to Nagel's works will be inserted into the text. The abbreviations used are: "PA" for *The Possibility of Altruism* (Princeton: Princeton University Press, 1970); and "VFN" for *The View from Nowhere* (New York: Oxford University Press, 1986).

a reason for anyone to promote the thing.[5] "Subjective" in this context is not meant to suggest "unreal" or "illusory." Subjective reasons are real and in one sense universal—they are alike for everyone—but they are personal property. Objective reasons, by contrast, are common property. Formally speaking, a subjective reason exists when the formulation of the reason predicate contains a "free-agent variable" and an objective reason exists when it does not (*PA*, pp. 90ff.).[6] Thus, suppose we say, "There is a reason for any agent to promote *her own* happiness." This gives me a reason to promote my happiness and you a reason to promote yours, but it does not give you a reason to promote mine or me a reason to promote yours. On the other hand, suppose we say, "There is a reason for any agent to promote *any person's* happiness." This gives each of us a reason to promote not only her own happiness but the other's as well.

Formulated in terms of values, it is tempting to say that subjective reasons capture the notion of "good-for," while objective reasons capture the notion of "good-absolutely." If there is a reason for any agent to promote *her own* happiness, then my happiness is good-for me and yours is good-for you. But if there is a reason for any agent to do what will promote any person's happiness, then any person's happiness is good-absolutely. Human happiness is an objective value which as such makes a claim on all of us. This way of putting the point, however, obscures an important distinction, which I will discuss in the next section.

In *The Possibility of Altruism*, Nagel argued that all subjective reasons and values must be taken to have objective correlates. If it is good-for me

---

[5] In *The Possibility of Altruism*, Nagel uses the terms "subjective" and "objective." But these terms are awkward because they are used in so many different ways. "Subjective" may be used in a metaphysical sense, to refer to *how things are for someone*, assuming that things might be different for others. Or it may be used in an epistemological sense, to refer to *how things seem to someone*, assuming that things might in fact be different from the way they seem. To avoid confusion, notice that in *this* sense the subjective need not be personal or individual. Something could seem the same way to every human being and yet not be that way from some more objective point of view. A mirage, although seen by everybody, is in this sense a subjective illusion; more controversially, one might say that colors are a feature of the subjective experience of creatures with color vision. In *The Possibility of Altruism*, Nagel uses "subjective" in a metaphysical sense: a subjective value is one that is good-for some individual. In *The View from Nowhere*, however, Nagel uses that term to refer to what *seems* to be a reason. Here his project is first to assert that it *seems* to us as if we had reasons and values (from a subjective or personal standpoint), and then to raise the question whether or not, from a more objective or impersonal standpoint, that appearance reveals itself as an illusion of the subjective standpoint (*VFN*, ch. 8). For this reason, Nagel borrows Derek Parfit's terms to cover his earlier distinction. What he had called a subjective value becomes an agent-relative value, which is a source of reasons for a particular agent, but not necessarily for others. What he had called an objective value becomes an agent-neutral value, which is a source of reasons for any agent (*VFN*, p. 152). Parfit introduces these terms in *Reasons and Persons* (Oxford: Oxford University Press, 1984), p. 143.

[6] James Dreier has pointed out to me that in styling my project an attack on the distinction between relative/subjective and neutral/objective, I might give the impression that I think this logical distinction in not exhaustive, which it obviously is. My quarrel, as will emerge, is really with Nagel's account of the source of these reasons, which suggests that values and reasons originate either from personal, idiosyncratic desires or from metaphysical realities of some kind. I thank Dreier for the point.

to have something, then we must regard it as good-absolutely that I should have it. I cannot do justice to Nagel's complex argument here, but its central idea can easily be conveyed. Nagel associates a commitment to the objectivity of value with a conception of oneself as one person among others who are equally real. I act on certain considerations which have normative force *for me*: they are subjective reasons. I am capable, however, of viewing myself from an impersonal point of view—as simply a person, one among others who are equally real. When I view myself this way, I still regard these considerations as having normative force.[7] This is especially clear, Nagel argues, when I consider a situation in which someone else fails to respond to my reasons. This is why we ask, "How would you like it if someone did that to you?" when we are trying to get someone to see the normative force of another's reasons. If I am tormenting someone, say a stranger, the question invites me to consider the case where a stranger is tormenting me. According to Nagel, I should see that I would not merely dislike this, I would also resent it, and my resentment carries with it the thought that my tormentor would have a reason to stop. That reason is the same as my reason for wanting it to stop: that I don't like it. I would expect my tormentor to respond to *my* reason (*PA*, pp. 82–85). And yet, to a stranger, I am just a person, some person or other. This shows that I view my reasons as having normative force simply insofar as they are a person's reasons, and expect others to do so as well. And that commits me to the view that other people's reasons have normative force for me.[8] Where there is a subjective reason, then, there is also an objective one, to which everyone should respond.

Later Nagel changed his mind about this conclusion. But before considering that, we must ask more exactly what this argument, if it works, establishes.

II. Two Interpretations of Agent-Neutral Value

Earlier I mentioned that there is a problem with understanding the distinction between relative and neutral values in terms of the distinction between good-for and good-absolutely. The problem is that the claim that something is a reason for everyone may be understood in two different ways, one of which the phrase "good-absolutely" tends to conceal.

An agent-neutral value might be a value that is not relative to what agents actually value. According to this interpretation, the goodness of, say, my happiness, has what G. E. Moore called an intrinsic value, a

---

[7] More accurately, Nagel's view is that if I do not, I will suffer from dissociation between the personal and impersonal views I can take of myself (*PA*, ch. 11).

[8] Or, as one might put it, that every person, being equally real, is a source of value. But Nagel does not put it that way: he moves, as we shall see, from a focus on the (equal) reality of people to a focus on the reality of their reasons. In one sense, I believe his mistake lies here, and that he would have arrived at a more Kantian and, as I think, more correct position if he had not made this move.

property that is independent either of my interest in promoting it or yours.[9] It provides a reason for both of us the way the sun provides light for both of us: because it's out there, shining down. And just as the sun would exist in a world devoid of creatures who see and respond to light, so values would exist in a world devoid of creatures who see and respond to reasons. I call this interpretation of agent-neutral values *Objective Realism*.[10] On a less metaphysical view, agent-neutrality does not mean independence of agents as such, but neutrality with respect to the individual identities of agents. On this reading, values are intersubjective: they exist for all rational agents, but would not exist in a world without them. I call this view of agent-neutral values *Intersubjectivism*.[11]

The difference between these two interpretations of neutral value is naturally associated with two other differences. First, the two views will normally involve a different priority-ordering between subjective or relative and objective or neutral values. According to Objective Realism, subjective values are *derived from* objective ones: an individual comes to value something by perceiving that it has (objective) value. Our relation to values, on this account, is epistemological, a relation of discovery or perception. According to Intersubjectivism, objective values are derived or, better, constructed from subjective ones. Our individual, subjective interests become intersubjective values when, because of the attitude we take towards one another, we come to share each other's ends.[12] On this view, our relation to values is one of creation or construction. The second and related difference concerns the possibility of adding and subtracting value across the boundaries between persons. On an Intersubjectivist interpretation, neutral reasons are shared, but they are always initially sub-

---

[9] See especially G. E. Moore, "The Conception of Intrinsic Value," in *Philosophical Studies* (London: Routledge and Kegan Paul, 1922). Values could be independent of agents in this sense and still always involve agents in another sense: agents and their experiences might always be parts of the complex "organic unities" which G. E. Moore thought were the loci of value. See note 24. I thank Arthur Kuflik for prompting me to be clearer about this.

[10] Another view makes good-for-ness objective in this sense. It is a fact about the universe that a certain thing is good for me or for you. I *think* that this is the view that G. E. Moore, from whom I borrow the idea of formulating these notions in terms of good-for and good-absolutely, found incoherent. See Moore, *Principia Ethica* (Cambridge: Cambridge University Press, 1903), pp. 97ff. I do not know whether it is incoherent, but it is not tempting.

[11] For another account of Intersubjectivism, see Stephen Darwall, *Impartial Reason*, part III.

[12] It may help to give examples of the sort of position I have in mind here. I am thinking, as will become clear, of Kant's claim that respect for the humanity in the person of another requires you to share his ends; or of Hume's view that the virtues get their value from a shared evaluative standpoint. According to Kant's argument, a person's subjective ends become objective ends in the eyes of those who respect his humanity; according to Hume's, the character traits subjectively valued by the members of a person's own "narrow circle" become objectively valued when viewed from a general point of view which we share. As I suggest below in the text, one may read Nagel's projects as forms of Intersubjectivist constructivism as well. I do not know whether an Intersubjectivist position *must* be one in which objective values are constructed from subjective ones, but the Intersubjectivist positions with which I am familiar do take this form.

jective or agent-relative reasons. So on this view, everything that is good or bad is so because it is good or bad *for* someone. This makes it natural for an Intersubjectivist to deny that values can be added across the boundaries between people. My happiness is good for me and yours is good for you, but the sum of these two values is not good *for* anyone, and so the Intersubjectivist will deny that the sum, as such, is a value.[13] But an Objective Realist, who thinks that the value is in the object rather than in its relation to the subject, may think that we can add values. Two people's happinesses, both good in themselves, will be better than one. Since consequentialism depends upon the possibility that values may be added, an Objective Realist about value may be a consequentialist, while an Intersubjectivist will not.[14]

This leaves us with some important questions. We shall want to know how Intersubjectivism could be true, and what there is to choose between it and Objective Realism. These are questions to which I will return in due course. More immediately, I want to raise a question about Nagel. Which kind of agent-neutral values did he intend to defend? This turns out to be a little difficult to establish. In a postscript he later attached to *The Possibility of Altruism*, Nagel says:

> This book defends the claim that only objective reasons are acceptable, and that subjective reasons are legitimate only if they can be *derived from* objective ones. I now think that the argument actually establishes a different conclusion: That there are objective reasons corresponding to all subjective ones. It remains possible that the *original subjective reasons from which the others are generated* retain some independent force and are not completely subsumed under them. (*PA*, p. vii; my emphases)

The first part of this is misleading, since nothing in *The Possibility of Altruism* really requires that subjective reasons be "derived from" objective

---

[13] This is not to say that there cannot be values that are best understood as "good for us." But these will not be the results of addition. They will exist when the two of us stand in a relationship to which the value in question is relevant. In this way the birth of a child might be good for a couple, or the conclusion of a treaty might be good for a nation. These are collective, not aggregative, goods.

[14] Obviously, the array of logically possible positions goes far beyond the two that are schematically described in the text. One could be an Intersubjectivist and yet think that values can be added across the boundaries of persons. One could be an Objective Realist and yet deny that values can be added — not only across the boundaries of people, but at all. In *Reasons and Persons*, for example, Derek Parfit explores the possibility that weighing and compensation cannot take place even within the boundaries of a life (pp. 342–45). I am not concerned to discuss all possible theories of neutral value, but only the two I find most natural. I shall assume throughout this essay that if there is any objection to adding values, it comes from the consideration that everything that is good or bad is good or bad for somebody, and that values can be added within individual lives. I shall also assume that the view that everything that is good or bad is good or bad for someone, is most naturally associated with some form of Intersubjectivism.

ones. What the argument establishes (if it works) is that if you are to act in harmony with a conception of yourself as one person among others who are equally real, then you must regard your own and others' subjective reasons and values as being objective as well. This is consistent with the view that the objective values are constructed from – or as Nagel himself says here "generated from" – the subjective ones, and so consistent with an Intersubjectivist interpretation.

In *The View from Nowhere*, Nagel says his project is to bring the method of objectivity to bear on the will (*VFN*, pp. 4, 138). You are to see, first, to what extent your motives are really reasons, with normative force for you, by seeing to what extent they may be confirmed or corrected when you view yourself more objectively, as simply a person, one person among others. You are then to see whether these agent-relative reasons can support a still more objective normative force, by considering whether from this point of view they could be taken to have normative force for everyone. This could describe a practical project: the project would be to bring our subjective motives into the impersonal point of view, conferring objective normative force or value upon them as far as that can consistently be done. The result would be Intersubjectivism, and sometimes Nagel sounds as if this is what he has in mind. But at other times he seems to think of it as an epistemological project, one of *discovering* whether what seem to us, subjectively, to be reasons are objectively real. He suggests that we should take reasons to be objectively real if (or to the extent that) the best account of why it seems to us that there are reasons and values is that they are really there (*VFN*, p. 141). This sounds like a form of Objective Realism, not about Platonic entities of some sort, but about reasons themselves. But it is not perfectly clear what Nagel thinks is involved in the existence of a reason.[15] He says that the existence of reasons is dependent on the existence of creatures who can see and respond to reasons:

> The reasons are real, they are not just appearances. To be sure, they will be attributed only to a being that has, in addition to desires, a general capacity to develop an objective view of what it should do. Thus, if cockroaches cannot think about what they should do, there is nothing they should do. (*VFN*, p. 150)

---

[15] Sometimes, Nagel seems to imply that all it amounts to for a reason to be "really there" *is* that it can be assimilated to the objective standpoint without contradiction or incoherence. This unites the practical and the epistemological projects described in the text, and the result would be an Intersubjectivist form of realism. Nagel's values would be part of reality because we put them there, rather the way that, according to Kant, causes are part of empirical reality. This view would have the merit of giving us realism without metaphysics. But it would require a transcendental argument for the category of objective value, and I do not myself see how, in the absence of Kant's own firm division between theoretical and practical reason, this is to be achieved.

This, however, is in tension with the claims Nagel makes when he is arguing for the existence of neutral values. For instance:

> The pain can be detached in thought from the fact that it is mine without losing any of its dreadfulness. It has, so to speak, a life of its own. That is why it is natural to ascribe to it a value of its own. (*VFN*, p. 160)
>
> . . . suffering is a bad thing, period, and not just for the sufferer. (*VFN*, p. 161)

An Intersubjectivist account of neutral values does not require that suffering be a bad thing in itself and not just for the sufferer. It requires only that suffering be a bad thing for everyone *because* it is bad for the sufferer. So here Nagel again seems to be an Objective Realist. But on a realist conception of the badness of pain, surely the pains of animals who cannot think objectively about what they should do must be bad in the same way as the pain of animals who can. If so, there would be reasons and values, even in a world without creatures who can see and respond to them.[16]

Finally, when discussing the temptation to think that a maximally objective account of values must be the best one, Nagel remarks:

> This idea underlies the fairly common moral assumption that the only real values are impersonal values, and that someone can really have a reason to do something only if there is an agent-neutral reason for it to happen. That is the essence of traditional forms of consequentialism: the only reason for anyone to do anything is that it would be better in itself, considering the world as a whole, if he did it. (*VFN*, pp. 162–63)

Evidently, Nagel thinks that the position that there are only agent-neutral values commits one to consequentialism. Relatedly, he thinks that agent-neutral values are correctly described as reasons for things to happen, reasons that are concerned with what is "better in itself." This again suggests Objective Realism. Nagel's position, I think, is not fully consistent. On the whole, it seems as if he takes himself to be defending the existence of agent-neutral reasons in an Objective Realist sense, although his project can be understood as an Intersubjectivist one.

It is not necessary to settle the question of how to categorize Nagel's position here. But two points are important to the rest of my argument. First, if we distinguish between agent-relative or subjective values on the one hand, and agent-neutral values *understood on the Objective Realist model*

---

[16] Nagel might reply that all that follows is that, if we exist, we have reason to stop the animal's pain. But if pain has a value of its own it seems more natural to say that there just is a reason to stop the animal's pain, although the animal cannot see and respond to it.

on the other, we leave out an important option. Values may be intersubjective: not part of the fabric of the universe or external truth, but nevertheless shared or at least shareable by agents.[17] Second, if the status of values is essentially intersubjective, then the question arises why we should suppose that a value must be shared by everyone—why Intersubjectivism must be universal. If values arise from human relations, then there are surely more possibilities. The claims springing from an acknowledgment of our common humanity are one source of value, but the claims springing from friendships, marriages, local communities, and common interests may be others.

III. WHY NOT ALL VALUES ARE AGENT-NEUTRAL

By the time he wrote *The View From Nowhere*, Nagel had decided that not all subjective values have objective correlates.[18] He argues that an individual may have agent-relative or subjective reasons which have a legitimate normative force for her, but which have no normative force for others.

Nagel was moved to modify his earlier position, I believe, by a general consideration and by reflection on certain familiar categories of value which seem to illustrate that consideration. The general consideration is familiar to us from criticisms of utilitarianism, especially those of Bernard Williams.[19] According to Williams, utilitarianism deprives the moral agent of her integrity or individual character, because it does not allow her actions to be guided by commitments to a set of people and projects that are distinctively her own. But these are the very commitments which make us who we are as individuals and give us reasons for caring about our own lives. A person may surely find that some project or person is the most important thing in the world *to her* without having to suppose that it is the most important thing in the world *absolutely*. A theory that

---

[17] One reason I take this option to be important is this: I think that its lack of ontological or metaphysical commitments is a clear advantage of Intersubjectivism; we should not be Objective Realists unless, so to speak, there is no other way. This is not just because of Ockham's razor. A conviction that there are metaphysical truths backing up our claims of value must rest on, and therefore cannot explain, our confidence in our claims of value. Metaphysical moral realism takes us the long way around to end up where we started—at our own deep conviction that our values are not groundless—without giving us what we wanted—some account of the source of that conviction.

[18] Nagel backed off from his earlier position by degrees. At the time he added the postscript to *The Possibility of Altruism* (quoted above), he had decided that it was possible that an individual's subjective reasons may sometimes have a legitimate normative force for her that goes beyond that of their objective correlates. If my happiness is good-absolutely, we both have a reason to pursue it, but perhaps I find an additional or a stronger reason in the fact that it is good-for me. This seems to be an intermediate position between the views of *The Possibility of Altruism* and *The View from Nowhere*.

[19] See J. J. C. Smart and Bernard Williams, *Utilitarianism: For and Against* (Cambridge: Cambridge University Press, 1973), pp. 100ff.; and Williams, *Moral Luck* (Cambridge: Cambridge University Press, 1981), pp. 1–19.

requires impartial allegiance to a system of agent-neutral values gives individuals insufficient space in which to lead their own lives. In Samuel Scheffler's words, it ignores "the independence and distinctness of the personal point of view."[20]

In *The View from Nowhere*, Nagel discusses three categories of values which, he thinks, must be understood as agent-relative for these reasons (*VFN*, pp. 164ff.). The first category springs from the agent's special relationship to his own projects. Nagel calls these "reasons of autonomy." He gives the example of someone with a desire to climb to the top of Kilimanjaro. This desire, he supposes, could give the person a good reason to make the climb, without giving others a reason to help him make it (*VFN*, p. 167). Because he has the desire, his climbing Kilimanjaro is good-for him, but this does not make it good-absolutely, nor need he suppose that it does. The second category, and the most difficult to understand, is the category of "deontological reasons." These are traditional moral restrictions, which forbid performing certain types of actions even when the consequences of doing so are good. According to Nagel, they spring from an agent's special relationship to his own actions. Although it may be best absolutely that someone should lie, or break faith, or kill another, because of the good consequences that will in this way be produced, it may be better *for him* not to do so (*VFN*, p. 180). The last category is "reasons of obligation" which, Nagel says, "stem from the special obligations we have toward those to whom we are closely related: parents, children, spouses, siblings, fellow members of a community or even a nation" (*VFN*, p. 165). Because of my special obligation to my own child, for instance, it might be the most important thing in the world *to me* that my child be successful or happy. I can have this attitude without supposing that my child is objectively any more important than any other child.

In each of these three cases, it appears as if an agent has excellent subjective reasons for doing things which from an objective point of view are either completely worthless or obviously inferior to other things which she might do. Of course, there are familiar strategies for dealing with these appearances, many of which have been generated by the utilitarian tradition. The most revisionist strategy is to dismiss them, and to castigate people who spend their time on worthless activities as irrational, and people who pursue the happiness of their loved ones at the expense of the greater good as selfish. A more moderate strategy is to produce extraneous justifications for giving one's personal concerns extra weight. The good is maximized, say, by everyone looking after her own special friends. But there are also well-known objections to these strategies.[21]

---

[20] See Samuel Scheffler, *The Rejection of Consequentialism* (Oxford: Oxford University Press, 1982), p. 41. I discuss Scheffler's views briefly in Section V below.

[21] Many of which can be found in the two pieces by Williams cited in note 19.

Rather than supposing that a special concern for your own projects, loved ones, and actions is either irrational or in need of an extraneous justification, Nagel thinks we should allow that there are some values which are purely agent-relative. Accordingly, in *The View from Nowhere*, he offers us explanations of why reasons of the first two kinds, reasons of autonomy and deontological reasons, might be thought to exist. In what follows I examine these accounts.

IV. AMBITION

In *The View from Nowhere*, Nagel suggests that some of an agent's interests and desires give rise to agent-neutral values and some only to agent-relative values. The obvious question is how we are to draw the line. Nagel expects the two categories to sort along these lines: Our interests in avoiding pains and having pleasures, in the satisfaction of what we would intuitively call basic needs, and in the possession of freedom, self-respect, and access to opportunities and resources, give rise to neutral values (*VFN*, p. 171). But more idiosyncratic personal projects, such as the desire to climb to the top of Kilimanjaro or to learn to play the piano, have only relative value. Rather than using Nagel's label "reasons of autonomy," I am going to call these idiosyncratic projects "ambitions."[22] The claim is that ambitions give those who have them reasons to do things, but do not give others reasons to help or to care whether these things get done. The question then is why the normative force of ambitions is limited in this way.

According to Nagel, it is a matter of how far an individual's authority to confer value may appropriately be thought to extend (*VFN*, p. 168). In order to explain this it is helpful to introduce another distinction. Nagel believes that values may differ in what he calls their degree of externality, their independence from the concerns of sentient beings (*VFN*, pp. 152–53). Some valuable things clearly get their value from their relation to people. Consider for instance chocolate. We could account for the value of chocolate in either of two ways. One is to say that its value is intrinsic, and that the reason why we like it so much is because we recognize that fact. If we failed to like chocolate, we would have failed to appreciate something of value. The other is to say that eating chocolate is valuable to human beings *because* we like it so much. In the case of chocolate, that seems like a much more sensible thing to say. Chocolate is not an independent value which our taste buds recognize (as if they

---

[22] Several readers have pointed out to me that this label, together with the example I go on to discuss, might suggest that all personal projects are in some way competitive. I do not mean to imply that, and in fact I discuss some noncompetitive ones below. But the choice of an example of a personal project which is competitive seems to me to be useful, since such projects are especially resistant to objectification of either an Objective Realist or an Intersubjectivist kind.

were an epistemological faculty, a way of knowing about values). Instead, chocolate gets its value *from* the way it affects us. We *confer* value on it by liking it.

In other cases it is less obvious whether this sort of analysis applies. Consider the value of a beautiful sunset or a work of art. Here, people are much more tempted to say that the value, the beauty, is in the object itself, and that what we do is recognize it. If we didn't like it, we would be failing to see a value that is really there. This is the kind of value that Nagel calls external.[23] Obviously, this kind of value is only possible if we accept an Objective Realist interpretation of agent-neutral or objective values. An Intersubjectivist must say that the value of beauty arises in the same way as the value of chocolate, only by a more complex process. In this case, aesthetic value would also be a value that we confer.[24]

Leave aside the question whether there are any external values. Suppose that we are talking about those values which we confer. Some of these values are conferred collectively—as aesthetics values are, if they are conferred—while others are conferred individually. This is the phenomenon which Nagel refers to as the individual's authority. The individual's authority is his right to confer objective value on something by desiring, or enjoying, or being interested in it. Whenever we say that an agent-neutral value arises from someone's desire, we in effect allow the agent to confer agent-neutral or objective value on some state of affairs. If all desires gave rise to agent-neutral reasons, every desire would be an act of legislation—it would create a value for the whole human race. The question therefore is how far the individual's right to legislate runs: what range of things an individual has the authority to confer neutral or objective value on.

Nagel believes that it is appropriate to give the individual the authority to confer objective value on her own inner states and the conditions that determine what living her life is like, but that it is not appropriate to give an agent the authority to confer objective value on things that are completely outside of herself (*VFN*, pp. 169-71). Suppose, for example, that it is my ambition that my statue should stand on campus. It seems very odd to say that everyone has a reason to work to bring this about

---

[23] Barbara Herman has pointed out to me that the external account works better for natural beauty than for art, since works of art are socially embedded and therefore their value seems more relative to our interests.

[24] One may wonder whether an Objective Realist can accommodate the cases of clearly relational value, like the case of chocolate. The answer is yes. The Objective Realist does not have to place the intrinsic value in the chocolate. He can place it in the experience of a human being enjoying eating the chocolate. That is to say, he can construct what G. E. Moore called an organic unity and place the value-creating relationship inside of it. (See Moore, *Principia Ethica*, ch. 6.) The trouble with this strategy is that it conceals the fact that the value is really relational, and the possibility, embraced by Intersubjectivism, that all values are really relational. For further discussion, see my "Two Distinctions in Goodness," *Philosophical Review*, vol. 92 (1983), pp. 169-95, especially 190-93.

merely because I desire it. Why should I be the right person to determine what state of the campus is objectively good?[25] On the other hand, I seem to be exactly the right person to determine what state of *me* is objectively good. If I'm not the person to determine this, who could possibly be? This is why everyone has a reason to help me to achieve things like pleasure and freedom, but no one has a reason to help me get my statue put up on campus.

Two facts complicate what I have just said — facts which we must notice in order to avoid confusion. The first is that the satisfaction of a desire often brings pleasure, and Nagel supposes that pleasure has neutral value. In one sense, then, you do have a reason to help me arrange to get my statue on campus, but the reason is not, directly, that I want it. It is that, given that I want it, it will give me pleasure. To see that these two reasons are different, we need only remind ourselves that desire and pleasure can be prized apart. We can have desires for the realization of states of affairs in which we will not personally take part, and desires whose satisfactions we will never even know about.

The other complication comes from one of Nagel's other categories of agent-relative reasons. It seems natural to believe that people have a special obligation to try to promote the projects of those with whom they have personal relationships (*VFN*, p. 168). If I am your friend, I should be concerned with whether or not you achieve your ambitions, regardless of whether your doing so serves some objective or neutral value.[26] To correct for these complications, we should imagine a case where all that is relevant is that some randomly selected person has an ambition, and ask whether that ambition, *in itself*, provides others with normative reasons, as it does the person who has it. Suppose I want my statue to stand on campus after I am dead (*VFN*, p. 169). I will not be one of those

---

[25] Of course, this way of putting it assumes that no one else has any desires about the campus that could weigh against mine. In that sense, it assumes that I am the only person in the world who cares about the campus. Some people, when they realize that, are tempted to think that under those improbable circumstances I *would* be the right person to determine what counts as a good state of the campus.

[26] This includes your happiness or pleasure, which perhaps makes what I say here controversial. I am claiming that if I care about you I want your ambitions to be fulfilled, and not only in order to make you happy. I want them to be satisfied simply because you do. This is why deathbed wishes are entrusted to loved ones. Of course, this does not mean that I will never oppose your pursuit of an ambition if I foresee that it will make you miserable. But that is a matter of weighing, not a matter of refusing to give the ambition any weight of its own. Something here depends on one's views about rationality. There are people who hold that it is only rational to fulfill those ambitions that will make us happy. If you hold this view about rationality, you are likely to encourage and help your friends only to do what will make them happy, just as you are likely to give up your own more dangerous ambitions. But if you hold that it is sometimes rational just to do what you think is important without regard for your happiness, you are likely to respect a friend's desire to do what he thinks is important without regard to his happiness as well. Of course, if you hold the view that happiness just consists in doing what you think is most important, these issues cannot even arise.

who uses or even sees the campus, nor will I even be around to enjoy the thought that my ambition has been achieved. Someone who takes this desire to be in itself the source of an objectively normative reason must be prepared to let me control campus aesthetics from beyond the grave. According to Nagel, my authority should not extend so far.

This way of putting the question makes Nagel's answer seem reasonable. But it ignores the fact that most people do not regard the value of pursuing their ambitions as grounded merely in their own desires.[27] Here it helps to appeal to a distinction Nagel himself used in *The Possibility of Altruism*—the distinction between unmotivated and motivated desires (*PA*, pp. 29ff.). An unmotivated desire is one which is simply caused in us; a motivated desire is one for which we can give reasons. In *The View from Nowhere*, Nagel says nothing about why his exemplar wants to play the piano or climb to the top of Kilimanjaro (*VFN*, p. 167). But most people *do* have reasons for their personal ambitions, and in this sense their ambitions are motivated.[28] Attention to this fact reveals that the structure of a reason of ambition is rather complex.

Suppose it is my ambition to write a book about Kant's ethics that will be required reading in all ethics classes. I do not care whether or not I live to see my book required. Following Nagel's analysis, we will say that this ambition is agent-relative, since it gives me a reason to try to bring it about that my book is required reading, but it does not give anyone else a reason to require my book. This seems to fit, for surely no reason for anyone to require my book could spring from the bare fact that I *want* it that way. The only conceivable reason for anyone to require my book would be that it was a good book.

But this way of describing the situation implies a strange description of my own attitude. It suggests that my desire to have my book required is a product of raw vanity, and that if I want to write a good book, this is merely as a means to getting it required. This does not correctly reflect the structure of my ambition. Part of the reason that I want to write a good book on Kant's ethics is that I think such a book would be a good thing, and my ambition is not conceivable without that thought. It is an ambition to do something good, and it would not be served by people's requiring my book regardless of whether it were good. For now, let us describe this by saying that I think *someone* should write a book on Kant's ethics good enough that it will be required reading. I think that this would have neutral value.

---

[27] On this point, see also Stephen Darwall, *Impartial Reason*, p. 139.

[28] When introducing the idea (in *PA*, p. 29), Nagel writes as if a motivated desire were one arrived at through deliberation. But on his own view prudence is a motivated desire, and most of us can hardly be said to have arrived at it through deliberation. You arrive at it through the simple recognition of a reason—that it is your own future—without deliberation. I am using the term in this looser sense; I do not think that most people arrive at their ambitions through deliberation.

This does not, however, mean that my ambition is just a disinterested response to that neutral value. It is essential not to sanitize the phenomena here, or we shall go wrong. I may be interested in personal adulation, I may really like the idea of my book's being required reading, and I may even harbor competitive feelings towards others engaged in similar projects. I do not just want it to be the case that someone writes the book. I want to *be the someone* who writes that book. That element in my ambition is ineliminably agent-relative; no one else, except possibly my friends, has a reason to care whether I write the book or someone else does.

So the structure of this ambition is not:

(1) I want my book to be required reading (where that is an agent-relative end);
(2) therefore: I shall write a good book (as a means to that end);

but rather:

(1) Someone should write a book on Kant good enough that it will be required reading (where that is an agent-neutral end);
(2) I want to be that someone (agent-relative motive).

In other words, to have a personal project or ambition is not to desire a special object which you think is good for you subjectively, but rather to want to stand in a special relationship to something you think is good objectively.

Ambition so characterized clearly does have an agent-relative component: you want to stand in a special relationship to what is good. Is this component the source of subjective reasons for action? On the one hand, the agent-relative component does seem to *motivate* me to do a lot of work I would not otherwise do. It is often true that without the personal element in ambition, people would not be able to bring themselves to carry out arduous tasks. There are, therefore, neutral reasons for encouraging the personal desires associated with ambitions. But should the agent herself treat these personal desires as the sources of reasons? If I took it seriously that my desire that *I* should be the one to write the book was a reason for action, then I would have a reason to prevent one of the other Kant scholars from writing *her* book. But in fact, neither I nor anybody else thinks I have a reason to do this, even if in competitive moments I am tempted to feel it. This is not an expression of ambition, but rather a very familiar perversion of it.

It is important to see that reasons of personal obligation characteristically have this form. Although I may not suppose that the happiness of my loved ones is objectively more important than that of anyone else, I certainly do suppose that their happiness is objectively good. The structure of reasons arising from love is similar to that of reasons of ambition. I think that someone should make my darling happy, and I want very much to *be that someone*. And others may have good reason to encourage me in this. But if I try to prevent someone else from making my darling happy or if I suppose that my darling's happiness has no value unless it is produced by me, that is no longer an expression of love. Again, it is a very familiar perversion of it.[29]

Where there is no agent-neutral value anywhere in the structure of the ambition—where the ambition is not an ambition to do something good—we might feel inclined to deny that it provides any kind of a reason, even an agent-relative reason for its agent. This is a plausible way of dealing with my ambition to have my statue on campus. That is just a stupid piece of vanity, and one might well think that such a desire does not provide even *me* with a reason for trying to arrange its satisfaction.

But there is an important objection to the way I have handled these cases. I have been trading on the claim that a good book on Kant's ethics would be an objectively good thing. You may of course deny that. But even if you accept it, you might point out that not every ambition is *in that way* an ambition to do or produce something good. Is someone who wants to climb a mountain "because it is there" committed to the view that someone ought to climb this mountain (as if it needed climbing), or perhaps that climbing a mountain is an intrinsically valuable action, whose occurrence everyone has a reason to promote? Does someone who wishes to collect stamps or coins or barbed wire, or to excel at bowling or billiards, have to believe that these are activities with an intrinsic value of their own?

Perhaps that does not seem quite right. But neither does it seem right to say that those who pursue such projects are in the grip of unmotivated desires, or view themselves as being so. There are reasons for caring about these things, reasons which are communicable and therefore at least potentially shareable. Ask a mountain climber why she climbs and she need not be mute: she may tell you things about the enlarged vistas, the struggle with the elements, the challenge of overcoming fears or surpassing physical limitations. She takes her desire to climb mountains to be a motivated desire, motivated by recognizably good features of the experience of climbing. She does not take the value of the climb to be conferred on it simply by her desire to do it. Someone who says "I *just* want to" is not offering you his reason; he is setting up a bulwark against in-

---

[29] I am not suggesting that there is something perverted about *sexual* jealousy. The desire to make love to someone is not primarily the desire to be the one who provides him with a certain kind of experience. The desire to make someone happy can be an expression of either morality or of love, but in neither case is it their essence. For further discussion, see my "Creating the Kingdom of Ends: Reciprocity and Responsibility in Personal Relations," in *Philosophical Perspectives 6: Ethics*, ed. James Tomberlin (Atascadero, California: Ridgeview Publishing Company, 1992).

comprehension. You may be the problem, or he may feel himself inartic-
ulate: many people do. But listen to the articulate talk about their projects
and you hear the familiar voice of humanity, not the voice of alien idio-
syncrasies.

Or if you don't, perhaps you should. For it is at this point that the difference between Objective Realism and Intersubjectivism becomes important. An Objective Realist interpretation of the value of climbing
mountains, or of collecting stamps or coins or barbed wire, or of excelling
at bowling or billiards, is not very tempting.[30] Neither, I think, is an Objective Realist interpretation of the value of a good book on Kant's ethics. These are not intrinsic values, already there in the universe, which
we have discovered, but rather are expressions of our own distinctively
human capacity to take an interest, and to find something interesting, in
whatever we find around us. To share another's ends, or at least to grant
that they could be shared, is to see them as expressions of that capacity,
and so as expressions of our common humanity. The Intersubjectivist
sees the other as human, and *therefore* shares or tries to share the other's
ends. That is why she helps others to pursue their ambitions. But the Objective Realist sees no reason to help unless he *first* sees the other's ends
as ones that he can share. His relationship to others is mediated by his
relationship to their ends. According to the Intersubjectivist this is not
only a mistake in moral theory but a moral wrong. We should promote
the ends of others not because we recognize the value of those *ends*, but
rather out of respect for the humanity of those who have them.

I am not here concerned to argue, as Nagel is in *The Possibility of Altruism*, that we are always obliged to promote everyone's ambitions, and
that therefore we must find some "combinatorial principles" for weighing up the many reasons they provide (*PA*, pp. 133ff.). I do not myself
believe that reasons *can* be added across the boundaries of persons. And
since we cannot always act for everyone's reasons, that cannot be our
duty. But according to this argument we are obliged to see the ends of
others as providing reasons for action, and this means that the claims of

---

[30] One may say that human talents and powers are developed and refined by these activities, and that this is an objective human good. Indeed, when people talk about what they
like about these activities, these are the things they talk about. But this does not mean that
what they care about are these supposedly objectively valuable features of their chosen activities rather than the particular activities themselves. Other activities, which people are not
always prepared to substitute for the ones they actually choose, may refine and develop similar human powers. And one may even accept these other activities as substitutes *if it is necessary* (as when one turns to a less strenuous sport in old age). But we should not take that
to mean that the "objective" goods embodied in the activities were all that the actors cared
about. The problem here is like the problem associated with the fact that we love particular people even though what we can say we love about them is general. You love a particular person, not just his warmth, intelligence, and sense of humor. It is not true that any
other person with these attributes would do just as well, even though it is true that if he
leaves you, you may seek another person with these attributes to replace him. No adequate
theory of value can ignore these complex facts.

proximity may bring them into play. Someone in your neighborhood, in immediate need of help in order to carry out his ambition, does present you with a reason to act. In that sense, reasons springing from ambitions are agent-neutral. But they spring from our respect for one another, rather than from our respect for one another's ends.

But one form of proximity is especially important. For of course it is also true that you might come to share the ambition of another in a deeper way. For if what I have said is right, you ought to be committed to the view that another *could* explain to you what is good about the world as she sees it through the eyes of her ambition.[31] You may come to see the value of mountain climbing, or philosophical ethics, or stamp collecting, and to take it as your own. And then, between the two of you, the value functions *as if* it were a value in the Objective Realist sense. It is a fact about your relationship that you both see this as a good thing, which you share a reason to promote. This is why those who share particular ambitions form communities which acknowledge special and reciprocal obligations to one another. In this way, Intersubjective values can come to function like Objective Realist values with respect to the very communities which they themselves create.

V. DEONTOLOGY

Deontological reasons are reasons for an agent to do or avoid certain actions. They do not spring from the consequences of those actions, but rather from the claims of those with whom we interact to be treated by us in certain ways. One who believes in deontological values believes that no matter how good our ends are, we are not supposed to hurt people, or tell lies, or break promises in their pursuit. Deontological reasons are the source of the traditional moral thou-shalt-nots.

---

[31] There are several ways to motivate this thought. Daniel Warren has pointed out to me, in conversation, that without this thought the requirement to share ends could be met by someone who took a sort of patronizing attitude towards the ambitions of others: "Oh, well, *you* like it, so I suppose we shall have to count it as good." Scott Kim points out that a parallel problem exists on the recipient's side: If you accept help from someone who does not in any way enter into your ambitions, you may be regarding him somewhat instrumentally. The point of these remarks is not to show that there is something *wrong* with either helping or accepting help among those who do not really enter into each other's interests, but that the moral attitude required of us is less than perfectly realized in such cases. This in turn shows that there is a kind of continuum between the sense of "shared ends" defined in the previous paragraph and the sense defined in this paragraph. One may share the ends of others in the sense of (i) agreeing to promote them because they are another's ends; (ii) trusting that there must really be something interesting about them because they are another's ends; (iii) seeing what is interesting about them; and (iv) coming to have them as your own ends. I thank Thomas Scanlon for prompting me to be clearer about this point, and Amélie Rorty for reminding me of the importance of the possibility that one may stop at step (iii); e.g., one may come to have a much better appreciation of what a certain school of art was trying to do without actually coming to enjoy the works or find them beautiful.

It is important to see why Nagel thinks these reasons must be agent-relative. Three other accounts of them, which construe them as objective or agent-neutral, may seem more plausible at first glance.

First, we might think that they derive directly from the agent-neutral or objectively valuable interests of the other people involved, the potential victims of wrongdoing. We might think that the reason not to hurt people is that it is objectively bad for them to be hurt, or that the reason not to lie to people is that it is objectively good for them to know the truth, or that the reason not to break promises springs from the objective badness of disappointed expectations. In short, we might think that wrongdoing is bad because of the *specific* harm that it does to the victim.

The second account of deontological values is modeled on one utilitarian account of them. John Stuart Mill argued that deontological principles are a kind of inductive generalization from particular utility calculations.[32] We apply the principle of utility directly in a large number of individual cases, and discover that, almost always, telling lies or breaking promises does more harm than good. Usually, this will be for the kind of reason mentioned in the first account—say, that pain, ignorance, or disappointment is bad—together with certain more long-range considerations, such as the bad effects of setting an example or making a habit of performing such actions.[33] The actions are bad because of the *general* harm which they do.

Third, we might think that the actions forbidden by deontological reasons are simply bad in themselves, objectively so—not (just) because of the harm that they do, but because of a specific form of badness, namely *wrongness*.

But there are problems with all of these attempts to construe deontological values as agent-neutral. To see this, consider Bernard Williams's by now famous example:

> Jim finds himself in the central square of a small South American town. Tied up against the wall are a row of twenty Indians, most terrified, a few defiant, in front of them several armed men in uniform. . . . The captain in charge explains that the Indians are a random group of the inhabitants who, after recent acts of protest against the government, are just about to be killed to remind other possible protestors of the advantages of not protesting. However, since Jim is an honored visitor from another land, the captain is happy to offer him a guest's privilege of killing one of the Indians himself. If Jim accepts, then as a special mark of the occasion, the other Indians will be let off. . . . [I]f Jim refuses . . . Pedro here will do what he was about to do when Jim arrived, and kill them all.[34]

---

[32] See John Stuart Mill, *Utilitarianism* (Indianapolis: Hackett Publishing, 1979), pp. 23–24.
[33] *Ibid.*, p. 22.
[34] Williams, in Smart and Williams, *Utilitarianism: For and Against*, p. 98.

Utilitarians are committed to the view that it is *obvious* that Jim should kill an Indian, but few people can imagine themselves in Jim's position without some sense of a dilemma. Many think that in Jim's shoes they would kill an Indian, but they do not see it as a happy opportunity for doing some good. Some think that Jim should not let the captain co-opt him into participating in a murder and should refuse. Still others think that it is essential to find out, if possible, what the Indians want Jim to do.[35] Nagel thinks that if all values are objective or agent-neutral we should have *no* sense of dilemma in cases like this, since that we do the *most* good by killing the Indian is obvious.

This problem can be dealt with in various ways. A consequentialist may claim that it is salutary for us to be subject to some hesitation to kill, even when the hesitation is irrational. Someone who favors the second account of deontological reasons, in terms of general harm, is especially likely to make this argument: killing is certainly something that usually does more harm than good, so a natural reluctance to do it has a consequentialist value of its own.[36] Another possible solution is suggested by the fact that the problem seems to depend on the assumption that values can be added across the boundaries between persons. If we deny this assumption, we may deny that killing twenty Indians is a worse thing than killing one. This move is not open to those who hold that the badness of a wrong act rests in the *general* harm that it does. But those who think that the badness rests in the specific harm to the victim, or in the wrongness of the act itself, may simply refuse to add. According to this view, not only hesitating but refusing to kill the Indian is perfectly intelligible.

But this does not entirely solve the problem. Suppose we do think that the badness of killing this Indian rests either in his own resulting death or in the badness of the act of killing him. We refuse to add values. Now it looks as if the badness is the same whether the Indian is shot by Jim or by Pedro: there will be a death, and a killing, either way. So perhaps Jim should flip a coin? This does not seem right either: most of us think that if Jim does not suppose he is going to do any good by killing the Indian then he *certainly* should not kill him. But if the same amount of evil is

---

[35] I think this point is sometimes overlooked in discussions of this example. Williams, to be fair, specifies that the Indians are begging Jim to accept the offer (*ibid.*, p. 99). But he obscures the importance of this point when he says that this is "obviously" what they would be doing.

[36] This is a familiar move: when reminded that a person is likely to experience a negative moral emotion such as guilt, regret, hesitation, or squeamishness about doing something which according to our theory is right, the philosopher points out that the action in question is *usually* wrong and that it is therefore healthy to be equipped with some reactions which will make it hard for us to do it or will make us think twice before doing it. The assumption seems to be that our emotions are clunkier, more mechanical, less sensitive to the details of a situation, and altogether less refined than our thoughts. This view seems to be a byproduct of the modern conception of the emotions; the emotions are conceived as feelings or reactions, not as perceptions. Aristotle, for instance, would not have said this about the trained emotions of the virtuous person.

done either way, then Jim's reason for declining to kill the Indian must be agent-relative.

To make the problem clearer, imagine a peculiar theory of value. According to this theory, value is always objective or agent-neutral, and the only thing that has value is the keeping of promises. This theory will not tell us always to keep our promises, surprising as this may seem. First, assume that we can add values. Then there could be a case like this: by breaking your promise, you could cause five other people to keep theirs; while, if you keep yours, they will break theirs. You produce more promise-keeping by breaking your promise than by keeping it, and so that is what the theory tells you to do. Second, suppose we say that the promise-breakings must be bad for someone, and that their badness cannot be added across the boundaries between persons. For whom are they bad? It does not matter which view we take. If the badness is for the victim, I have no reason to care whether I inflict it on him or you do. I should flip a coin. If the badness is for me, the agent, I may have a reason to care, but it could only be an agent-relative one.

Nagel concludes that deontological reasons, if they exist, are agent-relative. The special relation in which you stand to an action when you are the one who performs it carries a special weight, like the special relations in which you stand to your own ambitions or loved ones. In taking this position, Nagel joins Samuel Scheffler, who had earlier argued that deontological values are agent-relative. In *The Rejection of Consequentialism*, Scheffler argues for what he calls an "agent-centered prerogative," a right, under certain conditions, to neglect what will conduce to the overall good in favor of one's personal commitments.[37] Such a prerogative does the work of Nagel's "reasons of autonomy." But Scheffler finds the idea of an "agent-centered restriction"—that is, a deontological requirement—paradoxical. He claims that the idea that there could be a reason not to do certain actions which is not equally a reason to prevent them from being done has "an apparent air of irrationality," which any account of them must dispel.[38] Although Nagel undertakes to explain how deontological reasons arise, it is clear that he shares Scheffler's attitude. He characterizes deontological constraints as "obscure" and "peculiar"; he wonders how what we *do* can be so much more important than what *happens* (*VFN*, pp. 175, 180–81). At one point he says:

> One reason for the resistance to deontological constraints is that they are formally puzzling, in a way that the other reasons we have discussed are not. We can understand how autonomous agent-relative reasons might derive from the specific projects and concerns of the agent, and we can understand how neutral reasons might derive from the interests of others, giving each of us reason to take them

[37] Scheffler, *The Rejection of Consequentialism*, pp. 14ff.
[38] *Ibid.*, p. 82.

into account. But how can there be relative reasons to respect the claims of others? How can there be a reason not to twist someone's arm which is not equally a reason to prevent his arm from being twisted by someone else? (*VFN*, p. 178)

Despite his doubts, Nagel gives an account of why such reasons exist.

In cases where a deontological restriction is at issue, performing the *action* puts you into a direct relationship with another human being—your "victim" as Nagel puts it. In performing the action, you will have to aim directly at evil for your victim, even if your larger purpose is good. Robert Nozick, in his remarks on the apparent paradox of deontology, puts the point in more Kantian language. In violating a deontological requirement, you will have to treat your victim as a mere means.[39] I will come back to the question of what there is to choose between these two formulations. In any case, the force of deontological restrictions, according to Nagel, rests in the immediate badness of victimizing someone.

Nagel illustrates his point with an example (*VFN*, p. 176). You need the cooperation of a reluctant elderly woman in order to save someone's life, and you find that you can only secure it by twisting the arm of her grandchild so that his screams will induce her to act. You are faced with using the child as a means to saving a life, and in this case, that involves hurting the child. If the grandmother does not give in, you have to try to hurt the child more. You have to *will* to hurt the child more, and so, in a sense, to want to (*VFN*, p. 182). The louder the child screams, the better for you. But there he is, a child, a vulnerable human being to whom everyone owes protection. From your point of view, this is a terrible thing to *do*.

You might think that this analysis does not apply in some of the other cases I have mentioned. Consider Williams's Indians. The one you kill is going to die anyway, whether he is shot by you all alone or along with his compatriots by Pedro. So you are not bringing about an evil for him which he would not have endured otherwise. But there is still a sense in which *you* are aiming directly at his evil. You must pick up a rifle, aim it at his heart, and fire. You must be gratified if the bullet kills him, just as you must be gratified if the child screams louder. And, despite appearances, there is also a sense in which you are treating him as a mere means. You are killing him in order to save the others. The fact that he is going to die anyway does not really change the fact that this is what *you* are doing.

According to Kant, you treat someone as a mere means whenever you treat him in a way to which he could not possibly consent.[40] Kant's cri-

---

[39] See note 1.

[40] See Immanuel Kant, *Grounding for the Metaphysics of Morals* (Indianapolis: Hackett Publishing, 1983), p. 37; Prussian Academy edition, p. 430. For interpretation, see my "The Right to Lie: Kant on Dealing with Evil," *Philosophy and Public Affairs*, vol. 15 (1986), pp. 325–49; and Onora O'Neill, "Between Consenting Adults," *Philosophy and Public Affairs*, vol. 14 (1985), pp. 252–77.

terion most obviously rules out actions which depend upon force, coercion, or deception for their nature, for it is of the essence of such actions that they make it impossible for their victims to consent. If I am forced, I have no chance to consent. If I am deceived, I don't know what I am consenting to. If I am coerced, my consent itself is forced by means I would reject.[41] So if an action depends upon force or deception or coercion, it is impossible for me to consent to *it*. To treat someone as an end, by contrast, is to respect his right to use his own reason to determine whether and how he will contribute to what happens.

This is why it is important to establish, if you can, what the Indians themselves think should happen. Suppose the oldest Indian steps forward and says, "Please go ahead, shoot *me*, and I forgive you in advance." This does not make things wonderful but it does help. *Very* roughly speaking, you are not treating him as a mere means if he consents to what you are doing.[42] Of course, the Indian does not in general consent to be shot, and his gesture does not mean that after all he has not been wronged. In the larger moral world he has. But if you and the Indians are forced to regard Pedro and the captain as mere forces of nature, as you are in this case, then there is a smaller moral world within which the issue is between you and them, and in that world this Indian consents. On the other hand, suppose the Indians are pacifists and they say, "We would rather die than ask you, an innocent man, to commit an act of violence. Don't do what the captain asks, but go back up north, and tell our story; make sure people know what is happening down here." Now the decision *not* to shoot looks much more tempting, doesn't it? Now you can at least imagine refusing. But you may still take the rifle from Pedro's hands and say, "You cannot ask me to kill to save you, and yet I will," and pick an Indian to shoot. This is a different kind of decision to kill than the earlier one, for it involves a refusal to share the Indians' moral universe; from the perspective of the Indians who live, it has a slight taint of paternalism.

Surprisingly, the fact that you are treating someone as a mere means operates even in the peculiar cases of breaking a promise so that other people will keep theirs, or telling a lie so that others will tell the truth. You can see this by imagining the kind of case in which you could be faced with such a decision. If I tell the truth, I predict, three of you will

---

[41] There are familiar philosophical puzzles about all of these notions. This is perhaps especially true of coercion, notoriously hard to distinguish in any formal way from bribery or the mere offer of an incentive. This is not the place to take these puzzles up, but this should pose a problem only for readers who are actually skeptical about whether there is such a thing as coercion.

[42] That is a remark that needs *many* qualifications. Actual consent—in the sense of saying yes—can easily be spurious. As Onora O'Neill argues, a better test of whether someone was able to consent is whether the person had an authentic opportunity to say no. See Onora O'Neill, "Justice, Gender, and International Boundaries," in *The Quality of Life*, ed. Martha Nussbaum and Amartya Sen (Oxford: Clarendon Press, 1992).

tell lies that you should not tell. On what basis could I make this prediction? Perhaps I think that if I tell the truth I will reveal information which will show you that it is in your interest to lie, and I also think that you are unscrupulous people who will lie if it is in your interest. Or perhaps I believe that the truth will confuse you, and that you will tell the lies as a result of the muddle. Or perhaps I think you have a wrongheaded moral system, and knowing this particular truth will make you wrongly conclude that you ought to lie. However it goes, if I tell a lie in order to *get you* to tell the truth, I am treating you as somehow inferior creatures whose tendency to go wrong must be controlled by my superior wisdom. Since this is a way of being treated to which you could not possibly consent, I am treating you as a mere means. Here I am not necessarily aiming at anything evil for you: I may be paternalistic, protecting you from going wrong. This shows, I think, that Nagel is mistaken when he emphasizes that you are aiming at your victim's *evil*. The problem is that you are treating your victim as a mere means. But suppose that with this revision we accept Nagel's account. It is the particular badness of treating someone as a means that explains deontological reasons. It is the horribleness of looking right into a pair of human eyes, while treating their owner like an piece of furniture or a tool. And yet by violating the restriction you may be doing what is best. So the badness of violating it is a badness that is for you. The reason is agent-relative.

Now this does not seem right at all. Surely when you violate a deontological restriction, it is bad for your victim as well as for you. Your victim may surely object to being treated as a mere means, even when he understands the larger good which is thereby produced. And his objection is not only to being harmed; it is to being *used*. Nagel believes that his theory can accommodate the victim's right to complain. He says:

> The deontological constraint permits a victim always to object to those who aim at his harm, and this relation has the same special character of normative magnification when seen from the personal perspective of the victim that it has when seen from the personal perspective of the agent. Such a constraint expresses the direct view of the person on whom he is acting. *It operates through that relation.* The victim feels outrage when he is deliberately harmed even for the greater good of others, not simply because of the quantity of the harm but because of the assault on *his value* of having my actions guided by his evil. (*VFN*, p. 184; my emphases)

This is absolutely right. But the theory that deontological reasons are agent-relative or only subjectively normative *cannot* accommodate it. If the deontological reason were agent-relative, merely *my* property, my victim would not have the right to demand that I act on it. Consider a comparison. If you have an agent-relative reason to climb Kilimanjaro, and don't do it, I may entertain the thought that you are being irrational. I can see what your reasons are. But if I have no reason to bring it about that you climb Kilimanjaro, as Nagel supposes, then I have no reason to talk you into doing it. I have no reason to do anything about your relative reasons, even to think about them, although I may happen to. I certainly don't have a reason to complain of your conduct when you don't act on them, and if I do, you may justifiably tell me that it is none of my business. If deontological reasons were *agent*-relative, the same thing would hold for victims. My victim could entertain the thought that I have a reason not to treat him this way, but that thought would give him no grounds for complaint. Astonishingly enough, it turns out to be none of his business.

Earlier, I mentioned two reasons why you might be moved to do something by someone else's subjective or relative reasons. One is to give her the agent-neutral good of pleasure. The other springs from the third category of agent-relative reasons, the reasons of personal obligation. If you stand in a personal relation to someone, you may therefore interest yourself in her subjective reasons. This seems like a natural thing to say, and it has weight against the points I have just been making. Although we may resent it when strangers point out to us that we are not doing what we have reason to do, we do not resent such reminders from friends, and we do not tell them that it is none of their business.

Nagel suggests, in the passage quoted above, that the deontological constraint "operates through the relation" between agent and victim. So it is tempting to suppose that what he has in mind is something like this: the relationship of agents and victims, like that of love or friendship, is a *personal* relationship. Perhaps *that* is what gives the victim a stake in the agent's relative reasons, and so entitles him to complain.[43]

But the violation of a deontological constraint *always* involves an agent and a victim, and thus if this account is correct, deontological reasons are always shared reasons. They cannot be the personal property of individual agents. Instead, they supervene on the relationships of people who interact with one another. They are intersubjective reasons.

In fact, Nagel's primal scene, the confrontation of agent and victim, shows us how agent-neutral reasons are *created* in personal interaction. My victim complains; he says: "How would you like it if someone did that to you?" I see not merely that I wouldn't like it, but that I would resent it. I am treating my victim as a means, and it is the essence of treating another as a means that his consent is dispensed with. It would be impossible for me to consent to be so treated and so I would have to rebel. That is why I would feel resentment. "How would you like it if someone did that to you?" In asking me this question my victim demands that

---

[43] Thomas Scanlon has drawn my attention to a footnote in Nagel's paper "War and Massacre" in which Nagel mentions that Marshall Cohen says that according to Nagel's view, shooting at someone establishes an I-thou relationship. See *Mortal Questions* (Cambridge: Cambridge University Press, 1979), p. 69. I agree with Cohen, and think that so interpreted Nagel is *right*.

I either cease using him as a means, or give up my own claim not to be so used by others. But the latter is impossible: one cannot consent to be used as a means. And so *he obligates me* to desist, and to treat him instead as an end in himself.[44] This of course is a variant of Nagel's own argument in *The Possibility of Altruism* (*PA*, pp. 82ff.). And as his arguments there show, my recognition that others must be treated as ends in themselves explains altruistic reasons as well. We resent those who regard our plight with indifference, in much the same way that we resent those who use us as means.

But now we have arrived at a picture of neutral or objective value that is different from the one Nagel had intended to give us. According to this account, *all* neutral reasons for action arise from a category which Nagel had thought of as a source of relative reasons—the category of personal relationships. But this is no special category: for *all* human interaction is personal. It is because or to the extent that we regard one another as *persons* that we acknowledge the force of deontological reasons. As persons, others demand that we treat them in ways to which they can consent; as persons, we find we must respond to that demand. But we also express our respect for one another's humanity by sharing in each other's ends. As persons, we have a claim on one another's help when it can readily be given or is desperately needed. It is the status of humanity, as the source of normative claims, that is the source of all value. The argument, in other words, has brought us back to Kant.

VI. POSTSCRIPT

Let me conclude by going back to the thoughts with which I began. In both *The Possibility of Altruism* and *The View from Nowhere*, Nagel's arguments take an unexpected turn. In both he starts from recognizably Kantian ideas, working in *The Possibility of Altruism* with motivation derived from a metaphysical conception of the person, and in *The View from Nowhere* with a two-standpoints account. And yet in both he ends up having to construct elaborate arguments to fend off the conclusion that his ideas will lead to utilitarianism. Why does this happen? It happens because Nagel presupposes that the business of morality is to bring something about.[45] This presupposition infects Nagel's arguments in many

---

[44] Strictly speaking, this is only an account of what Kant would call the "incentive" of morality; we are not obligated until we acknowledge the necessity of adopting this incentive as law. A related point is this: several readers, among them Barbara Herman and Arthur Kuflik, have pointed out to me that this account says nothing about why I must recognize the other as a person, only about what follows from the fact that I do. For now, I can only acknowledge that the argument is incomplete in these ways. I hope to say more on these points elsewhere.

[45] A similar point, I think, can be made about Scheffler. He says that it is "natural" to interpret Nozick's defense of side constraints as an appeal to the disvalue, the badness, of violating those constraints (Scheffler, *The Rejection of Consequentialism*, p. 88). But it is only "natural" if you ignore Nozick's reminder that a moral constraint does not have to function as a moral goal—that is, only if you presuppose that the business of morality is the realization of goals.

ways. In *The Possibility of Altruism*, Nagel treats all reasons as reasons to *promote* something (*PA*, pp. 47ff.). In *The View from Nowhere*, he substitutes the idea of aiming at someone's evil for that of treating him as a means. Nagel is puzzled by deontology because he finds it odd that we could have reasons not to do things which are not equally reasons to *prevent* those things from being done (*VFN*, p. 177). He does not mention the difference between preventing an action by asking its agent not to do it or talking him out of it, and preventing an action by the use of force or tricks. If you suppose that all that matters is what you are bringing about, this is merely a difference in *method*. If morality is concerned with the character of human relationships, this difference is *everything*.[46] It is no accident that in order to explain deontology, Nagel must finally imagine his agents and victims *talking* to each other.[47] Nagel is in danger of ending up with consequentialism because that is where he started.

For the view that the business of ethics is to bring something about is the legacy of utilitarianism and, in turn, of the scientific aspirations of the utilitarian tradition. According to consequentialist conceptions of ethics, ethics is the most sublime form of technical engineering, the one that tells us how to bring about The Good. The questions that it answers are ques-

---

[46] Several readers have suggested to me that I am not really rejecting consequentialism but only proposing an alternative account of what we should aim at: decent human relationships. This suggestion is similar to the familiar consequentialist reply to standard counterexamples: "If justice matters, we can include it among the results." That kind of inclusion results in the curious view discussed above: that we should commit injustice if it will bring about more justice. Scheffler imagines his consequentialist saying: "And if you are worried that a violation of R [the deontological requirement] corrupts the relationship between the agent and the victim, and that the corruption of a human relationship is a bad thing, then why isn't it at least as permissible to corrupt one valuable relationship if that is the only way to prevent the corruption of five equally valuable human relationships?" (Scheffler, *The Rejection of Consequentialism*, pp. 89–90). A commitment to mutual respect in human relationships is not merely a commitment to bringing respectful relationships about, any more than a commitment to justice is merely a commitment to bringing justice about. For example: In the early stages of our friendship, I might be tempted to conceal things from you in order to help bring about a condition of mutual trust; I might be afraid that you will reject me too quickly if you find certain things out before you know me better. But if mutual trust is ever to be *achieved*, the day must come when my calculations about the effects of my telling you things stops: that is what it *means* for *me* to trust *you*. The point here is that having decent relationships with people is not the same as bringing them about, and to some extent is inconsistent with regarding them as things to be brought about. And my suggestion in this essay is that *having* decent human relationships, not bringing them about, is the primary concern of morality.

[47] Nor is it an accident that many of my own examples in this essay, especially the ones concerning Jim and the Indians, focus on what the protagonists might *say* to each other. Many of Rawls's arguments invite us to imagine people talking to each other, to consider what it would be like to say certain things to another person. His argument against the utilitarian account of what is wrong with slavery, in "Justice as Reciprocity" (in *Utilitarianism with Critical Essays*, ed. Samuel Gorovitz [Indianapolis: Bobbs-Merrill, 1971], pp. 242–68) in effect invites us to consider the absurdity of a slaveholder who says to a protesting slave: "But my gains *outweigh* your losses!" His consideration of the effects of publicizing principles of justice on people's self-respect are also related to this theme (see *Theory of Justice*, pp. 177ff). Part of the appeal of the difference principle is that it is the source of justifications which you can offer *to anyone* without embarrassment.

tions about what we should do with the world. These *are* the questions we must face when we confront issues of population control or the preservation of the environment, issues with which utilitarians have been nonaccidentally obsessed. But deontological restrictions predate these global issues, and were already recognized at a time when all we had to do with the world was to live in it together.

One way in which you might be tempted to describe the position I have defended in this essay leaves the distinction between neutral and relative values in place. It might be thought that I am defending this position: that persons have agent-neutral value, while all other values are agent-relative. And then I add that you express your sense of the neutral value of others by sharing in their agent-relative ends. This *is* close to the Kantian position I want to defend, but it is a misleading way to put it. It makes the value of persons a metaphysical reality, perhaps in need of a metaphysical defense; and to some minds, it will suggest that people are a good thing, and therefore that many people are better than a few. I do not believe these things.

Ask yourself, what is a reason? It is not just a consideration on which you in fact act, but one on which you are supposed to act; it is not just a motive, but rather a normative claim, exerting authority over other people and yourself at other times. To say that you have a reason is to say something *relational*, something which implies the existence of another, at least another self. It announces that you have a claim on that other, or acknowledges her claim on you. For normative claims are not the claims of a metaphysical world of values upon us: they are claims we make on ourselves and each other. It is both the essence of consequentialism and the trouble with it that it treats The Good, rather than people, as the source of normative claims.

The acknowledgment that another is a person is not exactly a reason to treat him in a certain way, but rather something that stands behind the very possibility of reasons. I cannot treat my own impulses to act as *reasons*, rather than mere occurrent impulses, without acknowledging that I at least exist at other times. I cannot treat them as *values*, exerting at least a possible claim on others, without acknowledging that other persons do indeed exist. That is the lesson of Nagel's own argument in *The Possibility of Altruism*. The title of this essay is a tautology: the only reasons that are possible are the reasons we can share.

Philosophy, Harvard University

REASONS FOR ALTRUISM*

By David Schmidtz

I. Regard for Others

This essay considers whether acts of altruism can be rational. Rational choice, according to the standard *instrumentalist* model, consists of maximizing one's utility, or more precisely, maximizing one's utility subject to a budget constraint.[1] We seek the point of highest utility lying within our limited means. The term 'utility' could mean a number of different things, but in recent times utility has usually been interpreted as preference satisfaction (and thus utility functions are sometimes called preference functions). To have a preference is to *care*, to want one alternative more than another.

People are self-regarding to the extent that they care about their own welfare. People are *purely* self-regarding if they care about no one's welfare other than their own and recognize no constraints on their pursuits beyond those imposed on them by circumstances: their limited time, income, and so on. The question is: Is it rational — is it *uniquely* rational — to be purely self-regarding? The instrumentalist model does not say. Nor, for that matter, does the instrumentalist model assume that people care about welfare (their own or that of others). For all the instrumentalist model says, a person could prefer the destruction of the world to the scratching of his finger.

The departures from pure self-regard that concern us here come in two varieties. First, we might care about other people, which is to say their welfare enters the picture through our preference functions. Indeed, a desire to help other people often is among our strongest desires. Second, the welfare of others can enter the picture in the form of self-imposed constraints that we acknowledge in the course of pursuing our goals. That is, an otherwise optional course of action may come to be seen as either forbidden or required, depending on how it would affect others. There

---

* I thank Neera Kapur Badhwar, Walter Glannon, Lainie Ross, and Elizabeth Willott for helpful comments on an earlier draft.

[1] The instrumentalist model is so standard that a viable alternative has yet to find its way into the literature of decision theory, but I am currently working on one in "Choosing Ends," unpublished. See Section II for brief remarks on the sort of consideration that might get an alternative model off the ground.

may be limits to what we are willing to do to others in the course of pursuing our goals.[2]

Insofar as one's other-regard takes the form of caring about other people's welfare, one exhibits *concern*. Insofar as one's other-regard takes the form of adherence to constraints on what one may do to others, one exhibits *respect*. As I see it, we manifest concern for people when we care about how life is treating them (so to speak), whereas we manifest respect for people when we care about how *we* are treating them, and constrain ourselves accordingly.[3]

I use the term *altruism* to characterize a certain kind of action. In particular, an action is altruistic only if it is motivated by regard for others.[4] Both concern and respect for others motivate departures from the pursuit of purely self-regarding satisfactions, and thus action motivated by other-regard clearly constitutes an interesting category from a rational-choice perspective. Whether altruistic action is coextensive with other-regarding action is, I suppose, a terminological matter. Some classify respect for others as altruistic; others would say that to respect others is merely to give them their due and thus cannot count as altruistic.[5] This terminological issue notwithstanding, it remains the case that the issue of substance is twofold. We have both concern and respect for others, which raises questions about whether these departures from pure self-regard are rational. This essay explores reasons for both departures, while acknowledging

[2] The distinction between self-regard and other-regard has often been applied to actions to mark a distinction between actions that affect only the agent and actions that affect others as well. (See John Stuart Mill's *On Liberty*, for example.) As applied to action within a community, the distinction has proven to be notoriously difficult to draw, at least insofar as it is meant to mark out a sphere of self-regarding activity with which society may not interfere. The problem is that a person seeking to justify interference with activities she dislikes can always claim she is being *affected* in some way or another. I do not, however, foresee analogous problems arising for the distinction between self-regarding and other-regarding concerns.

[3] Note that what motivates one kind of other-regard need not motivate the other. A person may think it out of the question to violate other people's rights, but may at the same time be unconcerned about other people's welfare. Or a person may be concerned about feeding the poor but have no qualms about taking other people's money to buy the food. In short, unconcerned people can be principled, and concerned people can be ruthless.

[4] Note that if I express concern or respect as a mere means to some other end, then the action is not altruistic. It is altruistic only if concern or respect for others is what motivates me to do it. Of course, people can act from mixed motives. Robin Hood may undertake a course of action in order to help the poor, make himself look good, and hurt the rich. His action is at once altruistic, self-serving, and vicious.

[5] This characterization leaves open questions about how altruism relates to justice and other essentially moral concepts. There is good reason not to use definitions to try to settle these questions. For example, if we try to use definitions to stipulate that altruism involves going beyond the requirements of justice, then we cannot count ourselves as observing instances of altruism unless we first settle what justice requires. Someone might wish to define altruism as other-regarding action that goes beyond the requirements of justice, but identifying members of the set of altruistic acts would then be fraught with difficulties, and pointlessly so. The difficulties would be mere artifacts of a bad definition.

that some people consider one or the other to be the canonical form of altruism.[6]

There is, of course, a sense in which to characterize altruism as I have done is already to have given reasons for altruism. To wit, people act altruistically—foregoing opportunities to satisfy purely self-regarding preferences—out of concern (or respect) for others. If we prefer on balance to act on our concern for others, then by that very fact we have reasons for altruism. The reasons are not purely self-regarding reasons, to be sure, but they are still reasons, and reasons from our points of view. It hardly needs to be said, though, that no one would be satisfied with an argument that stopped here. A satisfying account of our reasons for altruism will not take our other-regarding concern and respect as given. Nor will it suffice to offer a purely descriptive account of other-regard—an account of what (biologically or psychologically or sociologically) *causes* us to develop regard for others. Facts about our biology and psychology are relevant, but they are not enough. What we want is an account according to which it is rational for us to have concern and respect for others.

The interesting question, then, is this: If we did not already have reasons for altruism—if we were not already other-regarding—would it be rational to *nurture* our latent regard for others? What is the point in having anything other than purely self-regarding preferences? This section characterized altruism as action motivated either by respect or concern for others. My task now is to explain how someone who was not already other-regarding could be led by self-regarding concerns to cultivate concern and respect for others, how self-regarding agents might rationally come to have reasons for altruism.

II. HOMO ECONOMICUS

As already noted, to be rational in the instrumental sense is to be committed to serving preferences *of* oneself, but one may or may not be committed to serving preferences *regarding* oneself. The instrumentalist way of looking at rational choice is a problem, not because it excludes altruistic preferences from the picture, but rather because (regarding the preferences a rational agent might have) it does not exclude anything.

The instrumental model of rationality, however, is often combined in the social sciences with a stipulation that rational agents are purely self-regarding. The result is the *Homo economicus* model of rational agency. I mention this because I want to stress that the reasons I give to nurture other-regard are reasons for beings like us, not for beings like Homo economicus. The Homo economicus model leaves no room for altruism. The fact that the Homo economicus model assumes pure self-regard,

---

[6] The people I have polled usually agree that one of the two is the canonical form, but it turns out that they are evenly split on which one it is.

however, is only part of the reason why it leaves no room for altruism. The real problem lies in how the assumption of pure self-regard works when combined with the underlying instrumental model of rationality.

The instrumental model of rationality is incomplete insofar as it does not provide for rational choice among ends. But the problem goes beyond mere incompleteness, for the instrumental model of rational choice on which the Homo economicus construct is based is *static*, which is to say it lacks the resources to explain how preferences are formed, and why they change over time. Because the instrumental model is static, the conception of pure self-regard that we combine with it to produce Homo economicus is also effectively static. Static self-regard takes a preference function as given and considers only how to maximize the function's output. Accordingly, the only question for Homo economicus is: How much can I get? In contrast, a more dynamic model of self-regard and of rational choice emerges if we supplement the static model by introducing a new variable, namely the effect of our choices on the shape of our preference functions. We develop a more reflective understanding of our own interests as we come to see that the quality of our lives is a function not only of what we get, but also of what we are. And what we are, no less than what we get, depends on what we choose.[7]

Because the instrumental model of rational choice is silent on the question of how we come to have the ends we do, it will not be useful in explaining how we come to have ends that are other-regarding. But a *reflective* model of rational choice allows that ends as well as means can be criticized. And with this more reflective model of rationality comes a more dynamic conception of self-regard.[8] Even purely self-regarding human agents are unlike Homo economicus insofar as they are capable of a dynamic form of self-regard, a form of self-regard that does not take their preferences as given. Reflectively rational agents understand that their preferences can and will change over time, and so for them self-regard involves taking into account the effect their choices have on the shape of their preference functions. A more dynamic kind of self-regard will allow for the possibility of developing new and other-regarding concerns.

The crucial point is this: Homo economicus does not have to work at maintaining an attitude that her goals are worth living for, but we do. We need to worry about our goals in a way that Homo economicus does not. Our preference functions are fluid. Our very natures are to some degree contingent on our choices. Thus, we need to be reflectively rational in a

---

[7] I thank Jean Hampton for suggesting the contrast between what we get and what we are.

[8] I do not think a means-end conception of rationality should be thought of as entailing that our ultimate ends must be taken as given and beyond rational criticism. There is room even within the confines of the means-end model for reflective rational choice. But that is a story for another time. See "Choosing Ends," unpublished.

way that Homo economicus does not. We need to be alert to the fact that we are outcomes as well as makers of our choices.

To give nontrivial reasons for altruism, we need to go beyond the Homo economicus model of human agency, in particular moving from a purely instrumental conception of rationality to something more reflective, ranging over the choice of ends as well as means. The major point of this section, then, is that whether or not we intend to do so, we cultivate new preferences as we go, which creates the possibility that beings like ourselves might come to be other-regarding. The next section argues that the same fluidity and capacity for reflecting on our ends that makes the cultivation of other-regarding concern *possible* also makes it *important*. There are reasons to embrace and nurture our concern for others, reasons that have to do with what is conducive to our own health, survival, and growth.

III. Reasons for Concern

As Thomas Nagel points out: "Altruistic reasons are parasitic upon self-interested ones; the circumstances in the lives of others which altruism requires us to consider are circumstances which those others already have reason to consider from a self-interested point of view."[9] Altruistic reasons are parasitic on self-regarding reasons in a second way, insofar as reflective self-regard is the seed from which our regard for others must grow. Or perhaps the last claim is too strong. For all I know, respect and concern might be the phenotypic expression of a recessive gene. Still, it remains the case that we do not really give a rationale for other-regarding concerns until we explain how the concerns of a person who was not already other-regarding could lead her to cultivate concern for others. So other-regard is parasitic on self-regard for its rational reconstruction even if not for its literal origin.

Yet this is only part of the picture. On closer inspection, the apparently parasitic relationship between other-regard and self-regard turns out to be symbiotic. Insofar as other-regard has to be nurtured, we need self-regarding reasons to initiate the nurturing process. But self-regard is not automatic either. (It may be standard equipment, so to speak, but even standard equipment requires maintenance.) Our interests are not static. They wax and wane and change shape over time, and self-regarding interests are not exempt. An enduring self-regard is something that requires maintenance.

How, then, do we go about maintaining self-regard? Consider that our preference functions are, in effect, a representation of what we have to live for. To enrich the function by cultivating new concerns is to have more to live for. As we increase our potential for happiness, it may be-

---

[9] Thomas Nagel, *The Possibility of Altruism* (Oxford: Clarendon Press, 1970), p. 16.

come harder to attain our maximum possible happiness, but that is no reason not to expand our potential. New concerns leave us open to the possibility of new frustrations and disappointments, but also to the possibility of deeper and broader satisfaction. And one crucial way to nurture self-regard is to nurture concerns that give us more to live for than we have if we care only about ourselves.

It is rational for beings like us to be peaceful and productive, to try to earn a sense of genuinely belonging in our community. Not many things in our lives are more important to us than being able to honestly consider ourselves important parts of our community. When evaluating our goals, we have to ask whether pursuing them is an appropriate way to use our talents, given our circumstances and tastes. We also have to ask how valuable our services would be to others in the various ways in which we could employ our talents. The latter consideration is not decisive, of course, for if you are bored by computers and feel alive only when philosophizing about the nature of morality, then devoting yourself to computer programming might be irrational, even though your programming services are in greater demand. (What might make it irrational is that you would be responding to others at the cost of becoming unresponsive to yourself.) Nevertheless, much of the meaning in our lives stems from our importance to others. For beings like ourselves, to be rational is not so very far from being people who seek to be honest and productive parts of a community we respect. To create a place for ourselves in society as peaceful and productive members, we must have regard for the interests of others, for it is in serving the interest of others that we develop and give value to our own latent productivity.[10]

In saying this, however, I am not denying that when personal survival is an urgent concern, it can be quite sufficient to capture our attention. In that case, we may have no need for other-regarding concerns. We may not view ourselves as being able to afford other-regarding concerns either. To cultivate additional preferences when our hands are already full is to cultivate frustration. But when circumstances leave us with free time, a more reflective kind of rationality will weigh in favor of trying to develop broader interests. We begin with a goal of survival, but because we are reflective, we need to cultivate concerns other than survival. In particular, if there were nothing for the sake of which we were surviving, reflection on this fact would tend to undermine our commitment to survival.

Because we are reflective, it is conducive to survival to have a variety of preferences in addition to a preference for survival — preferences whose satisfaction gives significance and value to our survival that it would not

---

[10] As Phillip Bricker says (in "Prudence," *Journal of Philosophy*, vol. 77 [1980], p. 401): "[T]o be prudent is to effect a reconciliation between oneself and one's world." And, I may add, our world consists in large part of other people.

otherwise have. Accordingly, it can be healthy to cultivate preferences that cut against the pursuit of health. To care only about our health would be decidedly unhealthy. Developing concerns beyond the interest we take in ourselves is one way (Sections V and VI discuss other ways) of making ourselves and our projects important enough to be worth caring about.

Out of self-regard, we nurture the enrichment of our utility functions so that they come to incorporate other-regarding preferences. As these preferences become part of the function, they acquire a certain autonomy, becoming more than mere means to previously given ends. If they do not, we have not achieved our purpose in cultivating them, which is to have more to live for. We cultivate a richer set of concerns as a means to a further end, but we cultivate so as to reap new *ends*, not merely new means of serving ends we already have. (That we nurture our emerging ends for the sake of preexisting ends does not stop them from becoming ends we pursue for their own sake. The cultivation *process* is an effective means to existing ends only if the *things being cultivated* are more than that.) Our ultimate interest is in having something to live for, being able to devote ourselves to the satisfaction of preferences that we judge worthy of satisfaction. Not having other-regarding preferences is costly, for it drastically limits what one has to live for. A person may have no concern for others, but his lack of concern is nothing to envy.[11] Concern for ourselves gives us something to live for. Concern for others as well as ourselves gives us more.[12]

This section argued that, since we are reflectively rather than instrumentally rational, we cannot afford the poverty of ends with which pure self-regard would saddle us. Under conditions that leave us time for reflection, we need to have a variety of ongoing concerns with respect to which our survival — our selves — can take on value as a means to those ends. When these further ends are in place, survival comes to be more than a biological given; an agent who has further ends not only happens to have the goal of survival but can give reasons why securing that goal is important. As a biologically given end, survival can be a source of value insofar as various pursuits can take on value as means to the end of survival, but survival can also come to possess its own value insofar as it

---

[11] Making a similar point in a more elegant way, Gregory Kavka says that "an immoralist's gloating that it does not pay him to be moral because the satisfactions of morality are not for him [is] like the pathetic boast of a deaf person that he saves money because it does not pay him to buy opera records." See "The Reconciliation Project," in *Morality, Reason, and Truth*, ed. David Copp and David Zimmerman (Totowa, NJ: Rowman & Allanheld, 1984), p. 307.

[12] How much we have to live for has more to do with the intensity of our concerns than with their number. Sheer multiplication of ends gives us more to live for if we have time for them. But when we take on so many projects that they begin to detract from each other, forcing us to race from one half-hearted pursuit to another, we end up with less to live for rather than more.

comes to be a means to our emerging further ends. Survival thus becomes something we have rational reasons to pursue, quite apart from the fact that the end of survival is biologically given. The next three sections turn to the topic of other-regarding respect, and the more general phenomenon of commitment and counterpreferential choice. Section IV discusses how our self-imposed constraints (along with our preferences) change over time, and Sections V and VI discuss why we might want them to change.

IV. The Mechanism of Commitment

My distinction between concern and respect for others is like Amartya Sen's distinction between sympathy and commitment. Sen says that when a person's sense of well-being is psychologically tied to someone else's welfare, it is a case of sympathy, whereas commitment involves counterpreferential choice. "If the knowledge of torture of others makes you sick, it is a case of sympathy; if it does not make you feel personally worse off, but if you think it is wrong and you are ready to do something to stop it, it is a case of commitment." [13] I do not know if it is best to follow Sen in describing commitment as counterpreferential choice, but at the very least it involves a different kind of preference than does sympathy.

What I call concern for others is, I think, essentially identical to what Sen calls sympathy. [14] What Sen calls commitment, however, is broader than what I call respect for others. Commitment involves adherence to principles, whereas respect for others involves adherence to principles of a more specific kind, namely those that specify constraints on what we may do to others in the course of pursuing our goals. This section describes a process by which we become committed (in Sen's broad sense). Section V considers why it can be rational to cultivate commitments (in the broad sense), and Section VI explores reasons why commitment typically seems to involve the more particular kind of commitment that I call respect for others.

Geoffrey Sayre McCord once proposed a thought experiment in which we imagine we have an opportunity to choose whether we will have a disposition to be moral. "With one hand, say, we might pull a lever that

[13] See Amartya Sen, "Rational Fools: A Critique of the Behavioral Foundations of Economic Theory," in *Beyond Self-Interest*, ed. Jane Mansbridge (Chicago: University of Chicago Press, 1990), p. 31.

[14] Sen (*ibid.*) considers sympathy to be egoistic in an important sense, however, on the grounds that sympathetic action is still action done to satisfy one's own preferences. I disagree. Whether my preferences are egoistic depends on their *content*, not on the bare fact that I happen to *have* those preferences. But this difference between his view and mine is, I have to admit, relatively unimportant. (We are tempted to seize on minute differences between our work and its predecessors, and then seize on minute similarities between our work and what follows it. The first ploy helps us feel original while the second helps us feel influential.)

frees us of moral compunction and clears our minds of morality; with the other, we might pull a lever that gives us the will to do what we believe morality demands."[15] Which lever do we have reason to pull, all things considered?

The idea that we could choose a disposition is by no means merely a thought experiment. To borrow Sayre McCord's metaphor, our actions pull the levers that form our characters. We would not want to pull a lever whose effect would be to make us act as automatons. Nor can we, for we have no such lever. We would not want to pull a lever that would make us subject to absolute constraints. Nor can we. Again, we have no such lever. But many of us would pull a lever that would strengthen our disposition to be honest, for example, if only we had such a lever.

And in fact, we do. One of the consequences of action is habituation. Because we are creatures of habit, there is a sense in which pulling the lever is possible and a sense in which doing so can be rational. We decide with every action what kind of marginal effect we will have on our own character and on our self-conception. Character is a variable, one of the most important variables at stake when we make decisions. Matters are further complicated, however, by the fact that, as important a variable as character is, it is not subject to direct control. Actions that shape character are under our control. Character itself is not. It is neither fixed nor straightforwardly determined by choice, but it is a function of choice. Character is shaped by patterns of choice.

Because people are creatures of habit, then, time eventually leaves a person with the accumulation of dispositions that we think of as a character. We do not face new situations as blank slates. Yet our accumulation of psychological baggage can seem pretty obtrusive at times, which might leave us wondering *why* we are not blank slates. Why are we creatures of habit to begin with? We evolved as creatures of habit presumably because there is an advantage in having routines for coping with repeatedly encountered situations, thus husbanding our cognitive capacities for circumstances that are novel. But we do not need to do evolutionary history here. The point is that insofar as the advantage in developing routine responses is real, we need not regret being creatures of habit. If we are creatures of habit, shaping our characters as we go, then making sure we can live with the changing shape of our accumulation of dispositions will be an ongoing project.

Habituation, then, is a mechanism of commitment. We might wonder why we pay relatively little conscious attention to the ongoing process of habituation that internalizes our commitments and thereby makes them genuine. Why are we sometimes oblivious to the importance of cultivating good habits? Natural selection builds in a bias — a sometimes

---

[15] Geoffrey Sayre McCord, "Deception and Reasons To Be Moral," *American Philosophical Quarterly*, vol. 26 (1989), p. 115.

unhealthy bias — for the concrete. We have a potential for reflective rationality, but its flowering has not been a precondition of genetic fitness. People are built to worry about things that can draw blood, not about the decay of their characters. The cost of damaging our characters is easily overlooked, because it is not reflected in some obvious frustration of our preferences. Rather, it is reflected in something more subtle, in changes to the preferences themselves.[16] And so it turns out that when it comes to sorting out what is in our self-interest, we are relatively inept in situations where what is at stake is our character. Our ineptness notwithstanding, however, it remains possible for us to develop and reinforce our commitments, including commitments that embody respect for others. The next two sections offer reasons why we might want to do so.

V. REASONS FOR COMMITMENT

Section III undertook to show that we have reason to try to enrich our preference functions, for if we develop preferences that go beyond pure self-regard, we will have more to live for. Section IV explored habituation as a mechanism by which we might come to be subject to self-imposed constraints. Here I explain why we might consider some self-imposed constraints worth the price.

There is an important place in our lives for strategic behavior, that is, for seeking effective means to our current goals, given how we expect others to act and react. But this important place is not without limits. We want to achieve our goals, to be sure, but we also want to deserve to achieve our goals, and this is not at all like our other goals. (We care about what we are, not only about what we get.) We seek not merely to earn the respect and concern of others; more fundamentally, we seek to earn our own respect and concern. For whatever reason, it is a simple fact that a person of principle inspires more respect than a person driven by mere expedience. A person may duly note that the object of her attention is herself, but that fact is not enough to guarantee that the object will hold her attention. The motivating power of self-interest is not without limit and it is not fixed. The more worthy her self is of her interest, the better off she is. Consequently, there is this advantage in having a principled character: we become selves worth struggling for.

---

[16] Allan Gibbard notes that feelings can induce beliefs whose acceptance has the effect of making the feelings seem reasonable. See his *Wise Choices, Apt Feelings* (Cambridge: Harvard University Press, 1990), p. 276. I might add that the beliefs induced can amplify our original feelings in the course of supplying them with a rationale. Some of us, when angry at our spouses, for example, are tempted to begin dredging up a history of slights suffered at the hands of that person so as to justify our present feelings; and from there our new beliefs about that person's general inhumanity amplify our original anger to the point where our final blow-up is quite spectacular, and only barely intelligible to observers. We need to be careful about our negative feelings, for the beliefs they induce can do lasting damage to our characters.

As an example of an argument for the rationality of being principled, consider the discussion of justice in Plato's *Republic*. Plato took justice to consist of giving each citizen his due. Then he tried to argue that the citizen who did not give each part of himself its due would be at war with himself. The point of the argument was to connect justice to rationality (without reducing it to rationality). Few people have accepted Plato's argument at face value, of course, but even if Plato failed to connect rationality to justice, he did in the course of the argument connect rationality to integrity.

Integrity and justice are analogous insofar as both are species of the genus "giving each part of the whole its due." To have integrity is to be true to oneself, to give each part of oneself its due. To be just is to give each person, each part of the whole society, its due. Plato's argument went awry when he mistook this analogy for a case of identity, which might be one reason why his conclusion about the rationality of being just rings false.[17] But what rings true is that having integrity is rational.

I am not claiming that being a person of integrity is merely a good strategy, a matter of prudence. On the contrary, it is far more basic and far more important than that. Being a person of integrity may on occasion be wildly imprudent, but that is no objection to making such a commitment. Indeed, the point here is that people who have no commitment to integrity have less to live for, which in the long run tends to undermine their commitment to prudence as well. Although integrity may be incompatible with prudence in exceptional cases, it also rationally justifies prudence in ordinary cases. Integrity rationally justifies prudence because it involves committing oneself to having a self worth caring about.

A person who does not have commitments has little with which to identify himself. What we are is in large part what we stand for. We think of having to make a stand on behalf of our ideals or on behalf of our loved ones as frightening and painful, and it often is. Yet to make a stand for what we think is right is one of the most self-defining things we can do.

VI. Respect for Others

The reasons offered in Section III for cultivating other-regarding concern had to do with the value of enriching our set of goals. Our goals are what we have to live for, and enriching our set of goals gives us more to live for. Our constraints are not what we live for. Enriching our set of con-

---

[17] Lest this point be misunderstood, though, let me stress that, unlike the analogy between integrity and justice, the often-discussed connection between the soul of the state and the soul of the citizen is much more than a matter of analogy. Jonathan Lear has convinced me that Plato believed not only that the souls of citizens and the soul of the state are like each other but also that the reason they are like each other is because they are outgrowths of each other. The state is the milieu within which children grow up, while, at the same time, the state's ongoing evolution or devolution lies in the hands of its adult citizens.

straints does not directly give us more to live for, but it does help define *who* we are living for. In effect, our constraints help define what we are living with, what means we can employ while still remaining persons worth living for. Defining our constraints is prior to the strategy we formulate and execute within those constraints. It is a prerequisite of prudence.

Why, then, does having a principled character involve respect for others? There is an alternative, namely that we might accept a suitably demanding set of commitments to *ourselves*.[18] We might, for example, commit ourselves to achieving excellence in particular endeavors. This means that reasons for commitment per se do not automatically translate into reasons for commitments that embody respect for others. What then leads us to develop commitments of an other-regarding nature? Something like this, perhaps: We want more than to be at peace with ourselves. We also want more than to be liked and respected by others. We want to deserve to be liked and respected as well. Thus, being a liar can hurt us not only by disrupting our purely internal integrity, but also by precluding the kind of honest rapport we want to have with others, precluding our integration into the larger wholes that would otherwise give us more to live for. As Gerald Postema wisely observes:

> To cut oneself off from others is to cut oneself off *from oneself*, for it is only in the mirror of the souls of others that one finds one's own self, one's character. The pleasures and satisfactions of conversation and intercourse are essential to human life, because they are essential to a sense of one's continuity through a constantly changing external and internal world. . . . Thus, a truly successful strategy of deception effectively cuts oneself off from the community in which alone one can find the confirmation essential to one's own sense of self.[19]

Respect for others is part and parcel of having a principled character because integrity has external as well as internal components. That is, being true to ourselves ordinarily involves presenting ourselves truly to others. Further, integrity involves not only presenting ourselves to the world in an honest fashion but also *integrating* ourselves into the world, achieving a certain fit. We give ourselves more to live for by becoming an important part of something bigger than ourselves. A principled character lets us pursue this wider integration without losing our own identity.

---

[18] Since this is not an essay about morality, I will not stop here to consider whether some of these self-regarding commitments should be regarded as instances of moral principle, but see essays by Neera Kapur Badhwar and Jean Hampton, elsewhere in this volume.

[19] See Gerald Postema, "Hume's Reply to the Sensible Knave," *History of Philosophy Quarterly*, vol. 5 (1988), p. 35.

People with principled characters—those with nothing to hide—can seek integration on their own terms.

We may never quite manage to swallow Plato's conclusion that it is rational to give each part of one's community its due. Yet it surely is rational to give our own interests their due, and one of our main interests is in grounding in reality a conception of ourselves as decent human beings. We identify ourselves largely in terms of what we do, and therefore individual rationality requires us to do things that can ground the kind of self-conception we would like to have. This effects a certain convergence between *ex ante* and *ex post* conceptions of self-interested decision. In other words, being a person of integrity rather than an opportunist is rational not only as a prospective policy (that is, as something we anticipate would leave us better off in a long-run probabilistic sense). There is also something to be said for it on a case-by-case basis—indeed, even when we see in retrospect that we could have lied or cheated without being caught. We desire integrity not only in an internal sense but also in the sense of being well-integrated with a social structure, functioning well as part of the structure that largely comprises our environment. We seek real rapport with others, not merely a sham. We want to feel like we belong, and it is our real selves for which we want a sense of belonging, not merely our false facades.

So, how does that give us reasons to fall on grenades for the sake of our comrades? It may not. The considerations weighing in favor of having a principled character in ordinary cases need not do so in extraordinary cases. Nevertheless, ordinary cases are the crucibles within which characters are formed. It is in the ordinary course of events that we create the characters that we carry into the emergencies. And there is a certain precious dignity in having a character that will not crumble under pressure.

Our reasons for acting as we do in a given situation stem from concerns we bring with us to that situation. Thus, the rationality of nurturing a given concern cannot turn on consequences it has as a reason for action in a particular case. The relevant consequences are those that follow from a certain concern being part of one's life.[20] This is why the task of providing reasons for altruism is first and foremost the task of providing reasons for altruism of the more mundane variety. It is fine to consider

---

[20] An important article by Edward F. McClennen ("Constrained Maximization and Resolute Choice," *Social Philosophy & Policy*, vol. 5, no. 2 [1988], pp. 95–118) argues that one can be better off being a resolute chooser, i.e., a person who adopts plans and whose static preferences are thus contextually sensitive. Even though people in a Prisoner's Dilemma may prefer the free-rider *payoff* to the payoff from mutual cooperation, this does not entail that they prefer to *choose* free riding over mutual cooperation. But then one might ask, how is it possible for rational self-regarding agents to be resolute choosers? How can they possibly choose a less-preferred over a more-preferred payoff? My theory is that dynamically self-regarding agents can habituate themselves to virtue. "Resolve" is the sort of thing we can build up over time.

whether it can be rational to give up one's life fighting for a cause, but in truth, the central cases are cases of simply lending people a hand in the ordinary course of events. We stop to give people directions. We push their cars out of snowbanks. We hold open doors for people whose hands are full. And we walk away from these mundane encounters feeling grateful for the chance to be helpful.[21]

In nurturing concerns that give us more to live for, we develop concerns that can become more important to us than life itself. In the ordinary course of events, this is a splendid result, but in extraordinary situations, concerns worth living for can become concerns worth dying for. We may some day find ourselves in a situation where our other-regarding concerns dictate a course of action that seriously jeopardizes our purely self-regarding interests. The consequences might convince an observer to avoid developing similar commitments and concerns. But for us, already having the concerns we have, failing to act on them is what would be irrational. When the emergency comes that calls on us to pay the price of having our commitments, we no longer have the option of acting as if our slate of commitments were blank. We got the benefits of integrity by becoming actually committed, and when the emergency comes, we are actually committed.[22] It may never have been our intention to be self-sacrificing. We only meant to be altruistic, which is not the same thing. But we got unlucky, and now self-sacrifice is the best we can do by our current lights.

Altruism will involve self-sacrifice in exceptional cases, but not as a matter of routine. Altruism involves costs, of course, as does any action, but cost-bearing becomes self-sacrificial only when the agent prefers the value forgone to the value gained. Altruism is necessarily self-sacrificial only for purely self-regarding agents. For agents who have other-regarding concerns, acting on those concerns will be self-sacrificial if it costs too much, but it need not do so. Needless to say, we may regret giving up one value for the sake of another, even in cases where both values are of a self-regarding nature, and even when we have no doubt that the value gained is more important than the value lost. But however painful it feels, one is not sacrificing oneself when one sacrifices a lesser value for the

[21] Note that it would be a mistake to say something cannot be altruistic if you really enjoy doing it. This would put the cart before the horse. If you help other people for their sake, you are altruistic whether or not you like having the concern for others that your action expresses. In the *Grounding of the Metaphysics of Morals*, Kant said that whether you get joy out of an action affects the action's moral worth, which seems wrong, but even if he had been right, enjoying an action can affect its moral worth without changing the fact that the action is altruistic.

[22] Gregory Kavka points out that it might be prospectively rational to undertake a course of action that will lead one to develop a preference for falling on grenades in situations where that is the only way to save one's comrades. Developing such a preference is extremely unlikely to result in one's actually falling on a grenade, but much more likely to make possible the kind of rewards one reaps by developing that kind of love for one's comrades. See Kavka, "The Reconciliation Project," pp. 307–10.

sake of a greater value, and this is what altruism often amounts to for other-regarding agents.[23]

That also reveals the limits of rational altruism. It would be irrational to nurture commitments that lead to self-sacrifice as a matter of course. The point is to have more to live for, and to satisfy the prerequisites of prudence. We accomplish this by nurturing concern and respect for family, friends, neighbors, the strangers we meet, and so on. And there are certain kinds of respect that, under normal conditions, we can easily afford to extend to the whole world. But we have only so much capacity for genuine concern. If we tried to care about everyone, our lives probably would be impoverished rather than enriched. I think this has implications for morality as well as for rationality. Although I think morality requires us to respect everyone, I doubt very much that morality requires us to care about everyone.[24] I have not argued for that conclusion here, of course, but in any event, if morality does require us to care about everyone, then this is one area in which morality and rationality part company.

VII. Closing Remarks

People are not exclusively self-interested, at least not by any nontrivial standard of what it means to be self-interested. On the contrary, people sometimes go to extraordinary lengths to act against their self-regarding interests, driven by pride, for instance, or vengefulness, or plain malevolence. Most of us are quite prepared to brand irrational such deviations from self-regarding behavior. What, then, of altruistic behavior? Is that irrational as well? If so, then probably most of us are quite prepared to say: "So much the worse for rationality." But I have tried here to explore an account of reflective rational choice rich enough to allow for and even explain the development of other-regarding concern and respect.

As I reread the previous pages, even I remain unconvinced that concern and respect for others are rationally *required*. We are driven to cultivate concerns that go beyond mere survival, but perhaps more expansive sets of concerns and commitments could be fashioned that would be fulfilling and that would still count as purely self-regarding. Be that as it may, the project of giving reasons for altruism does not turn on whether we can prove that pure self-regard is irrational. It is enough to show that there are reasons that weigh in favor of developing concern and respect for others.

[23] I thank Lainie Ross for helping me to work out the connection between altruism and sacrifice.

[24] William Galston (elsewhere in this volume) points out important distinctions between progressively more expansive conceptions of altruism, and draws attention to the moral cost of what he calls "cosmopolitan altruism." For example, the concern expressed by rescuers of Jewish refugees in Nazi-occupied Europe was often part and parcel of a failure to express concern for family members thereby put at risk by the rescue effort.

Although the genesis of these new reasons for action is driven by instrumental reasons, this does not imply that the new reasons thereby generated are themselves instrumental reasons. The concern and respect for others that reflective self-regard leads most of us to nurture may be of an entirely wholehearted and uncalculating kind. Indeed, that is what we are striving for, for those are the most rewarding concerns a person can have.[25]

Finally, let me close by saying how this essay fits into the larger project of identifying connections between rationality and morality. There is a limit to how much other-regard is rational, but whether that opens a gap between rationality and morality is an open question, for there is also a limit to how much other-regard is morally required. This is in part a point about morality leaving room for agents to pursue their own projects, but it is also in part a reminder that the consequences of other-regard are only so good. Whether other-regarding action has better consequences than self-regarding action in a given case is an empirical matter. Paternalism, for example, is a form of altruism—an expression of concern for the welfare of other people—that overrides one's respect for their expressed or implied preferences. Altruistic though it might be, paternalism often is objectionable. To give another example, teachers should grade term papers on the basis of what they believe the papers deserve, not on what they believe the authors need. Anyone who has ever graded term papers knows how difficult it is to ignore one's concern for others, but there are cases in which one is morally required to make the effort. From the viewpoints of both the agent and those the agent might affect, neither self-regard nor other-regard is intrinsically exalted. A great deal depends on how a concern plays itself out.[26]

Gilbert Harman says moral absolutism is the view that there is some moral law that everyone has sufficient reasons to follow. Further, an agent has a sufficient reason to obey a law if and only if there is sound reasoning she could do that would lead her to decide to obey that law.[27] Harman thinks agents have sufficient reason to obey a law only if doing so serves their existing ends. And since people's ends can be quite different, there is a problem here for moral absolutism. But even if moral absolutism is false, and I am not sure it is, there is a weaker claim we might press against characters like Thrasymachus, who have sufficient reasons

---

[25] For an intriguing complement to my argument that reflective self-regard weighs in favor of cultivating other-regard, see Neera Kapur Badhwar's argument (elsewhere in this volume) that one cannot act in a wholeheartedly altruistic manner unless one is, in my words, reflectively self-regarding.

[26] Also, concerning the moral status of altruism, see Tyler Cowen's remarks on paternalistic altruism and Jean Hampton's remarks on how self-sacrifice can sometimes be a moral failure, elsewhere in this volume.

[27] See Gilbert Harman, "Is There a Single True Morality?" in Morality, Reason, and Truth, ed. David Copp and David Zimmerman (Totowa, NJ: Rowman & Allanheld, 1984), pp. 27–48.

to act only when doing so will satisfy their purely self-regarding ends. We might say that, because almost nothing counts as a sufficient reason for Thrasymachus to act (in particular, regard for others cannot move him to act), Thrasymachus leads a life that is impoverished in a certain way. He has fewer reasons to live than the rest of us. Perhaps the existence of creatures like Thrasymachus belies moral absolutism as Harman defines it. Even so, we can still say Thrasymachus lacks the kind of respect and concern for others that could have given him sufficient reason to pursue a range of goals. I realize that if Thrasymachus were here, he would laugh at me for saying this, for the range of goals I am talking about would mean nothing to him, but the fact remains that those goals could have enriched his life.

The larger project of which this essay is a part argues that sometimes we fail morally not so much because we lack sufficient reason to be moral as because we lack sufficient strength to be moral. We have a problem that Homo economicus does not: namely, we sometimes lack the strength of will to do what is in our best interest. Telling the truth sometimes takes more courage than we can muster, even when we foresee being intensely disappointed with ourselves if we lie.[28] Developing one's talents is also morally demanding; seeing where one's talents lie requires honest self-appraisal, and turning raw talent into practiced skill takes courage and perseverance. Being rational in a full-blooded sense — developing oneself in a way that is true to oneself — is a profoundly demanding activity.

Philosophy, Yale University

---

[28] Consider how weak we can be in situations where we are afraid or embarrassed to tell the truth. We react to the possibility of making a bad impression as if the situation were a threat to our physical health. This is a mistake, for what is really at stake is usually too subtle to be properly addressed by such reactions. Covering up the truth in over-reaction to perceived threats to our standing in other people's eyes is self-defeating; it walls off the possibility of our real selves being affirmed by those we are deceiving. Nevertheless, it takes a certain strength of character to act in our reflective self-interest.

THINKING AS A TEAM:
TOWARDS AN EXPLANATION
OF NONSELFISH BEHAVIOR*

By Robert Sugden

I. Altruism and Cooperation

For most of the problems that economists consider, the assumption that agents are self-interested works well enough, generating predictions that are broadly consistent with observation. In some significant cases, however, we find economic behavior that seems to be inconsistent with self-interest. In particular, we find that some public goods and some charitable ventures are financed by the independent voluntary contributions of many thousands of individuals. In Britain, for example, the lifeboat service is entirely financed by voluntary contributions. In all rich countries, charitable appeals raise large amounts of money for famine relief in the Third World. The willingness of individuals to contribute to such projects is an economic fact that requires an explanation.

Take the case of the lifeboat service. Many contributors, no doubt, occasionally risk being in need of a lifeboat—they go sailing, travel by ship, or walk on cliffs. Such people have a direct self-interest in the existence of the lifeboat service. But it is implausible to claim that this self-interest provides an adequate reason for them to contribute to the costs of the service. Suppose I contribute a small amount of money to the British lifeboat service. This will make life a tiny bit safer for fifty-seven million people, of whom I am only one. If instead I spend the same amount of money on changing my car tires more frequently or on fitting smoke detectors in my house, I can make my own life safer without having to pay for anyone else's extra safety. Unless the ratio of benefit to cost is millions of times greater for lifeboats than for new tires or smoke alarms, I will do better to ignore lifeboat appeals.

It might seem that this problem would be overcome if we assumed that contributors were altruistic. In economics, a person is altruistic if, other things being equal, he or she prefers outcomes in which another person enjoys greater consumption or utility. Altruism, then, is a property of a

* This essay was written as part of the Foundations of Rational Choice Theory project, supported by the Economic and Social Research Council (award R 000 23 2269). The ideas contained in it developed out of discussions with Robin Cubitt, Judith Mehta, Martin Hollis, and Chris Starmer. It was improved as a result of comments from the other contributors to this volume.

person's preference ordering over outcomes. Economists generally assume that altruists are *instrumentally rational*, just like other agents in economic theory: each individual acts so as to bring about the outcome that he or she most prefers. Assuming altruism, we might try to explain contributions to the lifeboat service on the hypothesis that each contributor has an altruistic preference for the safety of other people. On this hypothesis, contributors need have no self-interest in the project to which they contribute. Thus, the theory of the supply of public goods by voluntary contributions might be subsumed into a more general theory of charitable giving, based on the assumption of altruism.

Economists have built models in which populations of altruists are free to contribute towards charitable projects; each altruist acts in an instrumentally rational way, taking the contributions of other altruists as given. These models consistently generate counterintuitive results. A large number of puzzling "neutrality" theorems have been proved. A typical result is that if any one donor increases her contribution, there is virtually no net effect on total contributions. (Other donors decrease their contributions by an amount which almost exactly offsets the original increase.) Similarly, if a welfare service has a private charitable sector, changes in public-sector provision have negligible effects on total provision.[1]

More worryingly (since one explanation of a counterintuitive result is that our intuitions are wrong), these models of altruistic behavior fail to generate anything like the patterns of charitable giving that we actually observe. Econometric studies of aggregated charitable giving can give us estimates of the responsiveness of an average donor's gifts to changes in the donor's income. Such studies typically find that gifts increase with income, but by only a few cents for each extra dollar of income. Econometricians have also tried to estimate the responsiveness of an average donor's gifts to the total giving of others. Typically, no statistically significant relationship is found, which suggests that in this case, any responsiveness is very slight indeed. Intuitively speaking, these findings are perhaps not surprising. But they are inconsistent with the hypothesis that donors are instrumentally rational altruists.[2]

Why this is so can be shown by an example. Imagine an altruist whose income is $50,000 per year, who gives $100 per year to a charity whose total income from other donors is $100,000 per year. Let us call this Case 1. Now consider the same altruist, with the same preferences as before,

---

[1] See, for example, Robert Sugden, "Consistent Conjectures and Voluntary Contributions to Public Goods: Why the Conventional Theory Does Not Work," *Journal of Public Economics*, vol. 27 (1984), pp. 117–24; James Andreoni, "Privately Provided Public Goods in a Large Economy: The Limits of Altruism," *Journal of Public Economics*, vol. 35 (1988), pp. 57–73; and Tyler Cowen, "Altruism and the Argument from Offsetting Transfers," in this volume.

[2] I present this argument, and summarize the econometric evidence, in Robert Sugden, "On the Economics of Philanthropy," *Economic Journal*, vol. 92 (1982), pp. 341–50.

but suppose that her income is $49,999 while the charity's income from other donors is $100,001. Let us call this Case 2. How much will the altruist give in Case 2? If we use the econometric evidence, we can predict that her contribution will be within a few cents of $100. (In moving from Case 1 to Case 2, her income has decreased by one dollar, while the charity's income from other donors has increased by one dollar. Neither change will affect her contribution by more than a few cents.) But what does the theory of altruism predict?

In Case 1, the altruist's *feasible set* — the set of outcomes from which she is free to choose — contains all those outcomes in which her private (i.e., noncharitable) spending is in the range from 0 to $50,000 per year, and in which her private spending and the charity's total spending sum to $150,000 per year. By choosing to give $100, she chooses the outcome in which her private spending is $49,900 and in which the charity's spending is $100,100. We must infer that she prefers this outcome to every other member of the feasible set. In Case 2, the altruist's feasible set contains all those outcomes in which her private spending is in the range 0 to $49,999, and in which her private spending and the charity's total spending sum to $150,000. Notice that every outcome that is feasible in Case 2 was also feasible in Case 1, and that the outcome she chose in Case 1 is feasible in Case 2. Thus, if she is to be consistent, she must choose the same outcome in Case 2 as in Case 1: the outcome in which the charity's spending is $100,100. But if she is to bring about this outcome in Case 2, she must give only $99 (since the charity's income from other donors is one dollar greater in Case 2). This contradicts the implication of the econometric evidence, that her contribution will be within a few cents of $100.

The source of the problem is that, in the economic theory of altruism, each donor views her contributions merely as means of achieving the end of increasing the total spending of the charity. Thus, she views each other donor's contributions to the charity as perfect substitutes for her own. This leads to the implication that her own contributions are highly responsive to changes in other people's contributions. The evidence, however, tells us that the contributions of a real donor are much less responsive to changes in other people's contributions than the theory would lead us to expect. Real donors, it seems, recognize a distinction between their own contributions and those of other people. But what is this distinction?

One answer, often given by economists, is that each donor enjoys a "warm glow" from the knowledge that she has contributed to the charity. This warm glow is associated with the *act* of giving, and not with its results. It is usually interpreted as a sense of self-satisfaction deriving either from the knowledge that one has behaved in a morally praiseworthy fashion or from the knowledge that others know one has. Thus, James Andreoni introduces his theory of "impure altruism" by suggesting that donors may be motivated by considerations of "social pressure, guilt, sympathy, or simply a desire for a 'warm glow.' "[3] Similarly, Mancur Olson appeals to the "desire to win prestige, respect, friendship, and other social and psychological objectives"; Gary Becker appeals to the desire "to avoid scorn of others or to receive social acclaim."[4] But this sort of argument begs the question of *why* the act of giving to charity is morally praiseworthy. Why isn't it sufficient, from a moral point of view, for a person to be instrumentally rational and to have altruistic preferences on which she is willing to act? These versions of warm-glow theory, then, are parasitic on moral theories that enjoin us to behave in ways that are not instrumentally rational.

A different kind of answer can be given if we are prepared to reject the instrumental conception of rationality. Some forms of nonselfish behavior may reflect a morality of *cooperation* rather than of altruism. A cooperative morality enjoins each individual to *do her part* in achieving outcomes that are good for all. In some versions of cooperative morality, the individual's obligation to do her part is conditional on other people's doing theirs: these are theories of *reciprocity*.[5] In other, more Kantian versions, the obligation is unconditional. What is crucial about both versions of this kind of theory is that the individual does not ask whether her own actions, considered in isolation, yield preferred outcomes. Instead, she acts on rules which, when generally followed, yield preferred outcomes. Given this approach, it is clear that other people's contributions to charitable ventures are not substitutes for one's own. If we all benefit from the existence of a lifeboat service, and if others are bearing their share of its costs, then I have an obligation to bear my share. The fact that other people meet their obligations does not discharge me from mine. (Indeed, if we adopt a theory of reciprocity, the reverse may be true: my obligation to contribute may be conditional on others' contributing.)

The difference between theories of altruism and theories of cooperation might be summarized in the following way. Theories of altruism explain nonselfish behavior by invoking nonselfish preferences. Theories of cooperation explain such behavior by appealing to a noninstrumental connection between preference and action. Given the nature of this difference, it is not surprising that economists have tended to resist theories of cooperation, preferring to explain nonselfish behavior in terms of altruism and "warm glow." The instrumental conception of rationality is very deeply embedded in economic theory, while economists have tradition-

---

[3] James Andreoni, "Impure Altruism and Donations to Public Goods: A Theory of Warm-Glow Giving," *Economic Journal*, vol. 100 (1990), pp. 464–77.

[4] Mancur Olson, *The Logic of Collective Action* (Cambridge: Harvard University Press, 1965), p. 60; Gary S. Becker, "A Theory of Social Interactions," *Journal of Political Economy*, vol. 82 (1974), p. 1083.

[5] For example, Donald Regan, *Utilitarianism and Cooperation* (Oxford: Clarendon Press, 1980); Robert Sugden, "Reciprocity: The Supply of Public Goods through Voluntary Contributions," *Economic Journal*, vol. 94 (1984), pp. 772–87.

ally been open-minded about the content of people's preferences (provided only that certain formal conditions of consistency are satisfied). If nonselfish behavior can adequately be explained in terms of instrumental rationality, then economists are perhaps entitled to appeal to Ockham's razor in rejecting theories of cooperation.

In this essay, however, I shall argue that theories of cooperation have to be taken seriously. My strategy is to exhibit a class of problems in which the question "What ought rational individuals to do?" seems to have a perfectly obvious answer. I shall then argue that, although this answer is an immediate implication of a theory of cooperation, it cannot be derived from a theory based on instrumental rationality.

II. The Prisoners' Coordination Problem

Imagine a new version of the well-known Prisoner's Dilemma story. As in the original story, the two prisoners have jointly committed a crime. They are in separate cells, unable to communicate with one another. The district attorney does not have enough evidence to convict them, and they know this. Trying to extract confessions, the D.A. makes the following offer (which differs from the offer in the original story). If one prisoner confesses and the other does not, she will charge both of them and press for the maximum penalty of ten years in prison. If both confess, however, the main charge against them will be dropped: they will both be charged with a less serious crime, for which each can expect to be sentenced to one year in prison. If neither of them confesses, both will be released. All this is common knowledge. Is the D.A. being cunning, or is she just wasting her time? Has she presented the prisoners with a genuine problem?

This problem, the Prisoners' Coordination Problem, is set out in Table 1, which is drawn up on the assumption that utility is linear in years of imprisonment. It is tempting to say that the problem is trivial. There is no

TABLE 1. *The Prisoners' Coordination Problem*

| | | Prisoner B | |
		Stay silent	Confess
Prisoner A	Stay silent	0, 0	−10, −10
	Confess	−10, −10	−1, −1

conflict of interest: whatever happens, both will receive the same sentence. All they have to do to avoid the worst outcome of ten years imprisonment is to coordinate their strategies. There are two ways in which they could coordinate. They could both confess, in which case they both spend a year in prison, or they could both stay silent, in which case they are both released. Being released is clearly preferable to a year in prison. Therefore, it is rational for each prisoner to stay silent.

At first sight, this argument appears convincing enough. But it is remarkably difficult to justify the "therefore." I shall argue that, provided we stick with the conventional theory of rational choice, in which agents are instrumentally rational (and know one another to be instrumentally rational, and know that one another know this, and so on), we *cannot* justify it. The theory does not imply that staying silent is uniquely rational.[6]

The Prisoners' Coordination Problem is to be thought of as a *one-shot* game—as a game which is to be played only once. Many of the coordination games of real life, of course, take place repeatedly, so that in any particular interaction, the players can be guided by their experience of previous plays of the relevant game. If games are repeated, practices of coordination can evolve. (For example, many writers have suggested that the use of money evolved as a solution to a coordination problem.) As it happens, I think that the analysis of one-shot coordination games can throw some light on evolutionary processes;[7] but for my present purposes, that is beside the point. My concern here is with rational play in a one-shot game.

Suppose I am prisoner A and you are prisoner B. If I expect you to stay silent, it is clearly rational for me to stay silent: given that you will stay silent, my staying silent produces the best possible outcome—both for me and for you. But it is equally true to say that if I expect you to confess, it is rational for me to confess. Given that you will confess, my confessing produces the best possible outcome—both for me and for you. So it is rational for me to stay silent if and only if I attach a high enough probability to your staying silent. (Using the utility numbers of Table 1, and assuming that rationality requires the maximization of expected utility, it is uniquely rational for me to stay silent if I believe that the probability of your staying silent is greater than 9/19; and it is uniquely rational for me to confess if I believe that this probability is less than 9/19.)[8]

Thus, the question "What is it rational for me to do?" cannot be an-

---

[6] The argument I present here is similar to those of D. H. Hodgson, *Consequences of Utilitarianism* (Oxford: Clarendon Press, 1967); and Regan, *Utilitarianism and Cooperation*.

[7] Robert Sugden, *The Economics of Rights, Co-operation, and Welfare* (Oxford: Basil Blackwell, 1986).

[8] To see why, let p be the probability that B will stay silent. Then if A stays silent, A's expected utility is $-10(1 - p)$. If A confesses, A's expected utility is $-10p - (1 - p)$. The former expected utility is greater than the latter if p is greater than 9/19.

swered without first answering the question "What belief is it rational for me to hold about your decision?" But if I believe you to be rational, I must expect that you will choose whichever strategy is rational for you. If it is uniquely rational for you to stay silent, I must believe that you will stay silent. Equally, if it is uniquely rational for you to confess, I must believe that you will confess. Thus, the question "What belief is it rational for me to hold about your decision?" cannot be answered without first answering the question "What is it rational for you to do?" But, since your decision problem is exactly symmetrical with mine, we are no nearer an answer to the original question, "What is it rational for me to do?" The attempt to answer that answer leads to an infinite regress.

To put this another way, the claim that rationality requires both of us to stay silent is internally consistent but ungrounded. *If* it is uniquely rational for you to stay silent, then I have good reason to expect you to stay silent, and therefore, it is uniquely rational for me to stay silent. But it is equally true to say that if it is uniquely rational for you to confess, then I have good reason to expect you to confess, and therefore it is uniquely rational for me to confess. Thus, the claim that rationality requires both of us to confess is also internally consistent (and also ungrounded). The puzzle is that the standard theory of rational choice seems not to supply a reason for either person to play his part in a cooperative scheme that benefits both of them.

It is tempting to think that this analysis must be mistaken. Surely, one might object, the fact that the scheme of cooperation benefits both of us *is* the reason that we need. If we both stay silent, we will get to the best possible outcome for both of us. Let us call this fact "Cooperation is best for both," or CBB. What further reason do we need for staying silent?

But such an objection would miss the point. My claim is that CBB is not an adequate reason *within the conventional theory of instrumentally rational choice*. Within that theory, each individual tries to bring about the outcome that he most prefers, given his beliefs about what other individuals will do. This leaves nowhere for CBB to get a grip on individuals' reasoning. Conversely, if CBB is to get such a grip, then some feature of the conventional theory of rational choice has to be dropped.

At this point, it is useful to compare the Prisoners' Coordination Problem with the classic Prisoner's Dilemma, one version of which is shown in Table 2. (As before, it is assumed that utility is linear in years of imprisonment, so the entries in the matrix may be read either as utility numbers or as years to be spent in prison.) In the Prisoner's Dilemma, just as in the Prisoners' Coordination Problem, both players are better off if they both stay silent than if they both confess. But in the Prisoner's Dilemma, unlike the Prisoners' Coordination Problem, both players' staying silent does not lead to the best possible outcome for both of them. On the contrary, confession is the dominant strategy for both players. (That is, each player does better to confess, irrespective of whether the other confesses

TABLE 2. *The Prisoner's Dilemma*

| | | Prisoner B | |
		Stay silent	Confess
Prisoner A	Stay silent	−1, −1	−10, 0
	Confess	0, −10	−8, −8

or stays silent.) Thus, the conventional theory of rational choice prescribes that both players should confess.

A conclusion that is often drawn from the Prisoner's Dilemma is that the players fail to cooperate because their preferences are self-interested. Players with sufficiently altruistic concerns for one another, it is said, would not find themselves in Prisoner's Dilemmas. The familiar description of the outcomes of the Prisoner's Dilemma in terms of years of imprisonment does not in itself imply that confession is the dominant strategy for each prisoner: to reach this conclusion, we must add the assumption that each prisoner ranks outcomes in terms of the number of years *he* spends in prison. (That assumption is, of course, built into Table 2.) If, instead, it is assumed that each prisoner derives disutility from the other's imprisonment, then confession is not necesarily the dominant strategy. Indeed, if each prisoner derived as much disutility from the other's imprisonment as from his own, staying silent would be the dominant strategy. A game theorist would say that the problem faced by such altruistic prisoners would not be a Prisoner's Dilemma. Game theorists are continually pointing out that the utility numbers that appear in payoff matrices are to be understood as representing the objectives of the players, whatever those objectives may be. Altruism is just another kind of objective.

One of the interesting features of the Prisoners' Coordination Problem is that it is just as much a problem for altruistic players as for self-interested ones.[9] In setting up that problem, I have assumed that each prisoner's objective is to minimize the number of years he spends in prison.

---

[9] This feature is brought out by Hodgson, who considers a game similar to the Prisoners' Coordination Problem (see his *Consequences of Utilitarianism*). Hodgson's game is played by two act utilitarians, each of whom seeks to maximize the sum of all persons' utilities. Hodgson argues that act-utilitarian players would have no reason to cooperate. Regan discusses the same game and reaches a similar conclusion in his *Utilitarianism and Cooperation*.

But since each prisoner is certain to receive the same sentence as the other, this is exactly equivalent to assuming that each prisoner's objective is to minimize the average number of years the two of them spend in prison. It is also equivalent to assuming that each prisoner's objective is to minimize the number of years the other spends in prison. In the Prisoner's Dilemma story, self-interested players have conflicting interests, but a sufficient degree of altruism would change the problem into one in which they had common interests. In the Prisoners' Coordination Problem, in contrast, the players have common interests from the outset, but the theory of rational choice still does not provide them with a reason to cooperate. No amount of altruism will help them to find such a reason.

III. SALIENCE AND BOUNDED RATIONALITY

It is often suggested that coordination problems are solved by using ideas of "prominence" or "salience." This idea derives from Thomas Schelling, who argues that certain solutions to coordination problems have "some kind of prominence or conspicuousness" which allows people to recognize them as "focal points" on which their expectations can "converge."[10] Schelling provides many suggestive examples of salience, but never provides a full account of what salience *is*, or of how it comes to influence people's decisions. At crucial points in his discussion, he relies on metaphor and on unspecific appeals to the role of imagination as contrasted with logic. But even if his argument is incomplete, Schelling seems to be pointing to a significant phenomenon.

It might be argued that if one outcome in a game is better than every other for both players, then that outcome is salient by virtue of its being better. Such an outcome sticks out from the others in a way that each player is likely to recognize, is likely to expect the other to recognize, and so on, and this may provide the "clue" that the players need in order to coordinate their choices. Thus, in the Prisoners' Coordination Problem, each player's attention focuses on the outcome in which they both go free; and this somehow leads each of them to choose the strategy of staying silent.

Schelling discusses an intriguing class of *pure coordination games* in which the players have a common interest in coordinating their actions and are indifferent between alternative ways of doing so. (In the Prisoners' Coordination Problem, in contrast, one way of coordinating is preferred to the other by both players. Such games are coordination games, but not "pure" ones.) In Schelling's games, two players, who are not allowed to communicate with one another, are each asked an open-ended question. They are told that they will each win a prize if and only if they

---

[10] Thomas Schelling, *The Strategy of Conflict* (Cambridge: Harvard University Press, 1960), especially pp. 54–58.

both answer this question in exactly the same way. For example, the question might be: "Name a place in New York City in which to meet the other player."

On the basis of intuition and some "unscientific" experiments on a small sample of respondents, Schelling claims that people are often able to coordinate their responses to problems of this kind, and that they do so by choosing solutions that are salient. (In the New York City problem, a majority of his respondents chose Grand Central Station.) In many cases, the players of pure coordination games seem to choose the solutions that are ranked most highly along some dimension that, given the framing of the problem, is itself particularly salient. For example, British players presented with the problem "Name any mountain" overwhelmingly choose Everest; if the problem is to name any British town or city, they tend to choose London.[11] Similarly, Grand Central Station was perhaps the most commonly used meeting place in New York for Schelling's population of New Haven people in the 1950s. In these cases, the players seem to be making use of shared background knowledge. For example, in our culture it is conventional to rank mountains in terms of height, and most people know that Everest is the world's highest mountain. By making use of this common knowledge, players can coordinate successfully when asked to name a mountain, even though there is no absolute sense in which "Everest" is the correct response to "Name any mountain."

In a game like the Prisoners' Coordination Problem, in which different solutions offer different payoffs but the ranking of payoffs is the same for both players, this ranking might be said to be salient in much the same way that height is salient when comparing mountains and population size is salient when comparing cities. This analysis, however, fails to explain *why* players choose those strategies that are associated with salient solutions. David Lewis tries to answer this question. The core of his argument is contained in the following passage:

> The [players in a coordination game] might all tend to pick the salient as a last resort, when they have no stronger ground for choice. Or they might expect each other to have that tendency, and act accordingly; or they might expect each other to expect each other to have that tendency and act accordingly, and act accordingly; and so on. Or—more likely—there might be a mixture of these. Their first- and higher-order expectations of a tendency to pick the salient as a last resort would be a system of concordant expectations capable of producing coordination at the salient equilibrium.[12]

[11] These are among the findings of some experimental work I have done with Judith Mehta and Chris Starmer, which has not yet been published.

[12] David Lewis, *Convention: A Philosophical Study* (Cambridge: Harvard University Press, 1969), pp. 35–36.

The idea, I take it, is that an option can be salient in the sense that it impresses itself on the consciousness of an individual, independently of any calculation of the advantages of choosing it, but in a way that makes it more likely to be chosen. Let us call this property *primary salience*. Suppose, for example, that I am buying some type of good for the first time, and am faced with a choice of several, identically priced brands. As a result of my exposure to advertising, some of these brand names are more familiar to me than others. Even though I do not believe that there is any correlation between advertising and quality, I pick the brand whose name I have heard most often. If we are to explain why brand names work like this, we must look to psychology rather than to the theory of rational choice. In terms of that theory, I have no preference between the brands; primary salience is acting as an extra-rational tie-breaker. It might be possible to give a similar account of why someone who is asked to name a mountain, but has no reason to name any one rather than any other, gives the answer "Everest."

Now suppose we could say that the strategy of staying silent in the Prisoners' Coordination Game was primarily salient. Then two players, each of whom had no other reason for discriminating between strategies, would each be likely to choose to stay silent. This is the first possibility considered by Lewis. It is important to notice that, on this account, coordination is achieved as an unintended byproduct of nonrational behavior. The fact that both players do better if they both stay silent than if they both confess is not being viewed as a *reason* for either to stay silent. Lewis is well aware of the infinite regress described in Section II of this paper, and is invoking nonrational propensities as a means of escape from the regress.

The second possibility considered by Lewis is that each player knows that one strategy (say, staying silent) is primarily salient, and that each player believes that the other will choose the primarily salient strategy, having no other grounds for choice. Then each player *does* have a reason for staying silent, namely that staying silent maximizes his expected utility relative to his beliefs; but each believes that the other's choice will be determined nonrationally. We might say that in this case the players are motivated by *second-order salience*. Lewis's other possibilities have the same basic structure, but introduce nonrational motivations at more and more remote points in the chain of reasoning.

Notice that Lewis's argument is based on an assumption of imperfect or, in the language of economics, *bounded* rationality. Lewis's players do not reason like the players of classical game theory, who are perfectly rational and who have common knowledge of one another's rationality. At some point, Lewis's players cut off the chain of reasoning about what perfectly rational players would do, and substitute a psychological hypothesis about what a human player would do, if she had no rational grounds for choice. This hypothesis is then used to generate expectations about what the other player will do.

Significantly, however, Schelling seems to reject this kind of account of salience. He considers John Maynard Keynes's famous discussion of the newspaper competition in which the object is to pick the six prettiest faces from a set of a hundred, the winner being the competitor whose choices are closest to the average of all competitors' choices. According to Keynes:

> [E]ach competitor has to pick, not those faces which he himself finds prettiest, but those which he thinks likeliest to catch the fancy of the other competitors, all of whom are looking at the problem from the same point of view. It is not a case of choosing those which, to the best of one's judgement, are really the prettiest, nor even those which average opinion genuinely thinks prettiest. We have reached the third degree where we devote our intelligences to anticipating what average opinion expects the average opinion to be. And there are some, I believe, who practice the fourth, fifth, and higher degrees.[13]

Keynes's analysis of the competition uses the same kind of bounded-rationality approach as does Lewis's analysis of salience. Keynes seems to be presupposing that if a competitor had no other grounds for choice, he would pick the six faces he really thought prettiest. This is a hypothesis about nonrational behavior: prettiness is being treated as having primary salience. (For perfectly rational players whose only objective is to win, the fact that a face is pretty is not in itself a reason for picking it.) According to Keynes, sophisticated competitors use this hypothesis at the "third degree": they assume they are playing against opponents who assume they are playing against opponents who, on nonrational grounds, choose the faces they really think are prettiest.

Schelling comments that although Keynes is dealing with "exactly the problem dealt with here" (that is, with coordination games),[14] Keynes's conception of the solution "is *not* at all the same" as his own. This remark is appended to a discussion of a pure coordination game in which each player is asked to name a positive number. According to Schelling:

> [M]ost people, asked just to pick a number, will pick numbers like 3, 7, 13, 100, and 1. But when asked to pick the same number the

---

[13] John Maynard Keynes, *The General Theory of Employment, Interest, and Money* (London: Macmillan, 1936), p. 156.

[14] Strictly speaking, Keynes's competition is not a coordination game, since it is zero-sum (the object is to beat the other competitors). However, the first sentence in the quotation from Keynes could apply equally well to a coordination game, and this may be what Schelling has in mind.

others will pick when the others are equally interested in picking the same number, the motivation is different. The preponderant choice is the number 1. And there seems to be good logic in this: there is no unique "favored number"; the variety of candidates like 3, 7, and so forth is embarrassingly large, and there is no good way of picking the "most favorite" or most conspicuous. If one then asks what number, among all positive numbers, is most clearly unique, or *what rule of selection would lead to unambiguous results*, one may be struck with the fact that the universe of all positive numbers has a "first" or "smallest" number.[15]

Schelling is claiming (again, on the basis of a small and informal experiment) that, in a pure coordination game in which the players are instructed to write down any positive number, the number 1 will be the most frequent choice. Lewis (and, Schelling suggests, Keynes) would explain this by supposing that 1 is the number that would first come to mind for, and would be most likely to be chosen by, someone who had to pick a number and who had no reason for choosing any particular number rather than any other. Thus, for Lewis and Keynes, the salience of the number 1 is ultimately to be explained in terms of nonrational propensities. Schelling, however, claims that in the "just pick a number" case, 1 would be no more likely to be chosen than some other numbers. If he is right about this, but if 1 *is* chosen in coordination games, then 1's being chosen in coordination games cannot be attributed to the primary salience of 1. On Schelling's account, 1 is chosen by the players of coordination games because it has some property of uniqueness that is recognized by intelligent, reasoning players who are consciously trying to coordinate.

Two colleagues and I have tested this particular hypothesis of Schelling's. We divided 178 participants at random into two groups. The members of the first group were then divided anonymously into pairs to play pure coordination games. There were substantial money rewards for successful coordination. The members of the second group were given exactly the same questions as the first group, but their instructions said nothing about coordination, and it was made clear that any payments they received would be independent of the answers they gave. The point of this was to find out how each question would be answered by people who had no obvious reason to give any particular answer rather than any other, and who therefore, on Lewis's and Keynes's hypothesis, would give the answers that had primary salience for them.

One of the questions was Schelling's "Write down any positive number." In the group in which subjects were not trying to coordinate, there was a wide range of answers. The most common answer was 7, given by

---

[15] Schelling, *Strategy of Conflict*, p. 94

11.4 percent of subjects, followed by 2 (10.2 percent) and 10 (5.7 percent). The number 1 was only the fourth most frequent answer (4.5 percent). In the group in which subjects *were* trying to coordinate, however, 1 was by far the most frequent answer, given by 40.0 percent of subjects.[16] It seems that, as Schelling claims, the number 1 has some property which makes it "focal," but that this property is not the kind of primary or higher-order salience considered by Lewis.

IV. Following the Best Rule

How, then, are we to explain how some solutions to coordination games become focal points? One possible explanation is suggested by Schelling's question: "What rule of selection would give unambiguous results?" The thought seems to be that the players of coordination games are trying to find the rule that would be most successful in producing coordination. ("Unambiguous results" are valuable only because ambiguity reduces the probability of coordination.) More precisely, they are looking for the rule which, *if followed by both players*, would yield the best results for both. I shall call this rule the *best rule*. A solution is salient in Schelling's sense, then, if it is the one that would come about if all the players followed the best rule.

In the game of naming a positive number, one possible rule is: "Name the first number that comes to mind." Another is: "Name your favorite number." A third is: "Name the number that you think would be most likely to come to mind for an average person." None of these rules seems likely to be particularly successful in generating coordination, even if followed by both players. The range of numbers which are likely to come to mind, or which are likely to be favorites, is too large for either of the first two rules to give much chance of success. And unless the players are psychologists, they are unlikely to have enough knowledge to be able to use the third rule successfully.

Now consider Schelling's rule: "Name the number that is most clearly unique." (This can be taken as shorthand for: "Name the number whose claim to uniqueness is strongest, relative to standards of evaluation which can be expected to be common knowledge between the players." Every number, of course, is unique in *some* sense: 11 is the smallest prime number which has more than one digit; 26 is the day of the month on which Robert Sugden was born; and so on. But some forms of uniqueness are publicly regarded as more significant than others.) Schelling suggests that the players can expect the "most clearly unique number" rule to have a high chance of success, if they both follow it. This is because one positive number, namely 1, *is* more clearly unique than any other—at least, for people in our culture. If the "most clearly unique number" rule is indeed

---

[16] This was part of the experimental work referred to in footnote 11.

the best rule, and if 1 is the number that is picked out by that rule, then 1 is salient in Schelling's sense.

For my present purposes, the most significant feature of Schelling's analysis of salience is this: it depends on the presumption that if some rule is best for both players in a coordination game, then it is rational or reasonable for each player to follow this rule, and to expect that the other will do so too. Suppose we can agree that, in the set of all feasible rules, the rule "Name the number that is most clearly unique" would give the greatest probability of successful coordination *if followed by both players*. We may still ask why it is rational for either player to follow this rule. If each player is instrumentally rational, choosing the action that will achieve the outcome he most prefers in the light of his beliefs about what the other will do, then it will be rational for him to follow the best rule *if he expects the other to follow it*. But what grounds does he have for expecting this? If he believes the other player to be instrumentally rational, he will expect her to follow the best rule only if it is rational for her to follow it, which will be so, only if she expects him to follow it, and so on.

Notice that this is the same infinite regress as we found in the Prisoners' Coordination Problem. In that problem, we might say that there are two obvious rules, either of which, if followed by both players, would result in coordination. These rules are "Stay silent" and "Confess." It is clear that "Stay silent" is the better rule in Schelling's sense: it is the rule which, if followed by both players, would give the better results for both. But this does not seem to provide an adequate reason for either player to follow it.

It is significant that at least two attempts to construct a theory of salience—those of David Gauthier and Michael Bacharach[17]—begin from the principle that if one outcome is strictly preferred to all the others by both players, then it is uniquely rational for each player to choose the strategy that is consistent with that outcome. Bacharach is well aware that he has failed to provide an adequate justification for this principle: he merely hopes that some justification will eventually be found. Gauthier, in contrast, seems to see this principle, which he calls the "Principle of Coordination,"[18] as an almost self-evident principle of rationality. His

[17] David Gauthier, "Coordination," *Dialogue*, vol. 14 (1975), pp. 195–221; Michael Bacharach, "Games with Context-Sensitive Strategy Spaces," paper presented at International Conference on Game Theory, Florence, June 1991.

[18] Gauthier's Principle of Coordination is, in fact, slightly stronger than the principle I have just attributed to him. Gauthier's principle states that if an outcome is (i) a Nash equilibrium, (ii) Pareto optimal, and (iii) strictly Pareto preferred to all other Nash equilibria, then it is rational for each player to choose the strategy that allows this outcome to be brought about. (A Nash equilibrium is a combination of strategies, one for each player, such that each player's strategy is optimal for him, given the strategies of the others. One outcome is strictly Pareto preferred to another if all players prefer the former to the latter. An outcome x is Pareto optimal if there exists no feasible outcome y such that at least one player prefers y to x, and no player prefers x to y.) Since any outcome which is strictly Pareto preferred to all other outcomes must be a Nash equilibrium, Gauthier's Principle of Coordination implies the principle I have attributed to him.

defense of it is brief. It is made in the context of a game which is similar
to the Prisoners' Coordination Problem. Two players each choose "heads"
or "tails"; if they both choose heads, each wins five cents; if they both
choose tails, each wins nothing; if one chooses heads and the other tails,
each loses some money. According to Gauthier:

> Given this mutuality of knowledge and . . . interest, and the mutu-
> ality of knowledge of interest, each of us may treat the situation *as
> if* his decision were a common decision. If I choose to show heads,
> I choose the outcome which pays each of us 5¢; if I choose to show
> tails, I choose the outcome which pays each of us nothing. Hence as
> a rational maximizer I choose to show heads, and so do you.[19]

Gauthier says he is working "within the framework of an account of rational action, as rational action is commonly understood"; he interprets
rationality in terms of the maximization of expected utility and assumes
the rationality of the players to be common knowledge between them.[20]
Given these premises, Gauthier's argument seems fallacious. My choosing to show heads does not, in itself, bring about the outcome which pays
each of us five cents: that depends on what you do. In order to determine
what it is rational for me to do, I must form a belief about what you, as
a rational agent, will do. I can be confident that my choosing to show
heads will bring about the outcome in which we both show heads, only
if rationality requires you to show heads. But the proposition that rationality requires each of us to show heads is precisely what Gauthier's argument is intended to prove.[21]

So if we accept Schelling's analysis of salience, we need to be able to
show that it is rational for each player in a coordination game to act on
the rule which, if followed by both, would give the best results. But if we
try to show this within the conventional theory of instrumentally rational choice, we run into the infinite regress that is illustrated by the Prisoners' Coordination Problem. Clearly, then, it would be circular to appeal
to salience as a way of resolving the Prisoners' Coordination Problem.

V. Thinking as a Team

Perhaps the source of the problem lies in the *individualistic* nature of
agency in the conventional theory of rational choice. It might be said that

---

[19] Gauthier, "Coordination," p. 200.

[20] *Ibid.*, p. 196. In later work, Gauthier has developed a theory of "constrained maximization" which implies, among other things, that (in certain circumstances) it is rational to
cooperate in the Prisoner's Dilemma; see David Gauthier, *Morals by Agreement* (Oxford: Oxford University Press, 1986). A somewhat similar conception of rationality is proposed by
Edward F. McClennen in *Rationality and Dynamic Choice* (Cambridge: Cambridge University
Press, 1990). It is possible that the Principle of Coordination is a valid implication of this kind
of theory.

[21] A similar criticism is made by Margaret Gilbert in "Rationality and Salience," *Philosophical Studies*, vol. 57 (1989), pp. 61–77.

the problem arises because each player looks only for reasons that bear on *him*; the players seem to be overlooking reasons that bear on *them*.

Imagine you are writing a book of advice for bridge players. Notice that bridge is played by two-person partnerships, and that during the course of play, partners are not allowed to communicate with one another. It is impossible for bridge partners to agree in advance of a game about how they will respond to every possible contingency, but they can agree to follow certain general rules. Presumably a book of advice is an attempt to give some answers to the question of which rules are best. But how should that question be construed? The most natural way to construe it, I suggest, is as follows: Which rules, if followed by both partners, would give the partnership the best chance of winning its games? If this is the relevant question, then the advice will not be addressed to bridge players *as individuals*: an individual player has no reason to act on the book's advice unless his partner will be doing so too. The advice will be addressed to them *as members of partnerships*.

Now imagine that some reader of the book makes the following complaint: "This book is no use. I can see that if my partner and I both followed the rules set out in the book, we would improve our chances of winning, which we both want to do. My partner has read the book too, and she agrees. We can both see that it would be rational for me to follow those rules if I expected my partner to follow them, and that it would be rational for her to follow them if she expected me to follow them. But that doesn't explain why I should follow them, or why she should." In terms of the conventional theory of rational choice, this complaint is entirely justified, for reasons which should by now be familiar. Nevertheless, it is surely perverse. The obvious reply is that bridge books are written for readers who think as members of partnerships. The complainant and his partner are thinking as instrumentally rational individuals: the book is not intended for people like them.

The point of this example is that the players of a coordination game may be thought of as members of a team, jointly playing a game against nature. As in bridge, they are unable to communicate with one another during the course of play. On Schelling's analysis, the salient solution to a game is the one that would be reached if both players followed the best rule (defined as the rule which, if followed by both, would give the best results for both). That the players ought to follow the best rule is good advice in the same sense that the recommendations of the book on bridge are good advice: it is good advice for the players *as a team*.

The idea of giving advice to a team seems natural enough, but it raises difficult problems. If we can advise a team on what *it* should do, the implication seems to be that the team is an agent, acting in its own right. But what does this mean? The team's actions are still composed of the actions of individual team members. We need to understand what it means for an individual team member to act on advice that has been given to the team. How does this advice provide *him* with a reason to do one thing rather than another?

It is clear that we will get nowhere if we interpret "acting as a member of the team" as "acting in the best interests of the team." To adopt this interpretation is to treat each individual as an instrumentally rational agent in the conventional sense, who simply takes the team's objective as his own. The problem then, of course, is that no player can know which action on his part will best serve the interests of the team unless he can predict which action will be chosen by the other member: we are back with the infinite regress.

The most promising way of avoiding this regress, I think, is to think of "membership" in something like the old sense in which arms and legs are members of the body. To act as a member of the team is to act as a *component* of the team. It is to act on a concerted plan, doing one's allotted part in that plan without asking whether, taking other members' actions as given, one's own action is contributing towards the team's objective. (To insist on having that question answered in the affirmative before recognizing the rationality of doing one's own part would be to adopt an instrumental conception of rationality. Instrumentally rational agents would be trapped in the familiar infinite regress: we cannot show that it is rational for one member to do his part without first showing that it is rational for the others to do theirs.) It must be sufficient for each member of the team that the plan itself is designed to achieve the team's objective: the objective will be achieved if everyone follows the plan.

Susan Hurley illuminates this notion of membership by comparing the relation of cause to effect with the relation of part to whole. The person who acts in an instrumentally rational way evaluates actions in terms of cause and effect: for him, an action is rational to the extent that it causes good outcomes. The person who acts as a member of a team evaluates actions as parts of a whole that is made up of the actions of all the members of the team: for her, an action is rational to the extent that it is part of a set of actions which, taken together, cause good outcomes. As Hurley puts it:

> [It is wrong] to assume that when someone acts as a member of a group he must have made some mistake about the causal consequences of his act on the acts of the other members of the group, or have engaged in magical or superstitious thinking of some kind; such an individualistic assumption in fact distorts familiar forms of human motivation and agency. Someone's reason in acting may rather be that his act bears a constitutive relationship to a valuable form of agency. His contribution to its realization is not a causal one, but that of a part to a whole; it is hardly any less of a contribution, or irrational, on that score.[22]

[22] Susan L. Hurley, *Natural Reasons* (Oxford: Oxford University Press, 1989), p. 148.

The idea that it can be rational to act as a member of a team may seem to have an unpalatable implication. Consider the Prisoners' Coordination Problem. Suppose that player A construes his relationship with B as a relationship between team members in a game against the district attorney. If he acts as a member of this team, he will stay silent. He will not do this because he expects his own action to have good causal consequences for the team, but because it is part of a plan which, if followed by both members, would have good consequences. In saying this, are we saying that it would be rational for player A to stay silent, even if he expected player B to confess?

I think not. It is essential to the idea of acting as a team member that one does not choose an action *because*, taking the actions of other members as given, that action has good consequences. But the actions which one chooses for other reasons may still have good causal consequences, and one may act in the expectation that one will cause these consequences to come about. If there is to be a theory of rational action by teams, it should be expected to apply only to groups of individuals who *are* teams; and for a group of individuals to be a team in any genuine sense, their being a team must be mutually recognized. If this is accepted, then the possibility considered in the previous paragraph (that A might expect B to confess) cannot arise. If B acts rationally as a member of the team, he will stay silent. Thus, if it is a matter of common knowledge that A and B are rational members of the same team, then A will expect B to stay silent. Notice, however, that this expectation is not one of the *reasons* on which A acts. It is because players who think as a team do not need to form expectations about one another's actions that they can solve coordination problems.

This argument may seem to do no more than shunt the problem on. Originally, the problem was to explain how A and B form the mutual expectation that each will follow the best rule. The answer I have been canvassing is that, for individuals who mutually recognize themselves as members of a team, following the best rule is a principle of rationality. But this leaves the problem of explaining how A and B come to recognize themselves as members of a common team. Have we gotten any further?

I shall not try to argue that there is some procedure by which two individuals can rationally arrive at a mutual recognition of their comprising a team, starting only from common knowledge of the game, as described by its payoff matrix.[23] (Such a mutual recognition might, of course, be implicit in some other description of a game. For example, we might say

---

[23] In contrast, Hurley (*ibid.*, pp. 136–70) argues that, in games like the Prisoners' Coordination Problem, it is irrational for the players not to think as a team or, as she puts it, it is irrational for them not to participate in "collective agency." Her argument is that the unit of agency should itself be a matter of rational choice; if "it is a good thing for such collective agency to exist," then it is rational to participate in collective agency, and irrational not to (p. 157). I am inclined to think that the idea of rational choice is not meaningful until the unit of agency has been specified.

that two "partners" in a game of bridge who failed to recognize that they comprised a team had failed to understand what it means to play bridge as partners. But if that can be said, it is because the game of bridge is not fully described by its payoff matrix.) Thus, I shall not claim that rational players of the Prisoners' Coordination Problem will necessarily recognize themselves as members of a common team. But is the absence of such an argument any cause for concern?

Consider an analogy taken from the conventional theory of rational choice. Look at the game shown in Table 3. Conventional game-theoretic analysis gives the result that A should play "down" and that B should play "left." This leads to the outcome (1, 1), which is worse for both players than the (100, 100) that could have been achieved, had they chosen different strategies. But, given the usual assumptions about individual rationality, (1, 1) is the only outcome that can result from rational play. The proof works by dominance. For player B, "left" strictly dominates "right"; that is, the outcome for B is always better when B plays "left," no matter what A chooses to do. So if B is rational, she will play "left," irrespective of what she expects A to do. A knows that B is rational, and so knows that B will play "left." Knowing this, A maximizes his utility by playing "down."

Now suppose someone were to ask whether it would be rational for A to play "down" if he expected B to play "right." A game theorist would reply: "Of course not. In that case, he would be rational to play 'up'. But game theory assumes that both players are rational, and that both players know this. Under these assumptions, the case in which A expects B to play 'right' would never arise." But if the recommendations of the theory are conditional on its being common knowledge that the players are rational in the conventional sense, aren't we entitled to ask how the players arrive at this piece of common knowledge? Conventional theory can give us no answer: this is just one of the fixed points of the theory.

TABLE 3. *A Game That Can Be Solved by Dominance*

| | | Player B | |
		Left	Right
Player A	Up	0, 101	100, 100
	Down	1, 1	0, 0

One characteristic of the conventional theory of rational choice is that it does not recognize any kind of team agency: each individual pursues her own objective. The theory applies to the interactions of people who are rational in this sense. We might say that it applies only to people who recognize one another as *not* being members of a common team. I have suggested that a theory of team agency would apply only to people who recognized one another as belonging to a common team. The positions of the two kinds of theory seem quite symmetrical.

If the players in the Prisoners' Coordination Problem conceive of one another as people who act as members of a common partnership or team, they may be able to conclude that rationality requires them to stay silent. If, in contrast, they conceive of one another as individually rational in the sense of conventional rational choice theory, it seems that they cannot reason their way to that conclusion. These are two different ways in which the players could conceive of the relationship between them. Both are coherent and intelligible. To the question "Which is the rational one for the players to adopt?" there is, I think, no answer.

VI. Conclusion

The theory of instrumentally rational choice, as conventionally used in economics, does not provide us with adequate reasons to play our parts in cooperative arrangements that benefit us. This is true, even in such simple cases as the Prisoners' Coordination Problem, in which it is in each individual's interest to cooperate, provided he expects others to cooperate too. Yet, I think, most of us feel that we have adequate reason to cooperate in such cases. I have argued that reasons for cooperating do indeed exist, but that these reasons can get a grip only if we conceive of ourselves as members of a team. Whether or not we should conceive of ourselves in this way is a question that cannot be answered by appeal to rationality.

By restricting its attention to instrumental rationality, economics is neglecting a potentially significant form of human motivation. A theory in which individuals can act cooperatively, following rules which it would be in everyone's interest for everyone to follow, might explain much more than how people solve one-shot coordination problems. In particular, it might help us to understand nonselfish behavior.

Economics, University of East Anglia

ALTRUISM VERSUS SELF-INTEREST: SOMETIMES A FALSE DICHOTOMY*

By Neera Kapur Badhwar

Altruism is "an interest in other people *for their own sake.*"
Dictionary of Philosophy, ed. Antony Flew, 1979

Self-interest is an interest in yourself *for your own sake.*

"You shall love your neighbor as yourself."
Matthew 19:19

"[T]he good person must be a self-lover. . . ."
Aristotle, *Nicomachean Ethics,* 1168a28–29

"The noble soul has reverence for itself."
Nietzsche, *Beyond Good and Evil*

In the moral philosophy of the last two centuries, altruism of one kind or another has typically been regarded as identical with moral concern. When self-regarding duties have been recognized, motivation by *duty* has been sharply distinguished from motivation by *self-interest.*[1] Accordingly, from Kant, Mill, and Sidgwick to Rawls, Nagel, and Gauthier, concern for our own interests, whether long-term or short-term, has typically been regarded as intrinsically nonmoral. So, for example, although Thomas Nagel regards both prudence and altruism as structural features of practical reason, he identifies only the latter as a moral capacity, prudence be-

---

* This essay has profited greatly from the comments of Chris Swoyer, David Schmidtz, the other contributors to this volume, and its editors, as well as from the stimulating discussion following its presentation at the Department of Philosophy at the University of Oklahoma.

[1] Kant is the foremost example of a philosopher who makes room for self-regarding duties while firmly excluding self-interest from moral motivation. *No* empirical interest, according to Kant, can motivate moral concern, because all such interests—including our interests in others—reduce to self-interest. "All material practical principles are, as such, of one and the same kind, and belong under the general principle of self-love or one's own happiness" (Kant, *Critique of Practical Reason,* trans. Lewis W. Beck [New York: Bobbs-Merrill, 1956], p. 22). To love another's inclinations or empirical ends is to consider them to be "favorable to my own advantage" (Kant, *Groundwork of the Metaphysic of Morals,* Akademie ed., trans. H. J. Paton, in *The Moral Law* [London: Hutchinson and Co., 1948], p. 400). The moral attitude of respect (including self-respect) "is properly the representation of a worth that thwarts my self-love" (p. 401n).

ing merely rational, long-term egoism.[2] Similarly, John Rawls and David Gauthier contrast self-interest and other nontuistic interests — interests that are independent of others' interests — with moral interest.[3] We are morally *permitted*, no doubt, to act out of self-interest within certain constraints, but such acts can have no intrinsic moral worth. Pursuit of our own interests out of *duty* (if there is such a duty) does have intrinsic moral worth, but such pursuit, by hypothesis, cannot be motivated by self-interest.[4] Self-interested pursuit of our own interests as such, no matter how realistic, farsighted, temperate, honest, or courageous, cannot be intrinsically moral. And this remains the case even if self-interest motivates us to perform other-regarding acts: only those other-regarding acts that are (appropriately) motivated by others' interests count as moral, because only such acts are altruistic.

It is generally granted by philosophers who exclude self-interested motivation from moral motivation that altruistic acts often have self-interested consequences or, more strongly, that in the normal circumstances of human existence being moral is in most individuals' self-interest. It is even sometimes argued that if morality is to be rationally acceptable to an individual, it must be justified to her as a means to her own interests. It must be shown, as Gauthier puts it, that although "[d]uty overrides advantage . . . the acceptance of duty is truly advantageous" (*MA*, p. 2).

[2] Thomas Nagel, *The Possibility of Altruism* (Oxford: Clarendon Press, 1970), pp. 3, 15–16, 84, and 87. Egoistic interests, according to Nagel, include both self-interest and "the interest we may happen to take in other things and other persons" (p. 3). Nagel evidently does not accept Kant's claim that all interests reduce to self-interest; nevertheless, like Kant, he excludes all egoistic interests from moral motivation.

See also Laurence Thomas, *Living Morally: A Psychology of Moral Character* (Philadelphia: Temple University Press, 1989); Lawrence Blum, *Friendship, Altruism, and Morality* (Boston: Routledge & Kegan Paul, 1980); and Iris Murdoch, *The Sovereignty of Good* (New York: Schocken Books, 1971). Thomas states that he will "assume without really much argument that to be moral is to be altruistic" (p. vii), and contrasts altruism with self-interest (p. 67). Blum states that he "will not want to make any *general* claims about the distinction between moral considerations, judgments, and standpoints and non-moral ones," but that he "will want to maintain one distinction, namely the difference between concern for others and concern for self, and will want to see this distinction as having moral significance" (p. 9; see also pp. 91 and 213). In a more recent article, however, Blum is concerned to explore the *connection* between concern for others and concern for self, although he still stops short of saying that the latter can be a *moral* concern. See Blum, "Vocation, Friendship, and Community: Limitations of the Personal-Impersonal Framework," *Identity, Character, and Morality*, ed. Owen Flanagan and Amélie O. Rorty (Cambridge: MIT Press, 1990), pp. 173–97. The central concept in understanding morality or goodness, according to Murdoch, is realism rather than altruism, but the self and its concerns are still excluded from morality because, she explains, the self is the chief obstacle to realism. "The self, the place where we live, is a place of illusion. Goodness is connected with the attempt to see the unself, to see and to respond to the real world in the light of a virtuous consciousness" (p. 93).

[3] Nontuistic interests are what Nagel calls egoistic interests: independent interests *of* the self, whether in the self or in others. See John Rawls, *A Theory of Justice* (Cambridge: Harvard University Press, 1971), pp. 13, 127–29; and David Gauthier, *Morals by Agreement*, hereafter *MA* (Oxford: Clarendon Press, 1986), p. 7.

[4] Thus, according to Kant, we have an indirect duty to pursue our own happiness, because if we are happy we will be more likely to do our various duties.

But Gauthier joins in the general agreement that self-interest or advantage cannot be the *motive* of a moral act.[5]

I think this view is wrong: self-interest *can* be the motive of a moral act. Motivation by rational self-interest, i.e., an unselfdeceived, realistic, and coherent conception—implicit or explicit—of one's best overall interests, for one's own sake, can have moral worth. Since a person's conception of her rational self-interest can be mistaken, motivation by rational self-interest need not be identical with motivation by actual self-interest, but an act so motivated will still count as a self-interested act, and may still have moral worth.[6] As Joseph Butler puts it, "[s]elf-love in its due degree is as just and morally good as any affection whatever," because the goodness of an act depends on whether it is in accordance with our nature and the nature of the case, rather than on whether it is altruistic.[7]

However, this view of Butler's—unlike his argument against psychological egoism—has had little impact on moral philosophy since Kant.[8]

---

[5] Gauthier, *MA*, pp. 327–28. Despite the general agreement over the nature of moral motivation as (entirely or chiefly) altruistic, there is disagreement over the nature of altruism. For example, Nagel (*Possibility of Altruism*, p. 15) and Gauthier (*MA*, p. 238) see altruism as a purely rational capacity, i.e., a capacity which is independent of our other-regarding emotions such as fellow-feeling or compassion, whereas Thomas sees it as rooted in such emotions. Blum allows for the possibility that certain forms of concern for others, such as those expressed in justice, or perhaps even benevolence, may be purely rational, but insists on the moral worth of the concern that is motivated by sympathy or compassion (*Friendship, Altruism, and Morality*, especially pp. 121–24). Again, some philosophers regard genuine altruism as directly motivated by another's interests, whereas others—primarily Kantians—regard it as only indirectly motivated by such interests, via a commitment to some moral principle that requires altruistic concern. Finally, what different philosophers mean by *direct altruism* also differs. Thus, Blum's idea of direct (emotionally motivated) altruism is Nagel's idea of egoistic motivation, because emotions, for Nagel, are "intermediate" factors between others' interests and practical reason, factors that constitute part of the agent's own interests (pp. 84 and 87). Direct altruism, according to Nagel, is purely rational motivation by others' interests (pp. 15–16).

I cannot discuss these issues here, but it is important to note that psychological research does not support the idea of altruism as a purely rational capacity. On the contrary, studies of the psychopathic personality, as well as the altruistic personality, strongly support the idea that altruism is impossible without an adequate emotional capacity. See Hervey Cleckley, *The Mask of Sanity*, 5th ed. (St. Louis: C. V. Mosby, 1976) and the studies of altruism cited in n. 11 below. I share the view of those philosophers who think that most adult human emotions are not blind impulses but cognitive phenomena, and essential to moral perception, reasoning, and motivation. See Ronald de Sousa, *The Rationality of Emotion* (Cambridge: MIT Press, 1987); Blum, *Friendship, Altruism, and Morality*; and my "The Rejection of Ethical Rationalism," *Logos*, vol. 10 (1989), pp. 99–131.

[6] Hereafter, by "motivation by self-interest" I shall mean "motivation by rational self-interest" as defined above. And by "moral act" or "moral motive" I shall mean an act or motive that is morally good or right, and not merely one that is morally permissible.

[7] Joseph Butler, *Five Sermons*, ed. S. Darwall (Indianapolis: Hackett Publishing, 1983), preface, para. 39.

[8] The only contemporary philosophers I am aware of who defend self-interest as a *moral* interest are Jean Hampton, "Selflessness and the Loss of Self," in this volume; W. D. Falk, "Morality, Self, and Others," in *Morality and the Language of Conduct*, ed. Hector-Neri Castaneda and George Nakhnikian (Detroit: Wayne State University Press, 1963), pp. 34–39; and Edmund L. Pincoffs, *Quandaries and Virtues: Against Reductivism in Ethics* (Lawrence:

On the matter of moral motivation, most contemporary philosophers continue to reflect a worry often seen in the culture at large, that to the extent we are self-interested, we must be focused on ourselves to the exclusion of others, and must view both others and morality as, at best, mere means to our independent ends.[9] By contrast, many social scientists (especially economists), evidently unimpressed by (or unaware of) philosophical arguments against psychological egoism, continue to reflect another common belief, namely, that all human motives reduce to self-interest. When the thesis that self-interest can never be moral is combined — as it often is in the general culture — with the suspicion that all human motives reduce to self-interest, the predictable result is cynicism. This is reason enough to reexamine both the thesis and the suspicion. In this essay I do both, the first directly, the second indirectly. My chief concern is to argue that self-interested action — i.e., action motivated by rational self-interest — can be moral, but the data I use to argue for this also provide compelling empirical evidence that all human motives do *not* reduce to self-interest, that altruism *is* possible.

My main argument for the thesis that self-interest can be moral is that there is a kind of moral excellence, an intuitively recognizable excellence of character and action, which is at once a form of deep altruism and a form of self-interest. Such moral excellence may be exhibited over a lifetime, or over a brief span of a person's life; it may take the form of moral heroism or saintliness, or the more ordinary everyday form of an easy, cheerful, reliable goodness. An adequate description of this kind of moral excellence, I argue, is also a description of the person as someone motivated by self-interest, and of (the relevant portion of) her life as one that is well-lived or deeply satisfying. If the self-interested motivation were absent, something of moral worth would be lost. If I can show this, then I will have shown that self-interest can be a moral motive.

The example I use to illustrate and support these points is that of gentile rescuers of Jews in Nazi Europe, whose extraordinary heroism earned

---

University Press of Kansas, 1986). Falk argues that the precept that one ought to act on principles of courage and wisdom out of "proper care for oneself" is a moral percept, and Pincoffs argues that virtue considerations are both self- and other-regarding, and that both kinds of considerations are moral. I agree with both views, but my focus and line of argument are different. The psychologist Carol Gilligan has also made an important philosophical contribution to the recognition of concern for the self as a moral concern in *In a Different Voice* (Cambridge: Harvard University Press, 1982). Many feminist writers have rejected a morality of self-sacrifice as oppressive and exploitative, and as incompatible with genuine altruism, but without claiming that concern for one's interests, for one's own sake, can be intrinsically moral.

[9] An interesting example of the automatic equation of self-interest with immorality or amorality was provided recently by a student who stated that he saw no real *moral* difference between the view that virtue is choiceworthy because it is an essential component of happiness, and the view that virtue is *not* choiceworthy because it conflicts with happiness, because both views were equally selfish.

them the highest honors from Yad Vashem, and continues to evoke the admiration—and amazement—of students of the Holocaust.[10] Their characters and lives are the paradigms of altruism, and so learning about them has unusual potential to instruct us about the nature of altruism—and, as I argue, of self-interest. Rescuers have been the subject of several studies, most of which assume that if their motives were altruistic, they could not also have been self-interested. I use some of this research on rescuers to argue that many of the rescuers' altruistic actions were also deeply self-interested and, indeed, that this was essential to their full moral worth.

I begin, in Section I, with a discussion of a study of rescuers that was designed to test—and that eventually rejected—the assumption of rational actor theory, widely accepted in the social sciences, that all motives reduce to self-interest. In Section II, I discuss the hypothesis of this and other studies that rescue activity is best explained in terms of rescuers' conception of themselves as part of a common humanity, and the widespread assumption that such a conception is incompatible with strong self-interested motivations. I proceed to argue in Section III that having such a universalistic self-conception is compatible with having strong self-interested motivations, and that only an unduly restricted picture of self-interest prevents one from seeing this. Section IV is an attempt to show that if rescuers *had* been motivated by rational self-interest, they would have done exactly what they did because, given the content and structure of their interests, they could not have seen the refusal to help as being in their self-interest. Further, we have good reason to believe that rescuers were, in fact, motivated by self-interest and, indeed, that there was a necessary connection between their self-interested and altruistic motives. In Section V, I analyze altruistic and self-interested motives to show how they might be necessarily connected, and then argue that rescuers' self-interested motivations not only did not detract from the altruism of their acts, but were actually symptomatic of the strength and depth of their altruistic dispositions. I conclude in Section VI with a summary of my arguments, and an indication of some of the implications of the view that self-interest can be a moral motive.

I. RESCUERS AND RATIONAL ACTOR THEORY

In their study of rescuers, Monroe, Barton, and Klingemann (hereafter Monroe et al.) undertook to test rational actor theory, according to which all behavior, including altruistic behavior, is a means to the max-

---

[10] Yad Vashem is the Jewish organization that traces and honors the heroes and victims of the Holocaust. It honors those who assisted Jews with the designation "rescuer" only if it can verify that they acted without expectation of material or social rewards.

imization of the individual's own utility or preference satisfaction.[11] In particular, the researchers were concerned to show that the assumption of rational actor theory that self-interest is the dominant motive of all or most human behavior, including so-called altruistic behavior, was false. The researchers broke this theory down into several components and, on the basis of extensive interviews with thirteen rescuers, concluded that none of the components was applicable to rescue behavior.[12] Contrary to rational actor theory, they found that:

1. Rescuers' individual decisions to rescue Jews were *not* the result of a conscious calculation of costs and benefits — rescuers made their decisions spontaneously, in full awareness of the personal risk, and without expectation of reward, either material or social (honors, praise, and so on). Indeed, after the war several rescuers were greeted with ridicule or indifference ("Rescuers, 1990," p. 109).

2. Rescuers did not undertake their missions in order to feel good about themselves, i.e., they did not help as a means to psychological rewards ("Rescuers, 1990," p. 110).

3. Rescuers did not make their decisions in the hope of establishing fellowship with other rescuers, nor were they motivated by "clusters of altruists" who might appeal to their empathy or sense of duty; they made their decisions alone and, for reasons of safety, none discussed their rescue activities with anyone unless absolutely necessary ("Rescuers, 1990," pp. 112–14).

---

[11] K. R. Monroe, M. C. Barton, and U. Klingemann, "Altruism and the Theory of Rational Action: Rescuers of Jews in Nazi Europe," hereafter "Rescuers, 1990," *Ethics*, vol. 101, no. 1 (October 1990), pp. 103–22. A longer version of this article, hereafter "Rescuers, 1991," appears in Kristen R. Monroe, ed., *The Economic Approach to Politics* (New York: Harper & Row–Collins/Scott, Foresman, 1991), pp. 317–52. I will refer to this version only when the relevant point is absent from the earlier one.

Another relevant work by Monroe is a larger study of altruism, "John Donne's People: Explaining Differences between Rational Actors and Altruists through Cognitive Frameworks," *Journal of Politics*, vol. 53, no. 2 (May 1991), pp. 394–433.

An earlier major work on altruism and rescuers is Samuel P. Oliner and Pearl M. Oliner, *The Altruistic Personality: Rescuers of Jews in Nazi Europe*, hereafter Oliner and Oliner (New York: The Free Press, 1988). Oliner and Oliner interviewed 406 rescuers, of whom 95 percent were designated by Yad Vashem, and 5 percent were identified by Oliner and Oliner through interviews with rescued survivors (pp. 2–3). (However, on p. 2 the authors also claim that all 406 of the rescuers they interviewed were identified as rescuers by Yad Vashem.) In addition, they interviewed 150 survivors, and 126 nonrescuers and "actives" — those who claimed to have been resistance fighters or rescuers of Jews, but for whose claims Oliner and Oliner had no independent corroboration (pp. 3–4).

Another important work I shall use is Philip Hallie's account of the rescue effort mounted by the village of Le Chambon, *Lest Innocent Blood Be Shed: The Story of the Village of Le Chambon, and How Goodness Happened There*, hereafter *LC* (New York: Harper & Row, 1979).

[12] The names of the rescuers were supplied by Yad Vashem. The interviews, which took place between March 1988 and January 1990, ranged from two to almost twenty hours. The researchers also interviewed five nonrescuers and five entrepreneurs to serve as a contrasting baseline sample. See "Rescuers, 1990," pp. 103–7, for a summary of the research methodology.

4. Rescuers did not calculate how much they could or should give, and how much they should save for themselves—they accepted the most severe hardships to meet their Jewish guests' needs, making no distinction between their own or their families' needs and those of their guests ("Rescuers, 1990," pp. 114–15).

There is one other component of rational actor theory that the researchers found too vague to test reliably, namely, the idea that altruism is a "psychic good" for some people, so that in acting altruistically, such people act as a means to their own utility after all. The researchers did find that rescuers had been unusually altruistic before the war, and continued to be so after the war, but doubted that the fact of consistently altruistic behavior confirmed the psychic-goods idea ("Rescuers, 1990," pp. 110–12). They concluded that rescue activity challenges the theory that self-interest motivates all human behavior.

Some of the most important conclusions of this study—rescuers' awareness of risk, the absence of any expectation of material, social, or psychological rewards, the spontaneity of their choice to help, and the pattern of altruism in their lives—correspond to those of the other two studies mentioned above in footnote 11. Thus, Oliner and Oliner arrive at the same conclusions about most of the rescuers in their study, and Hallie about most or all of the rescuers.[13] There were probably many rescuers whose motivations were fully altruistic, but who had not been particularly altruistic before the war, and/or who made the decision to help only after a struggle. But those who helped spontaneously have, as I think will become clear in the course of this essay, a special moral significance. Hence in this essay I focus on these rescuers.

II. "Every Other Person Is Basically You. . . ."

What motivated the rescue activity of those who acted spontaneously, without the expectation of material, social, or psychological rewards, and despite an awareness of the risks involved? For most of them rescue activity lasted for years, years of constant strain and danger.[14] What is it that they had that nonrescuers lacked? One of the most significant facts

---

[13] Oliner and Oliner state that 54 percent of the rescuers in their sample reported a sense of extreme risk to their lives or welfare at the time of their first helping act, 23 percent said they had a sense of moderate risk, and only 18 percent said they had no sense of personal risk (pp. 126–27). Both during and after the war many rescuers in Europe are reported to have been severely ostracized, and many still seem to be in danger for their lives at the hands of neo-Nazi groups (Oliner and Oliner, pp. 1–2 and 225). On the matter of a consistent pattern of altruism in the lives of most rescuers, see Oliner and Oliner, pp. 170 and 245–47, and Hallie, LC. Hallie describes the attitude of the Chambonnais "as being *toujours prêt, toujours prêt à rendre service* (always ready, always ready to help)," and cites this to explain why Le Chambon became the safest place of refuge in Europe (p. 196).

[14] According to Oliner and Oliner, for most rescuers it lasted for between two and five years (p. 6).

about the rescuers interviewed by Monroe et al. was that they felt they had no option but to do what they did. A common response was "One cannot really act otherwise," or "What else could I do?" ("Rescuers, 1990," p. 118). This response was identical to that of the inhabitants of Le Chambon, who also rescued 1,500 Jews at great risk to themselves, but declared that they only did what they had to do.[15] And, again, this was also the response of most rescuers interviewed by Oliner and Oliner, who felt that it was only "natural" to have helped (pp. 169, 228). Indeed, it was so natural and obvious that it did not even seem to involve choice: "I don't make a choice. It comes, and it's there" ("Rescuers, 1990," p. 118). "It was not a question of reasoning. . . . There were people in need and we helped them. . . . People always ask how we started, but we didn't start. It started . . . very gradually. We never gave it much thought" (Oliner and Oliner, p. 216).[16] In Le Chambon, rescue activity started the night a refugee knocked on the door of the presbytery and asked if she could come in, and Magda Trocme, the pastor's wife, answered, "Naturally, come in, and come in" (LC, p. 120).

Rescuers also rejected the idea that their actions were extraordinary, deserving of special praise: ". . . what has all this to do with goodness? Things had to be done, that's all, and we happened to be there to do them" (LC, pp. 20–21). "I did nothing unusual; anyone would have done the same thing in my place" (Oliner and Oliner, p. 113). "I do not feel I am a hero. I feel that I only did my duty. I am not a hero" (Oliner and Oliner, p. 228). "We got them [decorations] for things that go without saying. If things had been right, all people would have acted this way" ("Rescuers, 1991," p. 342).

Those who acted spontaneously, then, acted with a sense that they had no alternative but to help, and that, under the circumstances, helping was nothing special. They knew that they were surrounded by people who watched the events as apathetic bystanders, or turned away Jews who came to them for help. Yet they saw themselves as unable to do anything but help. The rescue activity of those who helped unhesitatingly was, Monroe et al. conclude, a spontaneous manifestation of "deep-seated dispositions which form one's central identity" or character.[17] And central to rescuers' identity was a sense of themselves as part of a common humanity, as revealed in repeated remarks like: "You help people because you are human and you see that there is a need . . ." ("Rescuers, 1990,"

---

[15] Hallie reports that practically every person he interviewed responded in this fashion (LC, p. 20).

[16] Over 70 percent of the rescuers interviewed by Oliner and Oliner reported that the first time they helped, they took only minutes to decide (p. 169).

[17] "Rescuers, 1990," p. 121. See Aristotle: "[S]omeone who is unafraid and unperturbed in a sudden alarm seems braver than [someone who is unafraid only] in dangers that are obvious in advance; for what he does is more the result of his state of character, since it is less the outcome of preparation" (Nicomachean Ethics, 1117a17–20).

p. 118). "Every other person is basically you. . . . That's the kind of attitude you have for most of these rescues" ("Rescuers, 1990," p. 114). Oliner and Oliner also conclude that *inclusiveness* —experiencing others as part of the self —and a *universalistic orientation* —seeing oneself as part of a common humanity —were the salient factors in explaining rescue activity (pp. 165–66, 176, 178, 183, and 187). And in Hallie's account also, this inclusive and universalistic orientation emerges as an obvious trait of the central figures of the resistance in Le Chambon, Andre and Magda Trocme, as of the Chambonnais in general (see, in particular, *LC*, pp. 153–54, 159–63, and 194).

To borrow Thomas Nagel's words, rescuers had a conception of themselves as merely one person among others equally real.[18] This disposed them to be so keenly aware of, and so highly susceptible to, motivation by others' interests, that they felt they had *no choice but to help*. Their identity, as Monroe et al. correctly point out, "limited the options available *to them*" ("Rescuers, 1990," p. 118). So rescuers' claims that they had no choice but to help must be taken to mean that they felt that other choices were not possible *for them*, and not that they believed that other choices did not *exist*. Given who they were, given their sense of themselves, any other choice would have required "a fundamental shift" in their "basic identity construction" ("Rescuers, 1990," p. 121). Their choices served "more as self-affirmations and less as options" ("Rescuers, 1990," p. 122). Rescue activity enabled them to assert their humanity in a time of "moral anarchy" and, thus, "preserve their sense of integrity and identity" (Oliner and Oliner, p. 227).

Nonrescuers offer a study in contrasts. Like rescuers, most nonrescuers also felt as though they had no option but to do what they did. But unlike rescuers, what most *nonrescuers* saw as their only option was to stand by passively. *Their* common response was: "What could I do, one individual alone against the Nazis?" ("Rescuers, 1990," p. 119). The crucial difference between rescuers and nonrescuers, according to the three studies, did not lie in differences in religion, or degree of patriotism, or political affiliation, or role models, or views of human nature, or a communitarian versus individualistic world view.[19] Rather, it lay in their very different views of themselves in relation to others, in the extent of their identification with other human beings as human beings. Nonrescuers simply lacked the inclusive and universalistic orientation of rescuers.[20]

---

[18] Nagel, *Possibility of Altruism*, p. 14.

[19] Oliner and Oliner, pp. 156–60; "Rescuers, 1990," pp. 116–17; *LC*, pp. 66–67. Many rescuers were individuals to whom communal ties meant little or nothing and, like nonrescuers, most rescuers thought that human nature was a mixture of good and bad, and that self-interest was normal.

[20] Some nonrescuers also partially identified with the Nazis, despite compassion for the Jews and anger toward the Germans. As one nonrescuer said, "There was also a feeling of

But what exactly does having this orientation imply? Is an inclusive and universalistic orientation incompatible with a strong sense of oneself as a distinct individual and, thus, with strong self-interested motivations? It is often assumed that it is, an assumption shared by most of the researchers. Thus, Monroe et al. claim that rescuers did not "consider the individual the basic actor in society," that in viewing themselves as part of a shared humanity they did not view themselves "as individual beings, separate and distinct from others" ("Rescuers, 1990," p. 122). What Monroe et al. mean by this, I take it, is that rescuers did not see the individual—and hence themselves—as independently efficacious: the "basic actor in society," in their eyes, was not the individual but some larger entity. Accordingly, they also did not see themselves as separate and distinct individuals. But this interpretation of a universalistic identity seems seriously amiss: the mere fact that rescuers had a strong sense of oneness with others *as human beings* does not imply that they did not have a strong sense of their separate individuality *as individuals*. For there is no logical or psychological incompatibility between seeing oneself as part of a common humanity, and seeing oneself as a separate and distinct individual — or, for that matter, as a member of a cultural group, or city, or family. An individual's identity is multifaceted, admitting of multiple descriptions — as a person among others, a mother, a brother, a lover, a writer, a thinker, and so on. In different situations, different aspects of one's identity become relevant and assume primary importance; and while sometimes the different aspects may conflict, at other times they may be mutually supportive. This is best seen by the example of the rescuers themselves.

What the Nazis appealed to to justify their extraordinary inhumanity and brutality was the alleged lack of humanity of their victims; so what those who condemned Nazi inhumanity had to affirm was precisely the humanity of these victims. *This* was the relevant moral fact in that situation and not, say, the unique cultural identity of Jews. But to affirm the humanity of Jews was to say, in effect, that as human beings Jews were no different from anyone else; those who responded with outrage at the Nazi denial of this fact responded from a sense of their common humanity, from a sense of their oneness with Jews as human beings. Yet in acting on their sense of oneness with Jews they also had to see themselves as individuals with the capacity as well as the responsibility to act alone. Monroe et al. themselves tell us that the rescuers they interviewed acted alone, without the support of clusters of altruists. Indeed, most rescuers isolated themselves even from friends and family to protect them from

---

distance from the Jews. There was a part of me that also identified with the aggressor. . . . I felt threatened by what they did to Jews" (Oliner and Oliner, p. 118). And, perhaps, there were some who identified with the aggressor even more strongly. But not many: Oliner and Oliner report that more than 80 percent of the rescuers *as well as* of the nonrescuers denied that they saw any similarities between the Nazis and themselves (Oliner and Oliner, p. 175).

danger, as a result depriving themselves of practically every source of encouragement and emotional sustenance. So rescue activity must have tested to the utmost their confidence in the value of their mission, and in their own capacities for carrying it out.

The facts show, then, that rescuers had to have great confidence in their own judgment, intelligence, courage, and endurance, i.e., in themselves as independent actors.[21] Moreover, rescuers *had* to be aware, even if only implicitly, that they were somehow different from the vast majority who refused to help (or worse). For both these reasons, then, they had to be aware of their own separateness and distinctness.[22] Here, too, nonrescuers provide a sharp contrast to rescuers. Their typical response — "What could I do, one individual alone against the Nazis?" — showed their lack of confidence in their own independent abilities as individuals. On their own, they felt weak and helpless. It was nonrescuers, then, and not rescuers, who saw the group and not the individual as the basic actor in society, as the politically and morally empowered unit.

The claim of Monroe et al. that rescuers did not see the individual as the basic actor in society, or that they did not see themselves as separate and distinct, does not fit well with the data. It looks as though the researchers came to the data with the prior assumption that a sense of one's individuality and separateness is incompatible with a sense of oneness with others, and then concluded that since rescuers possessed the latter sense they must have lacked the former. And this assumption, in turn, may have been motivated by another widespread prior assumption, namely, that strong self-interested motivations (connected with a sense of one's individuality and separateness) and strong altruistic motivations (connected with a sense of oneness with others) are mutually incompatible.[23] This assumption is so widespread and so entrenched that it is of-

---

[21] The Oliner and Oliner study provides empirical evidence for this, as well as for what I say below about nonrescuers: significantly more rescuers than nonrescuers showed a sense of personal efficacy, a sense of being the authors of their actions (pp. 176–77).

[22] How, then, should we interpret the following remarks made by one of the rescuers, Tony: "I have very strong thoughts about altruism. . . . [O]ne of the most important teachings in Christianity is to learn to love your neighbor as yourself. And I was to learn to understand that you're part of a whole. . . . You should always treat people as though it is you. And that goes for evil Nazis as well as for Jewish friends who are in trouble or anything like that. You should always have a very open mind in dealing with other people and always see yourself in those people, for good or for evil both" ("Rescuers, 1991," pp. 346–47)? Did Tony really identify with Nazis and nonrescuers in the same way he did with the victims of the Nazis? If he did, then he could not have been aware of his own separateness and distinctness as an independent, responsible agent. However, the tone and language suggest that Tony was communicating his philosophical thoughts about the Christian dictum, rather than reporting how he had felt at the time of rescue activity. Furthermore, whatever he meant by *saying* that one should treat even a Nazi "as though it is you," he clearly *saw* a moral difference between "evil Nazis" and "Jewish friends," a difference that led him to act *for* the latter and *against* the former. In any case, as already noted, most rescuers denied that they saw any similarity between themselves and the Nazis (n. 20 above).

[23] See "Rescuers, 1990," p. 120, and also Hallie, *LC*, p. 10. Only Oliner and Oliner make no claims about a necessary incompatibility between altruism and self-interest (pp. 5–6).

ten taken to need no argument. Questioning it, however, will show both why it seems self-evident and why, without severe qualifications, it is simply false. Let us, then, start by asking how we should understand self-interest and the self-interested agent.

III. THE NATURE OF SELF-INTEREST AND THE SELF-INTERESTED AGENT

A common image of the self-interested agent is that of the rational calculator weighing the costs and benefits of various alternatives before deciding on the best means to her ends. The rescuers under discussion obviously do not fit this image. We have seen compelling evidence that they acted spontaneously, and that their rescue activity was not a means to a further end, such as avoiding guilt, feeling virtuous, earning honors, achieving fame, or gaining wealth. Rather, "[f]or the rescuers, the act was the end. Saving someone's life was reward enough" ("Rescuers, 1990," p. 109). But on the basis of these facts can we conclude, as Monroe et al. do, that rescuers were not motivated by self-interest, *simpliciter*? Or does this conclusion outstrip the evidence and the argument? I think it does.

First, concern for one's own best overall interests, for one's own sake, does not, in itself, require a cost/benefit analysis of different alternatives: if the content and structure of a person's interests make it immediately obvious to him where his interests lie, then the mere fact that he is aware of alternatives does not show that self-interest should, rationally, lead him to consider them, to treat them as live options, rather than to simply reject them as irrelevant. Secondly, self-interest is not exhausted by an interest in the kind of psychological, social, or material rewards cited above — feeling virtuous, becoming famous, gaining wealth, etc. A person may also have other, more fundamental interests — most notably, the interest in being true to himself and affirming the values central to his sense of himself, i.e., the interest in integrity and self-affirmation. The values in question may be intellectual, or artistic, or moral; but if the interest in preserving or affirming them is part of a person's conception of his overall interests, there is no principled way of denying that this interest also is a form of self-interest. Thirdly, the fact that an act is an end in itself is not enough to show that it cannot be motivated by self-interest: a self-interested act may be an *instrument* or *means* to an independent self-interested end, or an actualization of this end and, thus, an *end in itself*. So, for example, one may run for the sake of health or beauty, or simply for the sake of the pleasure inherent in the activity of running. The former act is a means to a logically independent end (since running is not logically connected to health or beauty), the latter, its own end (since running is logically connected to the pleasure of running). Yet both are equally motivated by self-interest. Once the notion of rational self-interest has been disentangled from its calculating and instrumentalist associations, and expanded to include the more fundamental interests in self-affirmation and integrity, it becomes both possible and plausible to argue that rescuers' acts were simultaneously altruistic and self-interested — and, indeed, that the two motives had a necessary connection. I shall do so below.

We have seen in the previous section that most of the researchers agree that by acting altruistically, rescuers satisfied their interest in self-affirmation. Monroe et al. also suggest that rescuers were *motivated* by this interest. But they (along with Hallie) explicitly deny that rescuers were motivated by self-interest, which implies that they do not see self-affirmation as a form of self-interest. Rescuers' acts, they say, were "motivated by a sense of personal identity in which choices serve more as self-affirmations and less as options," and rescuers' decisions were "a recognition, perhaps an inner realization, which reflects a statement of who one is at the most fundamental level of self-awareness" ("Rescuers, 1990," p. 122). However, this interpretation of their data needs to be supported by philosophical argument and reconciled with the claim that rescuers were motivated by altruism. This reconciliation is especially important if the interest in self-affirmation is, as I have argued, a form of self-interest.

I shall start by arguing in the next section that, given the nature of their selves, if rescuers had been motivated by rational self-interest, they could not possibly have refused to help. I shall then argue that, in fact, they were motivated by self-interest, and that this motivation had a necessary connection to their altruism. But this claim flies in the face of the common intuition that a fully altruistic act must be devoid of self-interested motivation. In Section V, I will examine this intuition, showing both why it seems true and why it is not true of all kinds of self-interested motivations. I shall conclude Section V by arguing that rescuers' self-interested motivations actually contributed to the moral worth of their acts, that had they had only altruistic motivations — or had self-interest been an independent motive with no necessary connection to altruism (as in an overdetermined act) — their acts would have had a lesser moral worth.

IV. The Refusal to Help and Self-Interest

Given who they were, could rational self-interest have led rescuers to refuse to help? It might be thought that this question is redundant because, given who they were, rescuers *had* to help, self-interest or no self-interest. Thus, according to Monroe et al., rescuers' "basic identity construct *necessarily entailed and precluded* certain kinds of behavior" ("Rescuers, 1990," p. 121; italics mine). But there is no reason to think that a person's identity makes certain choices literally *impossible* rather than simply *highly improbable*. If this were not the case, no one would ever act out of character, but clearly people do, both for good and for bad. Perhaps Monroe et al. think that rescuers could not have refused to save Jews, because such a refusal would have required "a fundamental shift in the actor's basic identity construction" (p. 121), a shift that they surmise some of the nonrescuers may have undergone (p. 121, n. 44). But a fundamental shift of identity can occur as the *result* of a choice that is contrary to one's identity or character and not, necessarily, as its precondition. So, for example, in a moment of cowardice, or under duress, a person may break down and betray his deepest values and thereby undergo a fundamental shift in his identity: witness the effects on Winston and Julia of their mutual betrayal in George Orwell's *Nineteen Eighty-Four*. And this may well have been the case with some of the nonrescuers, not to mention some Nazis.[24]

The fact that rescuers *could* have refused to help raises the question whether such a refusal could have been motivated by rational self-interest, rather than by fear or weakness. The answer to this question requires a closer look at the content and ranking of the values or interests that defined their selves.

We have seen that rescuers had a strong sense of oneness with all human beings qua human being. But, like nonrescuers, they also had a sense of oneness with some human beings qua friend, or parent, or child, or beloved. Their selves or character—their central dispositions of thought, emotion, and action—and their sense of themselves, were constituted by both their universalistic and their particularistic identifications. In normal circumstances their sense of oneness with their family and friends was doubtless stronger and more important to them, more central to their selves, than their sense of oneness with all human beings. In normal circumstances they cared first and foremost for the welfare of their family and friends, and were not willing to sacrifice them for the welfare of strangers. If they had retained this hierarchy of interests in the abnormal times under discussion, then the self-interested act would have been to refuse to help. This was likely the case with the vast majority of people who refused to help. But all the evidence points to the fact that rescuers' normal hierarchy of interests was sharply reversed when they were confronted with the need to save innocent lives from a monstrous threat.[25] When this happened, their interest in their own and their families' and friends' welfare was not only *subordinated* to their interest in saving innocent lives, it became *irrelevant* in arriving at the decision to help.[26] That this reversal should have taken place in such a time was

[24] Thanks to David Schmidtz for pointing out the latter possibility.

[25] This, as David Schmidtz has correctly remarked, would probably not have happened if the threat to innocent lives had come from, say, an infectious disease: it is important to remember that the threat that rescuers responded to was an extraordinary *moral* evil.

[26] As one rescuer explained, the interest in safety led him to be *cautious*, but the choice to help was made independently of considerations of safety. "[I]t's just like flying," he said. "I'm going to fly [next week]. I know we've just had three major air crashes and I really don't like flying. But what am I going to do about it? Not go on the trip?" ("Rescuers, 1990," pp. 108–9).

also a result and a sign of the kind of persons they were. People with less inclusive selves, with a weaker sense of their common humanity, might not have undergone such a reversal. Rescuers' interest in saving Jews expressed their sense of themselves as part of a common humanity, a sense that dominated their normally primary sense of themselves as parents, lovers, and friends. The thought of betraying this sense by refusing any help to Jews would have been seen as an expression of weakness, and the contemplated act as an act of self-betrayal. And the thought of undergoing an identity shift as the result of such an act of self-betrayal would have been the thought of an irreparable loss — a loss of self. So it seems that whereas a rescuer *could* have chosen to refuse all help to Jews, he could not have chosen this out of rational self-interest, out of concern for his own highest interests. Or at least this is the case if we assume that he could not have betrayed himself out of self-interest. But this assumption needs defense.

What I have said so far implies that self-interest depends on the nature of the self or character — the central dispositions of thought, emotion, and action — constituted by a person's fundamental values, and that these also constitute her sense of herself as the same individual in the past, present, and future. But in an obvious sense, the same person — the same historical individual, with the same memories, and the same desires for nourishment, rest, safety, companionship, etc. — endures even through a radical change in the values embodied in her central dispositions. Let us call the self that endures even through such a radical change the *permanent self*, and the self that can change, and that constitutes an individual's sense of herself, the *moral self*. It might be thought that a person could rationally decide to see her self-interest in terms of the values that define her permanent self, rather than in terms of the values that define her moral self. And it might be thought that this possibility provides a reason for saying that a rescuer could have betrayed her moral self out of self-interest. Thus (the argument might go) it is possible to imagine that even a rescuer who had, in the first instance, agreed to help might subsequently have gone through the following kind of calculation: "If I refuse to help, thereby betraying my deepest values — my very self — I may cease to feel the shame and loss after a number of years, whereas if I am true to myself the consequences may be so severe that the psychological devastation (if I'm still alive) will be total. And if *this* happens I'll become incapable of acting on my values anyway. So the self-interested thing to do, taking the future into account, would be to betray my present moral self and adopt or await a more expedient one."

But is it really possible to imagine this? I think not. One can imagine a rescuer wishing that she could become a different kind of person, the kind who did not feel that she had to help even at so heavy a price in terms of her permanent desires and needs. One can imagine her wishing this even if, immediately thereafter, she found her wish as alien, distasteful, and out of her power to act upon as a stranger's gratuitous proposal that she kill herself. But one cannot imagine a rescuer going through the kind of calculation described above, either consciously or unconsciously. One cannot imagine this, first, because it bespeaks a kind of detachment from the values in question that contradicts the premise that these values formed rescuers' very sense of who they were.[27] A person whose sense of self is given by a certain set of values, who sees herself as the same person in the past, present, and future *because* of these values, cannot regard the cost of betraying them as limited to a temporary sense of shame and loss. Secondly, rescuers could not have believed that betraying these values for the values that constituted their permanent self — the values they themselves regarded as less important — was *more* in their interest. The premise here is not that if a person regards certain values as being more important, then she *must* regard acting for their sake as being self-interested: the recurring literary theme of selling one's soul to gain the world makes it clear that this need not be so. Rather, the premise is that if a person *identifies* with values she regards as more important — if these values are embodied in her central dispositions of thought, emotion, and action — *then* her greatest interests will be identical with these values. If Faust is able to see the barter of his soul — his moral values — in exchange for experience of the world as a net gain, it is only because his soul is not a central part of his identity, of the man he is emotionally, intellectually, and practically. He may *believe* that his soul is more valuable, but he has not yet made this value fully his own, not yet fully *identified* with it. Hence, although it ranks high in his hierarchy of *values*, of the things he regards as important, it ranks low in his hierarchy of *interests*, of the things he desires and delights in. But rescuers identified with their hierarchy of values, and so their interests were identical with their values: they valued helping Jews more than they valued their own families' welfare, and this was also the priority of their interests. This single hierarchy of values and interests formed the core of their selves and their sense of themselves, and so they could not have betrayed their moral selves for the sake of their permanent selves out of self-interest.

Thirdly, one cannot imagine rescuers engaging in a cost/benefit calculation regarding their moral selves, because they had no *reason* to engage in such a calculation. To have a reason to do so a person must experience some alienation from, or ambiguity about, her moral self, so that the very dispositions that move her also seem to her to be not quite her own. The possibility of such alienation arises from the fact that the dispositions that

---

[27] This premise, it is important to remember, does not hold of *all* rescuers, but only of those who acted spontaneously and with a sense that they had no choice. There may well have been rescuers whose sense of themselves did not incorporate such a strong identification with other human beings and who, therefore, could conceivably have gone through the kind of reasoning described above, before deciding to act against their own judgment of their self-interest.

constitute one's moral self include both dispositions to evaluate and respond to particular situations in certain ways (first-order dispositions),
and dispositions to evaluate these dispositions (second-order dispositions). If a person cannot endorse certain of her own first-order dispositions and, thus, cannot identify with them, she may be led to ask whether
it would not be more in her interest to change them and bring them into
line with her second-order dispositions—or, alternatively, to change her
disapproving second-order dispositions and bring them into line with her
first-order ones. A person who felt this kind of ambiguity or alienation
could have reasoned in the way described above. But as we know, far
from being thus divided or alienated, rescuers' sense of themselves as
part of a common humanity was a central and enduring feature of their
identity, a feature without which they could not have envisaged their future moral selves. So they would have had no reason to engage in such
a cost/benefit analysis, much less to have seen acting contrary to their
moral selves as self-interested. Their deepest dispositions of thought,
emotion, and action—their deepest interests or values—led them to
think, feel, and act as though helping were the only response open to
them. "It is part of your body—the will is part of your body—you feel and
you do it" (Oliner and Oliner, p. 229).

Given the nature of their deepest interests, then, rescuers could not
have betrayed their moral selves out of rational self-interest. An act of
self-betrayal would have been an irrational act of weakness, not of rational self-interest, and refusing to extend any help to Jews would have been
an act of self-betrayal. If they had been motivated by self-interest, they
would have done exactly what they did. For in so doing, they actualized
their values, the values they endorsed and with which they were most
deeply identified. Many rescuers talked about their sense of inner satisfaction as a result of what they had done, and *none*, according to Oliner
and Oliner, regretted their actions.[28] In acting as they did, they satisfied

[28] Although a few did express disappointment at being forgotten by their beneficiaries
(Oliner and Oliner, pp. 234 and 239). Most rescuers, however, felt that they had been sufficiently rewarded—by a sense of inner satisfaction that they had done something to help
(although many felt they had not done enough), by the knowledge that their actions had
been successful, by their continuing relationships with the survivors, and by the appreciation they had received from the Jewish community (although many felt that they had not
done anything calling for such appreciation) (Oliner and Oliner, p. 239). One rescuer said,
"I think about these moments. Everything lives in me. I have good feelings about what I
did. I respect myself for doing it" (Oliner and Oliner, p. 227). Some expressed a sense of
thankfulness that their actions had borne fruit, and that the people they had saved were now
having children and grandchildren (Oliner and Oliner, p. 231). But it was Irene's testimony
that was probably the most poignant. Irene, who was held as a slave laborer in a German
army camp, and who had to become the Major's mistress in exchange for his silence when
he discovered that she was harboring Jews, told her interviewers, "[T]he older I get, the more
I feel I am very rich. . . . I would not change anything. It's a wonderful feeling to know that
today that many people are alive and some of them married and have their children, and
that their children will have children because I did have the courage and . . . the strength"
("Rescuers, 1990," p. 110).

a fundamental human interest, the interest in shaping the world in light of one's values and affirming one's identity. Moreover, I shall now try to show, there is good reason to suppose that they were also *motivated* by this interest.

Rescuers had a sense of oneness with others, and this sense was expressed in an altruistic disposition, a disposition to recognize the value of others and act accordingly. The spontaneity of their altruistic behavior, as well as the pattern of altruism in their lives, shows that this disposition was central to their selves and their sense of themselves. And this gives us at least three reasons for thinking that they were motivated not only by others' interests, but also by their interest in self-affirmation.

First, most of them already knew from past experience that altruistic action satisfied their need to affirm themselves. So one would expect this knowledge to enter into their motivations for acting altruistically. Second, there is a strong psychological connection between the interest in self-affirmation and being a good person, i.e., a person who feels, chooses, and acts "at the right times, about the right things, towards the right people, for the right end, and in the right way" (Aristotle, *Nicomachean Ethics*, 1106b21ff.). Someone who disapproves of her own disposition to feel, choose, and act rightly must be strongly motivated *not* to act rightly when the costs of doing so are high. The same applies to someone who is indifferent towards her own good dispositions, someone who lacks concern for her own character. Even in normal circumstances it is no more plausible to suppose that a person can lack concern for her own character and still consistently *be* good, than to suppose that a person can lack concern about reasoning well and still consistently *be* a good reasoner. For the ability to be good is not an ability that, once acquired, functions automatically, even in the face of the agent's own indifference.[29] The ability to feel and choose rightly is subject to constant pressure, so that, without a motivating interest in preserving and affirming this ability, it would be hard, if not impossible, to maintain it. But since rescuers did maintain it, even under the extraordinary pressure of living for years with strangers in their

[29] Moreover, if rescuers had been indifferent towards their own altruistic dispositions, then, since altruism is essential to moral agency, as moral agents they would have been selfless with the selflessness—and unreliability—of "wantons." See Harry G. Frankfurt, "Freedom of the Will and the Concept of a Person," *Journal of Philosophy*, vol. 68, no. 1 (January 14, 1971), reprinted in his *The Importance of What We Care About* (Cambridge: Cambridge University Press, 1988), pp. 11–25. "The essential characteristic of a wanton," says Frankfurt, "is that he does not care about his will"—the dispositions or desires that move him (1988, p. 16). Thus a wanton lacks a full-fledged self and sense of self. Everyone short of a wanton will have *some* attitude towards *some* of his own dispositions, and an interest either in affirming those dispositions (if the attitude is favorable) or changing them (if the attitude is unfavorable).

In *Autonomy: An Essay in Philosophical Psychology and Ethics* (New Haven: Yale University Press, 1986), Lawrence Haworth identifies the interest in self-affirmation with the interest in autonomy, and argues that the interest in autonomy is a fundamental, natural interest. Autonomy, as he says eloquently, is inseparable "from our sense of ourselves, not just our sense of what we happen to be, but our sense of being at all" (p. 185).

midst — strangers who constituted a threat to their own and their families' lives — we have good reason to believe that they did have this motivating interest in preserving and affirming their altruistic dispositions.[30]

The third, and strongest, reason for thinking that rescuers were motivated by an interest in affirming their own altruistic dispositions is that thinking otherwise implies that these dispositions could not have been central to their selves or sense of self, so that they could not have acted as they did, spontaneously, naturally, and reliably. For the absence of the interest in self-affirmation implies the absence of a second-order disposition to endorse one's first-order dispositions. So if rescuers had not had an interest in affirming their altruistic dispositions, they would have either *disapproved* of or been *indifferent* towards them. But if rescuers had disapproved of or been indifferent towards their altruistic dispositions, they would have failed to identify with them. And so these dispositions would not have been central to their selves or sense of self, and they would not have acted as they did.

The connection between the centrality of a disposition and the interest in self-affirmation implies that the latter is not limited to altruistic dispositions or, even, only positive dispositions — a coward who prizes his own safety above all else, rejecting courage as boastful foolishness and endorsing his own cowardice as hard-headed realism, will have this interest no less than the courageous person. Thus, a coward may want to appease his superiors not only for the sake of getting ahead, but also for the sake of affirming himself as the kind of person who "sees it as it is." Similarly, the courageous person — the person who is disposed to face up to danger to achieve his ends, and who values being so disposed — will have an interest in acting courageously not just for the sake of achieving those ends, but also for the sake of being true to himself and affirming himself. Hence, he will sometimes act courageously even when the only value of doing so is the value of self-affirmation. A dramatic illustration of this can be found in Bruno Bettleheim's *The Informed Heart*.[31] Bettleheim tells of the condemned woman who, ordered by the commanding SS officer to dance for him before entering the gas chamber, danced up to him, seized his gun, and shot him dead (p. 259). Bettleheim remarks that there were several other cases of this kind of attempt by prisoners to exercise their autonomy before going to their deaths (pp. 258–59). Life and literature are replete with similar examples of people who will court disgrace, financial ruin, or death in order to affirm themselves.

[30] In *Quandaries and Virtues*, Pincoffs points out that for "the reflective agent there is . . . always the subjective side" of questions of right and wrong: "the concern with the sort of person one has been, is, and is becoming; the sense of direction or the lack of it; the strengthening or weakening of will . . ." (p. 116). He suggests that moral considerations could not "have any leverage" on a being who cared nought about any of this (p. 129). The good person, as Aristotle notes, is a self-lover (*Nicomachean Ethics*, 1168b28–33).

[31] Bruno Bettleheim, *The Informed Heart: Autonomy in a Mass Age* (New York: The Free Press, 1960).

Rescuers' strong sense of oneness with others was central to their selves and their sense of themselves. This implies that they had an interest in acting altruistically not only for the sake of affirming others, but also for the sake of affirming, and being true to, themselves. The data provided by the studies used in this essay bear out this conclusion. Some rescuers tried to help even when they expected their efforts to prove futile.[32] Several rescuers remarked that they could never have lived with themselves — could never have forgiven themselves — if they had done nothing to help (Monroe, "John Donne's People," p. 404; Oliner and Oliner, p. 168). Doing nothing to help would have been an act of self-betrayal. Helping, on the other hand, they had found to be "very satisfying," for it had allowed them to express their sense of efficacy as actors and, in particular, their sense of themselves as responsible for others (Oliner and Oliner, pp. 169, 177, and 220). Helping those in need was, in Magda Trocme's words, a way of "handling themselves," a way of maintaining their identity.[33] Andre Trocme was grateful to refugees for giving him a chance to help because, as Hallie suggests, it enabled him to express his profound conviction of the value of every human being (*LC*, pp. 159–60). After they had embarked on their perilous missions, several rescuers prevented the Jews they were hiding from giving themselves up or leaving their hideout for the sake of their benefactors' safety, because allowing them to do this would have meant defeat in their missions. As Oliner and Oliner put it: "To maintain the life of someone targeted for death was itself a consummate statement of autonomy and resistance" (p. 85). Rescuers' deep-seated altruism thus had a self-interested dimension.

But this claim, as I noted earlier, flies in the face of the common intuition that a fully altruistic act must be devoid of self-interested motivation. In the next section I shall take this intuition into account by analyzing the notion of a fully altruistic act, discussing various kinds of self-interested motivations that are incompatible with the motivation of a fully altruistic act, and then showing that self-affirming motivations need *not* be so incompatible. Indeed, I shall argue, the presence of such motivations may be indicative of the greater *depth* and *strength* of a person's altruistic motivations. A fruitful way to begin is by unpacking the idea, central to the

---

[32] Oliner and Oliner remark that "the main goal" of those with a *principled* orientation (as distinct from a *normocentric* or *empathic* orientation), was to "reaffirm and act on their principles" as a way of keeping them alive (pp. 188 and 209). But although I do not think this was *the* main goal, the fact that it was *a* main goal can help to explain why they sought to help even when they expected failure. And the same may be said of rescuers with a normocentric or empathic orientation: they also sought to reaffirm the norms or empathy central to their sense of themselves.

[33] Magda Trocme told Hallie: "I do not hunt around to find people to help. But I never close my door, never refuse to help somebody who comes to me and asks for something. This I think is my kind of religion. You see, it is a way of handling myself" (*LC*, p. 153).

notion of a fully altruistic act, that such an act must be for another's good, for his own sake.[34]

V. ALTRUISM AND SELF-AFFIRMATION

An act done for another's good, for his sake, must be motivated solely or primarily by a perception of his interests. That is, the necessary and sufficient motivation of a fully altruistic act must be the perception of another's good. This has two implications:

1. If B does something for A's good, for A's own sake, B must be motivated by the desire that A's good be brought about, and not only or primarily by the desire that she, B, perform the act. If the desire that A's good be achieved were weak or absent, then, whatever the explanation for the act, it could not be that it was motivated by A's interests.[35]

2. If B does something for A's good, for A's own sake, B's act must be an end in itself, and not only or primarily a means to a further end — not even if that further end is altruistic with respect to a third party or parties. For example, if saving A's life were only or primarily a means to the well-being of the people A serves as, say, the local pharmacist, then A's good would be neither necessary nor sufficient for the act. B would have saved A even if A's own good had demanded that he not be saved, and would have refused to save A had the good of A's clients' demanded that A not be saved. Hence, an instrumentally motivated act that seeks A's good cannot be said to be altruistic with respect to A.

In summary: A fully altruistic act is an act that is motivated primarily by a perception of another's interests, where such motivation implies (1) the desire to bring about that person's good, and not merely to be the agent of the altruistic act, and (2) the desire to bring it about as an end in itself.

Are self-interested motivations incompatible with either of these desires? Some kinds, yes. Those who saved Jews in exchange for monetary or social rewards, and would not have helped them in the absence of such rewards, offer an obvious example of such motivation.[36] Some of them may well have sympathized with Jews, and believed that saving

---

[34] Altruism is the "willingness to act in consideration of the interests of other persons, without the need of ulterior motives" (Nagel, *Possibility of Altruism*, p. 79). Altruism is "a regard for the good of another person for his own sake, or conduct motivated by such a regard" (Blum, *Friendship, Altruism, and Morality*, pp. 9–10). Altruism is "an interest in other people *for their own sake*" (*Dictionary of Philosophy*, ed. Antony Flew [New York: St. Martin's Press, 1979], p. 11).

[35] Kant thought that excluding motivation by empirical interest, even *another's*, was the only way to ensure that an act was an end in itself and not, ultimately, a means to one's own ends. But what such an act — an act not motivated by another's interests — cannot be is an act for another's good, for his own sake.

[36] These individuals are not, of course, among the group under discussion in this essay, or among those designated as rescuers in any of the studies I have used.

their lives was a good thing to do for its own sake, but this sympathy and belief were not enough to motivate them. Their rescue activity was primarily a means to their own prior ends, and not an end in itself.

The same is true of those who helped Jews primarily for the sake of psychological rewards such as avoiding guilt or feeling good about themselves. No doubt there was a significant moral difference between those who helped for the sake of psychological rewards and those who helped for the sake of external rewards: the former not only sympathized with the victims of Nazism and believed that saving them was a good thing to do, but also felt that not doing so was shameful. They felt personally implicated in a way that those who needed external rewards to help did not, so that the thought of not doing the thing they recognized as good was cause for shame, and the thought of doing it without external rewards was cause for self-congratulation. All the same, their acts were not fully altruistic, because they, too, acted primarily as a means to a further end: if they had been able to get the psychological reward through, say, evasion or rationalization, then they would not have helped. It is important to recall, therefore, that rescuers uniformly rejected the suggestion that they acted for the sake of avoiding guilt or of feeling good about themselves.[37]

There is yet another kind of self-interested motive that is incompatible with altruistic motivation, namely, the desire to benefit another primarily for the sake of becoming a more altruistic person, the kind of person who habitually acts altruistically. Here, too, the act is undertaken as a means to an independent end of the agent's, and not as an end in itself: if the agent did not have this end, her desire to benefit another would be weak or nonexistent. Once again, there are important moral differences between this case and the previous one. For one thing, in this case the end itself — moral improvement — is intrinsically moral. On achieving the end of becoming a more altruistic person, the individual would finally become able to habitually act altruistically. For another, unlike the previous case, acting to benefit another is morally and psychologically necessary for moving oneself towards the goal of becoming more altruistic. There may, indeed, be moral analogues of religious revelations and conversions: dramatic events that change one's moral character radically and permanently.[38] But revelations and conversions are not in the hands of the person who seeks to become more altruistic: *her* only choice insofar as she has this goal is to *act* for others' good. What prevents such acts of hers from counting as fully altruistic is that the interests of those to be benefited are not sufficient to motivate her. Here, again, it is instructive

---

[37] "Rescuers 1990," p. 110; Monroe, "John Donne's People," pp. 423–24.

[38] As, for example, in George Eliot's story of Silas Marner, an embittered, lonely miser who regains his trust in human goodness when chance makes him father to the abandoned orphan, Eppie (*Silas Marner*, 1861).

to note that none of the rescuers cited an interest in becoming a better person as a primary motive for helping.[39] Most also denied that their activities had changed their perception of themselves,[40] which showed that moral improvement had not only not been the primary aim of their activity, it had not been its result either. Rather, their activity had been a "natural" expression of the kinds of persons they were. Some did say that they felt proud of themselves — "inside, just for me" — or enriched by what they had done when they contemplated the results of their actions,[41] but such feelings do not reveal a changed perception of oneself as a person.

To differing degrees, then, acts motivated by such self-interested desires — the desire for external rewards, or for psychological rewards, or for self-improvement — are at odds with full altruism. Acts that are motivated primarily by one of these self-interested desires are acts for which altruistic motivations are neither sufficient nor, in some cases, even necessary. Rather, they are primarily means to one's own good, contrary to condition (2) of fully altruistic acts (see above).

Self-affirming acts, on the other hand, are not means to further ends, but ends in themselves. So, for example, a helping act motivated by the desire to affirm one's sense of oneness with others is not a *means* to one's end of self-affirmation but, rather, an *expression* or *actualization* of that end. There may, however, be an objection to regarding a helping act motivated by an interest in self-affirmation as being fully altruistic, namely, that such an act is motivated by the desire that the agent be the one to help, rather than by the desire that the beneficiary be helped. The beneficiary of such an act, the objection might continue, is a mere occasion for the agent's act of self-affirmation: if, for some reason, *he* could not be the one to help, he would have little or no interest in seeing the potential beneficiary helped. And this violates condition (1) of a fully altruistic act (see above).

If self-affirming acts were necessarily thus focused on the self, this criticism would be well-taken. And if it were, then we would have to say that rescuers' acts were *either* self-interested acts of self-affirmation *or* altruistic, but not both. However, whether and to what extent a self-affirming act is self-focused depends on what it affirms. A creative act such as writing a poem typically expresses an individual's need to create, a need whose existence and expression is independent of the world's need for more poems, and whose satisfaction may be largely independent of the

---

[39] Andre Trocme might seem like a counterexample to this claim, because walking in the footsteps of his moral exemplar — Jesus — was a strong motivating force in his life (LC, pp. 161–62). But Trocme is not really a counterexample, because he was already a person with an acute sense of the worth of each life, and this was sufficient to motivate him to help the refugees who came to Le Chambon (LC, pp. 159–62).

[40] Monroe, "John Donne's People," p. 423.

[41] Ibid., p. 424.

world's enjoyment of the product. Such an act is highly self-focused, for it is motivated by an interest that, by its very nature, is wholly or largely independent of the interests of others: if the individual had not written this particular poem, he would have had little or no interest in its existence, for almost its entire value to him lies in the fact that it is *his* creation. Again, there are acts of love that are purely expressive of that love: for example, a mother may write a story for her son not because *he* needs that particular story, or because there are no other stories available to tell him, but because *she* wants him to have a story written by *her*, as an expression of her love. It matters to her, of course, that he *enjoy* the story, so this act is less self-focused than the purely creative act. But, as in that case, the important thing is that she write the story, and not that this story exist—the same story by someone else would hold no special interest.

If a self-affirming act is to be fully altruistic, it cannot be thus self-focused. For a necessary condition of an altruistic act is that it be motivated primarily by the desire that another's good be brought about, rather than by the desire that *I* be the one to perform that act. But is it possible for an act to be self-affirming without being focused on the self in the manner of the acts discussed above? An examination of rescue activity shows that it can.

One of the questions that Monroe et al. asked rescuers had to do with precisely this issue. The question was whether the important thing to them was that Jews be saved, or that they be the ones to save Jews. Rescuers invariably answered that it was the former rather than the latter ("Rescuers, 1991," p. 326). Most of them, as we know, responded to requests for help instead of initiating help: "because they came to us and had nobody else, we helped them."[42] But even those who initiated help stated that what was important to them was that Jews be helped, rather than that they be the ones to help. Rescuers' altruistic dispositions made the plight of Jews salient to them, focusing them on *their* needs rather than their own. They helped insofar as doing so was the best way to bring about the desired end: had their attempts created more danger for Jews, they would not have attempted to help. Again, had a rescuer thought that someone else was in a better position to help a particular individual, she would have let that person do it.[43] In an obvious sense, then, what was important to rescuers was that Jews be saved, rather than that they be the ones to save them.

---

[42] "Rescuers, 1991," p. 326. See also *LC*, pp. 152–53 and 204. According to Oliner and Oliner, 67 percent of rescuers were asked for help and only 32 percent initiated rescue activity, but the significance of this, they point out, is limited by the fact that a person was asked only because he or she was seen as the kind who was likely to help (p. 250).

[43] As Magda Trocme did in the case of the first refugee to come to Le Chambon (*LC*, pp. 120–24).

But this does not mean that being the ones to save Jews was *unimportant* to rescuers. In light of the data and arguments in Section IV, we must interpret rescuers' answers as reflecting the judgment that seeing Jews helped was *more* important to them than being the ones to help Jews, but that to the extent that the latter was compatible with the former, it too was important. For as we have seen, saving Jews enabled them to express their sense of themselves as part of a common humanity. Helping those in need was a way of "handling themselves," a way of being in the world. There were differences among rescuers in the way they did this: most merely responded to particular situations as they arose, others sought them out; some approached it as a practical task, others as a labor of love; some were guided only by their empathy and principles, others also by the image of some moral exemplar.[44] But when the time came, they all felt that it was imperative that they help, a feeling that came not only from their perception of the needs of the persecuted, but also, evidently, from their need to direct their lives in a certain way, to affirm their sense of oneness with others. In later years many rescuers felt that they had not done enough (Oliner and Oliner, p. 239), a feeling that expressed not only their assessment of the Jews' need for help vis-à-vis how much they had done, but also, evidently, of their own need to help vis-à-vis how much they had done.[45] And their need to help and affirm their sense of oneness with others was not only compatible with, but *necessarily* compatible with, their altruistic motivations, for acting out of the self-interested desire to affirm their own altruistic identity *required* that they also act out of their altruistic motivations. If their self-affirming acts had been self-focused, they could not also have been fully altruistic, i.e., motivated by a desire to bring about others' good for their sake. But since their acts *were* fully altruistic, their self-affirming motivations could not have been self-focused. Their unambiguous sense of themselves as part of a common humanity gave them *both* an altruistic desire for affirming others *and* a self-interested desire for being true to this sense of themselves.

We are now in a position to see how rescuers' self-interested motivations, far from *conflicting* with their altruism, were actually symptomatic of the *depth* of that altruism. It would have been possible for rescuers to act fully altruistically even if their altruistic values had not been central to their selves and even if they had, consequently, not found their altruistic acts self-affirming. This might have been the case with some of those

---

[44] In Hallie's portrayal, the first of each of these alternatives is exemplified by Magda Trocme, the second by Andre Trocme. Andre Trocme emerges as a profoundly energetic, creative man, overflowing with love for people, and inspired by the example of Jesus (*LC*, pp. 157–62), Magda Trocme as a practical, no-nonsense woman, uncomfortable with talk of love and goodness, and skeptical of theology and religion (*LC*, pp. 152–56).

[45] As noted above, Andre Trocme was grateful to the refugees for giving him a chance to help.

who helped only after a struggle. But it is because, and only because, rescuers' altruistic values *were* thus central and they *did* have this self-interested motive for acting altruistically, that they could do so spontaneously, naturally and (in a literal sense) *wholeheartedly*, i.e., from an undivided sense of the desirable and the desired, and an undivided desire for their own good and others' good. Altruistic motivations alone would have been sufficient to make their acts fully altruistic, but the self-interested desire to affirm their altruistic identity was necessary to make their acts wholeheartedly altruistic. And it is only because their altruism *was* thus wholehearted that it can truly be said of them that they loved their neighbor as themselves and not just as an other.[46]

To recapitulate: Because altruism was a central and unambiguous part of their very identity, rescuers had an interest in helping others not just for the sake of those others, but also for the sake of being true to themselves and affirming themselves. And the two motivations had a necessary connection because each was part of a wholehearted altruism, acting from which meant that in acting on the one they would also, necessarily, act on the other. Without this necessary connection between their concern for others and their concern for themselves, they could not have loved their neighbor as they loved themselves.

VI. CONCLUSION

I have argued that self-interest can be a moral motive by showing (1) that self-interest includes the interest in being true to oneself and affirming one's altruistic dispositions; (2) that acting from such an interest implies acting out of altruism; and (3) that acting from such an interest is necessary for acting in a wholeheartedly altruistic manner. If this interest were absent, something of moral worth would be lost. I have used the research on rescuers both to support and to illustrate these points. Although I have explicitly argued only for the moral worth of the self-interested disposition to affirm one's *altruistic* dispositions, I have not meant to suggest that it is only *this* self-interested disposition that is moral. If this were the case, then self-interest would be moral only by virtue of its dependence on altruism. In fact, however, the rhetorical thrust of this essay has been in the opposite direction, namely, to highlight the way that even *altruism* achieves its highest moral worth only by virtue of its con-

---

[46] There is another sense of loving another as oneself that I have not discussed, namely, loving another not just as a human being but as a particular individual, as one does a beloved friend, or child, or sibling. Such loving relations did arise between many rescuers and rescued over time, and they supplied an additional self-interested motivation to help—the desire to help a beloved individual not just for the sake of that individual's happiness, but also for the sake of one's own. But obviously this kind of personal identification and self-interested motivation could not have been present at the time of most rescuers' initial decision to help.

nection with self-interest. And, I would argue, in the absence of the right kind and degree of self-interest, altruism would not be a virtue at all. In the remaining space I will provide a sketch of such an argument.

It is not only because altruism has moral worth (other things being equal) that the interest in affirming one's altruistic self has moral worth; it is also because the interest in self-affirmation has moral worth (other things being equal) that the interest in affirming one's altruistic character has moral worth. The interest in self-affirmation may have as its object not only character-defining dispositions, altruistic or nonaltruistic, but also commitments to people or projects that give shape and meaning to one's life. Whether the interest in self-affirmation has moral worth depends on whether the commitment that is its object has moral worth, but whether the commitment has moral worth does not depend on whether it is altruistic, i.e., motivated primarily by altruistic considerations. It can have moral worth even if it is motivated primarily by self-interested considerations, by considerations of the meaningfulness and interest of one's life to oneself, for one's own sake. Such, for example, might be a commitment to building futuristic buildings that will change the urban landscape. Most self-interested commitments do, of course, also involve others, and when they do, both altruistic and self-interested considerations are relevant to determining the moral worth of the commitment. So, for example, if my commitment to building futuristic buildings is unmindful of others' legitimate interests, so that I care not if the buildings are safe for their inhabitants — or deluded, so that I think I can build lasting structures on the sand — or motivated by trivial considerations, so that my only reason for building them is to get my name in *Who's Who* — or rooted in self-deception about my own interests or abilities — then my commitment is morally unworthy, and so, too, my interest in affirming myself with respect to this commitment. But if a commitment is itself unselfdeceived, significant, realistic, and mindful of others' legitimate interests, then, I would argue, it has moral worth, and so, too, the interest in affirming oneself with respect to this commitment. For such a commitment and interest express one's sense of self-worth, of the importance one places on making one's life meaningful and worthwhile, for one's own sake. And this sense of the importance of one's life, for one's own sake, is at the core of self-respect and integrity. Someone who lacked this sense, this fundamental interest in the self for his own sake, would also lack self-respect and integrity. And this, surely, is a moral lack.

One can, no doubt, understand self-respect without reference to self-interest. Thus, one can conceive of self-respect as a distinctively *moral* attitude, with no conceptual connection to self-interest, conceived of as an intrinsically *nonmoral* attitude. But I think this distinction is doomed without recourse, à la Kant, to the distinction between a moral (noumenal) and a nonmoral (phenomenal) self. So, if one finds this Kantian metaphysics unacceptable, one must, I think, acknowledge that self-interest is at the core of self-respect. And then one can better understand why certain character traits and ways of life, no matter how altruistic in intent and effect — as, for example, blind deference to, and abject self-sacrifice for, someone of superior intelligence and talent — are commonly regarded as morally deficient.

A person who leads such a self-sacrificial life has abdicated or never developed her own independent judgment and ends. If others did not wish to use her for their own ends, she would have nothing to live for. *Others* she sees as ends in themselves; herself, as only a means to their ends. Lacking a sense of self-worth, she has discounted the importance of her own interests, the interests that a person naturally acquires as a result of her encounters with the world. It is this radical failure of interest in herself for her own sake — this radical lack of *self* — that explains why, in her, even altruism fails to be a virtue.

Philosophy, The University of Oklahoma

COSMOPOLITAN ALTRUISM*

By William A. Galston

Introduction

This essay focuses on what I shall call "cosmopolitan altruism"—the motivationally effective desire to assist needy or endangered strangers. Section I describes recent research that confirms the existence of this phenomenon. Section II places it within interlocking sets of moral typologies that distinguish among forms of altruism along dimensions of scope, interests risked, motivational source, and baseline of moral judgment. Section III explores some of the relationships between altruism—a concept rooted in modern moral philosophy and Christianity—and the understanding of virtue and friendship characteristic of Aristotelian ethical analysis. Finally, Section IV argues that cosmopolitan altruism does not represent moral progress *simpliciter* over other, less inclusive views, and that the widening of moral sympathy to encompass endangered strangers entails significant moral costs.

I. The Actuality of Altruism

The debates over altruism during the past generation revolved around two issues: the *possibility* of altruistic behavior, and the *desirability* of such behavior. The relationship between these issues was clear enough. If altruism was impossible (as the proponents of "psychological egoism" insisted),[1] it was not much use arguing about its merits. Indeed, all talk of altruism would be diversionary if not obfuscatory. (Nietzsche's understanding of the Sermon on the Mount as expressing the concealed, vengeful self-love of the powerless is an extreme but by no means illogical working-out of this possibility.)

In part because the debate over the possibility of altruism was so strongly empirical as well as conceptual, it proved possible to make progress. In fact, it has now been resolved: in a series of recent articles artfully blending open-ended interviews and rigorous hypothesis-testing, Kristen Monroe has demonstrated the existence of a class of individuals

---

* I want to thank the other contributors to this volume, and its editors, for searching comments without which I could not even have begun to revise the initial draft of this essay. I am under no illusion that I have responded adequately in every case.

[1] For general discussion, see Ronald D. Milo's introduction to *Egoism and Altruism* (Belmont, CA: Wadsworth, 1973).

(gentile protectors of Jews during World War Two) whose acts simply cannot be explained through any nonvacuous account of self-interest.[2]

Monroe's procedure is ingenious but straightforward. She begins by defining a class of "rescuers" whose acts on behalf of endangered Jews continued over an extended period, required enormous sacrifice of resources, entailed huge risks to liberty and life itself, and yielded condemnation and even ostracism from family and former friends and associates. She then inventories the numerous theories from various disciplines (economics, sociology, developmental psychology, evolutionary biology, and anthropology, among others) that seek to explain apparently altruistic behavior as the product of deeper self-interest, variously understood. She tests these theories against evidence developed from interviews and surveys administered to individual rescuers (identified through Yad Vashem, an Israeli agency established to honor Holocaust victims and those who sought to save them) as well as to individuals identified as entrepreneurs, philanthropists, and heroes. The evidence clearly indicated differences of psychology and outlook among these four groups, and it failed to support, let alone confirm, any of the self-interest theories of altruism. Monroe concludes, plausibly, that the rescuers did indeed act altruistically, and she traces their acts to a distinctive sense of personal identity that erodes typical divisions between self and others. While various methodological questions can be raised about this line of research, I shall proceed on the assumption that its principal conclusions are (at least roughly) valid.

The fact that altruism is possible for some individuals does not prove that it would be possible for all, even under the most favorable formative circumstances. On the contrary: I do not have a knock-down argument, but I defy anyone to read Monroe's depiction of the rescuers without seeing just how exceptional they are, and how misguided it would be to expect such behavior of everyone. The diversity of human character-types constitutes an obstacle to any understanding of altruism as a universal moral obligation. The dictum that "ought implies can" must be applied in a manner that is sensitive to deep differences of individual moral capacity. For example, the solitary, self-willed courage most rescuers displayed would simply be beyond the powers of most individuals. I would hazard the conjecture that this crucial difference is not (entirely) the product of upbringing or social context but represents the expression of deepseated differences of temperamental endowment. If true, this conjecture would not reduce our admiration for the rescuers, but it would relax the

[2] See Kristen Monroe, "John Donne's People: Explaining Differences between Rational Actors and Altruists through Cognitive Frameworks," *Journal of Politics*, vol. 53, no. 2 (May 1991), pp. 394–433; and Monroe, Michael C. Barton, and Ute Klingemann, "Altruism and the Theory of Rational Action: Rescuers of Jews in Nazi Europe," *Ethics*, vol. 101, no. 1 (October 1990), pp. 103–22.

rigorous judgment we might otherwise want to pass on those who had, but out of fear failed to seize, the opportunity to rescue.

Moral diversity also complicates relations between ethics and politics. If political theorists (or political actors) expect too much of the citizenry taken as a whole, the result is bound to be unappealing. From the French Revolution, to the "New Soviet Man," to Mao's Cultural Revolution, the history of utopian efforts to require constant selfless dedication to the common good on the part of everyone suggests that failure is inevitable, and that efforts to avert it are bound to turn tyrannical.

But there is an opposing error—expecting too little of human beings and citizens—to which anti-utopians (and most economists) often fall prey. From the fact that altruism will be the exception rather than the rule, it does *not* follow that the rest of us will be guided by naked self-interest. "Selfishness/altruism" describes, not a dichotomous set of possibilities, but rather a behavioral continuum ranging from complete indifference to the interests of others (at one extreme) to complete responsiveness (at the other), with innumerable gradations in between. For all but the most insensate, the suffering of others constitutes, not just a reason, but also a felt motive, for other-directed acts. The question then becomes how strong or effective that motive is—*how much* cost, or risk, the agent is willing to accept while acting on behalf of others.

By thus characterizing a behavioral continuum, I do not want to be taken as endorsing a conceptual opposition between self-interest and altruism. In some cases, at least, a high degree of responsiveness to others is so integrated into individuals' character that altruism coincides with self-affirmation. As Neera Kapur Badhwar rightly suggests, there are forms of moral integrity or self-expression that are not self-focused.[3] The fact remains (as Badhwar recognizes) that most forms of self-interest—financial, psychic, even self-perfective—*are* self-focused in a way that hinders their integration into altruistic behavior;[4] it is this fact that gives rise to the commonplace, if overly sweeping, assertions of opposition between altruism and self-interest.

There is a second potential misunderstanding I wish to avoid. In offering a selfishness/altruism continuum, I do not mean to suggest that acts of agents necessarily improve morally as they move away from the former pole toward the latter. Indeed, I shall later argue that certain kinds of concern for others are rooted in a lack of concern for, or undervaluing of, oneself that is more nearly a vice than a virtue. I quite agree with Jean Hampton that not all self-sacrifice is worthy of moral commendation, and

---

[3] Neera Kapur Badhwar, "Altruism Versus Self-Interest: Sometimes a False Dichotomy," in this volume.
[4] *Ibid.*

in particular, not the self-sacrifice that stems from self-abnegation.[5] Our judgment must not be blanket, but rather case-by-case: it will depend, not only on the specific sacrifice, but also on the constitution and circumstances of the self performing that sacrifice.

Distinguishing between selfishness and altruism in behavioral terms brings us to the classic distinction between act and motive. We may wish to reserve the term "altruism" for acts in which the inner impulse to assist others comes to dominate self-regarding desires that counsel inaction. If so, we shall have to employ some other term (perhaps "empathy" would do) to characterize the very real effects the interests of others may produce even when we are not sufficiently moved to act. One sign of this is the discomfort many of us feel when we fail to go to the aid of someone who appears to be in need. The fear (of injury, financial loss, emotional entanglement, or whatever) that holds us back may seem reasonable enough, but it does not erase the empathy that initially posed the choice for us.

This conception of the behavioral continuum, in which empathy may (but need not) prove strong enough to issue in altruistic acts, relies on two propositions defended most persuasively by Thomas Nagel. The first is that human beings simultaneously experience the force of subjectivity and objectivity; that is, they put themselves at the center of the universe and see themselves as but one entity, or point of view, or claimant, among myriad others. The question then becomes how these two standpoints are to be integrated into a single way of seeing or acting. The mode of integration, the balance struck, will vary from individual to individual. Some (the full-blown altruists) will give pride of place to the "view from nowhere"; others (the full-blown egoists) will focus exclusively on their personal standpoint; the rest of us will give weight to both, with the balance shifting in response to particular circumstances and to the vagaries of what might be termed our moral mood.

It is not the case, however, that the balance can be purely subjective or personal. This brings me to Nagel's second proposition: some interests have objective value (or disvalue) regardless of the identity of individuals to whom they are linked at any given moment, and these interests therefore make a rational claim upon us regardless of our personal relation to them. Because pain is objectively bad from an impersonal standpoint, my desire for the cessation of my pain at least overlaps my desire for the cessation of your pain. I may well give more attention to my plight than to yours, but that does not mean that I am, or can reasonably be,

---

[5] Jean Hampton, "Selflessness and the Loss of Self," in this volume. It is worth pointing out, however, that the self-abnegation Hampton and I both reject might well be more positively valued within certain religious traditions. Here as elsewhere, the decision to conduct moral analysis within a secular philosophic frame carries with it assumptions (typically tacit and even invisible) concerning the weight properly accorded to the self.

wholly indifferent to yours. Indeed, I can ignore yours only at the cost of undermining the rational basis on which I care about my own.[6]

This is not to say that all interests have impersonal or objective value. Some are valuable only because they have been adopted as ends by individual agents. As T. M. Scanlon has argued, such agent-relative values make far weaker claims, if any, on others who may be in a position to aid or to frustrate their achievement. For me to take your agent-relative interests as grounds for action is, as Nagel puts it, "a matter of personal sympathy rather than objective acknowledgement."[7] This distinction may help draw the line between the kinds of regard for others that are to some degree required and those that are purely optional or supererogatory.

The distinction between impersonal and agent-relative interests is far from exhaustive. A third possibility is that needy agents can simply be mistaken about their interests, or about the specific steps that might promote them. Similar mistakes are possible on the part of those who are motivated to assist those who appear needy. It seems odd to say that well-intentioned acts built on such mistakes cease to be altruistic. The point is rather that there is a gap between acting with the intention of benefiting others and actually doing so; successful altruism includes a cognitive dimension (of practical and moral understanding) that may be less common than is the raw impulse to do good.

One may object, more radically, to Nagel's entire framework. Christine M. Korsgaard argues that an ambiguity lurks in the concept of impersonal or agent-neutral values. On one interpretation (Objective Realist), an agent-neutral value would be independent of agents in general; on the other (Intersubjectivist), such values would exist equally for all rational agents but would be neutral with respect to the individual identities of agents. On Korsgaard's preferred Intersubjectivist view, the projects Nagel characterizes as agent-relative are not rightly understood as brute or unmotivated; "there are reasons for caring about these things, reasons which are communicable and therefore at least potentially shareable." And if the desires that provide A with reasons to act are shareable, then they provide B with reasons to help A—at least if B happens to be in A's neighborhood.[8]

---

[6] Thomas Nagel, *The View from Nowhere* (New York: Oxford University Press, 1986), pp. 159–62. Nagel's point is not that empathetic identification with the interests of others necessarily depends upon the construction of a rational argument, but rather that certain kinds of self-preference with regard to certain interests are self-contradictory. Once subjected to challenge, Nagel claims, exclusive self-preference concerning (say) pain cannot be maintained as a rational moral stance.

[7] *Ibid.*, pp. 166–68. The argument Nagel discusses is advanced in T. M. Scanlon, "Preference and Urgency," *Journal of Philosophy*, vol. 72 (1975), pp. 655–69.

[8] Christine M. Korsgaard, "The Reasons We Can Share: An Attack on the Distinction between Agent-Relative and Agent-Neutral Values," in this volume.

This is a persuasive argument as far as it goes, but it generates a new ambiguity of its own. Reasons can be "shareable" in the sense that I can (come to) understand why you care about your project, or in the sense that I (come to) care about what you care about. The former sense is necessary for the latter, but not obviously sufficient. The gap between them mirrors the practical force of Nagel's agent-relative/agent-neutral distinction. In the first sense of shareability I am enabled to take an interest in your interests; in the second sense I am all but compelled to do so, on pain of losing touch with my own. This does not mean that I am always required to act in support of your agent-neutral interests. It does mean that when confronted with such interests, I must have reasons for not coming to your assistance far weightier than the reasons that would justify not helping with your more optional projects. (This is not to deny that it would be wrong for me *never* to help neighbors or associates with personal projects.)

It would be absurd to suggest that the primary threat facing European Jews during World War Two was interference with optional life-plans. The threat was to family ties, security, and life itself — hard-core agent-neutral interests. What distinguished the rescuers from others who stood by was their ability to give their own agent-neutral interests no greater weight (in many cases *less* weight) than the comparable interests of endangered strangers. In Nagel's terms, they were unusually capable of adopting the impersonal standpoint as the basis of moral action, and of setting aside the kinds of personal considerations that proved decisive for most people. The question is no longer whether they behaved in that fashion — Monroe's work has settled that — but rather how it was possible and what we can learn from it.

II. Dimensions of Altruism

To bring these issues into sharper relief, I want to turn more systematically to problems of description and conceptualization. "Altruism," I want to argue, is not the name of a specific moral requirement or pattern of behavior. Rather, it points toward a family of possibilities.

The objects of altruism. To begin with, altruism can vary in its objects. Three main variants may be discerned. *Personal* altruism is directed toward individuals near at hand, such as family members and friends. *Communal* altruism is directed toward groups of individuals possessing some shared characteristics: members of an ethnic group, coreligionists, and fellow citizens, among others. *Cosmopolitan* altruism, by contrast, is directed toward the human race as a whole, and hence toward individuals to whom one has no special ties. (One could imagine a fourth variety — a *comprehensive* altruism directed toward all entities with interests. This possibility raises important issues that I cannot explore in this essay.)

The steady expansion of scope from the personal, to the communal, to the cosmopolitan does not (necessarily) represent moral progress. While the form of altruism directed toward family and friends may be more common than is altruism embracing all humanity, it does not follow that the former is in any simple sense less worthy than the latter. This point is of particular importance because, as we shall see, forms of altruism can come into conflict with one another. While philosophic discussion typically induces us to focus on the clash between self-interest and altruism, conflicts between competing objects of altruism are equally pervasive, and perhaps even more wrenching. (As a parent, one wishes the best for one's child; as a citizen, one may believe in forms of military conscription that place that child at risk; and so forth.) If enlarged scope does not translate into moral priority, there may be no way to resolve such clashes without moral loss; each course of action, including the all-things-considered best, may require the agent to forego some significant impersonal good.

Varieties of sacrifice. Forms of altruism can vary, second, with regard to the kinds of personal goods agents are willing to sacrifice on behalf of others. In differing circumstances, altruism may entail the sacrifice of life, wealth, liberty, convenience, or many other goods. This variation is significant because individuals may find it less difficult to act altruistically along some dimensions than others. I know people, for example, who freely donate their time and energy to others but who cannot bear to part with their money. This phenomenon of good-specific altruism suggests intriguing links with the traditional vocabulary of the virtues. Risking one's life for others might be thought akin to (or at least to depend upon) a species of courage; the sacrifice of wealth, liberality; of pleasure or personal convenience, moderation; and so forth.

Motives for altruism. Forms of altruism also vary in their personal source or motivation. One form seems rooted in some individuals' highly developed capacity for *sympathy*. Because they cannot maintain emotional distance, because they keenly feel the pain and suffering of others, they are more inclined than are most of us to come to the aid of those in need.[9] Another form reflects *rationality* — the capacity to understand the ways in which claims made on one's own behalf can entail equally valid claims by others, and to act on the basis of that understanding.[10] A third, perhaps less familiar, form rests on *identity*. Monroe's study of rescuers, for example, found that these individuals without exception acted instinctively rather than reflectively, expressing a perception of self as at one with all mankind: "Their perception of themselves as part of a common human-

[9] See especially Lawrence A. Blum, *Friendship, Altruism, and Morality* (London: Routledge & Kegan Paul, 1980).
[10] See especially Thomas Nagel, *The Possibility of Altruism* (Oxford: Clarendon Press, 1970).

ity formed such a central core of their identity that it left them no choice in their behavior toward others."[11]

This conception of identity-based altruism combines two dimensions, which I shall call "expression" and "identification." The former is the idea of a kind of action that directly and spontaneously reflects the character of the agent, such that to act otherwise would be to deny what one is. The latter is the idea of a special sense of self in which the customary boundary between self and others becomes indistinct.

The baseline for altruism. The foregoing varieties of altruism are dimensions of observed empirical variation. I want to turn now to a conceptual issue: the baseline relative to which altruistic behavior is defined. I have already observed that the mix of self- and other-regarding motives generates a continuum of possibilities rather than a two-valued choice. Still, there are a number of competing conceptions of full or complete altruism.

The first, and probably the most stringent, is self-abnegation: your actions are wholly defined by (your perception of) the interests of others, and your own interests are given less weight than those of others, perhaps no weight at all. Examples of this would include some of the sacrifices parents make for their children.

A less stringent but nonetheless quite demanding baseline is the requirement, characteristic of utilitarian theories among others, that we regard ourselves as but one among equals and give our own interests the same weight as those of others. Altruism then means making the point of view of the impartial spectator effective as a motive of personal conduct. On this understanding, self-abnegation is not only not required, but is not even regarded as supererogatory — it is actually ruled out as arbitrary and irrational.

Less stringent still is a baseline defined relative to justified self-regard. On this account, morality itself incorporates a measure of self-preference: you are permitted to give your own interests greater weight than those of others — up to a point. If you and someone else are contending for a good that only one of you can get, and if there is no special factor that gives your foe a superior moral claim, then you are not required to be impartial. You are not, for example, required to resolve the matter through some randomizing device such as a coin-toss. The fact that you are one of the contending parties makes a moral difference that you are allowed to take into account. But while self-preference is permitted, it is hardly required. You may recede from permissible self-preference in the direction of (say) giving equal weight to self and others, and this moral shift would count as a species of altruism.

Still another variant of altruism might be termed "justice-based." Assume that some theory of justice plausibly defines your just share S of some good. You could be said to act altruistically whenever, and to the

[11] Monroe et al., "Altruism and the Theory of Rational Action," p. 119.

extent that, you claim less than S for yourself and are willing to surrender the remainder to others. (I assume here that you are acting on principle; surrendering a portion of your share out of fear, or confusion about what you are entitled to, or desire to curry favor with someone else can hardly be considered altruistic on any interpretation. I also assume what can in principle be denied, that those who receive the portion of your share that you have relinquished are better off as a result.)

Justice-based altruism connects up in interesting ways with classical accounts of the virtues. The primary Greek antonym of justice was *pleonexia* — grasping, overreaching, claiming more than one's share. Aristotle does discuss the other possible antonym — claiming less than one's due — in his account of "equity," but he does not there explain the basis of such conduct (*Nicomachean Ethics* [hereafter *NE*], 1137a32–1138a4). The explanation is suggested, rather, in the discussion of *megalopsychia*, "greatness of soul." Some human beings are justifiably proud: they think well of themselves, for good reason. Others are foolishly arrogant, thinking better of themselves than the facts would warrant. Still others err in the reverse direction by undervaluing themselves (*NE*, 1123b). While Aristotle does not make the connection explicit, on the level of moral psychology a link is at least implied between undervaluing and underclaiming. From this standpoint, what I have called justice-based altruism would have to be regarded, not as a virtue, but rather as the outgrowth of a vice.

But this is not the end of the matter. To think well of oneself, Aristotle believes, is also to care less about the external goods that less-confident individuals crave as sources of identity, worth, and power. So self-undervaluing can also lead to *over*claiming. By contrast, great-souled individuals may be more willing to yield their share of resources, opportunities, and even life itself. Something that looks like altruism can be the byproduct of diminished concern for the usual objects of desire.

This is not to say, however, that great-souled individuals are selfless. Rather, their concerns are so focused on a single external good — honor — that the importance of other goods is diminished (*NE*, 1124a, 1136b). More generally, it is not clear that Aristotle's moral psychology has room for the uncompensated surrender of individual advantage on behalf of another.

III. Altruism, Virtue, and Friendship

This gesture toward the classical virtues may well seem inconclusive, but it suggests something important about the moral geography of altruism. As we have seen, "selfishness/altruism" names a moral continuum along which the relative weight of self- and other-regarding motives shifts. Omitted from this calculus are substantive differences among the selves to which the interests of others are counterposed. On one interpretation, for example, the Aristotelian virtues constitute an account of self-perfection, that is, of self-interest rightly understood. And yet this higher-order self-interest can yield patterns of conduct not easily distinguished from regard for others. The interests of the purified self are likely to be more compatible with the interests of others than are those of the brute, unrefined self, especially if, as Aristotle argues, justice is a part of rational self-perfection.

Still, a gap remains. Of all the classical virtues, friendship most closely approaches the contemporary understanding of altruism. Yet here too, self-regard, even rightly understood, places limits on what we are willing to wish, or to do, for our friends. True friendship requires equality, and thus, Aristotle suggests, we would not hope that our friends would achieve a degree of excellence or perfection that would move them outside the circle of possible friendship with us: "One will wish the greatest good for his friend as a human being. But perhaps not all the greatest goods, for each man wishes for his own good most of all" (NE, 1159a11–13).

This might seem to mark the limits of possible reconciliation between altruism and the classical virtues. But it turns out that the boundaries of the self whose good is primarily sought can shift in morally significant ways. In a remarkable passage, Aristotle reflects on the relation between friendship and self-love. The good man (indeed, *only* the good man) truly loves himself; but "he has the same attitude toward his friend as he does toward himself, *for his friend is really another self*. . . . [T]he extreme degree of friendship can [thus] be likened to self-love" (NE, 1166a30–b2). Because the self whose interests we seek to promote can come, in the best case, to include the interests of others, the boundary between self-regarding activities and what I earlier called particular altruism begins to blur.

The question is how this merger of self and other can occur. Aristotle suggests a triadic model: two individuals are brought together through their common possession, or pursuit, of something each regards as objectively good. This triadic (or classical) model contrasts with a dyadic (Romantic) account in which individuals become directly merged with, lost in, one another without the mediation of an independent good. In the two-person case, romantic love, this takes the form of mutual intoxication.

This experience, while real, is notoriously hard to sustain in the absence of truly shared tastes, activities, or objectives. Children can provide the third pole; so can commonalities of religion, creed, and ethnicity. From this point of view, while the practice of arranged marriages constitutes an extreme anti-romanticism, it is not entirely crazy. It reflects the belief that if due attention is given to objective commonalities, the individuals chosen for one another will come over time to experience sharing subjectively.

As Aristotle emphasizes, the triadic account rests on a distinction between competitive and noncompetitive goods — that is, between (on the one hand) finite or inherently scarce goods and (on the other) inexhaustible goods whose possession by one individual does not impede their acquisition by others. This is why Aristotle lays such stress on knowledge and virtue as those shared goods most conducive to enduring friendship: my attainment of (some part of) virtue or wisdom does not diminish (may even enhance) your opportunity to attain the same objective good.

Of course, this cannot be said of the external rewards (such as public honor) that may be attached to these goods. For example, in a particular military situation that calls forth extraordinary heroism, it is unlikely that more than one individual will be considered for the Congressional Medal of Honor, even if several have behaved in an exemplary manner. Even more dramatic examples occur in the arena of knowledge, when the identity of the first discoverer of some phenomenon or theory (differential calculus in the seventeenth century, the AIDS virus today) becomes a matter of intense controversy. (The competition to make the discovery is correspondingly intense; recall James D. Watson's narrative of the race for DNA in *The Double Helix*.) When an inexhaustible good is valued, not just for itself, but also as a means to a finite good, such conflicts are all but inevitable.

This triadic account of the extended self gives rise to perplexities. For example, why isn't the common pursuit of an inexhaustible good the adult version of the side-by-side but unengaged ("parallel") play characteristic of very young children? How does it lead to a partial merging of separate selves? The answer lies, I would suggest, in the shared awareness that the other person is having an experience akin to one's own, and in the sense of identification this awareness can produce. As an analogy, consider two people on a beach watching a gorgeous sunset. Each experiences, not only the sunset, but also the fact of its being shared by and with another. The result is a kind of merged consciousness — partial and fleeting, to be sure, but nonetheless real and significant.

A deeper perplexity is whether, and how, the kind of self-extension based on shared participation in an objective good can become particularized. If the commitment is to the good, then why does it not extend to all persons similarly situated with respect to that good? The answer is that it does, *to some extent*. Aristotle describes the kind of sentiment ("good will") that is apt to arise whenever we become aware of individuals or groups who possess what we take to be desirable attributes, whether or not we know them. This good will represents the universalizing tendency inherent in the classical account.

The difficulty, according to Aristotle, is that this wide-ranging feeling lacks "intensity and desire." The bearers of good will "only wish for the good of those toward whom they have good will, without giving them active assistance in attaining the good and without letting themselves be troubled in their behalf." While good will activates altruistic sentiments, it is insufficient to motivate altruistic deeds (*NE*, 1166b33–1167a5).

The reason, Aristotle argues, is rooted in the finitude of our consciousness. Acting on behalf of others requires effective identification with them, which requires in turn that we be able to experience their feelings as our own. But it is "difficult to share the joys and sorrows of many people [not just a few friends] as intensely as if they were one's own . . . [for example,] it might well happen that one would have to share the joy of one friend and the grief of another all at the same time" (*NE*, 1171a5–8). That we effectively identify with one virtuous individual rather than another may be an accident of personal history, but once the available psychological space has been filled, it is impossible to further broaden the sphere of deep connection.

Let me translate this thesis into the typologies developed earlier in this essay. Aristotle is arguing, in effect, that rational altruism provides at most a motive for desiring the good of others, but not for acting on that desire. The movement from desire to action is mediated by sympathy, but sympathy is inherently limited in scope. Full-blown altruism is necessarily particular altruism; full-blown cosmopolitan altruism is virtually inconceivable.

This is not to say that there is nothing corresponding to cosmopolitanism in the classical understanding. Not only can good will link us to strangers; there is a kind of fellow-feeling based on common membership in the human species: "That is why we praise men for being humanitarians or 'lovers of their fellow men.' " This sentiment goes well beyond the specific feeling ("concord") that can arise through common membership in a political community: "Even when traveling abroad one can see how near and dear and friendly every man may be to another human being" (*NE*, 1155a21).

Still, this is a far cry from Monroe's rescuers—cosmopolitan altruists who not only care about strangers qua fellow human beings but who are ready to risk everything to save them. How are we to explain this apparent gap in Aristotle's account? One possibility is that the principle of rational altruism extends farther than he thought. Human beings can share an orientation, not just toward lives lived in particular ways, but also toward human existence itself. The fact (and Aristotle takes it to be a fact) that most of us prize our own existence may lay the foundation for considering the existence of other human beings, and threats to that existence, with utmost seriousness, and for assisting threatened individuals. Not everyone will go to the aid of an endangered stranger (as the Kitty Genovese case so graphically demonstrated),[12] but some will, at least some of the time.

Another possible explanation would expand the sphere of potential sympathy. On this account, Aristotle erred in believing that our psychic space could accommodate only a small number of intense relationships. In fact, at least some people are capable of extended sympathy and of act-

---

[12] In this notorious New York City incident, Genovese was assaulted within earshot of dozens of people living in a nearby apartment building. No one came to her assistance — including individuals who were not only hearing but actually witnessing the assault. For an extended period, no one even bothered to call the police!

ing in response to the suffering of distant strangers. Those individuals have the capacity Aristotle questioned, to feel a wide range of joys and sorrows more or less simultaneously.

One may at least speculate about the link between this enlarged capacity and the spread of Christianity. The picture of Jesus, who could feel the sufferings of all humanity and who made the ultimate sacrifice so that others might be redeemed, powerfully influenced the European moral imagination. Conversely, Christianity appealed to aspects of human moral capacity that classical philosophy had largely overlooked. And of course, the idea of the impartial and benevolent spectator, though turned to secular use, drew much of its force from the understanding of divinity as aware of and concerned about individual human beings, which Aristotle's Unmoved Mover assuredly was not.

A third possible explanation is that Aristotle may have overstated the extent to which the understanding of the self and its interests is congruent with the physical boundaries of individuals. His assumption was that individuated self-love was the universal norm and that only intense particular relationships could come close to overcoming it. But if Monroe's findings are to be believed, for at least some individuals this is simply not the case: the ordinary boundaries between self and other are relocated, and numerous physical individuals are seen as within the perimeter of the psychological self.

These three explanations track the trichotomy of reason-based, sympathy-based, and identity-based altruism sketched earlier. They need not be viewed as mutually incompatible or, for that matter, as jointly exhaustive. My point is only that because the actuality of cosmopolitan altruism implies its possibility, some relaxation of Aristotle's rigorously skeptical view is necessary, and that these three hypotheses are among the most plausible ways of proceeding in that direction.

IV. The Vicissitudes of Cosmopolitan Altruism

The discussion thus far has revolved, albeit at varying distance, around the question of possibility. The second large issue I mentioned at the outset — the desirability of cosmopolitan altruism — raises different questions. Even if (or when) not obligatory, such altruism might still be (and frequently is) considered exemplary. For example, while Richard Rorty is at pains to debunk traditional philosophical accounts of moral cosmopolitanism, he has no doubt that "there is such a thing as moral progress, and that this progress is indeed in the direction of greater human solidarity," where solidarity means the ability to identify with, and respond to, the pain and humiliation of others.[13] At the end of Rorty's road is a world in which our capacity for solidarity overrides boundaries of family, class,

[13] Richard Rorty, *Contingency, Irony, and Solidarity* (Cambridge: Cambridge University Press, 1989), p. 192.

ethnicity, politics, and religion—everything that can distance us from the sufferings of the most distant strangers.

Rorty seems to believe that cosmopolitan solidarity represents an unqualified gain over other, less inclusive principles. In his optimistic view, we can indefinitely widen the circle of our concern without giving up any previously held value. I doubt it, for all the reasons Isaiah Berlin has so memorably expressed: not only is moral value pluralistic and multidimensional, strong gains along one dimension almost always involve costs along others. As Berlin puts it: "If, as I believe, the ends of men are many, and not all of them are in principle compatible with each other, then the possibility of conflict—and of tragedy—can never wholly be eliminated from human life, either personal or social."[14] There are general considerations, rooted in what Nagel calls the fragmentation of value, for believing this to be so. And there are particular reasons, based on empirical research, for believing it to be true in the case of cosmopolitan altruism.

I want to distinguish this argument from another with which it can easily be conflated. In her "Moral Saints," Susan Wolf argues that moral perfection (of which altruism is a species) does not constitute a model of personal well-being toward which it would be rational or good to strive. There is human value other than moral value—wit, charm, or general agreeableness, some excellences of skill, some aspects of self-perfection, *inter alia*—that the moral saint cannot achieve.[15] While I believe there is much to be said in favor of this proposition, my claim is different: without invoking nonmoral goods, even within what we would all regard as the sphere of morality, there are grounds for doubting that cosmopolitan altruism represents a comprehensively worthy ideal.

I build my case on three features of this moral stance that emerge from Monroe's research. First, the rescuers were willing to place at risk, not only their own lives and well-being, but those of their families as well, frequently over the family's passionate objections.[16] This would not be troubling if cosmopolitan altruism could be understood as a universal moral obligation, but (as we saw above) there are many reasons to believe that it cannot be—that it is not a general moral possibility and must instead be regarded as extraordinary, hence as supererogatory. It is, to say the least, morally questionable to compel others to risk profound sacrifices that they are not required to make and to which they have not consented.

These doubts only deepen when we reflect on the identity of those forced to run risks against their will. It is one thing for me to be indiffer-

---

[14] Isaiah Berlin, *Four Essays on Liberty* (London: Oxford University Press, 1969), p. 169.

[15] Susan Wolf, "Moral Saints," *The Journal of Philosophy*, vol. 79, no. 8 (August 1982), pp. 419–40.

[16] "Several rescuers had to go against critical loved ones in order to rescue Jews" (Monroe et al., "Altruism and the Theory of Rational Action," p. 113). In more than one case, rescuers hid their activities from relatives and spouses who were nonetheless implicated and paid with their lives (*Ibid.*, pp. 113 n. 30, 115).

ent between my own life and that of a stranger, quite another to be indifferent between that stranger and my own brother. Cosmopolitan
altruism seems to require the negation of particularistic obligations and
the attenuation of special emotional ties, but these forms of human connection can hardly be set aside without moral loss.

Another feature of cosmopolitan altruism points in the same direction.
Monroe reports, astonishingly enough, that the rescuers felt they had
done nothing extraordinary.[17] From an internal perspective, this is easy
to understand. The rescuers' personal identity was so intimately bound
up with others that their altruistic behavior was direct, immediate, and
unreflective. They felt that they had no choice but to help the endangered
Jews, whatever the risk. Their acts expressed their identity in a manner
that they experienced as natural and unforced—the reverse of the kind
of exertion experienced as demanding and extraordinary.

From an external point of view, however, the rescuers' view constitutes
an astonishing absence of moral perspective. They seem not to understand that their personal no-man-is-an-island definition of selfhood *is* extraordinary. Precisely because they identify so closely with others, they
lose sight of the profound differences between themselves and others. We
may speculate that this lack of perspective contributed to their willingness
to place the lives of family members at risk: the rescuers may have assumed that, *au fond*, their kin were just like themselves.

In part because they denied the extraordinariness of their deeds, the
rescuers tended to be indifferent to—and in several cases rebuffed—postwar efforts to honor them.[18] This is the third feature of cosmopolitan altruism I find troubling. After all, what could be more natural than the
desire of those rescued, and of their communities, to recognize and thank
those who had saved them? The victims' sense of gratitude and desire to
do what they could to express it—to equalize the moral balance-scales as
best they could—was overwhelming. But the rescuers found it difficult
if not impossible to respond to these desires in the ordinary human way.

Once again, it is not difficult to understand why. To do what they did
during the war, the rescuers had to disregard the opinions of others—
not only of family and friends, as we have seen, but also of the broader
community in which they had grown up.[19] It was their strong, inwardly
sustained sense of self that enabled them to do this, and it was this in-

---

[17] Monroe, "John Donne's People," pp. 423–24: "Most rescuers shrugged off their rescue actions as 'no big deal'."

[18] Monroe et al., "Altruism and the Theory of Rational Action," p. 109: "The honors or
thanks the rescuers received were not sought and were as often as not a source of embarrassment as one of pride. . . . [For example,] Leonie refused the Yad Vashem award, saying she had not really done enough to deserve it."

[19] Badhwar is quite right to emphasize the great confidence rescuers displayed in their
own judgment, intelligence, courage, and endurance—in themselves as independent actors
("Altruism Versus Self-Interest"). But I do not believe (as she does) that Monroe et al. meant
to deny this. The point is rather that the rescuers' capacity to identify with humanity as a

ward self that continued to guide their postwar behavior. The very source of their extraordinary wartime conduct generated a kind of imperviousness to ordinary human connections afterwards.

I want to stress that these observations are not intended as a case against cosmopolitan altruism. Speaking as a Jew, I am thankful for the rescuers' existence; I only wish there had been more of them. My point is rather that their moral excellence was not comprehensive, that the inner constitution that enabled them to risk their lives on behalf of endangered strangers was intimately connected to what might well be regarded as moral deficiencies. Precisely because moral worth is multidimensional, extraordinary excellence along one dimension is apt to produce loss along others.

To avoid misunderstanding, let me restate what I hope is already clear: moral loss is hardly a phenomenon confined to cosmopolitan altruism, but rather is characteristic of a very wide range of moral choices. The identification of forms of moral loss characteristic of cosmopolitan altruism does not in itself constitute, and is not intended as, a criticism of that choice or an argument for some other choice. The point, rather, is this: Because cosmopolitan altruism is not infrequently regarded as a peak of moral excellence, it is especially important (and perhaps even surprising) to discover that it too encompasses acts and attitudes that may well be judged less than fully admirable.

The proposition that moral loss is ubiquitous, moreover, does not entail the casually relativistic conclusion that no choices can be rationally preferred to others. Some alternatives may straightforwardly dominate others: B may simply outrank A along every relevant moral dimension. And even if there is no single dominant option, even if qualitatively diverse dimensions point in different directions, there may still be an identifiable right thing to do, all things considered. If, as seems plausible in most cases, the morally relevant dimensions cannot be reduced to a common measure, then all-things-considered judgment rests on trained moral deliberation, a fully adequate account of which is as yet unavailable.

This is not the occasion to enter into a full substantive discussion of the rescuers' decisions from the standpoint of the moral pluralism just sketched. Still, one may venture some proposals. For example, if rescuing cannot be understood as obligatory, it would appear questionable at best for rescuers knowingly to endanger others without their consent. I do not believe that it is right to place one's children at risk in this manner. It is certainly not right to conceal one's activities from (say) one's fiancé, depriving him even of the opportunity to offer considered approval

---

whole gave them the inner resources to resist the pressure of family, neighbors, and the political community. This might be taken as an instance of the more general hypothesis that the ability to resist social pressure, to develop and display true individuality, must somehow be rooted in potent countervailing forces.

to deeds in which he is likely to be implicated. Identification with all of humanity can be an admirable ground for personal action, but by itself it does not entitle the agent to act for, or involve, others.

The principal conclusion I draw from the ubiquity of moral loss concerns, not the substance of moral choices, but the manner in which they should be made. Within a given situation, the fact that some considerations override others does not mean that the losers simply vanish without a trace, morally speaking. The considerations that could not be reflected in our action retain a claim on our attention. Moral choices, I want to suggest, should be made and carried out with continuing awareness of, and sensitivity to, their costs. If we find ourselves compelled to disregard certain personal or communal ties in the name of cosmopolitan considerations, we should nonetheless experience the continuing force of those ties. When the considerations that determine our choices also dominate our consciousness, the result can often be a dangerous moral tunnel-vision.

This is not to say that we ought to feel regret or guilt when we do what is right, all things considered. When we do what is right, we have done the best we can, given (so to speak) the structure of the universe. We have done nothing for which to reproach ourselves. While we may yearn for a less pluralistic world in which moral loss is less pervasive, that loss is neither our product nor our responsibility. The point is rather that we should not seek to gratify our understandable desire for moral harmony by obliterating our awareness of unavoidable moral costs.

I close with two suggestions concerning the sources of moral loss within cosmopolitan altruism. First, moral universality is (can only be?) purchased at the cost of moral particularity; the ability to act on behalf of strangers conflicts with, and may often crowd out, other forms of human connection. Second, there is, if not classic egoism, at least a form of self-centeredness, in self-expressive action, for through such action individual inwardness is in a sense imposed on the world. Thus, while the rescuers' personal identity encompassed humanity as a whole and their acts expressed that inclusiveness, their moral stance was nonetheless unresponsive to the moral sentiments of human beings unlike themselves.

This unresponsiveness was necessary. As we have seen, if the rescuers had been effectively responsive to family and community, they could not have done what they did. Still, an important variant of moral inclusiveness is being able to take seriously other human beings, not as abstract homogenized entities identical to oneself, but rather as particularized individuals who may be very different. Responsiveness to particularity may undermine cosmopolitan altruism, but it may also pave the way for other worthy forms of moral action.

Philosophy, School of Public Affairs, University of Maryland at College Park

SELFLESSNESS AND THE LOSS OF SELF*

By Jean Hampton

> The biggest danger, that of losing oneself, can pass off in the world as quietly as if it were nothing; every other loss, an arm, a leg, five dollars, a wife, etc. is bound to be noticed.
>
> Soren Kierkegaard, *The Sickness Unto Death*[1]

Sacrificing one's own interests in order to serve another is, in general, supposed to be a good thing, an example of altruism, the hallmark of morality, and something we should commend to (but not always require of) the entirely-too-selfish human beings of our society. But let me recount a story that I hope will persuade the reader to start questioning this conventional philosophical wisdom. Last year, a friend of mine was talking with me about a mutual acquaintance whose two sons were in the same nursery school as our sons. This woman, whom I will call Terry, had been pregnant with twins, but one of the twins had died during the fourth month of pregnancy, and the other twin had just been born prematurely at six months with a host of medical problems. We were discussing how stressful this woman's life had been while she was pregnant: she was a housewife, and her two boys, aged three and five, were lively, challenging, often unruly—a real handful to raise. Her husband worked long hours in a law firm, so the vast majority of the childcare and household chores fell on her shoulders. "You could see that she was exhausted by the end of the first trimester," I maintained, "because her eyes were tired, and her cheeks were sunken—she looked almost like a cadaver." My friend agreed. I went on to blame her exhaustion on the fact that she had to do too much during a pregnancy that anyone would have found difficult. "I don't understand her husband," I maintained. "Surely he could see how badly she looked. If he had concern for his future children, why didn't he do something to help her so that the pregnancy had a chance of going better? And if he loved *her*, why didn't he cut down his hours so that he could help out at home? Surely he could see just by looking at

* I have been greatly benefited by a number of people in the course of writing this essay. The impetus to write it came from a discussion of a related paper of mine at Yale Law School's Legal Theory Workshop. I also wish to thank Neera Badhwar, Jules Coleman, David Schmidtz, Elizabeth Willott, the other contributors to this volume, and its editors, for all their comments, criticisms, and ideas. (I trust their help was authentically offered!)

[1] Soren Kierkegaard, *The Sickness Unto Death*, trans. Alastair Hannay (Harmondsworth: Penguin, 1989), pp. 62–63.

her that she was in trouble." My friend said nothing at the time, but after a week she called me, and told me that my criticism of this woman's husband had bothered her all week. "You're wrong about Terry's husband not caring enough about her. They have a good marriage," she insisted, and then she continued: "You know, you're not like us. We accept the fact that we should do most of the childcare and housework. Terry's husband wasn't doing anything wrong expecting her to take responsibility for that side of things."

What troubled me most about my friend's remarks was her assumption that it was not only permissible but appropriate for "her kind" to care for other people, even to the point where they were endangering their own health (and in this case, also the health of those they were responsible for nurturing). And I realized that Terry herself bore some of the responsibility for these events: not only had she harmed those fetuses by insisting on carrying the entire burden of care in the family, but she had also harmed herself by putting enormous stress on her body, in a way that had bad physical and, one suspects, bad psychological repercussions.

Often philosophers who commend altruism assume that someone who cares for another even at the expense of her own welfare is an impressive and highly moral figure. But surely the story I have just told indicates that the truth is much more complicated: not all self-sacrifice is worthy of our respect or moral commendation, and not all such sacrifice really benefits those at whom it is aimed. Often men and women who give to others at their own expense are called "selfless," and I find that a revealing term, because "selfless" people such as Terry are in danger of losing the self they ought to be developing, and as a result, may be indirectly harming the very people for whom they care.

This essay attempts to explore the sort of "selfless" act that is bad, and the sort of "selfish" conduct that is good. I am using the terms 'good' and 'bad' in the preceding sentence as moral terms, so my understanding of what counts as 'moral' is unconventional. The adjective 'moral' is normally understood to be a term referring to traits of character or actions that are, in either a direct or indirect way, other-regarding. But this paper attempts to pursue what might be called the "self-regarding" component of morality, a component which has been curiously neglected over the years.

I. Two Conceptions of Morality

I want to begin by exploring traditional conceptions of what morality is, and how they tell us to evaluate altruistic action. By the term 'conception of morality' I do not mean any particular theory (such as Kantianism or utilitarianism) justifying or attempting to define moral conduct. I mean the deeper understanding of morality which moral theories are *about* — our intuitive sense of what morality is, which we use to recognize moral actions and about which we develop moral theories to defend or precisely define it. There are two conceptions of morality that have undergirded moral theories in modern times, both of which, I shall argue, are problematic.

In order to flesh out these conceptions, I will make use of Carol Gilligan's interviews with two children — interviews that address real or hypothetical moral problems, which she has presented in a number of forums, most prominently in her book *In A Different Voice*. On the basis of interviews such as these, Gilligan argues that in our society there are currently two different "moral voices," which she calls the "ethic of justice" and the "ethic of care," and she finds some evidence (albeit controversial) associating the first with men and the second with women.[2] Now Gilligan's work is that of a psychologist, and thus she is not concerned to be very clear about what a "voice" is, nor does she attempt to use the resources of moral philosophy to clarify or define any theoretical details involved in these voices. But as a philosopher I have found her work valuable because it takes seriously the moral views and perspectives of everyday people, and thus offers us a way to uncover what I am calling "conceptions of morality" by exposing the deep-seated assumptions people in our society have about what morality is, what it requires of us, and the nature of its authority over our lives. And (as I shall show at length in a discussion of the work of one philosopher below) such conceptions are an important source of the intuitions upon which we philosophers are subtly relying when we generate moral theories. Hence, in this section I want to present Gilligan's two voices, and then go on to discuss how they can be understood as (in my sense) two different moral conceptions.

As I have noted elsewhere,[3] two of Gilligan's interviews with older children clarify these two "voices" nicely. Gilligan originally initiated these interviews in order to test Lawrence Kohlberg's theory of moral development, which Gilligan believed did not adequately describe the moral development of many females. Eleven-year-old Jake, whose answers to the interviewers earned him high marks on Kohlberg's moral-maturity scale, gave the following answer when asked: "When responsibility to oneself and responsibility to others conflict, how should one choose?" He replied with great self-assurance: "You go about one-fourth to the others

---

[2] See Carol Gilligan, *In A Different Voice* (Cambridge: Harvard University Press, 1982). She has revised and expanded her ideas since then. See a variety of articles about Gilligan's recent work in *Mapping the Moral Domain*, ed. Carol Gilligan, Victoria Ward, and Jill McLean, with Betty Bandige (Cambridge: Center for the Study of Gender, Education, and Human Development, 1988). And see Carol Gilligan, "Moral Orientation and Moral Development," in *Women and Moral Theory*, ed. Eva Feder Kittay and Diana T. Meyers (Totowa, New Jersey: Rowman and Littlefield, 1987), pp. 19–33.

[3] The discussion of Jake and Amy is partly drawn from my paper "Feminist Contractarianism," in *Analytic Feminism*, ed. L. Antony and C. Witt (Boulder: Westview Press, 1992).

and three-fourths to yourself."[4] When asked to explain his answer to the question about responsibility to himself and others, Jake replies:

> Because the most important thing in your decision should be your-self, don't let yourself be guided totally by other people, but you have to take them into consideration. So, if what you want to do is blow yourself up with an atom bomb, you should maybe blow your-self up with a hand grenade because you are thinking about your neighbors who would die also.[5]

As this remarkable example shows, he regards "being moral" as pursuing one's own interests without damaging the interests of others, and he takes it as a matter of moral strength not to allow the interests of others to dictate to him what he ought or ought not to do. For Jake, morality defines the rules governing noninterference.

Contrast the following answer to the same question given by eleven-year-old Amy, whose answers to the interviewers earned poorer marks on Kohlberg's scale:

> Well, it really depends on the situation. If you have a responsibility with somebody else [sic], then you should keep it to a certain extent, but to the extent that it is really going to hurt you or stop you from doing something that you really, really, want, then I think maybe you should put yourself first. But if it is your responsibility to some-body really close to you, you've just got to decide in that situation which is more important, yourself or that person, and like I said, it really depends on what kind of person you are and how you feel about the other person or persons involved.[6]

When asked to explain this answer, Amy replies:

> . . . some people put themselves and things for themselves before they put other people, and some people really care about other peo-ple. Like, I don't think your job is as important as somebody that you really love, like your husband or your parents or a very close friend. Somebody that you really care for — or if it's just your responsibility to your job or somebody that you barely know, then maybe you go first. . . .[7]

Whereas Jake's remarks take for granted the idea that being moral means following rules that preclude interference in other people's pursuit of

---

[4] Gilligan, *In A Different Voice*, pp. 35–36.

[5] *Ibid.*, p. 36.

[6] *Ibid.*, pp. 35–36.

[7] *Ibid.*, p. 36.

their interests, Amy's remarks make clear that for her, moral conduct is beneficent involvement that may require, at times, self-sacrifice. And her discussion of other moral problems reveals the assumption that being moral means actively pursuing the well-being of others. Whereas Jake sees others' interests as constraints on the pursuit of his own ends, Amy believes others' ends are ones that morality obliges her to help pursue.[8]

Many feminist theorists maintain that, in contrast to the ranking Kohlberg would assign to them, the kind of moral voice Amy exemplifies is clearly "higher" or more advanced than Jake's.[9] On Jake's view, morality is seen as—to use Annette Baier's term—"traffic rules for self-assertors,"[10] and Baier argues plausibly that such a perspective on morality is neither a sophisticated nor a mature moral perspective. It appears to derive from the mistaken assumption that each of us is self-sufficient, able and desirous of "going it alone." Amy is surely right that this is false. Her perspective on morality, which emphasizes caring for and fostering the well-being of others, appears to be a richer, sounder theory of what genuine moral behavior is all about. Such a perspective is one which women (and especially mothers) are frequently thought to exhibit more than men.

However, Amy's conception of her moral role is certainly not beyond criticism. *Maybe* she can put herself first, she says, if not doing so would mean losing out on something that she "really, really" wants. But only maybe. Jake is convinced not only that his interests count, but that they count far more than other people's (three quarters to one quarter). Amy appears to be having trouble figuring out whether or not her interests count at all. Even in a situation where she takes her responsibility to others to be minimal, she finds it difficult to assert the priority of her own interests.

On the basis of these children's observations and remarks, we can outline two conceptions of morality which they are assuming as they answer the interviewers' questions; and we will see that neither of the conceptions is fully acceptable. First, although they disagree in many ways, both children accept the following tenet:

(1) Moral behavior is almost exclusively concerned with the well-being of others and not with the well-being of oneself.

In his discussion of Marx's criticism of morality, Allen Wood argues that something along the lines of tenet (1) must be included in any adequate understanding of what morality is. Although he admits that the word

---

[8] I am indebted to Elizabeth Willott and David Schmidtz for this way of contrasting the children's moral outlooks.

[9] Annette Baier, "What Do Women Want in a Moral Theory?" *Nous*, vol. 19, no. 1 (March 1985), p. 62.

[10] *Ibid*.

'morality' can be used to include certain forms of self-regarding behavior, nonetheless he writes that

> there is a narrower and I think more proper sense of 'moral' in which we distinguish *moral* goods and evils from *nonmoral* ones. We all know the difference between valuing or doing something because conscience or the 'moral law' tells us we 'ought' to, and valuing or doing something because it satisfies our needs, our wants or our conceptions of what is good for us (or for someone else whose welfare we want to promote — desires for nonmoral goods are not necessarily selfish desires).[11]

Both children seem to agree with Wood that "nonmoral goods" include most of what we want for ourselves, goods whose pursuit often competes with activities that we "ought" to do for others — activities that most of us tend to find less compelling precisely because they do not lead to self-benefiting goods.

However, although they both accept tenet (1), Amy and Jake have very different conceptions of what it means to be "other-regarding." Amy assumes it means caring for others, and accepts the following tenet:

> (2A) A perfectly moral person is one who actively seeks out ways of benefiting others, and offers her services and/or her resources in order to meet others' needs.

In contrast, Jake assumes that "being moral" primarily involves not hurting others. Although he is prepared to choose to be responsible toward others "one quarter" of the time, when he gives an example of moral behavior, it is a "noninterference" example: i.e., do not interfere with others when you are engaged in your pursuits (in his example, the pursuit is "blowing yourself up"!). So for Jake, being moral is primarily perceived as a negative activity; he accepts the following tenet:

> (2J) A perfectly moral person does not do anything to interfere with or injure other people or their (noninjurious) activities.

Now Amy would certainly agree that (2J) is part of being moral, but only because it is implied by (2A). However, Jake would likely reject (2A) as being *too* responsive to other people; after all, he insists, we are permitted to put ourselves ahead of others "three quarters" of the time.

Because they have different conceptions of how moral behavior benefits others, Jake and Amy have different understandings of what altruistic behavior is, and how it should be commended. Because Jake believes

---

[11] Allen Wood, *Karl Marx* (London: Routledge & Kegan Paul, 1981), pp. 126–27.

that morality generally only requires him to refrain from hurting people, he is convinced that this is a realizable ideal, allowing him plenty of room for his own activities. Now he is prepared to go beyond this and offer help (giving other people one quarter of his attention, and reserving for himself three quarters), but I would suspect, if he did so, that he would often perceive this help to be something over and above the demands of morality—analogous to "moral extra credit." The tone of his remarks makes it clear that he would not feel terribly bad about refraining from performing costly care, since such care is not, strictly speaking, morally required in any case (morality is primarily about not hurting others), and thus an "extra" that any of us can forego with a fairly easy conscience. Therefore, someone with Jake's conception of morality accepts the possibility that there are what philosophers call "supererogatory acts." To put it precisely, such people believe:

> (3J) There are acts that benefit other people which are morally commendable but not morally obligatory (i.e., supererogatory acts).

However, for people such as Amy, foregoing beneficial activity is not so easy. *Any* beneficent involvement in another's life is mandated by morality, and because so many people are in need in our world, Amy is the sort of person who will constantly feel the tug of conscience, chastising her for not doing more to care for others. Of course, many of these obligations may be defeasible, given other obligations she is under; but the point is that they would still be *obligations*, as opposed to mere "moral recommendations." This means that Amy accepts:

> (3A) Any act that could benefit another person is a *prima facie* moral obligation.

One who accepts (3A) believes that there is no such thing as a morally supererogatory act (or "moral extra credit").

Although Gilligan's research suggests that people divide on gender lines in their advocacy of either of these conceptions, in fact it is interesting to note that over the centuries there have been entirely male-developed moral theories that have drawn from both conceptions. Consider, for example, that for the utilitarian, the fundamental business of the moral person is the pursuit of the happiness of the community, which is a difficult and demanding task. And while this pursuit may allow or even require one to serve one's own interests on occasion, it may also require considerable self-sacrifice. Moreover, at least one utilitarian has recently championed something like (3A); recognizing that the beneficence required of the utilitarian leaves no room for moral extra credit.[12]

---

[12] See Shelly Kagan, *The Limits of Morality* (Oxford: Oxford University Press, 1988).

On the other hand, there are also plenty of Jake-like theories. Consider, for example, Locke's formulation of what he takes to be the fundamental law of nature:

> Every one as he is *bound to preserve himself*, and not to quit his Station wilfully; so by the like reason when his own Preservation comes not in competition, ought he, as much as he can, *to preserve the rest of Mankind*, and may not unless it be to do Justice on an Offender, take away or impair the life, or what tends to the Preservation of the Life, Liberty, Health, Limb or Goods of another.[13]

At first, it seems Locke perceives morality as an active and beneficent activity when he calls on people to do as much as they can to preserve others; but when he gives instances of moral activity later on, each prescribes a form of noninterference. In general, he tells us, do not "take away or impair" others' ability to preserve themselves, and this seems to be what he means by the phrase "preserve the rest of Mankind." Finally, note that he gives permission to behave in ways that can be damaging to others' lives if one's own preservation requires it ("when his own Preservation comes not in competition"). So while Locke, like Jake, perceives morality as an other-oriented activity, he does not perceive it to be so demanding that it would require one always—or even usually—to choose to serve others' needs over one's own. He even seems prepared to sanction behavior that is destructive of others' interests if one's own preservation requires it.

Let us return, then, to the topic of altruism: on one conception, there are altruistic behaviors that are recommended but not required; on the other conception, all altruistic behaviors are prima facie moral obligations, to be performed unless there is a higher altruistic obligation in place. But note one interesting fact: *both* conceptions assume that if one has a choice between doing something self-regarding or doing something that is *genuinely* beneficial for others, the beneficent act can never be immoral. This is most obviously true for the utilitarian—assuming, of course, that the community would benefit more from your service to others than it would from your service to yourself: and any action that would further the happiness of the community according to the utilitarian calculation, is a moral action, and thus an action to be morally commended, no matter what it might do to you. Moreover, while Locke gives his readers moral permission to choose themselves over others when their own self-preservation is at stake, he never considers the possibility that someone who did the reverse might be an immoral person. And this is probably because he assumed that such a person would be even more moral "than normal" in-

---

[13] The quote is drawn from section 6 of the Second Treatise in *Two Treatises of Government*, ed. Peter Laslett (Cambridge: Cambridge University Press, 1960), p. 311.

sofar as he would be choosing to serve others even when permitted not to do so.

II. Morality's Hegemony

Which conception of morality is right? Although philosophers have tended to line up on both sides, and have rigorously debated this issue, we should consider how we react to the two children's articulation, in crude but pure terms, of the moral conception each accepts: we think each conception is wrong, and indeed, immature. But if we criticize both conceptions of morality, shouldn't we also criticize any moral theories that are based upon the assumptions of either of these conceptions?

We should. I have already alluded to Annette Baier's attack on Jake-like moral theories, which I will discuss later in this section. But we can just as easily criticize Amy-like moral theories; in fact, without realizing it, Susan Wolf develops such a criticism in her "Moral Saints."[14] In a nutshell, Wolf argues that two leading moral theories, utilitarianism and Kantianism, along with the "common-sense" morality accepted by nonphilosophers, all regard moral activity as almost exclusively other-regarding and beneficent, so that were a person to become perfectly moral (i.e., a moral saint) as defined by any of these approaches, he would be so focused on pursuing the well-being of others that he would have neither the time nor the "moral permission" to develop a variety of the talents, skills, traits of personality, and vocations that make each of us an interesting and well-rounded person:

> If the moral saint is devoting all his time to feeding the hungry or healing the sick or raising money for Oxfam, then necessarily he is not reading Victorian novels, playing the oboe, or improving his backhand. . . .
> . . . There are, in addition, a class of nonmoral characteristics that a saint cannot encourage in himself for reasons that are not just practical. There is a more substantial tension between having any of these qualities unashamedly and being a moral saint. . . . For example, a cynical or sarcastic wit, or a sense of humor that appreciates this kind of wit in others, requires that one take an attitude of resignation and pessimism toward the flaws and vices to be found in the world. . . . [A]lthough a moral saint might well enjoy a good episode of *Father Knows Best*, he may not in good conscience be able to laugh at a Marx Brothers movie or enjoy a play by George Bernard Shaw.[15]

[14] Susan Wolf, "Moral Saints," *Journal of Philosophy*, vol. 79, no. 8 (August 1982), pp. 419–39.
[15] *Ibid.*, pp. 420–21.

Wolf goes on to argue that human institutions such as *haute cuisine*, high fashion, interior design, and perhaps even fine art could not be said to be worth as many resources as we standardly put into them, given how these resources could be used in many morally superior ways. Hence, she concludes that although morality is a highly valuable and important human activity, it cannot be said to be always authoritative over all nonmoral options: in particular, there are, she insists, judgments that are neither moral nor egoistic, about what would be good for a person to do or be, which are made from a point of view outside the limits set by the moral values, interests, and desires that the person might actually have. These judgments arise from what she calls the "point of view of individual perfection," and are governed by ideals and values that have nothing to do with morality. She argues that, like moral judgments, these perfectionist judgments claim for themselves a kind of objectivity and a grounding in a perspective which any rational and perceptive being can take up. Unlike moral judgments, however, the good with which these judgments are concerned is not the good of anyone or any group other than the individual himself.[16] She insists that we are sometimes (perhaps even often) permitted to choose this perfectionist good over the values and dictates of morality. So, Wolf's conclusion in "Moral Saints" is that the unrelenting pursuit of morality is a bad thing, where 'bad' must be understood in some sense other than 'immoral'.

Now Wolf claims that *all* contemporary moral theories fall prey to her criticisms, and her attack on the currently popular moral approaches is supposed to reveal the mistake that pervades all contemporary approaches to morality. But the analysis in the preceding section of the two divergent conceptions of morality in our society should make it clear that Wolf is actually criticizing only *one* "common-sense" conception, namely, the "Amy-like" one. To see this, consider that Wolf takes it for granted that all three conceptions she criticizes have a highly active, "caring" conception of morality. Thus, she takes it for granted that, on any of these views, a perfectly moral person would be going out in the world looking for ways of benefiting others, offering her services, using her money for philanthropic gestures, constantly surveying her world to see how she could help, either by using her time and personal skills, or by using her financial resources. Moreover, Wolf assumes, along with Amy, that this beneficent involvement is not only commendable but also morally required. It is not surprising that Wolf finds it easy to argue against such an exhausting and self-limiting ideal. Our intuitive rejection of the ideal of the moral saint she describes is not unlike our alarm at the kind of person Amy says she wants to become: Amy and the moral saint are so taken up with the needs of others that they seem to have no time to de-

---

[16] *Ibid.*, p. 436.

velop into interesting, distinctive (and not always "nice") human beings in their own right.

However, Wolf's criticisms do not seem to work against those moral theories and common-sense views that are more Jake-like. If you assume a Jake-like conception of morality, you view being moral as primarily a negative activity, requiring only that you refrain from hurting others, and not demanding that you do everything and anything you can in order to benefit them. So on this conception, the ideally moral person is both practically and logically able to pursue many nonmoral ideals. Admittedly, this conception would still preclude development of certain character traits or participation in certain activities that are harmful or interfering in the affairs of others, for example, the development of a caustic and wounding wit or a taste for clothing made by processes that injure workers. But many would insist — contra any claims to the contrary that Wolf might make — that this is not a drawback of this conception because such traits and activities are, in their view, correctly viewed as morally inappropriate.

Indeed, it is possible to interpret Kant's moral views so that they are more like Jake's than like Amy's, thereby allowing the Kantian theory to escape many of Wolf's criticisms. Consider that Kant seems to conceive of his moral law as that which merely *checks* the moral permissibility of one's behavior ("Could this action be a universal law of nature?" one is supposed to ask), and not something used to *uncover* beneficent, nurturing behaviors that might not otherwise occur to one without the help of the law. We are told that *after* we have consulted our (nonmorally defined) desires to formulate a maxim about what to do, we should use the law to find out if the maxim is morally permissible; we are not told to use morality in a more positive fashion, to formulate our maxims directly. So we could use Kant's law appropriately to evaluate our maxims for action and still be oblivious to a variety of ways that we could actively help others, if such ways of helping never occur to us. Indeed, why would they occur to us if desires are the source of all maxims and these ways of helping are opposed to the satisfaction of our desires?

So Kant's theory seems to leave plenty of room for the pursuit of individual perfection, but note that it does so only because, on this interpretation, it is a "reactive" rather than a "proactive" theory, unable to pick out and require the beneficent involvement in others' lives which might never be proposed by our desires, but which common sense tells us is nonetheless morally required.

However, just because Kant's theory, so interpreted, escapes Wolf's criticisms, does not mean that it is a successful portrayal of morality. To think of morality along Jake-like lines gives us *too much* room for self-development; such an approach assumes that we should look out for and respect others only insofar as they happen to be in the way of our own plans for self-gratification; it does not encourage us to see ourselves as having some responsibility for fostering others' plans for self-gratification apart from any impact those plans might have on us. Hence, it discourages us from recognizing and coming to the aid of those who are in need, and misleads us about the extent to which any of us can satisfy his or her own desires without the help and support of others. (Some of us may like to be so mislead, finding it unpleasant to remember that each of us starts life as a helpless infant, and ends life "sans teeth, sans hair, sans taste, sans everything." [17]

I regard this Jake-like way of reading Kant as disappointing, and I will develop an alternative way of using at least some of his moral views in the next section. The challenge is to develop a conception of morality that recognizes the importance of beneficent involvement in other's lives, but which not only "leaves room" for the development of one's self, but also makes that development a moral requirement. In what follows, I will maintain that Wolf's moral saint is not only a failure from the standpoint of individual perfection, but also from the standpoint of morality itself, properly understood.

III. Human Worth, Human Flourishing, and Human Self-Authorship

The ability of Jake-like people to incorporate room for themselves in a moral life is, I believe, the best part of their moral conception. On the other hand, as it stands, that conception fails (as I have noted above) to capture genuine morality. In what follows, I will contend that in order to understand what an ideally moral person would look like, we must define a new conception of morality which recognizes that any "altruistic" behavior is morally wrong when it prevents one from paying moral respect to oneself.

What does it mean to be a moral respecter of yourself? I want to argue that such respect involves having the following three characteristics:

(a) a sense of your own intrinsic and equal value as a human being,
(b) a sense of what you require, as a human being, to flourish, and
(c) a sense of what you require, insofar as you are a *particular person*, to flourish as that particular person.

Let me explicate each of these in turn.

First, a person's conception of his own worth as a person is derived from his overall conception of human worth. Such a conception defines for this person how human beings are to be valued, and how to appraise each individual's value. Philosophers have varied in how they have un-

---

[17] From Shakespeare's *As You Like It*, Act III (in a speech by Jacques).

derstood the nature of human value; for example, Hobbes regards human value as no different from the value of any commodity: "the value of each person," he insists, "is his price." [18] So on his view our value is entirely instrumental: we are worth what anyone would give to make use of our skills, labor, or other characteristics. Naturally, such a position is going to accord people different values, depending upon the marketability of their various traits.

There are a variety of noninstrumental conceptions which grant people inherent or intrinsic worth on the basis of one or more characteristics. Many such conceptions are inegalitarian, granting human beings (unequal) value depending upon their sex, or race, or caste, or alternatively, on the basis of how intelligent, or accomplished, or morally worthy they are. Others are egalitarian, insisting that people are equal in worth insofar as they all share certain critical, worth-defining characteristics. One popular egalitarian theory is that of Kant, who grants each of us equal worth insofar as we are all rational and autonomous. Now Kant does not deny that we can be evaluated in ways that make us unequal—noting, for example, that some of us are vastly better, and morally more worthy, than others. Nonetheless, he takes all such inegalitarian evaluations— including assessments of moral worth—as *irrelevant* to defining the kind of moral respect a person deserves. On his view, our moral obligations to people do not increase with, say, their moral virtue; instead, we are obliged to respect our fellow human beings equally, no matter the state of their moral character, insofar as each of us is an autonomous, rational being (although Kant would certainly maintain that how this respect should be demonstrated can vary depending upon the state of a person's moral character).[19] This "democratic" conception has been highly popular in the modern world (some arguing that it is the offspring of Judeo-Christian religious teaching).[20]

I want to propose that our conception of morality is properly understood to involve a Kantian conception of worth, i.e., a conception of human beings as intrinsically and equally valuable, where that value is not straightforwardly capable of aggregation in the way that some utilitarian

[18] See Thomas Hobbes, *Leviathan*, ed. C.B. Macpherson (Harmondsworth: Penguin, 1968), chap. 10, para. 16, p. 42.

[19] For example, Kant maintains that those who are morally bad can deserve punishment, but he is also well-known for insisting that punishment is a way of respecting a person's autonomy, and represents neither a violation nor a suspension of that autonomy.

[20] See Jeffrie Murphy, "Afterword: Constitutionalism, Moral Skepticism, and Religious Belief," in *Constitutionalism: The Philosophical Dimension*, ed. H. Rosenbaum (New York: Greenwood Press, 1988), pp. 239–49.

I was struck recently by how many people in American culture accept this view of worth when I read a letter written by parents of children in a Tucson-area elementary school, calling upon the school to foster the idea that "all people are equal." In attempting to explain this equality, the authors of the letter noted that although each of us is different, our differences do not affect our equality. As they put it: Just as $3 + 3 + 1$ is different from but equal to $3 + 4$, so too are we different from, but equal to, one another.

doctrines characterize it. If this conception of our value is adopted, one must respect the value not only of others but also of oneself, and must therefore reject any roles, projects, or occupations which would be self-exploitative. So the first, and most important, way in which morality involves self-regard is that it demands of each of us that we take a certain kind of pride in ourselves—not the pride that, say, a white supremacist takes in his alleged superiority, but the pride that arises from a sense of our own inherent worthiness in a world of intrinsically valuable equals. Henceforth, I shall say that to call us "persons" is to accord us this kind of intrinsic and equal worth.

It is this sort of pride which people such as Terry in my earlier example do not have. They perceive themselves as subordinate, a different kind of human being whose role is to serve others. Unable to put their interests and concerns first, they struggle to feel satisfied as they care for others. And to those (especially their children) who observe them, they teach the permissibility of their own exploitation by submitting to, and even supporting, their subservient role. Often these beneficent "saints" are revered by those whom they serve because of their caring ways, but the appropriateness of their devotion to the service of others at their own expense is never questioned or challenged, probably because those who revere them unconsciously recognize that such people are highly useful to them, given their own self-interested concerns. What better way to promote this useful servitude than by continually commending such people as "moral," "saintly," "devoted," "virtuous"?

The second way in which morality involves self-regard concerns what I will call the conception of the legitimate needs of human beings. If you respect others' value, you make sure that they have what they need to thrive as human beings and as persons, where that includes air, water, food, shelter, clothing, and medical care to meet physical needs, along with a decent measure of freedom, self-control, and love to meet psychological needs. But those who respect their own value will be just as concerned that these needs be met in their own cases. Leaving aside conditions of severe scarcity where resource allocations are agonizing and highly controversial, the saint who devotes herself and virtually all the resources at her disposal to benefiting others is in danger of damaging herself, and in this way failing to respect her own needs as a human being. In Terry's case, her persistent service to her family left her little time to rest, to the point where her body became severely stressed. Rather than understanding that she should rightfully demand time off from her childcare and household duties given her physical problems, she continued her regimen of care. To those readers who, like Jake, find it easy to put themselves first, it may seem fantastic that a person could be so other-regarding that she would literally make herself sick rather than take time out to care for herself. But Terry's behavior is not unusual. As another example, consider that Virginia Woolf's life and the content of her novels (especially *To The Lighthouse*) were strongly influenced by the example of the early death of her mother, Julia Stephen, which, according to Woolf, resulted from exhaustion brought on by caring unceasingly for seven children and a demanding husband.[21] Woolf's novels strongly suggest that such behavior is connected to a conception of self as servant, which makes one a less-important, second-class kind of person. Indeed, that self-conception would figure in a general explanation of why it does not seem more obvious to obsessive care-givers that in order to be able to care for others properly, they must care for their own needs, since the importance of these needs is never clear to them.[22]

Of course, not all self-denying care-givers are female. One colleague of mine told me about her father's insistence on helping his friends and relatives to the point of risking his health and well-being (for example, throwing out his back helping a neighbor repair her fence, or risking the severing of his fingers helping his daughter move a freezer into the basement). Indeed, his desire to help has been sufficiently extreme that he once locked his daughter out of the garage so that he could unload her luggage from the trunk of a car! How do we explain his obsessive, self-damaging, and (for the recipients) frequently suffocating interest in "helping"? Part of the explanation seems to be that he, and others like him, not only have a poor sense of self-worth and a poor grip on what they owe to themselves in order to meet their objective needs, but also a dearth of plans, projects, and goals that are uniquely their own. Thus, they decide to satisfy the ends of others because they have so few ends of their own to pursue.[23] This explanation accounts for why those of us who have received help from such obsessive care-givers frequently resent and feel violated by the help: it is as if our own ends of action have been seized and taken away from us by these "helpers" when they insist on pursuing them for us.

Such behavior illustrates a third way in which morality involves self-regard: namely, it requires us to ensure that we have the time, the resources, and the capacity to develop the characteristics, skills, plans, and projects that make us unique individual selves. One of the traits that mark us out as human beings is our capacity to develop distinctive personalities. Granted, some of the distinctiveness that differentiates us from one another is the product of the environments in which each of us grows up—our families, schools, religious organizations, political institutions, and so forth. And some of it is the product of biological characteristics,

---

[21] Woolf's account of her mother's life can be found in autobiographical fragments published as "A Sketch of the Past," in *The Virginia Woolf Reader*, ed. Mitchell Leaska (New York: Harcourt, Brace, Jovanovich, 1984).

[22] This obvious lesson is often missed. Consider that airlines find it necessary to teach parents that if oxygen masks are necessary during flight, they should place the masks over their own noses and mouths first, and only then help their children to secure *their* masks.

[23] I am indebted to Elizabeth Willott for this way of putting the point.

destined to develop in us because of our genetic make-up. But some of that distinctiveness is what I shall call "self-authored." There are many times in our lives when we choose what we will be. For example, when a young girl has the choice of entering into a harsh regimen of training to become an accomplished figure skater, or else refusing it and enjoying a more normal life with lots of time for play, she is being asked to choose or author whom she will be. When a graduate student decides which field of her discipline she will pursue, or when a person makes a decision about his future religious life, or when someone takes up a hobby—all of these choices are ways of determining one's traits, activities, and skills, and thus ways of shaping one's self—of determining one's self-identity. Nor are these self-determining choices always earthshaking or major. In small ways we build up who we are: if we successfully forgive a friend a misdeed, we thereby become a little more generous, or if we give way to anger and hit a loved one, we do a little bit more to build an abusive personality. Just as a sculptor creates a form out of a slab of rock, so too do people (in concert with their environment and their biology) create a distinctive way of interacting with, thinking about, and reacting to the world. It is this distinctiveness which each individual plays a major role in creating, that I am calling the "self." Whereas we say that we respect one another as "persons," we say that we love or hate, approve or condemn, appreciate or dislike, others' selves.

This self-authorship is not only something that we do, but also something that it is deeply important for us to do; through self-authorship we express our autonomy and prosper as human beings. To be prevented from self-authorship is to undergo brutal psychological damage. Therefore, morality requires that others give each of us the opportunity to author ourselves, and it requires of each of us that we perform that self-authorship. But the objective requirement of self-authorship is satisfied by an individual when she *subjectively* defines who she is, what she wants, and what she will pursue in her life. Whereas the conception of legitimate needs is objectively defined, reflecting a theory of what it is that each of us requires, as a human being, to flourish (where this includes, among other things, the ability and opportunity to engage in self-authorship), the conception of "personal needs" sets out what one requires as a particular personality or self, and is subjectively defined, arising from a person's decision to be a certain way, to have certain aspirations, and to undertake certain projects—all of which are up to her to determine.

So who I am is partly "up to me." Nonetheless, to make sense of self-authorship each of us needs to understand when we are genuinely engaged in self-defining, as opposed to self-denying, activities. I shall now argue that in order to define what counts as genuine self-authorship, we require objective constraints. The subjectivity of preference formation only counts, from a moral point of view, as self-authorship if that preference formation occurs in a certain way, when a person is in a certain kind of state. In the discussion that follows, I will attempt to suggest the rough nature of these objective constraints, but this is theoretically difficult terrain, and as the reader will see, I will leave many questions unanswered.

IV. UNDERSTANDING SELF-AUTHORSHIP

To determine the nature of self-authorship, we must answer a number of questions. First, we need to know what state a person must be in, such that *he*, and not some other person or thing, is doing the self-authoring. That is, we need to know when the plans and preferences are genuinely subjectively defined (i.e., defined by the subject), and not by something (some drug or other agent) other than the subject. Consider Ulysses before, during, and after his interaction with the Sirens. Before and after he heard their song, Ulysses preferred to stay on course with his ship, rather than steer towards the rocks where the Sirens sung. But while they were singing, his preference was reversed. Now it is natural to say[24] that Ulysses *really* preferred staying on course rather than steering towards the rocks, and presumably that judgment rests on the idea that the person who was in thrall to the Sirens was in some way "out of his mind"—not the *real* Ulysses, and thus not capable of forming a genuinely authentic preference. But making this evaluation requires developing objective criteria for what counts as a real and satisfactorily operating person. I want to suggest that we use such criteria often, as when, for example, we discount the preferences of seriously ill people, or those whom we consider to be insane or in some way mentally defective (e.g., because they are on mind-altering drugs), or when we discount some (but certainly not all) of the preferences of very small children (who can get very confused, overtired, or over-emotional). Specifying what state a person has to be in, such that he or she can be considered capable (at that time) of generating authentic preferences, is highly difficult, and I will not attempt to elaborate such an account here. Suffice it to say that such an account is morally required if we are to understand what self-authorship is actually like, and would certainly involve specifying what we take to be at least a minimally rational person.

But once we have such an analysis, we are not done. To be self-authored, it is a necessary condition that a preference be subjectively defined, but it is not a sufficient condition. I want to propose that there are objective constraints on what can be the *content* of an authentic self-authored pref-

---

[24] For a prominent discussion, see Jon Elster, *Ulysses and the Sirens* (Cambridge: Cambridge University Press, 1979); the fact that Elster takes for granted the idea that Ulysses's desire to steer the ship toward the rocks is not a genuine desire is noted, and criticized, by Don Hubin, "On Bindings and By-products: Elster on Rationality," *Philosophy and Public Affairs*, vol. 15, no. 1 (Winter 1986), pp. 82–95.

erence. This means that not everything that a self decides to pursue or prefer can count as a preference we are prepared to attribute to that self. This is *not* to say that morality should play any significant role in defining our vocations, or avocations, or skills, or personality traits (which is one point Susan Wolf certainly wants to make).[25] But morality does place constraints on what we can legitimately choose to pursue, and different moral theorists disagree both about how strong these constraints can be and about the role political institutions should play in enforcing them.

I shall argue that it is a necessary condition of a preference's being self-authored that its content not conflict with what is required to meet that person's objective needs as a human being. The following example illustrates this point: I once knew friends of a man who appeared to author the desire to be tied and beaten during sexual relations with young men. The violence in his desire makes it repulsive to most of us, and it is certainly in conflict with common-sense understandings of legitimate human needs. But it is at least arguably authentic insofar as it was a subjective preference of this human being (who was not obviously impaired or irrational). Nonetheless, most of his friends discounted the legitimacy of this desire, and attempted to interfere with his actions to satisfy it, partly because of what they saw as the reason he had the desire. According to them, this man was periodically filled with self-loathing (in virtue of a number of cruel deeds he had committed over the years), and it was during such a bout of self-loathing that he would solicit this kind of experience which, tragically, his friends concluded, only increased his self-loathing when it was finished. So in their view, he solicited the experience as a kind of self-punishment.

In what sense did this man "want" to undergo this experience? We are rightly uneasy in straightforwardly attributing to him a desire for it in the way that we might attribute to him, say, the desire to play chess. We want to discount it, in the same way that we want to discount the desire of, say, the addict for his drug. Why? I believe this is because, as Aristotle would say, we believe that subjectively defined preferences are only authentic if their content is consistent with what we take to be the objectively defined needs of human persons *qua* human persons. To the extent that one is renouncing or repudiating the meeting of these needs (as this masochist did), one will be incapable of authoring authentic preferences. Indeed, in an interesting passage in Book IX of the *Nicomachean Ethics*, Aristotle suggests that this is true of anyone whom we criticize as bad or evil:

> And those who have done many terrible deeds and are hated for
> their wickedness even shrink from life and destroy themselves. And

[25] See again her "Moral Saints."

wicked men seek for people with whom to spend their days, and shun themselves; for they remember many a grievous deed, and anticipate others like them, when they are by themselves, but when they are with others they forget. And having nothing lovable in them they have no feeling of love to themselves. Therefore also such men do not rejoice or grieve with themselves; for their soul is rent by faction, and one element in it by reason of its wickedness grieves when it abstains from certain acts, while the other part is pleased, and one draws them this way and the other that, as if they were pulling them in pieces.[26]

If Aristotle is right, the harmful preferences of people not only toward themselves but also toward others cannot be considered authentic preferences of those selves, because they are the product of people in turmoil, who cannot author preferences satisfactorily. Because they are unable to understand or secure what it is they owe to themselves as human beings, they are unable to function effectively as human beings, and hence become impaired in their ability to develop preferences that accurately reflect who they are and what they require as persons. Or at least so I would like to argue. Actually developing such an account would involve developing Aristotelian-style criteria for what is objectively required for human flourishing—which is, to put it mildly, no easy task.

Note that to say a preference is not genuinely self-authored or "authentic" is *not* to say that one is not responsible for it. While it is "his" preference in the sense that he chose it, and thus must bear the consequences for having done so, it is not "his" preference in the sense that it is genuinely self-creating or self-expressing. This last remark assumes some kind of idealized conception not only of what a flourishing human being is like but also of what it is to be a particular, distinctive human person. Flourishing human beings will be different from one another, in their traits, activities, projects, and skills, in part because flourishing human beings are interested in and capable of defining themselves in distinctive and original ways.

The preceding remarks aim to disqualify the preferences of the wicked as self-authored. But I also believe they disqualify the preferences of people such as Terry as self-authored. Terry is certainly not what we would consider a wicked person, but like a wicked person or like the masochist in the example above, she has made choices about what to do and how to be that are personally destructive. "I love looking after my kids," Terry might insist, or "I love the domestic arts," or "I love helping out at the nursery school." But we would be suspicious of such enthusiasm for ac-

---

[26] Aristotle, *Nicomachean Ethics*, Book IX, 1166b22–24. The quote is drawn from the W. D. Ross translation in *The Basic Works of Aristotle*, ed. R. McKeon (New York: Random House, 1941).

tivities someone of her gender and class is "supposed" to like, and that suspicion would be confirmed if we found her life to have little in it that she "wants for herself." Her statements would therefore have all the hallmarks of inauthenticity. It is not so much that her preferences and activities are inauthentic because she has chosen to define herself by stepping into a (societally defined) role—after all, each of us must live life by choosing roles to some extent, e.g., when we choose our careers, or when we choose (or decline) to be married, or to have children, etc. Moreover, as I shall discuss in the next section, it is perfectly possible for a woman to make the *authentic* choice to be a housewife and mother. But in Terry's case, what primarily justifies our criticism of her choice as inauthentic is that her role, as she understands it, permits her to have very few ends other than those of her family, and thereby makes her, at virtually every turn, their servant. Although none of them wants to hurt her, they make use of her so thoroughly that she is not only unable to meet many of her objective needs as a human being, but also has very little room for engaging in self-expressing or self-defining activities outside that role.

There is something else that troubles us about Terry's choice. Many women make that choice in contemporary American society; whether or not these women work outside the home, they conceive of themselves as being responsible for most (and sometimes all) of the care-giving in the family (and those who work sometimes suffer enormous guilt to the extent that their jobs preclude them from doing what they are convinced they ought to do). These women's choice of this role therefore seems to be, in part, a social phenomenon, one that they have made in order to avoid the disapproval of their friends, or family, or church, or colleagues, who expect them to make it. So even if Terry had redefined her role in the home so that her objective needs could be met, we would still reject the idea that the choice was authentic if we perceived it to be a choice she made in order to avoid such social disapproval.

Consider, in this regard, a male example of an inauthentic choice resulting from social pressure: in the spring of 1991, American newspapers recounted the story of an investment banker who, as a teenager, wanted to be a clown. His parents strongly discouraged it, regarding it as inappropriate for someone of his background and abilities, so he went to MIT and got a job working in Silicon Valley in computers. Still he was dissatisfied and decided things might go better if he had an MBA. With this degree he got a job on Wall Street making a lot of money in a high-powered investment bank. But one day, he claimed, he woke up realizing that if he kept working on Wall Street, he would end up close to death never having gone to clown school. So he quit his job, and did exactly that. This is a nice story of someone who struggled to author himself, while under pressure to be what people in his social group expected of him. Like Terry, he faced pressure to submit to a social role, to take on preferences,

interests, and projects that he did not really want. He experienced understandable relief when he reclaimed himself.

These examples illustrate how people can choose *not* to author themselves. Self-authorship involves more than an autonomous choice: it involves a decision to develop the traits, interests, and projects that are not
only consistent with meeting your objective human needs but that are
also ones *you* want, and not ones that others prefer that you want (and
perhaps try to persuade you to want). When Terry and the MBA gave up
the chance to author themselves early in their lives, they "sold out" to certain societal groups that believed they had the authority to determine
who and what these individuals should become. Such "selling out" has
been a common subject of story and legend in many cultures. Consider,
for example, Stravinsky's *L'histoire du Soldat*, a work based on the story
of a soldier who sells his violin, representing his soul, to the devil for
money. Only when he reclaims that violin and gives away all his
money—repudiating all that led him away from who he really was—does
he reclaim his soul. It is perhaps hard for the MBA or for women such as
Terry to see that they too have sold out by accepting the particular social
role our society has created for them. And this may be particularly hard
in Terry's case: how can embracing such a caring, beneficent role be a
devilish act, or be considered "selling out"? Yet is it so much better to give
up the ability to define your own life in order to avoid sanctions from social groups you fear, than to give it up in order to secure money or
power? And is it any easier for Terry or the MBA to reclaim themselves
than it was for the soldier? Not only must they reconsider and redefine
their goals and projects, but they must also reconsider and redefine their
conception of who has the authority to determine or even criticize what
they would pursue in life.[27]

These last remarks suggest that, like the MBA and the soldier, women
such as Terry bear responsibility for succumbing to the temptations of
embracing a self-denying social role. Many feminists may question how
fair this is, given the societal assault on people such as Terry, and the
high cost such women must pay if they do not succumb. The extent to
which women must take responsibility for "selling out" is an issue discussed in novels, such as those by George Eliot and Jane Austen (think
of Austen's Anne in *Persuasion* in contrast to Charlotte in *Pride and Prej-
udice*, or think of Maggie Tulliver in Eliot's *Mill on the Floss*). And the most
striking discussion of this point by a philosopher is by Kierkegaard.[28] In
The Sickness Unto Death Kierkegaard argues that sin is a kind of despair,
generated by the failure to be who we are, and he distinguishes mascu-

---

[27] I am indebted to David Schmidtz for this last point.
[28] Catherine Keller discusses Kierkegaard's views in this context in her *From a Broken
Web: Separation, Sexism, and Self* (Boston: Beacon Press, 1989), p. 12.

line and feminine forms of sin. Whereas the masculine form is a kind of defiance—a failure to accept the limits of selfhood, the feminine form, he says, is a kind of *weakness*, a loss of self, which he links to the woman's service to others.[29] Such devotion he takes to be a kind of sinful self-abnegation: "the woman in proper womanly fashion throws herself, throws her self, into whatever she abandons herself to. If you take that away, then her self vanishes too, and her despair is: not wanting to be herself."[30]

To call this loss of self "sinful" is to suggest that the woman—a woman like Terry—is responsible for it, no matter how much she tries to excuse herself by appeal to "social pressure." But it is surely reasonable to wonder how far she, or indeed the MBA, can be blamed for making choices which her parents, teachers, and community members may be prepared to enforce with severe social sanctions (involving not only ridicule but also ostracism). Although I will not be able to pursue this point further, the possibility of self-authorship would seem to be as much the responsibility of society as it is of the individual; it would seem that society must not only be prepared to respect a variety of nonstandard choices, but must also provide what each person needs (e.g., educational opportunities, health care, etc.) in order that she be able to engage in self-authorship.

V. Altruism

Let us return to the issue of altruism. I have argued that service to others is only morally acceptable when it arises from an authentically defined preference, interest, or project undertaken by one who pursues her legitimate needs as a human being, and who accepts a Kantian conception of human value. So one who lives up to these requirements not only accepts severe constraints on what she can do to others, but also on what she can do to herself. Such a person can certainly have authentically defined preferences leading her to serve others, but she will refrain from such service when it will lead her to become (to use a Hobbesian term) "prey" for those whom she serves.

But can't there be people who authentically choose to help others at some cost to themselves, and whom we are right to praise for their unusual generosity and fellow-feeling? For example, can't there be women who really want to stay home to care for their children, even while knowing that this will set back their career for years and mean a substantial loss of income, and whose choice we ought to value? Aren't there people (such as Mother Theresa) who are genuinely devoted to the poor at considerable cost to their own comfort, and who seem to be exceptionally

---

[29] See Soren Kierkegaard, *Sickness Unto Death*, pp. 80–81n.
[30] *Ibid.*, p. 81n.

fine people? Haven't major religions continually celebrated the martyrdom of saints and heroes who die for the benefit of others and their
cause? Does my argument require that we cease our commendation of
such people, and even criticize them for their self-sacrifice?

It does not, as long as that sacrifice is authentic and done out of love,
as I shall now explain.

I have a friend whom I consider to have made an authentic choice to
be a housewife and mother and who lives a life very different from that
of Terry. She stayed home to care for her children because she adored
them, and she genuinely liked the control over her own time that the life
of a housewife gave her. Moreover, she has been quite capable of limiting her care to her family over the years whenever she thought they were
demanding too much, by using a kind of prickly sarcasm they have been
loath to experience. Her life has always included all sorts of projects and
plans (e.g., involvement in art organizations and women's organizations;
self-study projects that have made her an expert in the flora and fauna of
her region) that she greatly enjoys and that have helped to make her a
fascinating individual to know. So she is a richly developed person, and
her care of others is a natural result of what she has chosen to love in her
life.

Nonetheless, I do not believe she deserves any special commendation
for crafting this kind of care-giving life; those whose life-choices do not
include caring for children, or the aged, or the infirm are not thereby less
impressive. We value genuine, richly developed persons, and that development can take all sorts of forms, only some of which involve extensive
care-giving. Susan Wolf assumes that when we value those people who
are not care-givers, our valuing must be nonmoral. But this is importantly
wrong: we morally value *all* people with authentic lives, whether or not
they are care-givers, when we appreciate that each has had the strength
to respond morally to herself, and thus has resisted pressure to make her
life into something that is not authentic. It is abusive to demand of everyone (and in particular all females) that they lead a life with considerable
service to others—and just as abusive to demand that no one, and in particular no female, should lead a life with *any* considerable service to others: such demands fail to recognize the diversity of talents and pleasures
that make more or less care-giving lives appropriate for different people.
Those who yield to such demands can become disabled from developing
an honest and authentic life.

Indeed, such demands may actually reflect the self-serving interests of
the community. There is a doctor I know whose service to his community
has been extraordinary: as a young man he became interested in drug ad-
diction, and finally founded a free clinic in Northern California to treat ad-
dicts and provide medical service to the poor. What is striking about this
doctor is that he will tell you that he has always *enjoyed* dealing with ad-
diction problems, and has been very happy in his medical career. Thus,

his service has always been authentically and happily given. Clearly he deserves our deep appreciation. But does he really deserve more praise than a doctor whose authentic choices are such that he intensely dislikes dealing with such problems, runs a medical practice that gives a decent share of free service to the poor but primarily serves the medical needs of the middle class, and who vastly prefers rock-climbing to volunteering in Oakland drug clinics? Doesn't our community betray its *own* selfishness if it calls the first doctor "better" than the second, insofar as the services of the first are rarer and thus instrumentally more valuable to the community than those of the second? Many of our commendations of what look to be altruistic behavior may be more self-serving than we realize.

But what about people who devote their entire lives to serving the poor, or parents who risk their lives to save their children: don't these extraordinary acts of altruism spring from authentic preferences, and yet don't they involve great harm to self? Shouldn't we commend them as highly moral and hold up those who perform them for emulation, or at least consider the acts supererogatory and hence morally fine even if not morally required?

I am inclined to argue *against* doing either. Such behavior is morally commendable and *only morally permissible* when it is done authentically, out of a love that unifies the one who serves with the one who is being served. The love about which I am talking is not a feeling (although a feeling may often accompany it), but a point of view, a way of conceiving of oneself in connection to others, and it comes in more than one form. Those who experience such love are so unified with those whom their acts are attempting to benefit that what they regard as good for themselves is what will be good for those with whom they are unified.

From a moral point of view, the most important form of this love is that which connects us to our fellow human beings by virtue of our common humanity, such that we will naturally recoil at others' suffering and desire (authentically) to stop it. It may be that 'love' is not a particularly good word to use to describe this point of view (although it is commonly used for this purpose in Christian literature).[31] More particular and frequently more powerful forms of love are experienced by parents for their children, and by friends and spouses for each other; in these relationships there is an intimate connection between the parties—to the point where the pleasures of each are advanced when the other's needs and desires are satisfied. Contrast this kind of loving care to the self-sacrificing service of a reluctant benefactor who performs his caring deeds only because he believes it is his "duty" to do so: when we know that our benefactor believes he has brought (uncompensated) damage upon himself by serving us, not only do we take no joy in that service, but we may also feel

---

[31] Christian theology uses the Greek word *agape* to denote this form of love.

guilty and undeserving of help purchased at this cost, and we may be angry at how little our own good is a good for the reluctant benefactor, and thus regard his help with resentment. (There is nothing that kills the pleasure from a gift quite so much as the gift-giver's intimations that he has suffered a great deal too much in order to give it to you.) This sort of selfish and dishonest altruism deserves no commendation.[32]

However, those who feel *no* love for others, and thus (quite authentically) refuse to help them, are not thereby exempted from moral criticism. There are situations when moral criticism of them is appropriate, not because they did not help (their refusal is, after all, honest and authentic), but because they did not have the love — by which I mean the perception of connection with others, and not a mere feeling — from which such help would inevitably spring. (The appropriateness of such a connection is something that Amy can teach Jake.)[33] On my view, when we commend real altruists, we celebrate not only the authenticity of their choices, but also the point of view they have (authentically) adopted that has resulted in them wanting to make such choices. We commend their deeds *not* because these deeds are extraordinary acts of self-sacrifice; they *aren't* — real altruists do not understand their actions in this way. As Neera Kapur Badhwar makes clear in her essay "Altruism Versus Self-Interest,"[34] most of the rescuers of the Jews in Europe during World War II told interviewers that it was "easy" to decide to help the Jews, because they felt a deep sense of union with them as fellow human beings. Hence, they refused to understand their deeds as self-sacrifices or acts of martyrdom. When we commend the acts of such altruists, we are actually commending *these people*, and the point of view they took toward their fellow human beings.

Does morality require that all of us take a loving point of view toward all of our fellows? This is a theoretically difficult question, for it is surely right that *some* fellow-feeling is morally required of all of us (which is the point Christianity tries to make), and yet the strength of the love the rescuers had for those whom they saved is extraordinary and unusual. To expect such love from everyone would seem to be unrealistic given the diversity of human personalities, and to socially pressure people to try to develop such love would likely result only in dishonest approximations of the real thing. Nonetheless, we are prepared to criticize severely those

[32] But there may be times when a person serves reluctantly because he has a conflict between his love for others and his own self-regarding interests. I discuss such conflicts in the next section.

[33] So my position is not so anti-Kantian as it might initially appear. Like Kant, I agree that morality requires service to others, despite one's self-regarding interests. But I see that service as commendable only if it is connected in a certain way not only to that person's will but also to his conception of himself.

[34] See Neera Kapur Badhwar, "Altruism Versus Self-Interest: Sometimes a False Dichotomy," in this volume. I am indebted to Badhwar for helping me to develop many of the ideas in this paragraph.

who aided the Nazis for their appalling lack of fellow-feeling. Moreover, there are certain situations where we do think that morality demands that people develop *particular* forms of love. For example, a parent who risks his life to enter a burning building to save his children strikes us as animated by an appropriate love binding him to his children, whereas a parent who refuses to do so insofar as he takes himself to be removed from, and more important than, his children strikes us as (deeply) criticizable.

It is impossible in this essay to explore when and how each of us is morally required to make various loving commitments to others (or when those commitments surpass such requirements), although our response to the examples of the rescuers and the parents risking their lives for their children illustrates that we believe such requirements exist,[35] constraining the territory over which morally acceptable authentic choices can be made. As I noted before, commendable authentic choices always operate subject to moral constraints. If Aristotle is right, we should not regard these constraints as unwelcome limits on what we can choose, but rather as directives which, when followed, will make our own lives better.

However, even love is not sufficient *by itself* to make such service worthy of our commendation. To be commendable, one's service to others must be performed in a way that fully recognizes one's own worth and distinctiveness. Terry may have thought that her self-sacrificing service to her children arose from her love for them, but since she was unable to bring a sense of herself and her own importance to her union with her family, she not only inflicted harm on herself but also on them. Commendable, effective love does not mean losing oneself in a union with others; instead, it presupposes that all parties to the union have a self, which they understand to be important, and which they share with one another.

It may even be that *real* love—and the sort of love that deserves moral commendation—only exists if this sense of self accompanies it. Consider, in this regard, the following Victorian poem about mothers—of the sort Terry is:

> There was a young man loved a maid
> Who taunted him, "Are you afraid,"
> She asked, "to bring me today
> Your mother's head upon a tray?"

---

[35] I cannot pursue here the difficult question of when (and in what way) human beings should establish connections of love with others. It cannot be morally required that we become friends with everyone, or that everyone become some kind of parent, although the kind of universal connection with fellow human beings experienced by the rescuers does seem to be morally required of us all. I have argued elsewhere that answering this question will involve, among other things, considering issues of justice (to oneself and others); see my "Feminist Contractarianism."

He went and slew his mother dead,
Tore from her breast her heart so red,
Then towards his lady love he raced,
But tripped and fell in all his haste.

As the heart rolled on the ground
It gave forth a plaintive sound.
And it spoke, in accents mild:
"Did you hurt yourself, my child?"[36]

To love another deeply should not mean to lose all sense of oneself in another's personhood and to be unable to make any independent claims of
one's own. Self-sacrifice cannot be commendable if it springs from self-
abnegation. That Kierkegaard calls it a sin is rightly suggestive of the way
it is immoral, a way of being deeply disrespectful to oneself. If we are so
"altruistic" that we become unable to develop and express our selves
properly, we become unable to give to others what they may want more
than anything else.

Real care for others looks and feels much different from any socially encouraged, self-damaging imitation. We see the real thing in a story of a
mother and her family who waited in a shelter in Texas while a tornado
destroyed their home: as they waited, the mother sat and worked on a
quilt, recalling later, "I made my quilt to keep my family warm. I made
it beautiful so my heart would not break."[37] This mother's care for her
family that day came from enormous strength and self-confidence, as she
looked disaster in the eye and insisted that her family believe, despite the
destruction, that something good would prevail. She used her talents and
gifts as an individual to create a sign of that good. The service of such a
mother is neither reluctant, nor soul-destroying, and may be extraordi-
narily important to those who receive it.

Real care may also come from human beings who do not in any way
appear to be altruistic, saintly, or "good." A minister I know once told a
story about a man named Doc that makes this point:[38]

> Where I spent a good deal of my childhood in a small New England
> town, the meanest man in town owned the garage and fixed every-
> thing mechanical that went wrong. He was a foul mouthed, hostile
> fellow who had been brought up as a state boy. After going through

---

[36] Quoted by Sara Ruddick, "Maternal Thinking" in *Women and Values: Readings in Recent Feminist Philosophy*, ed. Marilyn Pearsall (Belmont, CA: Wadsworth, 1986), p. 340; from J. Echergaray, "Severed Heart," quoted by Jessie Bernard in *The Future of Motherhood* (New York: Dial, 1974), p. 4.

[37] Quoted by Sara Ruddick, "Maternal Thinking," p. 344; original story told to Ruddick by Miriam Schapiro.

[38] This story was told during a sermon by the Rev. John Snow, delivered at the Harvard University Chapel, in 1978. I am quoting from the text of that sermon.

numerous foster homes he had ended up as the foster child of the town's auto mechanic. He and his foster father got along badly, but he turned out to be an automotive Einstein, a total genius with any kind of machinery, and he learned everything in *this* line that his foster father had to teach him. When he got to be eighteen he was convicted of armed robbery and sent to prison for five years. By the time he got out, his foster father had died, but the foster father had left him the garage. The mythology of the town was that he had returned to arrange for its sale, but that he had decided suddenly and impulsively to stay and run the garage when he discovered that the townspeople greeted him warmly and even solicitously. And he had stayed, and he had run the garage. From the early 1930's to the middle 1950's you knew that if you lived in that town and ran out of gas late at night you could call Doc and he would arrive half drunk in his wrecker mumbling obscenities about anyone that idiotic, but Doc would arrive with a can of gas, or if your car had broken down, with the needed tow.

People, especially kids, were a little scared of Doc, but the farmers knew that if their equipment broke down during mowing or if they got into any kind of mechanical jam, Doc would stay up all night fixing what needed to be fixed. People were willing to put up with Doc's awful temper and acid remarks because he was utterly trustworthy.

As Doc grew older, his rages resolved into mischievous wit which, though not often kind, was always funny. The boys and young men of the town went back to hanging around the garage and many of them absorbed the mechanical skills which Doc possessed in such abundance. They also learned something about trustworthiness and dedication to service they might not have learned otherwise. Eventually Doc married, and he and his wife had two children. He even took to going to church occasionally.

This is hardly the portrait of an Aristotelian man of practical wisdom. But it *is* a portrait of a real altruist, someone who cared deeply about people in his community and who served them hard, long, and well—in large part out of gratitude for their acceptance of and faith in him. In no way do we see his caring as self-destructive, but indeed as quite the opposite—a way of coming to terms with himself, his anger, his frustrations, and his losses as a child. This is certainly not a man who serves others in order to fulfill some kind of social role. His caring is the real thing.

VI. Authenticity and Conflict

There is a contemporary song by Tracy Chapman, which recounts the story of a young woman who faces a choice between living an authentic life of her choosing but abandoning her alcoholic father whom she loves, or serving the father but thereby accepting a life of poverty, drabness, and frustration. What ought she to do? If her love for her father is authentic and deep, she may choose to stay with him, and in those circumstances, that action would be self-authored. Indeed, to do anything else might mean she would be full of regret the rest of her life. Yet this decision will allow her few of the resources necessary to develop skills, talents, projects, and traits of character that are the mark of a well-developed self. Hers is a nasty choice, and in many respects, a deeply unfair one. Compare it to the choice of the character that Jimmy Stewart plays in the movie "It's a Wonderful Life," who has an authentic desire to help the poor of his town, but satisfying this desire requires such self-denial on his part that he comes close to suicide later in his life.

Note that both desires here are authentic—so authenticity alone does not help us to resolve how we ought to act in life in order to be respectful not only to others but to ourselves. The problem is that each of us has a *set* of authentic desires, and the other-regarding ones can require that we do things that preclude the self-regarding ones. So how do we choose? Conventional wisdom celebrates the other-regarding choice in these sorts of situations (although it may not always require it). But why should "being moral" always involve choosing in favor of others—why can't it sometimes involve choosing in favor of oneself?[39]

In situations where self-development and service to others conflict, we have the familiar problem of balancing moral claims. Normally that problem is perceived as involving the conflicting moral claims of people other than yourself, all of whom have some call on you. In a conflict between your needs and others' needs, service to others has normally been considered the moral choice—either morally required, if you think as Amy does, or else merely recommended (but not required) if you think as Jake does. But I want to argue that in these situations, choosing in favor of yourself can be a morally permissible choice, and perhaps in some circumstances the morally required choice.[40]

Hence, I do not agree that all community-benefiting, other-regarding

---

[39] Life is filled with such unfairness, but we ought to blame our social systems for some of that unfairness if we live in a society that persistently puts people of a certain class, or gender, or race, or caste in the position of having to choose between caring for those whom they love and developing themselves as persons. Granted, it is hopelessly utopian to strive for a world in which individuals never have to compromise their own development in order to care for others whom they authentically love. But surely it is reasonable at least to strive for a world in which society is not persistently doing things that encourage such dilemmas for only some of its members.

[40] Might this be a way to explain why many people regard as morally permissible Gauguin's choice to leave his family and go to Tahiti to develop as an artist? It strikes me as preferable to Bernard Williams's explanation that we commend the choice only because Gauguin prospered as an artist in Tahiti, and thus was "morally lucky." See Williams's discussion of this example in his "Moral Luck," in *Moral Luck* (Cambridge: Cambridge University Press, 1981).

actions are morally required, and I believe that the advocates of the concept of supererogation are right to maintain that we are sometimes morally permitted not to choose an altruistic, self-sacrificing act, but to act, instead, to benefit ourselves. However, this is true, on my view, (only) in situations where either choice is morally acceptable—that is, (only) in situations where duty to others and duty to self are opposed and we are morally permitted to choose either one. Moreover, I have also argued that in some situations in which duty to others and duty to self are opposed, the self-regarding choice is actually the morally superior and obligatory choice. To be "impartial" from a moral point of view does not always mean excluding oneself and one's own needs from moral deliberation. To treat all people equally does not mean giving everyone but oneself equal concern. Moral people do not put themselves to one side; they include themselves in the calculation and give themselves weight in the determination of the right action to take.

How much weight? To know the answer to that question is to have a moral theory that correctly adjudicates conflicting moral claims not only between others but also between oneself and others. I have no such theory (nor does any other philosopher!).[41] But surely Jake is wrong to think that we can answer the question with some kind of easy formula; how that balance should be struck depends upon many things, including the circumstances and context of our lives (so, for example, that balance should rightly be struck one way if one is a student fighting to get a degree, and another way if one is the parent of a newborn infant). And it is just as easy for many of us to overestimate the weight our interests should get, as it is to underestimate it. If, after all I have said in the name of self-authorship, it still seems unsettlingly wrong to spend $200 per person at a fancy New York restaurant in the name of individual self-expression when so many people in our society and around the world are unable to meet their most minimal human needs, then maybe that's because it really is wrong to do such a thing. I am arguing that we should

---

[41] This is partly because contemporary moral philosophy has been fixated on other-regarding moral duties, to the serious neglect of self-regarding ones. What explains this fixation? A Marxist explanation (which was suggested to me by Christine Korsgaard) is that the call for equal rights by those who have been in lower class, "servant" groups (e.g., women and African Americans) has alarmed the rest of society sufficiently that they have encouraged servile conceptions of morality that would, if accepted by these people, keep them in their servile roles—and such conceptions have (wittingly or unwittingly) been accepted by moral philosophers (who have traditionally come from more powerful, nonservile social groups). An alternative explanation (which is potentially consistent with the first) is that moral philosophy, up until very recently, has been done almost exclusively by males, who commonly hold a Jake-like understanding of morality, and who are attracted to an other-regarding conception of morality as they become aware that their highly self-regarding conception of their connection to other people needs correction (not realizing that many people might need a very different kind of correction). Moreover, recent feminist celebrations of women's propensity to care have certainly encouraged this tendency to think of morality as almost exclusively other-regarding.

not allow ourselves to be pressured — by society, by our religion, or by some philosopher's conception of our "moral duties" — to become the servant of others; but I do not want to deny that many of us who are privileged err in the other direction, and serve ourselves too much and others too little.[42] The art of living well is to know how to balance competing moral obligations — some of which are to yourself.

Philosophy, University of Arizona

[42] Thus, I do not mean to be hostile to the currently popular celebration by feminists of women's persistent interest in caring. I only wish to put caring in its proper moral place. There are a number of women that have sounded similar themes recently; e.g., Susan Moller Okin, *Justice, Gender, and the Family* (New York: Basic Books, 1989); and Marilyn Friedman, "Beyond Caring: The Demoralization of Gender," in *Science, Morality, and Feminism*, ed. Marsha Hanen and Kai Nielsen (Calgary: University of Calgary Press, 1987). See also my "Feminist Contractarianism."

ABORTION, ABANDONMENT, AND POSITIVE RIGHTS: THE LIMITS OF COMPULSORY ALTRUISM*

By Roderick T. Long

I. INTRODUCTION

Let us imagine that we accept the following three propositions:

(1) Every person has the right not to be treated as a mere means to the ends of others.[1]

(2) A woman who voluntarily becomes pregnant but later changes her mind has the right to abort her unborn child.

(3) A woman who voluntarily bears a child but later changes her mind does *not* have the right simply to abandon her child, but must care for it until she can arrange for a substitute caretaker.

This is particularly easy for me to imagine, since I do in fact accept them. Not everyone will be so inclined, for the propositions are hardly uncontroversial. Nevertheless, since many people do accept them, it is worthwhile finding out whether they are compatible; for there are good prima facie reasons for believing that there is, if not a logical inconsistency, then at least a serious tension among these three propositions—a tension that might well make us doubt the possibility of a plausible moral perspective that could accommodate all three. Defenders of the three propositions thus have an interest in showing that they are compatible; and opponents of (some or all of) the propositions might well have an interest in showing that they are incompatible.

My first aim in this essay, then, is to explain why the three propositions might seem to be incompatible, and to argue that there is nevertheless a plausible moral view which reconciles them.[2] My second and broader

* An earlier version of this paper was presented to the Research Triangle Ethics Circle (Chapel Hill, North Carolina), whose participants provided useful and stimulating discussion. I am also grateful to David Schmidtz and Ellen Frankel Paul for helpful written comments.

[1] I take (1) to make a narrower claim than (1*): "Every person has the right to be treated as an end in him or herself." Proposition (1*) seems to require taking positive action on behalf of the rights-holder, in a way that (1) does not.

[2] Am I arguing for the *truth* of these three propositions, or merely for their *compatibility*? Somewhere in between, actually. I shall not argue for the truth of (1), but I take it to be a plausible moral principle; and I shall argue that that principle, together with what I take to be plausible moral assumptions, yields (2) and (3) as consequences.

aim is to take some preliminary steps toward answering the question: *Under what circumstances is it legitimate to force someone to act on behalf of the welfare of others?* In other words, my second aim is to sketch a theory of positive rights, and so to determine the limits of compulsory altruism. These two aims are connected: the first aim depends on the second because my solution to the apparent incompatibility of the three propositions depends on my views about positive rights; and conversely, my second aim depends on the first because I regard it as a desirable constraint on any theory of positive rights that it give (what I regard as) the "right answer" to the questions raised by the three propositions. Moreover, in treating the issues of abortion and abandonment I hope to give some content to my theory of positive rights by showing how it handles important moral dilemmas. The question "How much may we ask a woman to do for her unborn or newborn child?" is a special case of the broader question "How much, in general, may we ask one person to do for another?" An attempt to answer the general question should help to illuminate the specific one, and vice versa; and our responses to these two questions must be brought into harmony with one another if we are to have any confidence in either. Hence the dual focus of this essay.

II. Rights: Some Preliminaries

The three propositions under consideration employ the language of rights. We ought to get clear, then, about what we are saying when we ascribe (or deny) rights to people. I take it that having a right typically involves one or more of the following components:

(A) The moral value, or at least the moral permissibility, of one's doing/having that to which one has a right.

(B) The obligation of others to let/help one do/have that to which one has a right.

(C) The legitimacy of forcing others to let/help one do/have that to which one has a right.

From these three components it is possible to construct seven distinct varieties of rights: A-rights, B-rights, C-rights, AB-rights, AC-rights, BC-rights, and ABC-rights.[3]

---

[3] Discussions of rights sometimes founder on a failure to distinguish these varieties from one another. When Marthe's mother claims a right to Marthe's gratitude, she is presumably claiming an AB-right but not a C-right; Marthe ought to be grateful to her mother, but it would be illegitimate to enforce such gratitude at gunpoint. On the other hand, when Hector's friends tell him that he has no right to complain about the restaurant since he's the one who insisted they come there, they are denying him an A-right, but as First Amendment devotees they would no doubt grant Hector's BC-right to complain. Yet again, when Hobbes

Of which sort are the rights at issue in our three propositions? I think
they are best understood as *political* rights, in the broad sense of being
those rights that a just political system would respect and enforce.[4] And
if such rights are to be supported by legal sanctions, they will have to include component C. Furthermore, it would be difficult to characterize as
just a political regime whose prescriptions and proscriptions one generally had no moral reason (apart from fear of punishment) to accept; so we
may also assume that political rights (usually or always) include component B. I shall therefore take the rights at issue to be BC-rights,[5] and by
"right" without prefix I shall henceforth mean "BC-right."

My having a right (i.e., a political or BC-right), then, involves two components: the obligation of others to treat me in a certain manner, and the
legitimacy (moral permissibility) of forcing them to treat me in that manner. Let us call an obligation *enforceable* just in case it would be legitimate
to force the bearer of the obligation to act in accordance with it.[6] We may
thus define the (relevant) notion of a *right* as follows:

(4) S has a right against O to be treated in manner M if and only if
O has an enforceable obligation to treat S in manner M.

(5) S has a right (*simpliciter*) to be treated in manner M if and only if,
for every O, S has a right against O to be treated in manner M.

So defined, a right is a right to be *treated* in a certain way; the object of
the right is a certain sort of behavior on the part of other people.

---

argues (*Leviathan*, part I, ch. 14) that in the state of nature everyone has an equal right to
everything, he is asserting an AC-right, not a B-right. And so on. (In particular, discussions
of abortion often fail to make clear whether it is A-rights or BC-rights that are at issue.) Traditional distinctions between perfect and imperfect rights, or between liberty-rights and
claim-rights, capture some of the relevant distinctions, but not, I think, all of them.

[4] That is, a just political system would refrain from violating these rights itself, and also
protect its citizens from having these rights violated by others. In calling these rights "political rights," I do not mean to suggest that their existence depends on or is an artifact of
political institutions or conventions. I mean only that these are the sorts of rights with which
a legal system might properly be concerned, whereas the right to gratitude, say, is not.

[5] That is, political rights are *at least* BC-rights. A different issue is whether all BC-rights
are also ABC-rights. On a liberal conception of politics, the answer will be no, since legal
protection for some morally impermissible actions has a basis in one of the central tenets
of liberalism, that political institutions should be neutral (at least in a broad range of cases)
among their citizens' competing conceptions of the good. (It does not follow that this liberal neutrality may not itself be founded on a particular conception of the good.) But the liberal doctrine of institutional neutrality is often challenged; for example, a popular slogan
among supporters of Pat Robertson's 1988 presidential campaign was: "People should only
have a right to do what is right." For the purposes of this essay I shall leave it an open question whether BC-rights must also be ABC-rights—though proposition (1) does seem to favor a reply in the negative.

[6] I here ignore a possible complication, which is that it may be legitimate for some people, but not for others, to enforce the obligation in question. (In particular, the person to
whom the obligation is owed might conceivably have different rights of enforcement from
those enjoyed by third parties.)

Now we surely do sometimes think of rights as having quite different objects; sometimes the object of the right is a potential action of its bearer (I have the right *to vote*, or *to speak freely*), and sometimes the object is a thing (I have the right *to food*, or *to the money I earn*). But these rights may all be understood in terms of the right to certain sorts of treatment; the right to take certain actions is the right to be allowed, or helped, to perform those actions; and the right to a thing is the right to be given, or not to be prevented from obtaining, that thing. Hence every right must specify what (enforceable) obligations it entails for others.[7]

The rights claimed in propositions (1) and (2), and denied in proposition (3), are thus not grants of moral permission. Rather, they are rights that assign other people enforceable obligations to treat the bearers of such rights in certain specified ways.

Moreover, the rights of one person entail the absence of certain rights in other people. Suppose I have the right to be treated in manner M. That means that other people have an enforceable obligation to treat me in manner M. So it would be legitimate (morally permissible) to force everybody to treat me in manner M. So there is no obligation (and *a fortiori* no enforceable obligation) *not* to force everybody to treat me in manner M. And so nobody has a *right* not to treat me in manner M. If other people did have such a right, then I would have no right against them to be treated in manner M. Claims ascribing rights to one person automatically yield claims denying other rights to everybody else.[8]

Rights (i.e., BC-rights) are commonly divided into positive and negative rights. One natural way of drawing the distinction might look like this: A positive right is one whose correlative obligation is the obligation to take some positive action on behalf of the right's bearer; a negative right, on the other hand, is one whose correlative obligation is merely the obligation to refrain from interfering in some way with the right's bearer. Rights are positive or negative insofar as they involve positive or negative obligations on the part of others, where the objects of positive and negative obligations are *doings* and *allowings*, respectively.[9]

(6) S's right to be treated in manner M is a positive right if and only if manner M involves taking positive action on S's behalf.

---

[7] The lack of such specification can lead to seriously ambiguous rights-claims. For example, is the right to life the right not to be killed? Or the right to be provided with the necessary means of survival? Or the right to be brought into existence? Is the right to work the right to guaranteed employment, or merely the right not to be interfered with in seeking a job? And interfered with how? And so on.

[8] I am treating rights as all-things-considered rights rather that as prima facie rights. It follows that, on this understanding, conflicts of rights (that is, of BC-rights) can never occur. It may well be that this would justify placing some qualification or exception clause on (1).

[9] For the purposes of this essay I shall assume without argument that a principled distinction can be drawn between doing and allowing (e.g., between killing and letting die).

(7) S's right to be treated in manner M is a negative right if and only if manner M does not involve taking positive action on S's behalf.

Nevertheless, I suspect that (6) and (7) do not succeed in capturing our intuitions about positive and negative rights.[10] Suppose I claim that I have a right to cut off your arm—by which I mean that you have an enforceable obligation to let me cut off your arm. By definitions (6) and (7), the right I am claiming is a negative right, not a positive right. But this seems strange: surely the point of the distinction is that positive rights go beyond the mere right to be left alone in one's personal space, as it were. Negative rights build fences around people; positive rights break down fences. When I claim the right to cut off your arm, the right I am claiming is more plausibly thought of as a positive, fence-breaking right, rather than a negative, fence-building one. I suggest, then, that definitions (6) and (7) be replaced by (8) and (9), which do a better job of capturing the intuitions behind the positive/negative distinction:

(8) S's right to be treated in manner M is a positive right if and only if (a) manner M involves taking positive action on S's behalf, or (b) manner M involves letting oneself be used by S.

(9) S's right to be treated in manner M is a negative right if and only if (a) manner M does not involve taking positive action on S's behalf, and (b) manner M does not involve letting oneself be used by S.

Note that (8) is a disjunction, while (9) is a conjunction. With these preliminaries out of the way, let us turn to the heart of our problem.

III. The Problem

Proposition (1) says that we never have a right to treat people as mere means to the ends of others. And this in turn seems to entail that nobody ever has an enforceable obligation to let himself or herself be treated as a mere means to the ends of others. But if that is true, it is hard to see how anyone could ever have any positive rights. For if I have a positive right against you, then you have an *enforceable* obligation (not merely to refrain from interfering with my activities but) either to let yourself be used by me or to take some positive action on my behalf; and it follows that it would be legitimate for me (or a third party) to *forcibly* use you, or to *force* you to take such action on my behalf. But in so reducing you to an object, or to involuntary servitude, it seems that I am treating you as a mere means to my ends—and that, proposition (1) tells us, can never be legitimate. Hence proposition (1), we may well infer, is inconsistent

[10] I will be appealing to intuitions a lot. My epistemologist says that's okay.

with the existence of positive rights.[11] And if there are no positive rights, then (1) yields the following negative right: the right not to be forcibly used, or to be forced to take positive action to promote the welfare of others.

Now proposition (1), understood as denying the possibility of positive rights, sits rather oddly with propositions (2) and (3). For proposition (2) endorses the right to abortion, while proposition (3) denies the right of abandonment. The problem is that abortion — causing the death of the unborn child — seems like a case of *doing* or *killing*, whereas merely abandoning the child after it has been born seems like a case of *allowing* or *letting die*. If it is a violation of a person's rights to treat him or her as a mere means to one's own ends, then surely it is a violation of an unborn child's rights to abort it; for in aborting her child, is not the mother treating it as a mere means to her own ends? And on the other hand, if it is a violation of a person's rights to force him or her to take positive action to promote the welfare of others, is it not a violation of the mother's rights — indeed, a form of involuntary servitude — to require her to care for her child once it is born?

Proposition (1), in short, appears to require the rejection of both (2) and (3). Proposition (1) yields a negative right not to be killed (and so not to be aborted), thus contradicting (2); and (1) also denies any positive right to be cared for (and so not to be abandoned), thus contradicting (3). That is, proposition (1) seems to give exactly the opposite answers on the abortion and abandonment questions from those expressed in (2) and (3). Our three propositions have apparently turned out to be incompatible, and with a vengeance!

IV. Basic Versus Derivative Positive Rights

I think this conclusion is too quick. To see why it is too quick, we need to take a closer look at the argument from (1) to the denial of positive rights. That argument claimed that *since* X has an enforceable obligation not to treat Y as a mere means[12] — not to violate Y's negative right to freedom from servitude — X can have no positive rights against Y. But

---

[11] The suggested claim is not that people never have positive obligations to act on behalf of others, or to let themselves be used by others; the claim is rather that such obligations, if they exist, are not legitimately *enforceable*. On this view, there may be positive B-rights, but no positive BC-rights. Positive rights are sometimes rejected, not because they violate (1), but because they are allegedly nonuniversalizable; but Andrew Melnyk, "Is There A Formal Argument Against Positive Rights?" *Philosophical Studies*, vol. 55 (1989), pp. 205–9, has argued persuasively against that view.

[12] By "means" I shall henceforth mean "means to the ends of others." I leave open the question of whether it is possible to treat someone as a means to his *own* ends without his consent. If so, then (1) appears to permit paternalism; if not, then it doesn't. I should think that the intuition behind (1) at least creates a serious presumption against paternalism, but I shall not argue for that claim here.

what if it should be the case that, since X has an enforceable obligation not to treat Y as a mere means, Y will turn out to have positive rights against X?

The right not to be run over is a negative right if anything is. To run over somebody is to treat that person as pavement for one's wheels, to subordinate him or her to one's ends.[13] Well and good. But suppose Frieda is careening around the corner in her Lamborghini and suddenly sees Roscoe ambling across the road a short distance ahead. At her current speed, she has only two choices: (a) she can run over Roscoe, or (b) she can swerve around him. Running over Roscoe would be a violation of his negative rights; so Frieda has an enforceable obligation not to run over him. In the circumstances, what that amounts to is an enforceable obligation to swerve around him. But that obligation is not an obligation to sit back and do nothing; it is an obligation to take positive action, and a very specific positive action at that: she must turn the steering wheel in order to avoid running over Roscoe. Here we have a case, then, in which Frieda has an enforceable obligation to take positive action on Roscoe's behalf—but only because that is the only way she can avoid violating her negative obligation not to treat Roscoe as a mere means. Roscoe's right against Frieda not to be run over has generated, in the circumstances, a further right against her that she turn the wheel in a certain way. The first right is a negative right, one licensed by proposition (1); the second right is a positive right, but since it follows from a negative right endorsed by (1), it seems that it too is endorsed by (1). Let us call such a right a *derivative* positive right, as opposed to a *basic* positive right.

(10) A derivative positive right is a positive right that is generated by the requirements of some negative right(s).

(11) A basic positive right is a positive right that is not derivative.

Does (1) rule out derivative positive rights? If so, then (1) is simply incoherent. For if everyone has a right against everyone else not to be treated as a mere means, then by the same token everyone has an enforceable obligation to refrain from treating anybody as a mere means. And if everyone has an enforceable obligation to so refrain, then everyone has an enforceable obligation to take whatever positive steps are necessary to avoid treating others as mere means. If the end is mandatory, the means to that end are mandatory as well. If forcing people to take

---

[13] One might deny that running someone over counts as a violation of (1), since in running you over I may not be *using* you as a means (mere or nonmere) to any further end; I may simply be trying to drive through the space you are standing on, and killing you is not a means to, but rather a byproduct of, my pursuit of that goal—a foreseen but not intended consequence. This is true enough if the notion of "using as a mere means" is understood very narrowly; but surely I am forcibly subjecting or subordinating you to my ends, and that is what I take to be the central point of the notion.

such positive steps counts as treating them as mere means, then (1) cannot license any rights at all, positive or negative.

Fortunately, we need not draw this conclusion. The enforcement of positive rights involves treating others as means, but it need not therefore involve treating others as *mere* means. Some such distinction must be available if (1) is to be plausible at all; after all, when I pay a barber to cut my hair, the barber and I are using each other as means, but (Marxist worries aside) there is presumably nothing wrong with this. In order to make sense of (1), then, we need to be able to draw a distinction between the use of people as mere means and the use of people as nonmere means.

The barber example might suggest one natural way of drawing the distinction:

(12) S uses O as a mere means if and only if S uses O as a means without O's consent.

(13) S uses O as a nonmere means if and only if S uses O as a means with O's consent.

According to this way of drawing the distinction, forcing the barber at gunpoint to cut my hair would be a violation of (1), while persuading him (e.g., with offers of money) to cut my hair voluntarily would not.

The problem with this way of drawing the distinction is that it does not do what we wanted it to do: it does not make room for derivative positive rights. If Frieda has an enforceable obligation to turn the steering wheel and so avoid killing Roscoe, then it would be legitimate to *force* her to turn the steering wheel; but in forcing her to turn the wheel we would be using her as a means *without her consent*, and so — according to (12) — we would be using her as a *mere* means, thus violating (1). If there are derivative positive rights, then it is sometimes legitimate to use people as means without their consent; so if we want to maintain the truth of (1), we need to find a way of drawing the distinction between mere and nonmere means other than that expressed in (12) and (13).

I think we will have a better shot at the idea we are trying to hit if we think of (1) as specifying certain boundaries around people. All actions that involve using S as a means (whether mere or nonmere) fall within the boundary around S; all actions that do not involve using S as a means lie outside S's boundary.

(14) S's action lies within O's boundary if and only if S's action involves using O as a means (whether mere or nonmere) to the ends of others.[14]

[14] The notion of "use" needs to be clarified somewhat. Suppose Professor Kant is so regular in his daily walks that the townspeople set their watches by him. Are the townspeo-

Now we cannot interpret (1) as prohibiting all actions that lie within another person's boundary, for that would exclude derivative positive rights. Nor can we interpret (1) as prohibiting all actions that lie within another person's boundary and are undertaken without that person's consent; for that too would exclude derivative positive rights. But among actions that lie within another person's boundary, we can draw a distinction between those that *violate* that boundary and those that merely *repel* the person from one's own boundary.

Let us draw some distinctions:

(15) S *crosses* O's boundary if and only if S performs an action within O's boundary.

(16) S *invades* O's boundary if and only if S crosses O's boundary without O's consent.

(17) S *violates* O's boundary if and only if (a) S invades O's boundary and (b) invading O's boundary (in that way) is not necessary to end any boundary-invasion on O's part.[15]

(I shall be using "action" broadly, to include involuntary as well as voluntary behavior.) Now boundary-*violations* seem to be a clear case of treating others as mere means, and so run afoul of (1) if anything does. But what about boundary-invasions that are not boundary-violations? Is it legitimate to end S's boundary-violation by invading S's boundary in turn?

The dilemma here is analogous to that in Shakespeare's *The Merchant of Venice*. Antonio owes Shylock a pound of his flesh, but he does not owe Shylock any blood; yet of course Shylock cannot claim his pound of Antonio's flesh without taking some of Antonio's blood as well. Portia reasons that since Antonio does not owe Shylock any blood, Shylock has no right to take Antonio's blood, and so has no right to take the pound of flesh either (since, although he has a right to the pound of flesh, he cannot exercise that right without doing something he has no right to do — namely, take Antonio's blood). Shylock, on the other hand, reasons that since Antonio does owe Shylock the pound of flesh, Shylock has the right

---

ple *using* Kant as a means (with or without his consent) to their own ends? Does their action lie within Kant's boundary? Surely not. The townspeople are not doing anything *to* Kant; they simply accept, and make use of, the information that he distributes *gratis*. (Recall the fable of the rich man who tried to sue his poor neighbor for enjoying the smells that emanated from the rich man's kitchen.) Using another person must involve *subjecting* him to one's ends, in a way that the Kant case does not. (See previous note.)

[15] I take it that threatening to invade someone's boundary is itself an invasion of that person's boundary (since in announcing my intention of using you as a means I am already treating you as the sort of thing it is legitimate to use as a means). Therefore, the right to forestall a threatened invasion would follow from the right to end an actual one.

to take it, and so has the right to take the blood too (since that follows from something Shylock has a right to). By analogy, we might distinguish two possible principles to govern boundary-invasions:

> *Shylock's Principle:* If S violates O's boundary, O (or O's agent) has the right to invade S's boundary in whatever way is necessary to end S's violation of O's boundary.

> *Portia's Principle:* O (or O's agent) has no right to invade S's boundary, even if invading S's boundary is necessary to end S's violation of O's boundary.

Is Portia's Principle correct? If so, then there are no derivative positive rights. But we have seen that in accepting (1) we are committed to accepting the existence of derivative positive rights. Since we are looking for a view that accommodates (1), we must therefore reject Portia's Principle.

Should we then accept Shylock's Principle? Shylock's Principle may be consistent with the letter of (1); but it certainly conflicts with its spirit. Am I justified in killing you if that is the only way to stop you from violating my boundary in some trivial way (e.g., stepping on my toe)? My response seems disproportionate[16] to the seriousness of the violation; and insofar as it does so, I might justifiably be taken to treat you as a mere means to my convenience, thus violating (1). I therefore suggest that the following principle does a better job of capturing the intuitions behind (1) than either Portia's or Shylock's Principle does:

> *Principle of Proportion:* If S violates O's boundary, O (or O's agent) has the right to invade S's boundary in whatever way is necessary to end S's violation of O's boundary, so long as O's (or O's agent's) invasion of S's boundary is not disproportionate to the seriousness of S's violation of O's boundary.

And if we accept the Principle of Proportion, the most plausible way of drawing the mere/nonmere distinction is as follows:

> (18) S uses O as a mere means if and only if either (a) S violates O's boundary or (b) S invades O's boundary and either (b1) S's invasion of O's boundary is not necessary to end any wrongful boundary-invasion on O's part, or (b2) S's invasion of O's boundary is disproportionate to the seriousness of any wrongful boundary-invasion on O's part.

---

[16] By "disproportionate" I mean, of course, disproportionate on the side of excess, not of deficiency.

(19) S uses O as a nonmere means if and only if (a) S crosses O's
boundary and (b) S does not violate O's boundary and either
(c1) S does not invade O's boundary or (c2) S invades O's
boundary and S's invasion of O's boundary is necessary to end
some wrongful boundary-invasion on O's part and S's invasion
of O's boundary is not disproportionate to the seriousness of
O's boundary-invasion.[17]

A "wrongful boundary-invasion" is one that either falls under (18a) — i.e.,
is an actual boundary-violation — or else falls under (18b).

In summary, then, Shylock's Principle, Portia's Principle, and the Principle of Proportion represent the three most plausible positions one could
take in attempting to apply (1) to the issue of derivative positive rights,
and the Principle of Proportion captures the spirit of (1) more faithfully
than either of the other principles does. The Principle of Proportion furthermore yields (18) and (19) as the most plausible interpretations of the
notion of being used as a means, as that notion appears in (1). So (1) may
now be rendered as, or taken to be equivalent to:

(20) Every person has the right not to have her boundaries violated,
and also not to have her boundaries invaded unless such invasion is necessary to end some wrongful boundary-invasion of
hers, and such invasion is also not disproportionate to the seriousness of her boundary-invasion.[18]

So the problem of reconciling (2) and (3) with (1) is now the problem of
reconciling (2) and (3) with (20).

V. Welfare Rights: A Digression

Before we proceed to that task, however, it is important to get clear
about what the implications of (20) actually are. Proposition (20) licenses
derivative positive rights, while denying the existence of basic positive

---

[17] These definitions entail that any use to which the used person consents is not a case
of being used as a mere means. This follows from (1), since if it were a violation of my rights
for you to cross my boundary even with my consent, then you would have an enforceable
obligation not to cross my boundary even with my consent, which means that it would be
legitimate to force you not to cross my boundary even with my consent, which in turn
means — by definition (17) — that it would be legitimate to violate your boundary; and (1) prohibits boundary-violations if it prohibits anything. This does not entail, however, that all
noninvasive boundary-crossings are morally permissible.

[18] Proposition (20) is probably not true without exception as it stands. I am not so extreme a rights fanatic as to deny that minor boundary-violations may occasionally be morally permissible in order to prevent some great evil. But I do not think this qualification
affects the central arguments of my essay.

rights. Some may be reluctant to accept (20) because, in denying the existence of basic positive rights, it appears to deny the existence of welfare rights. Others may be eager to accept (20) for precisely the same reason. But I think either reaction would be mistaken, or at least premature.

Property rights are negative rights.[19] That is, my right to my property is not in the first instance a right to be given positive aid; it is simply a right not to have my property taken from me, and not to have my use of it interfered with in certain ways. But these negative rights generate derivative positive rights. If you (intentionally or accidentally) take my umbrella, you acquire an enforceable obligation to take positive steps to return it to me. For example, you must walk back to my house, or you must mail the umbrella to me, or you must call me to let me know where I can pick it up. You cannot refuse to take these steps without violating my right not to be deprived of my property without my consent.

I suggest that welfare rights should be treated as a variety of property rights. We may regard theories of property rights as individuated, at least in large part, by principles of just acquisition and transfer. One way in which property rights are traditionally taken to be transferred is through voluntary gift or voluntary exchange. If Frieda gives Roscoe her Lamborghini, either *gratis* or for a consideration, we take Frieda to have lost, and Roscoe to have gained, a property right in the Lamborghini. Furthermore, such transfers of property rights need not involve an actual transfer of physical possession. If Frieda signs her title over to Roscoe, then Roscoe suddenly becomes the new rightful owner of Frieda's Lamborghini, even if the Lamborghini is still sitting at home in Frieda's garage. The car in Frieda's garage is now Roscoe's rightful property, and Frieda has an enforceable obligation to surrender it to him (which may involve a derivative positive obligation to deliver the car to him, or to give him the key to the garage).

Such transfers need not always be voluntary. Another way in which property rights can be transferred is through rectification or compensation. If Frieda uses her Lamborghini to run over Roscoe, she may acquire an enforceable obligation to compensate him (or his beneficiaries), and so Roscoe (or his beneficiaries) may acquire a property right to some share of Frieda's resources. Once again, the money becomes Roscoe's rightful property *before* she hands it over to him, so if she holds on to it she is guilty of theft; hence, she has a derivative positive obligation to hand the money over, stemming from her negative obligation not to hold on to someone else's rightful property.

---

[19] I leave aside the question of whether there *are* property rights, and if so, what their foundation might be. If, as Aristotle, Locke, Hegel, and Marx thought (in very different ways), one's property is in some sense an extension of oneself, then (1) will entail the existence of property rights. (For a recent defense of such a view, see Samuel C. Wheeler III, "Natural Property Rights as Body Rights," *Noûs*, vol. 16 [1980], pp. 171–93.) But much more remains to be said.

In both these cases, the transfer is triggered by some action of Frieda's; but other cases can be imagined. I suggest that proponents of welfare rights should be understood as claiming that property rights can be transferred in yet a third way. Suppose that the facts that (a) Roscoe is in need of financial assistance, and (b) Frieda is in the best position to provide such assistance, jointly generate in Roscoe a property right to some share of Frieda's resources.[20] In that case, circumstances outside either Roscoe's or Frieda's control can trigger a transfer of property rights from Frieda to Roscoe. Some of the resources that previously were rightfully Frieda's are now rightfully Roscoe's, and Frieda—as in the previous cases—now has an enforceable obligation to take positive action to ensure that Roscoe receives his rightful property. If there are welfare rights, they are best understood as derivative positive rights arising out of negative property rights whose transfer conditions are sensitive to financial need. There is thus no need to invoke *basic* positive rights in order to ground the possibility of welfare rights.[21]

I have not argued that welfare rights exist, or indeed that property rights of any sort exist. My point is merely that the acceptance of (20) does not commit us one way or the other on the question of welfare rights, and thus that our positions—whether favorable or unfavorable—with regard to welfare rights should not affect our willingness to accept (20).

It originally seemed that (1) committed us to rejecting all positive rights per se. Since a woman's right to abort her unborn child would have to be a positive right, and since a newborn infant's right not to be abandoned would also have to be a positive right, we would then have been unable to countenance such rights, and so—in accepting (1)—would have to reject (2) and (3). But if the intuition behind (1) is best expressed as (20), then what seemed a general prohibition on positive rights turns out to be a prohibition on basic positive rights only; derivative positive rights are allowed. Propositions (2) and (3) may be salvaged, then, if it is possible to construe them as claiming derivative, rather than basic, positive rights. To that task I now turn.

---

[20] Such a view of property rights has an unlikely source in Locke; see his *First Treatise of Government*, ch. 4, section 42, where welfare rights are treated as derivative positive property rights licensed by something like (1).

[21] It might be objected that (1)'s ban on basic positive rights is toothless, since the case of welfare rights suggests that all basic positive rights can be rewritten as derivative positive rights. But that is a mistake. In order for a positive right to be admitted as derivative and so permissible, it must be possible to identify a specific *negative* right from which the putative positive right is supposed to arise; and there is no guarantee that such a negative right can be found in every case. From what negative right, for example, could a positive right to health care derive? (I am speaking not of a right to be enabled to purchase health care—as in Medicare, etc.—but of an actual right against some doctor that he or she expend labor in treating the patient—as in the alleged right, defended by J. S. Mill in the penultimate paragraph of *Utilitarianism*, to "kidnap, and compel to officiate, the only qualified medical practitioner" in order to save a life.)

VI. The Right Not To Be Abandoned:
A Derivative Positive Right

Let us first consider the case of abandonment. The proposition at issue is the following:

>   (3) A woman who voluntarily bears a child but later changes her mind does *not* have the right simply to abandon her child, but must care for it until she can arrange for a substitute caretaker.[22]

The claim that a willing mother has no right of abandonment means that it is not the case that others have an enforceable obligation to let her abandon her child. This by itself is insufficient to generate in the child a right against its mother not to be abandoned; the child has such a right only if the mother has an enforceable obligation not to abandon the child. Now the absence of the right of abandonment means that others can legitimately use force to prevent her from abandoning her child, which in turn means that *if* she has an obligation not to abandon her child, that obligation is indeed enforceable. But this does not suffice to show that she in fact has such an obligation. However, the further claim that the mother "must" care for the child until a substitute caretaker is found *does* indicate an obligation (whether enforceable or otherwise); and her liability to legitimate coercion by others in this regard ensures this obligation's enforceability. Therefore, (3) claims that the woman has an enforceable obligation not to abandon her child; and that does invest the child with a positive right against its mother not to be abandoned.

Now this right cannot be a basic positive right, for (20) rules out the existence of such rights. It must therefore derive from the requirements of some negative right; but what could that right be? (It cannot be a welfare or property right, because nobody can have property rights in another's labor without running afoul of [1] or [20].)

The answer lies in the fact that the mother in (3) gave birth *voluntarily*.[23] In doing so, I suggest, she undertook an obligation not to abandon the child. Why so? And why is this obligation enforceable?

---

[22] Proposition (3) leaves open the question of *how much* the mother must do to secure such a caretaker. Must she locate a willing and suitable guardian? Or may she simply leave the infant in a shopping mall, confident that someone will take care of it? It is not my aim in this essay to determine precisely the *most* that others may ask of her (that is, the most that others may *enforce*; the mother's unenforceable obligations may well extend beyond her enforceable ones). The point of (3) is to set at least *some* lower limits: the mother may not, for example, abandon her infant in a deserted area, or dispose of it in a dumpster.

[23] I do not see any way of generating an enforceable obligation not to abandon a child if that child was born against the mother's will. An unwilling mother might well have an obligation to care for the child until a substitute caretaker could be found, but that obligation could not be *enforced* without violating (1) or (20).

Suppose that Stan is a pilot for Clouds-R-Us, a charter airline company. Now ordinarily Stan is under no obligation, enforceable or otherwise, to work as a pilot; he has a right to go on strike at any time. But now suppose that Stan decides to go on strike in midflight: he abandons the controls, dons his parachute, leaps out the door, and leaves his planeload of passengers (none of whom can pilot a plane) to fall to their doom. (Clouds-R-Us does not waste money on frills like copilots.) When Stan is accused of murder he is indignant: "What do you mean, murder? I didn't *kill* my passengers. I merely *let them die*. Since there are no basic positive rights, I was not under any enforceable obligation to take positive action on behalf of my passengers' welfare; I was merely obligated to leave them alone. And that's precisely what I did: I *left them alone*. What am I, my passengers' keeper?"

This response is clearly inadequate; but why? The answer, I think, is that Stan's relation to his passengers is importantly different from, say, an innocent bystander's relation to an accident victim. When one is merely a bystander, one's failure to take positive action counts as letting die, not as killing. But it is a different story when one is not a bystander but the *pilot*.[24] The fact that all these passengers are traveling at a high speed, thousands of feet above the ground, is not simply an interesting situation to which Stan is a latecomer. *The passengers are way up in the air because Stan brought them there.* And the passengers consented to being brought there *on the understanding* that Stan would return them safely to the ground; they would not have consented to be carried upward if they had known that Stan was going to bail out. Thus, if Stan bails out, he has violated the conditions under which the passengers' ascent was voluntary; and so Stan's total behavior toward the passengers (carrying them upward and then leaving them there) counts as a violation of their negative right not to be killed without their consent. Therefore, once Stan and the passengers are aloft, it would be legitimate to force Stan to return the passengers safely to the ground before resigning his post at Clouds-R-Us. (And this is because Stan carried the passengers aloft voluntarily; if a gun had been held to his head from the beginning, it is not clear that he would have an *enforceable* obligation not to bail out.)

The moral we may extract from Stan's story is this:

> (21) If S voluntarily places O in a situation where S's failure to take positive action on O's behalf will result in O's death, then such a failure on S's part is a killing, not merely a letting-die.

Now when a woman voluntarily gives birth—i.e., voluntarily brings a child into the world—she is voluntarily moving it from a situation in which it has an automatic life-support system to a situation in which it

---

[24] Cf. Aristotle, *Physics*, II.3.195a11–14.

does not.[25] In other words, she is cutting it off from its life-support system and placing it in a situation where it depends on her care for survival—just as Stan, by carrying his passengers aloft, was cutting them off from earthbound safety and placing them in a situation where they depended on his piloting for survival. And since she is voluntarily placing her child in a situation where he will perish without her positive assistance, if she were to refuse that assistance, her action—according to (21)—would be a killing rather than a letting-die; that is, it would be a boundary-crossing. But the child has not consented to be killed; so if she abandons her child, she will be not merely crossing but *invading* her child's boundary. Since that invasion is not necessary to counteract any invasion on the child's part (the child is merely lying there, newborn, not invading anything), her invasion of her child's boundary, according to (17), counts as a *violation* of that boundary—and so is prohibited by (20). Hence, if a woman gives birth voluntarily (where the availability of safe, inexpensive abortion may be among the criteria of voluntariness), she has an enforceable obligation[26] not to abandon her child until she can find a substitute caretaker to take over for her—just as Stan has an enforceable obligation to ensure his passengers' safety before he bails out.

VII. THE RIGHT TO ABORT: A DERIVATIVE POSITIVE RIGHT

I have argued that a newborn infant's right not to be abandoned by its mother is a derivative positive right rather than a basic one, and that such a right is accordingly licensed by (20). I shall now argue that the same is true of a woman's right to abort an unwanted fetus.[27]

> (2) A woman who voluntarily becomes pregnant but later changes her mind has the right to abort her unborn child.

It is sometimes argued that abortion is justified because a fetus is not a person. If that were true, then the right to abortion would simply be a negative right, not a positive one, and would follow from (1) and (20). If a fetus is not a person, but simply a mass of human tissue, like a cancer-

---

[25] It may seem odd to speak of "voluntarily giving birth," when the actual biological process of birth proceeds independently of the mother's will. But it is clear enough what is meant: if the mother wants to give birth, and has deliberately chosen to do so, in the face of opportunities to terminate her pregnancy, then she gives birth voluntarily. The same remarks apply to voluntary conception. (One can likewise be struck by lightning voluntarily, if one deliberately stays on the roof during a storm, holding up a pitchfork in the hope of getting hit.)

[26] I leave aside the question of what responsibilities the father might have to assist her in fulfilling this obligation.

[27] As will be obvious, my treatment of the abortion issue is greatly indebted to Judith Jarvis Thomson, "A Defense of Abortion," *Philosophy and Public Affairs*, vol. 1 (1971), pp. 47–66.

ous growth, then in aborting it a woman would simply be doing something to her own body, and the right to control one's own body (so long
as one does not invade others' boundaries in the process) is clearly licensed by (1). If I forcibly interfere with your use of your own body, I am
violating your boundaries and may legitimately be restrained by force.

But is it true that fetuses are not persons? I think it is clearly true in the
early stages of pregnancy, for the possession of psychological capacities
of some sort is essential to personhood. Nothing counts as a person if it
lacks psychological capacities; an early fetus lacks neurophysiological
structures sophisticated enough to ground psychological capacities; therefore, an early fetus is not a person,[28] and so may be killed without violating any rights.[29]

Nor will it do to protest that an early fetus is at least a *potential* person,
and is deserving of moral concern in virtue of that status. For the claim
that an early fetus is potentially a person is ambiguous; and the sense in
which the claim is true is different from the sense needed by the opponent of early abortion. The claim might mean that the early fetus is potentially *identical* with a person, just as I am potentially identical with a
grandfather; or it might mean that the early fetus is potentially *constitutive* of a person, just as clay is potentially constitutive of a statue. The
claim that the early fetus is potentially identical with a person might make
it an object of moral concern (although it is far from obvious that it would
do so); but such a claim is simply false. Whatever is a person is essentially
a person; the change from person to nonperson or vice versa is not a
change that anything could survive.[30] So the early fetus cannot be regarded as becoming a person; either we must regard it as going out of existence when the person comes to be (in the same way that an organism
goes out of existence when a corpse comes to be), so that an early fetus
is *replaced* by a person, or else we must regard the early fetus as persist-
ing as the underlying *matter* of the person. In the latter case, an early fetus does turn out to be a potential person, but only in the pickwickian

---

[28] It might be claimed that an early fetus is a person because, as a potential person, it has
psychological *capacities*; it just cannot exercise them yet. But this is to confuse remote with
proximate potentialities. Suppose that Pierre is a Francophone, and Zeke is not. Yet Zeke
is capable of learning French; Zeke is a potential Francophone. So both Pierre and Zeke have
the potentiality to speak French; but that does not make them both Francophones. Pierre's
potentiality to speak French is proximate, while Zeke's is merely remote. Being a Francophone is defined in terms of the *proximate* potentiality to speak French, so Pierre is a Francophone while Zeke is not. So even if an early fetus has remote psychological capacities,
it is not thereby a person, since being a person is defined in terms of (more) *proximate* psychological capacities.

[29] Aquinas, following Aristotle, regarded the soul as the form of the body, and denied
that a fetus could become ensouled until its matter had been sufficiently worked up to enable it to be informed by a human soul; accordingly, he did not regard early abortion as murder. Late abortion was another matter. (See *On the Sentences*, IV.31.2; *On the Politics*, VII.12;
Summa of Theology, II.II.64.8.2.)

[30] While a non-Francophone could become a Francophone, no nonperson could become
a person.

sense of potentially *constituting* a person; and there is no reason to suppose that something becomes an object of moral concern merely in virtue of *constituting* a person. The right to abort an early fetus, then, is an unproblematic negative right.

But while this argument serves to justify most abortions (and would certainly justify the use of "morning-after" abortifacients), it does not justify late abortions.[31] Personhood may not begin at conception, but it does appear to begin before birth; there is no significant difference between the psychological capacities of a newborn infant and those of a late fetus. If we deny that the late fetus is a person, we must also deny that a newborn infant is a person, and therefore justify infanticide. But this conclusion, apart from its morally unpalatable character, also runs afoul of (3); if a newborn infant is not a person, it does not have any rights, and so may legitimately be abandoned. (The worst thing one could say about it is that it might be a case of littering.) One might respond by claiming that newborn infants can have rights even if they are *not* persons; but in that case the argument for (2) fails. The claim that late fetuses are not persons counts as an argument for (2) only if personhood is necessary for rights; and in that case (given the similarity between late fetuses and newborn infants) we do not get a view that accommodates both (2) and (3) — which is what we were looking for. So the denial that late fetuses are persons seems like an unpromising strategy.

Let us grant, then, that late fetuses are persons. If that is so, what could justify aborting them? The answer to that question will turn on the answer to a broader question: When, in general, does one have the right to kill a person? Or, more specifically, when does one have the right to kill a person without that person's consent?[32] Well, killing a person without that person's consent is a boundary-invasion by definition (16), and the general rule governing boundary-invasions was laid down by (20):

(20) Every person has the right not to have her boundaries violated, and also not to have her boundaries invaded unless such invasion is necessary to end some wrongful boundary-invasion of hers, and such invasion is also not disproportionate to the seriousness of her boundary-invasion.

To prohibit abortion is to invade a pregnant woman's boundary. According to (20), such a prohibition will be illegitimate unless it is necessary to counteract some wrongful boundary-invasion on her part. Now aborting a (late) fetus is certainly a boundary-invasion; but such invasions cannot

---

[31] Since I am ultimately going to argue that all abortions are justified, I do not need to worry about fixing the precise temporal cutoff between early and late.

[32] Since killing a person *with* that person's consent is only a boundary-crossing, not a boundary-invasion, such a killing presumably does not violate (20).

be prohibited unless they are wrongful, where such wrongfulness is itself defined as the violation of (20). Therefore, to show that a woman has the right to abort an unwanted fetus, it will suffice to show (a) that such an abortion would not involve a boundary-violation, and (b) that such an abortion is necessary to end some wrongful boundary-invasion on the part of the fetus, and is also not disproportionate to the seriousness of the fetus's boundary-invasion. But by (17), (b) entails (a). So all we need to show is (b): that aborting an unwanted fetus is necessary to end some wrongful boundary-invasion on the part of the fetus, and is also not disproportionate to the seriousness of the fetus's boundary-invasion.

Here is the quick version of the argument (which I shall go on to defend in more detail): Suppose Miriam is pregnant, and Joshua is her unwanted fetus. Joshua is using Miriam's body as an incubator; so Joshua is crossing Miriam's boundary. Miriam wants Joshua out; so Joshua's boundary-crossing counts as a boundary-invasion. Joshua's invasion of Miriam's boundary is not necessary to counteract any invasion on Miriam's part, so Joshua's invasion is a boundary-violation. By (20), Joshua has no right to violate Miriam's boundary; so Joshua's boundary-violation is a wrongful boundary-invasion. Aborting Joshua is necessary to end his wrongful boundary-invasion of Miriam, and is not disproportionate to the seriousness of the threat; therefore, Miriam has a derivative positive right to abort Joshua.[33] The right to abortion is a special case of the right to self-defense.[34]

Opponents of the right to abortion find this style of argument repellent. How, they ask, can one treat a fetus as some sort of alien parasite, and pregnancy as an unnatural violation, when pregnancy is the most natural thing in the world?[35] Well, sexual intercourse is also the most "natural" thing in the world; but when it is involuntary, it becomes rape.

---

[33] I am not arguing that abortion is morally permissible, but only that a woman has a BC-right to abortion. The view I am defending is thus compatible with any of the following three positions:

  (a) A woman has a moral obligation to let an unwanted fetus use her body as an incubator, but it would be illegitimate to enforce that obligation. (I take this to be the position of a majority of the American public.)
  (b) A woman has no moral obligation to let an unwanted fetus use her body as an incubator, but it would be morally praiseworthy (albeit supererogatory) for her to do so. (This is Thomson's position.)
  (c) Not only has a woman no moral obligation to let an unwanted fetus use her body as an incubator, but she actually has an obligation (an unenforceable one, of course) *not* to saddle herself with the physical and psychological burden of an *undesired* pregnancy and childbirth — an obligation stemming from her duty to care for herself and to make the most of her life. (This is the position to which I incline.)

[34] Self-defense is a derivative positive right; my positive right to fight off a mugger derives from my negative right not to be attacked by him in the first place.

[35] For this style of argument, see John T. Wilcox, "Nature as Demonic in Thomson's Defense of Abortion," *New Scholasticism*, vol. 63 (1989), pp. 463–84. Since Wilcox's conception of the "natural" is avowedly statistical (rather than, say, teleological), it is difficult to see how it can bear the normative weight with which he wants to invest it.

Likewise, when the "natural" process of pregnancy is involuntary, it too becomes an alien intrusion or violation.

Yet if the case of Miriam and Joshua is to justify (2), we must add the supposition that Miriam became pregnant *voluntarily*. [36] And if Miriam's pregnancy is voluntary, then Joshua's boundary-crossing is not a boundary-invasion, and so the argument for Miriam's right to abort Joshua cannot get off the ground.

We must, however, distinguish between pregnancies that were *initially* voluntary and pregnancies that are *currently* voluntary. Suppose that Miriam's pregnancy began in as voluntary a fashion as one could ask for: she voluntarily engaged in intercourse with the deliberate intention of conceiving a child. [37] But now she has changed her mind, and no longer wishes to carry Joshua to term. Her pregnancy was originally voluntary, but now it is involuntary. The same is true of sexual intercourse: a woman who begins intercourse voluntarily but then changes her mind has the right to back out halfway through; if her partner fails to respect this wish, he is guilty of rape, even if he (and she) have been socialized not to think of it that way. [38] Consent, to justify, must be sustained. [39]

[36] What makes the difference between voluntary and involuntary pregnancies? Pregnancies that result from rape are clearly involuntary; but pregnancies that result from failed contraception are a more difficult case. Proponents of the right to abortion usually argue that pregnancies that result from failed contraception are clearly involuntary, since steps are taken to avoid them. (Recall Thomson's "people seeds" example in "A Defense of Abortion.") On the other hand, opponents of the right to abortion usually argue that such pregnancies are voluntary, so long as intercourse was engaged in with full knowledge of the risk (just as actions performed under the influence of an intoxicant are voluntary if the intoxicant was taken voluntarily with full knowledge of the possible results; see Aristotle, *Nicomachean Ethics*, III.5.1113b21–1114a21). Until recently, I was extremely suspicious of the latter argument; it struck me as analogous to the claim that a rape victim was "asking for it" by walking in a high-crime neighborhood or going on a date. But I have been made somewhat less confident by Wilcox's observation that if (as I believe) fathers have responsibilities with regard to pregnancies that they cause, even when those pregnancies are the result of failed contraception, then such pregnancies cannot be treated as mere bolts from the blue. It seems that fathers could have such responsibilities only if engaging in intercourse with knowledge of the risks somehow made even pregnancies resulting from failed contraception voluntary in Aristotle's broad sense. And if they are voluntary for the father, are they not voluntary for the mother? I need not decide this issue, however, since I shall argue that pregnancies may be terminated whether or not they were (initially) voluntary.

[37] It may be objected that, in the context of the overt and covert pressures and attitudes of a male-dominated society, no act of heterosexual intercourse is fully voluntary on the woman's part, and so no pregnancy resulting from such intercourse could be voluntary either. I think this objection, while insightful, is overstated, and slights women's capacity to achieve and express genuine autonomy even in the face of an adverse social climate; but for those who accept this objection, it still makes sense to ask whether abortion *would* be justified in a society that was not male-dominated, and my discussion may be taken as relevant to that question at least.

[38] To borrow an example that I believe I heard in a lecture by Claudia Card: If I start to eat a meal and then change my mind halfway through, you cannot use my original intention to eat the entire meal as an excuse to force the rest of the food down my throat.

[39] Does this undermine the possibility of contractual obligation? No, but that is a long story which I cannot get into here. The short answer is that if I do not do what you paid me to do, I may not legitimately be forced to do so, but I do have a derivative positive obligation to give you back your money (plus, perhaps, another derivative positive obligation to

When Miriam's pregnancy was voluntary, Joshua's occupation of her body was a mere boundary-crossing; but now that Miriam has changed her mind, that occupation has become a boundary-invasion.

Yet what distinguishes Miriam's case from the case of Stan the airline pilot, or from the case of the initially willing mother who later abandons her baby? Cannot Stan say that he started the flight as a willing pilot, but has since changed his mind, and thus that forcing him to continue piloting would be involuntary servitude? (And likewise for the abandonment case?) It seems that (2) and (3) have come into potential conflict once more. Either we grant Miriam the right to change her mind, in which case it is unclear how we can deny the same right to Stan or to the abandoning mother; or we deny Stan and the abandoning mother the right to change their minds, in which case it is unclear how we can grant that right to Miriam. What could justify giving different answers in the two cases?

Recall that in denying Stan the right to abandon his passengers, and in denying an initially willing mother the right to abandon her child, we appealed to principle (21), which establishes that such abandonments are killings rather than mere lettings-die. That is, we showed that abandonment in such cases is a boundary-crossing — and therefore, since the victims did not consent, a boundary-invasion. But that was only part of the story. In order to show that Stan's passengers and the newborn infant have the *right* not to be abandoned, it was necessary, according to (20), to show that the boundary-invasion in question would be a wrongful one. This we were able to do by showing that no such boundary-invasion was necessary to counteract any wrongful boundary-invasion on the part of the passengers or of the infant; a boundary-invasion that lacks such an excuse is a boundary-violation, and (20) prohibits all boundary-violations. But in Miriam's case, killing Joshua is necessary in order to counteract his wrongful invasion of her body,[40] and so Miriam's act of aborting Joshua is not a boundary-violation. That is the crucial difference between abortion and abandonment.

But although the fact that abandonment is a boundary-violation shows that it is prohibited by (20), the fact that abortion is *not* a boundary-violation does not show that it is licensed by (20). For (20) also prohibits some boundary-invasions that are not boundary-violations — namely, those boundary-invasions that are disproportionate to the seriousness of the threat they are designed to counteract. (Once again, I do not have the right to blow you away in order to prevent you from treading on my toe,

---

compensate you for taking it under false pretenses). For useful discussion, see Randy E. Barnett, "Contract Remedies and Inalienable Rights," *Social Philosophy & Policy*, vol. 4, no. 1 (1986), pp. 179–202.

[40] If killing Joshua were *not* necessary — if Miriam could remove him from her body without killing him — then she would, I think, be bound by (20) not to kill him. See Thomson, "A Defense of Abortion," p. 66.

even if no lesser measure would succeed.) In order to show that abortion is licensed by (20), then, we will need to show that Miriam's killing Joshua is not disproportionate to the seriousness of the threat posed by Joshua to Miriam.

One might try to show this by appealing to the fact that the process of childbirth is (a) life-threatening, and (b) extremely painful.[41] (If the pain involved in childbirth were induced by other means, it would generally be recognized as a form of torture, and a nation that required women to undergo it would be found in violation of Article V of the United Nations Universal Declaration of Human Rights.)[42] As things stand, then, abortion is not disproportionate to the seriousness of the threat it counteracts, and so is not a wrongful boundary-invasion; we surely have a right to kill in order to avoid being tortured. (It might be objected that killing can never be a proportionate response to any threat short of death. But our concern is with proportionality in moral seriousness, not proportionality in physical effect; to claim that defensive killing can be morally proportionate only to a threat of death is to assume, between aggressive force and defensive force, a moral symmetry difficult to square with [20].) But what if medical science eventually renders childbirth safe and painless? Should abortion still be permitted under those circumstances? A robust defense of (2) should strive to vindicate the right to abortion in general, without relying on historically contingent facts about the level of advancement of medical technology. In what follows I thus forgo any appeal to the risk or painfulness of childbirth.

So let us pretend that pregnancy poses no risk to the mother's life, health, or comfort. If the threat posed by an unwanted pregnancy is not one of pain or physical injury, then how could killing the fetus *not* be a disproportionate response to the seriousness of the boundary-violation posed by such a pregnancy? How could anything less than a threat of pain or physical injury justify *killing* one's assailant in self-defense?

To answer this question, it is useful to consider the analogy of rape. A woman is clearly justified in killing a rapist in self-defense (assuming no lesser measures would be successful). Rape is one of the most profound and traumatizing assaults on one's personhood that it is possible to inflict; so killing is not a disproportionate response to the seriousness of rape. But a rape need not involve physical injury or pain; if the rape victim is intimidated into failing to resist, then in purely physical terms a rape may be indistinguishable from normal, consensual intercourse. Rape need not be violent in any overt sense.[43] Yet it is a rape for all that; for

---

[41] In most cases anesthetic does not fully counteract the pain, and often cannot be administered early enough anyway.

[42] "No one shall be subjected to torture or to cruel, inhuman or degrading treatment or punishment."

[43] "The essence of rape isn't violence, but *trespass*." J. Neil Schulman, *The Rainbow Cadenza: A Novel in Vistata Form* (New York: Avon Books, 1986), p. 190.

any sexual use of another person's body without that person's consent is a rape. What gives a woman the right to kill a rapist in self-defense, then, is not that he threatens her with pain or injury, but that he uses her body in the most deeply intimate and personal way, without her consent (even if she originally consented, then changed her mind). And it is *precisely this same fact* that gives Miriam the right to kill her unwanted fetus Joshua: not that he threatens her with pain or injury, but that he uses her body[44] in the most deeply intimate and personal way, without her consent (even if she originally consented).[45] Hence abortion is not a disproportionate response to the seriousness of the boundary-violation it counteracts. My argument for abortion rights may be expressed, then, by the following syllogism:

(a) One has the right to kill in self-defense if the threat is sufficiently serious.
(b) The threat posed by an unwanted fetus is sufficiently serious.
(c) Therefore, one has the right to kill an unwanted fetus in self-defense.

My analogy between fetuses and rapists will strike many opponents of abortion rights as absurd. Doesn't this analogy ignore a vitally important difference — namely, that the fetus is *innocent*? The fetus did not *choose* to violate its mother's boundaries; the violation occurred as a result of nat-ural processes over which the fetus, in the nature of the case, could have had no control (since these are the same natural processes that produced *it*).

Yes, this is of course an important difference; but it is not important in the relevant way. An unwanted fetus is an innocent threat, but is a threat nonetheless.[46] A boundary-violation does not cease to be a boundary-vi-olation just because the boundary-violator was acting involuntarily; nor does such involuntariness transform a profoundly personal intrusion into a minor inconvenience. Proposition (20) therefore licenses the killing of innocent threats in self-defense.[47] To be sure, considerations of the threat's innocence or guilt may legitimately affect judgments of the moral

---

[44] I do not mean to imply that the fetus is a voluntary agent; Joshua may "use" Miriam's body in the same sense that a Venus' flytrap "uses" flies, mindlessly subjecting them to its ends. But nothing in the definition of boundary-violations requires them to be voluntary acts.

[45] The frequently heard claim that women who have abortions are sacrificing human life merely for the sake of their own "convenience" overlooks the profoundly intrusive nature of the fetus's boundary-violation. Such remarks are on a par with the advice to rape victims to "lie back and enjoy it."

[46] If it is wrong to kill an innocent threat, it is difficult to see how the presence of evil thoughts in the threatening agent's head could suddenly make such a killing legitimate, given that nobody has rightful jurisdiction over the contents of another person's mind.

[47] I leave aside the question of whether (20) also licenses the killing of innocent shields. For the distinction between innocent threats and innocent shields, see Robert Nozick, *Anarchy, State, and Utopia* (New York: Basic Books, 1974), pp. 34–35.

proportionality of the response. But when the threat is as personal and intrusive as an unwanted pregnancy, it is difficult to see how the innocence of the fetus could make enough of a difference to justify forcing the mother to quietly endure nine months of what is tantamount to rape. Analogously, even if someone has been involuntarily hypnotized into becoming a *literal* rapist, his victim still has the right to kill him in self-defense.

Objection: Not if she's the one who deliberately hypnotized him. Reply: Yes, even then, I think. A woman never has an obligation—or at any rate, never has an enforceable obligation[48]—to let herself be raped. That is moral bedrock if anything is. The notion of an enforceable obligation to let one's body be used by a rapist is a moral obscenity; and the same holds for the notion of an enforceable obligation to let one's body be used as an incubator by a fetus, even if the mother is responsible for the fetus's presence there in the first place.[49] The right to abortion, like the right not to be raped, is *inalienable*; one cannot legitimately enslave oneself by waiving in advance one's right to control one's own body. This follows from (20); since boundary-violations are prohibited, the only way Miriam could alienate her right to her body is by placing her body outside her own boundary, so that someone could use her body as a mere means without using *her* as a mere means. But unless Miriam has acquired the knack of astral projection, this is impossible.[50]

Yet another disanalogy may be urged between a rapist and an unwanted fetus: Joshua is Miriam's *child*, and we have special obligations to our children that we do not have to strangers.[51] Miriam may have a right to deny strangers the use of her body, but it does not follow that she has the right to deny such use to her child, when his very survival depends on being allowed to use her body. The right to abortion, so this objection runs, is inconsistent with the existence of parental obligations.[52]

---

[48] I would be willing to defend the stronger claim, but for the purposes of this essay the weaker claim will suffice.

[49] It is true, of course, that a woman who deliberately hypnotized a man into attempting rape, and then killed him in self-defense, would be blameworthy for his death; but that is presumably because she violated his rights in the first place by voluntarily placing him in a situation where she would be justified in killing him. There is no analogous rights-violation in the pregnancy case; we surely do not violate a person's rights merely by bringing him or her into existence.

[50] If Miriam were to voluntarily cut off or surgically remove some part of her body, she would then be able to alienate her right to that part (as organ donors do), since it would be possible to use the part without using Miriam. But as long as the part is organically attached to Miriam, she and it are a package deal, and her right over the part is inalienable. (One can never place *oneself* outside one's own boundary. Hence, the real problem with selling oneself into slavery is that such a contract is *fraudulent*; the seller offers something that cannot be delivered.)

[51] For this objection, see Wilcox, "Nature as Demonic"; and Francis J. Beckwith, "Rights, Filial Obligations, and Medical Risks," *American Philosophical Association Newsletter on Philosophy and Medicine*, vol. 89 (1990), pp. 86–88.

[52] Beckwith inexplicably calls these *filial* obligations. Surely a filial obligation is owed by a child to a parent, not the other way around.

I would hardly deny the importance of parental obligations; but it is generally recognized that adoptive parents have the same obligations as biological parents—and that, conversely, either biological or adoptive parents may divest themselves of their (*enforceable*) obligations by putting their child up for adoption. Hence a parent's enforceable obligations appear to stem from his or her voluntary acceptance of the rights and responsibilities of guardianship, and not from a merely biological tie. Hence an appeal to parental obligations in the case of abortion misses the mark, since a woman seeking abortion is ipso facto not a willing guardian.

But even if we were to assume, implausibly, that Miriam has assumed the parental responsibilities of guardianship toward Joshua (e.g., in virtue of having conceived him voluntarily), does it really follow that she has no right of self-defense against him? Until fairly recently, it was widely held (and still is, in some of the world's more benighted recesses)[53] that a woman does not count as having been genuinely "raped" if the assailant is her husband. The "parental obligations" objection to abortion, like the refusal to recognize rape in marriage, appears to stem from a traditional attitude that refuses to acknowledge women as autonomous individuals, and regards their bodies as mere resources to be used by family members.[54] On this view, a woman is not an independent moral being worthy of respect in her own right, but instead exists only for the sake of her family relationships, and has her moral identity and standing only within that context. Simply by virtue of being a family member, then, a husband or fetus is imagined to possess a rightful claim to use her body. A woman is only a tenant in her body, not its rightful proprietor.[55] But this view is wrong, and (1) is one way of expressing the fact that it is wrong. Family relationships are important, but they do not give some people the right to use other people as mere means to their own ends.[56]

---

[53] One of these recesses is the mind of Alaska Senator Paul Fischer, who remarked in 1985: "I don't know how you can have a sexual act and call it forcible rape in a marriage situation. . . . I still believe in the old traditional bond of marriage." Quoted in Susan Moller Okin, *Justice, Gender, and the Family* (New York: Basic Books, 1989), p. 42n. Thank you for sharing that with us, Paul.

[54] In ancient Athens every woman was assigned a *kurios*, a "boss"—either her husband or a male relative. Today, opponents of abortion may be viewed as assigning to the fetus the status of *kurios*.

[55] One is reminded of Herbert Spencer's insightful remark that opponents of the full and equal rights of women are clinging to an evanescent form of the doctrine that women have no souls. See Herbert Spencer, *Social Statics: The Conditions Essential to Human Happiness Specified, and the First of Them Developed* (New York: Robert Schalkenbach Foundation, 1970), p. 143.

[56] Does this essay's stress on rights and individual autonomy, rather than on relationships of caring and connectedness, express an androcentric perspective inappropriate to the needs and concerns of women, and thus irrelevant to the abortion debate? (See Carol Gilligan, *In a Different Voice* [Cambridge: Harvard University Press, 1982].) I hope not. To say that people have rights is simply to say that there are some things one should not be allowed to do to others; whoever grants the importance of that fact is committed to granting the importance of rights. Relationships of caring and connectedness are important as well; but if they are not to turn into a self-sacrificial trap, they must operate within a framework of rights. As for individual autonomy, it is precisely this that women have traditionally been

What Jefferson said of men is likewise true of women: "[T]he mass of mankind has not been born with saddles on their backs, nor a favored few booted and spurred, ready to ride them legitimately, by the grace of God."[57]

VIII. SUMMARY

We began with three propositions: that people have a right not to be treated as mere means to the ends of others, that a woman who voluntarily becomes pregnant nevertheless has the right to an abortion, and that a woman who voluntarily gives birth does not have a right to abandon her child until she finds a substitute caretaker. These propositions initially seemed inconsistent, for the prohibition on treating others as mere means appeared to rule out the possibility of positive rights, thus making it impossible to countenance the right to abort or the right not to be abandoned (both of which, it was argued, are positive in form).

But we have seen that the prohibition on treating people as mere means to the ends of others is best understood as ruling out basic positive rights while permitting derivative ones. Since a willing mother is responsible for bringing her child into the world in the first place, she cannot abandon it without violating its negative right not to be killed, and so such a child has a derivative positive right not to be abandoned. A pregnant woman, on the other hand, has a negative right not to have her body invaded, and from this negative right derives a positive right to abort her fetus, so long as doing so is not disproportionate to the seriousness of the threat (as it is not in the case of involuntary pregnancy, or of pregnancy which has become involuntary). Therefore, far from being in conflict, propositions (1), (2), and (3) have been shown to be in harmony with one another, the latter two being plausibly grounded in the first. Insofar as we have reason to accept (1), then, we have reason to accept (2) and (3). Moreover, we have seen that a proper understanding of (1) allows us to embed (2) and (3) in a larger moral perspective in which the limits of compulsory altruism are firmly drawn: enforceable rights to the use or assistance of others may be allowed into the moral domain only if they are "sponsored" by some negative right. Every putative positive right must find such a sponsor, or perish.

Philosophy, The University of North Carolina at Chapel Hill

---

denied, with devastating results. Women have been classified as objects, as resources, as property, and have been routinely subordinated to the will of others. A principle that grants every person the right not to be used as a mere means to the ends of others is a feminist principle if anything is. (For a defense of the importance of a "justice perspective" to feminist concerns, see Okin, *Justice, Gender, and the Family*, p. 15, and indeed the entire book.)

[57] Letter to Roger C. Weightman, 24 June 1826, in *The American Enlightenment: The Shaping of the American Experiment and a Free Society*, ed. Adrienne Koch (New York: George Braziller, 1965), p. 372.

THE RIGHT TO WELFARE AND THE
VIRTUE OF CHARITY*

By Douglas J. Den Uyl

> As each individual abandons himself to the solicitous aid of the State,
> so, and still more, he abandons to it the fate of his fellow-citizens.
>   Wilhelm Von Humboldt, *On the Limits of State Action*

Are the right to welfare[1] and the virtue of charity compatible? Consider this argument: *Since the right to welfare is an enforceable (not to mention enforced) duty, and since virtuous acts require uncoerced voluntary choice to qualify as virtuous, the extent to which welfare rights are exercised is the extent to which the virtue of charity is absent.* If "incompatibility" means that the presence of one thing requires the total absence of the other, then the right to welfare and the virtue of charity are not made incompatible by this argument. But the same thing cannot be both voluntary and compulsory at the same time, so it would seem that the right to welfare and the virtue of charity would be incompatible in the sense of "being incapable of simultaneous exercise."

The argument, nevertheless, has at least two obvious problems. The first is that some economic literature suggests that people will be less charitable if there is a total absence of coerced giving (e.g., due to a free-rider problem). Unfortunately, the *incentives* for and against giving cannot be a concern of this essay.[2] The second problem is that the argument seems to ignore what is central. Of course coerced action cannot count as virtuous, but the real problem is not establishing that compelled actions are virtuous, but rather showing exactly where the dividing line between justifiable coercion and noncoercion lies. The real problem, in other

---

*I wish to thank Stuart Warner, Loren Lomasky, Susan Feigenbaum, and Neil DiMarchi for preliminary help on this essay. I am especially grateful to Douglas Rasmussen, to the other contributors to this volume, and to its editors for their extensive critical comments.

[1] I am using the term "right" very loosely here to mean any claim of justice coupled with a correlative duty which is coercively sanctioned by the state. There may be rights without duties, but they would have little bearing on our problem here, since we are concerned with legitimate redistribution of resources in response to a rights claim. More importantly, not all defenses of redistribution are formulated in the language of rights. I have tried to keep the notion of "rights" loose enough to include those normative proposals which require state-sanctioned redistribution, but which for some reason prefer not to defend that redistribution by using the language of rights. In these cases, "rights" is a shorthand expression.

[2] For a discussion of some of the issues and literature on this problem, see Susan Feigenbaum, "The Case of Income Redistribution: A Theory of Government and Private Provision of Collective Goods," *Public Finance Quarterly*, vol. 8, no. 1 (January 1980), pp. 3–22.

words, concerns finding that point at which we can no longer say that what is done is "up to us," but rather that what we do is *owed* to another as a matter of right and can accordingly be compelled if we fail to respect that right.

It might be argued that there is additionally a third obvious problem with the opening argument, namely, that the argument is logically uncompelling, since people might not have to exercise their right to welfare because of the prior, free, and uncoerced benevolence of the givers. In other words, although giving *could* have been compelled, those who transferred their resources did so willingly and without a thought to the compulsion that might have been brought to bear if they had failed to give. In such cases, the right to welfare would not seem to be in conflict with the virtue of charity. Yet despite appearances, there is a problem with this sort of analysis. For if one has a *right* to welfare, the provision of that benefit cannot be a virtue separate from justice (even if done with a "smile"), because the provider would only be offering to another what is the other's due. So although some commentators are quick to point out that justice and charity cannot be distinguished on the basis that one is owed while the other is not (since that begs the question about what is or is not owed),[3] it can still be said that if the benefit is owed to another, rendering it is not an act of charity. There is no virtue beyond that of justice in "rendering to each his due."

One of the purposes of this essay, then, is to indicate how arguments which attempt to blur or abandon the distinction between justice and charity end up dismissing charity altogether. This is because the normal frameworks, both moral and political, used for discussing aid to those in need are at odds with approaches that would be conducive to the virtue of charity. Consequently, charity gets relegated to the dustbin of the supererogatory and becomes increasingly unimportant. To resuscitate this virtue we need to understand something of its historical meaning and context, the conceptual framework in which it is likely to be significant, and the ways in which it has been dismissed by other theories.

I. Adam Smith, Liberalism, and the Distinction between Justice and Charity

Allen Buchanan writes that

[t]he view that duties of justice are always negative, while those of charity are (generally) positive, is perhaps the least satisfactory attempt to distinguish justice from charity since it simply begs one of the most hotly disputed questions in the theory of rights, the ques-

---

[3] See Allen Buchanan, "Justice and Charity," *Ethics*, vol. 97, no. 3 (April 1987), p. 573.

tion of whether there are positive as well as negative (general) rights.[4]

Buchanan seems to understand the issue of distinguishing justice from charity as a dispute about rights. Yet in the history of liberal political theory the distinction was forcefully asserted by Adam Smith without any mention of rights and presumably with an appeal to some standard of evaluation other than rights (i.e., sentiment). Consider these passages from Smith's *Theory of Moral Sentiments*:

> Beneficence is always free, it cannot be extorted by force, the mere want of it exposes to no punishment; because the mere want of beneficence tends to do no real positive evil. It may disappoint of the good which might reasonably have been expected, and upon that account it may justly excite dislike and disapprobation; it cannot, however, provoke any resentment which mankind will go along with.[5]

> There is, however, another virtue, of which the observance is not left to the freedom of our own wills, which may be extorted by force, and of which the violation exposes to resentment, and consequently to punishment. This virtue is justice: the violation of justice is injury: it does real and positive hurt to some particular persons, from motives which are naturally disapproved of. It is, therefore, the proper object of resentment, and of punishment, which is the natural consequence of resentment. . . . The person himself who meditates an injustice is sensible of this, and feels that force may, with the utmost propriety, be made use of, both by the person whom he is about to injure, and by others. . . . And upon this is founded that remarkable distinction between justice and all the other social virtues, . . . that we feel ourselves to be under a stricter obligation to act according to justice, than agreeably to friendship, charity, or generosity; that the practice of these last mentioned virtues seems to be left in some measure to our own choice, but that, somehow or other, we feel ourselves to be in a peculiar manner tied, bound, and obliged to the observation of justice. (*TMS*, II.ii.I.5)

In Smith's system, justice and beneficence are motivated by the corresponding sentiments of resentment and benevolence. These are entirely different sentiments which attach themselves to what must as a consequence be rather different virtues. But in pointing this out I do not mean to suggest that the move from the language of rights to that of sentiment solves Buchanan's problem. For a possibility that Smith himself may not

[4] *Ibid.*, p. 559.

[5] Adam Smith, *The Theory of Moral Sentiments*, ed. D. D. Raphael and A. L. Macfie (Indianapolis: Liberty Classics, 1982), II.ii.I.3. I shall refer to this work hereafter as *TMS*; references will be given parenthetically in the text.

have adequately considered is that the sentiments of resentment and benevolence could attach themselves to rather diverse (even contradictory) sorts of circumstances. The person of little means raised under a Marxist ideology could possess every bit the resentment towards his capitalist "exploiters" as the libertarian may show towards the leaders of the redistributive state. In this respect, sentiment begs all the same questions that Buchanan claims the rights perspective does. Nevertheless, Buchanan's way of presenting the issue *is* indicative of a problem of moral reductionism to be discussed momentarily.

In any case, it does not follow from the fact that a line is difficult to draw, that there is therefore no line to be drawn at all. For however relative or difficult it may be to determine the line between justice and charity, the passages from Smith indicate that such problems are not sufficient to remove the distinction itself. For surely, the fact that some things are freely given to others, while other things are given because they are owed or due, marks a distinction that can be maintained in spite of any difficulties there may be in deciding the exact dividing line.

Smith's own ethics is an attempt to continue something of the classical conception of virtue within a decidedly modern orientation.[6] He can be read as pointing to the need to maintain a *significant* place for virtue within his otherwise liberal framework. If what is freely given has only personal, idiosyncratic, or supererogatory worth, then the distinction between justice and charity would not be one which parses equally valuable realms of moral concern, but would rather be a distinction which separates the morally important or primary (justice) from the morally secondary, unimportant, or heroic (charity).

In Smith's case, both justice and charity have significant roles to play. The principles of justice represent principles *necessary* for social life to occur. Virtues such as charity, on the other hand, contribute to a society's well-being or happiness, but their absence does not necessarily dissolve society, as the absence of justice would (*TMS*, II.ii.3.3). Each virtue, then, provides something different, though equally necessary, to the full flourishing of society, with justice being given the foundational, yet by no means morally superior, position.[7]

---

[6] That Smith wishes to do this is evident not just from his constant use of "virtue" throughout *TMS*, but also from his vast knowledge of, and interest in, ancient moral theory and its role in ethics (e.g., *TMS*, VII), and from his focus on propriety throughout *TMS*. Smith's classical orientation is established by Charles Griswold in "Rhetoric and Ethics: Adam Smith on Theorizing about the Moral Sentiments," *Philosophy and Rhetoric*, vol. 24, no. 3 (1991), pp. 213–37. The Smithian idea that there may be more to liberal orders than a commitment to justice is also reflected in Stephen Macedo's *Liberal Virtues* (Oxford: Clarendon Press, 1990), especially pp. 278ff.

[7] Smith's point is causal, not evaluative. Principles of justice are needed to get society off the ground. They are not necessarily superior or more admirable principles. In this connection, Smith throughout *TMS* accords benevolence and the actions it produces the highest praise from the impartial spectator, but he does not regard it as the most common motive in human life or the basis upon which to structure a social order.

However, appreciating the role of virtues other than justice may require that we see ethics as concerned with more than the prevention of harm or the promotion of utility.[8] There is no hope, for example, for a virtue like charity when morality is understood as, "fundamentally (though not exclusively) concerned with avoiding states of affairs that are harmful for individuals."[9] The avoidance or prevention of harm is some distance from the promotion or exhibition of virtue, which, even if not "excluded" from morality, would nevertheless require the sort of proactive and perfecting conduct that is not adequately captured by issues of harm or avoidance. Further, such a conception of ethics makes every ethical issue a matter of some form of justice; for the prevention or avoidance of harm (justice), while necessary, is neither ennobling nor always laudatory, though it may be, at least with respect to avoidance, always due. And this problem is not overcome by expanding "justice" to include so-called "positive" rights. For whether one respects another's rights by forbearance or by positive action, one still renders only that which is due and thus exhibits no virtue but that of justice.[10]

It should be no surprise, then, that Buchanan can plausibly claim at the end of his article that the distinction between justice and charity plays no significant role in the prominent moralities of our era (e.g., in utilitarianism and contractarianism) and that nothing important is lost by the absence of this distinction.[11] Maybe so; but it is patently false to claim that the avoidance or prevention of harm is the essence of ethics,[12] or that such a view represents the bulk of the history of this subject. Moreover, it is equally problematic to suppose that all virtues can, in quasi-Platonic fashion, be reduced to one form of the good, namely justice. That sort of moral reductionism is, in effect, what the willingness to abandon the distinction between justice and charity amounts to when otherwise charitable acts are said to be owed to someone as a matter of right.

---

[8] It is worth noting that for Smith, as reported by John Millar to Dugald Stewart (introduction to the Oxford edition of *TMS*, p. 2), questions of utility or benefit were categorized under the heading of "expediency" and came after the subjects of natural theology, moral theory, and jurisprudence.

[9] Buchanan, "Justice and Charity," p. 561. A number of the points I am making here and below seem to parallel those made elsewhere by Loren Lomasky in "Justice to Charity," unpublished manuscript.

[10] This is true even of Jeremy Waldron's unique approach to the problem of charity. The adoption of his principle 'Q' ("Nobody should be permitted ever to use force to prevent another man from satisfying his very basic needs in circumstances where there seems to be no other way of satisfying them") in no way takes his solution out of the realm of justice and into a defense of some other virtue, for Q still describes what is owed to others. See Jeremy Waldron, "Welfare and the Images of Charity," *Philosophical Quarterly*, vol. 36, no. 145 (October 1986), pp. 463–82.

[11] Buchanan, "Justice and Charity," pp. 574–75.

[12] I have argued for this point at length in *The Virtue of Prudence* (Bern: Peter Lang, 1991), ch. 1 and *passim*.

Of course, to fully appreciate the foregoing point requires some modification of the contemporary abuse of the term "virtue." Today the term is often used interchangeably with any term of positive moral value as determined by one's moral theory. Hence an act which promotes the "greatest happiness" is called virtuous, as is one which prevents a harm, fulfills a duty, or ennobles a character. If this is not a trivialization of the term "virtue," it is certainly removed from its classical conception. As Smith himself recognized,[13] virtue consists in excellence of character. Actions alone may confer benefits, but they often tell us little about the person's character. By the same token, virtue is not simply a matter of so-called "intentions." Not only must there be something of a settled nature to our dispositions, but also insight into the appropriateness of certain forms of conduct must be demonstrated. Fundamental, however, is the idea of self-directedness. No matter how appropriate, insightful, or beneficial an action may be, it can only qualify as virtuous if freely chosen. (The reverse, of course, is not the case; that is, not all freely chosen actions are virtuous.) On this understanding, therefore, the fact that an action either confers a positive benefit, prevents harm to another, or contributes to social cooperation, is neither necessary nor sufficient for describing the action as virtuous. These things may be accomplished without excellence of character and without contributing to such excellence, as, for example, when one feigns benevolence in conferring a benefit but has ulterior motives.

The foregoing point about the nature of virtue in general is thereby true of the virtue of justice as well. If a certain amount of aid to our fellows in need is owed to them, one does not demonstrate the virtue of justice by being compelled to make the transfer. If, on the other hand, one recognizes it as one's obligation to transfer the resources that are owed and is thereby motivated to render aid for that reason (treating the compulsory element as a safety net against moral backsliding), then the term "virtue" may be appropriately applied to one's character and conduct.[14] The difference between the virtue of justice and that of charity, then, cannot rest on voluntary performance, which is required of both virtues, but rather

---

[13] See, for example, *TMS*, I.i.5 and VII.ii.

[14] Cf. Lawrence Becker, *Reciprocity* (Chicago: University of Chicago Press, 1990), p. 148. In a different type of approach to our question, Becker manages to avoid reducing all virtues to justice (while at the same time giving virtue an obligatory character) by restricting the idea of justice. For him, justice is restricted to special cases of "competing or conflicting interests." Reciprocity—the obligatory virtue—is more basic than justice because it is not so restricted. Apart from being what I would regard as an overly narrow conception of justice, the move simply substitutes one term for another as far as my point here goes. The broader issue, however, is more interesting. Can one be obliged to another without that being an issue of justice? Can charity be obligatory and still remain a distinct virtue on a par with justice? My answer to this comes later and amounts to something like, "Yes, provided that the ethical approach is classical."

on whether when one makes a transfer one is "rendering [to someone] his due" *and* on whether compulsion is the appropriate response to a failure to act according to the virtue.[15]

In Smith's own brand of liberalism, the foregoing issue of whether the virtue of charity has a significant and independent role to play in his liberal regime does not initially present itself as a problem. Consider the following:

> A *superior* may, indeed, sometimes, with universal approbation, oblige those under his jurisdiction to behave, in this respect, with a certain degree of propriety to one another. The laws of all civilized nations oblige parents to maintain their children, and children to maintain their parents, and impose upon men many other duties of beneficence. The civil magistrate is entrusted with the power not only of preserving the public peace by restraining injustice, but of promoting the prosperity of the commonwealth. . . . [H]e may prescribe rules, therefore, which not only prohibit mutual injuries among fellow-citizens, but command mutual good offices to a certain degree. (*TMS*, II.ii.I.8; emphasis added)

Notice that according to this passage it is permissible for a superior to coerce an act of "charity" on the part of an "inferior." It is the inequality that matters here, for as Smith points out, "for equals to use force against one another, would be thought the highest degree of insolence and presumption," and "the mere want of beneficence seems to merit no punishment

---

[15] It is actually my view that not all matters of justice are enforceable by coercion, and in this there may be some difference between my final view of the nature of justice and that of some classical liberals such as Smith. It may be, in other words, that something is owed to another for which the failure to deliver that good is unjust but does not call for coercion (e.g., as when one unfairly criticizes another and owes that other an apology). I am not, therefore, convinced that justice is limited to *enforceable* duties. I am, however, convinced that all basic moral *rights* are enforceable duties. This then raises the issue of whether justice and rights are coextensive. For purposes of this essay (since it is about the *right* to welfare), I shall take them to be coextensive, because part of the moral reductionism I have been speaking of is the conflation of justice with "social" justice or at least with an exclusively other-oriented conception of justice. It might be the case, however (as Douglas Rasmussen has suggested in comments on this manuscript), that we would need to distinguish between various sorts of justice (e.g., the justice of "rendering each his due" versus the justice of rights respecting conduct versus justice as a virtue or constituent part of a self-perfective life). Yet in light of what I say below, the sort of justice which constitutes the "right to welfare" is strictly social and "demand-sided," since it involves what *others* may legitimately require of us independently of virtually any acts or projects of our own. Charity, on the other hand, is a thoroughly "supply-sided" virtue. Justice and charity would therefore remain distinct at an essential or general level. That is all I need here, for my purpose is to show that if justice and charity are collapsed into something like the "right to welfare," the self-directed ("supply-sided") character of the virtue of charity is at risk. Perhaps within a strictly self-perfective ethical paradigm the distinctions between various senses of justice and between justice and charity would have to be more subtle. At the moment, however, it is more the confrontation between paradigms that concerns me.

from equals" (*TMS*, II.ii.I.7, 9).[16] Apparently, then, the distinction between justice and charity—that justice can be forced while charity cannot—holds steadfast for Smith only when we are speaking of relations among equals.

Smith's reference to inequality in this context seems a holdover from classical political theory, where inequality was central to that theoretical enterprise. Superiors, because of some natural endowment, extraordinary merit, or other discriminating factor, knew what was best for people, and due to their unequal and thereby authoritative status, were entitled to command certain actions that were good, even if those actions were not accompanied by the appropriate motivation or disposition. In addition, the inequality in some sense gave the rulers the "right" to command certain kinds of actions, because it was their responsibility to directly promote the welfare of the individuals or groups under their charge. In Smith's case, the inequality turns out to be rather convenient, for it allows the justified compulsion of welfare without having to obliterate the distinction between justice and charity.

The problem here is that modern political theory does not seem to countenance the idea of the centrality of inequality, but rather its opposite. And elsewhere Smith himself seems to regard human beings as by nature equal, with inequalities being only the result of circumstance and focused effort.[17] If we are all by nature equal, then rulers are not our superiors but our equals; they simply have various administrative duties to perform on our behalf. Morally speaking, we are all the same; there are no "natural slaves" or "philosopher kings" who by their extraordinary qualities deserve to rule over us and guide us in "appropriate" directions. This conception is at the very heart of liberalism—whether it be of the classical or "new" variety. It also has interesting implications for our topic; for given the premise that beneficence cannot be coerced among equals, the following principle seems to hold: *If we are all equal, then either none of us can be commanded to be beneficent (charitable) or all of us must be* (e.g., by imposing the requirement equally upon ourselves). Is this not indeed what we find in the literature of liberalism today—one side claiming a universal right to welfare and the other saying there is no such thing?

Although Smith himself is reluctant to reduce all virtues to justice, there is nonetheless a tendency in that direction by the time we get to our

---

[16] The indented passage above could be read as saying that by some social contract "superiors" have been entrusted to make certain that various services are provided. That, of course, would not sound foreign to modern ears; but apart from the fact that Smith is not a contractarian in any normal sense of that term, the lines just cited give a better sense of the context of that passage and thus that it was the *inequality* that mattered.

[17] Adam Smith, *An Inquiry into the Nature and Causes of the Wealth of Nations*, ed. R. H. Campbell and A. S. Skinner (Indianapolis: Liberty Classics, 1981), I.ii.4–5. I shall refer to this work hereafter as *WN*; references will be given parenthetically in the text.

own era. That tendency can now (speculatively) be explained by saying that Smith was right; that is, *charitable* conduct really cannot be coerced among equals. So if we want to ensure the legitimacy of some forced transfers, we need to make them matters of justice. Indeed, if we want to *ensure* the sort of conduct that would result from the presence of any virtue, we would need to make that virtue (or the degree of it we find desirable) a matter of justice as well. This is because liberalism allows the state to legitimately use its power of coercion only in those cases where force is inherently appropriate, and such cases are almost by definition matters of justice.

All this raises the more general and deeper problem of whether the reductionist tendency is inherent in liberalism itself, and whether liberalism in the end has any place for virtue at all.[18] For if we can generate the sort of conduct we want by first reducing all moral virtues (or their appropriate parts) to justice, and then using the enforcement power such a reduction now renders morally permissible, what need (or room) could there be for an appeal to the types of exclusively self-directed actions virtue requires? But what is at issue here is not just whether liberalism has any role for virtues like charity. It may be that liberalism has actually succeeded at the *expense* of such virtues! Smith tells the following story about the impact of commerce, a central feature of liberal orders, on the institution of charity:

> In the antient state of Europe, before the establishment of arts and manufactures, the wealth of the clergy gave them the same sort of influence over the common people, which that of the great barons gave them over their respective vassals, tenants, and retainers. . . . Over and above the rents of those estates, the clergy possessed, in the tythes, a very large portion of the rents of all the other estates in every kingdom of Europe. The revenues arising from both those species of rents were . . . paid in kind. . . . The quantity exceeded greatly what the clergy could themselves consume; and there were neither arts nor manufactures for the produce of which they could exchange the surplus. The clergy could derive advantage from this immense surplus in no other way than by employing it, as the great barons employed the like surplus of their revenues, in the most profuse hospitality, and in the most extensive charity. . . . They not only maintained almost the whole poor of every kingdom, but many knights and gentlemen had frequently no other means of subsistence

---

[18] In this connection, Leo Strauss has noted: "The soul of modern development, one may say, is a peculiar realism, consisting in the notion that moral principles and the appeal to moral principles — preaching, sermonizing — are ineffectual, and therefore that one has to seek a substitute for moral principles which would be much more efficacious than ineffectual preaching." Strauss, "Progress or Return," in *The Rebirth of Classical Political Rationalism*, ed. T. Pangle (Chicago: University of Chicago Press, 1988), p. 242.

than by travelling about from monastery to monastery, under pretence of devotion, but in reality to enjoy the hospitality of the clergy. . . . The hospitality and charity of the clergy . . . increased very much the weight of their spiritual weapons. . . . Every thing belonging or related to so popular an order . . . necessarily appeared sacred in the eyes of the common people, and every violation of them, whether real or pretended, the highest act of sacrilegious wickedness and profaneness. . . .

The gradual improvements of arts, manufactures, and commerce, the same causes which destroyed the power of the great barons, destroyed in the same manner, through the greater part of Europe, the whole temporal power of the clergy. In the produce of arts, manufactures, and commerce, the clergy, like the great barons, found something for which they could exchange their rude produce. . . . Their charity became gradually less extensive, their hospitality less liberal or less profuse. Their retainers became consequently less numerous, and by degrees dwindled away altogether. . . . The ties of interest, which bound the inferior ranks of people to the clergy, were in this manner gradually broken and dissolved. . . . The inferior ranks of people no longer looked upon that order, as they had done before, as the comforters of their distress, and the relievers of their indigence. On the contrary, they were provoked and disgusted by the vanity, luxury, and expence of the richer clergy, who appeared to spend upon their own pleasures what had always before been regarded as the patrimony of the poor. (*WN*, V.i.g.22–25)

If the charity of the clergy is more a function of their economic opportunities than their moral character, one cannot help but wonder what role the virtue of charity could possibly play in a well-ordered liberal economic system. For although there may still be some who possess that virtue as a quality of their character, they would be few in number and not of any significance to the workings of the economic system. And although there may also be those who are too weak, infirm, or otherwise distressed to function in this type of economy, these groups could be easily handled by a rather minimal provision of welfare. The bulk of the population in a well-ordered liberal society would conduct their affairs in a market system where the real standard of living for the lower classes would be improving and the wealth of the upper classes would always be subject to market tests that tend to keep that wealth employed in ways that benefit society at large. This was certainly Smith's picture of the effects of the "system of natural liberty" as described in *The Wealth of Nations*. And if this is really how the picture looks, why should we care about the virtue of charity? After all, people are much better off than they were under the medieval order of systematic "charity and hospitality" offered by the barons and clergy. And if the charity that will exist will only be present at the margins anyway, why not join Buchanan and simply be done with the whole issue by making it all a matter of justice? Given the relatively low cost of maintaining marginal members of society, it would seem that only the pedantry of some philosophers stands in the way of conceding that in liberal regimes everyone has the right to a certain form of minimal subsistence.

We have now reached a point where we need to take stock of where we are. On the one hand, it would seem that we require some sort of distinction between justice and charity to help us separate what is owed from what may be freely given, and possibly also to enliven the virtues generally. On the other hand, liberalism seems to incline towards moral reductionism or the division of the moral landscape into issues of justice on one side and matters of personal preference or supererogatory conduct on the other. Thus, the further question was raised as to whether liberalism has room for virtue at all. For after getting desirable conduct under the rubric of justice, and after designing appropriate incentive systems (i.e., the market) to handle that which we do not presently compel, there seems to be no need for classical virtue, except as a form of moral heroism.

It is undoubtedly the case that the issues we have raised are too vast to be dealt with fully here. It is not just the relationship between justice and charity that is now before us, but the role of virtue in general. It may be, for example, that the loss of virtue is not to be lamented, especially if all the goods we want are provided in its absence. But let us at least understand something of what is being lost if virtue is to be abandoned. The remaining sections of this essay should provide at least some of that understanding. I believe, however, that the choice we face is not so exclusionary. Consequently, I wish to draw a provisional conclusion that can serve, when applied to charity in particular, as a kind of thesis for the rest of the essay: For *virtues to have a significant chance of flourishing in liberal orders where all persons are morally equal, every effort must be made to distinguish those virtues from the virtue of justice.* The first step in lending some support to this thesis is to see charity in its historical context. Indeed, one of my conclusions, which is only partially supported in this essay, is that the classical (self-perfective) paradigm in ethics can offer us a way of conceiving of virtue as being significant while also being compatible with the principles of ("classical") liberal order. This may have been Smith's insight as well.

II. The Roots of the Virtue of Charity

The virtue of charity has its roots in the Christian era. Although such Aristotelian concepts as "friendship" are at least partially incorporated into charity, this virtue was regarded as one of the three great "theological" virtues (along with "faith" and "hope") in the Christian Middle Ages and beyond. These theological virtues were superior to the so-called "four cardinal virtues" of "prudence," "justice," "courage," and "temperance." The four cardinal virtues were, nonetheless, the four basic moral virtues which all others were either derived from or subordinated to.[19] For purposes of this essay, the fact that charity was a theological and not a moral virtue is of little significance. The philosophical aspects of the virtue are easily identified, and it is the philosophical heritage that interests us here. In this respect, it seems only natural that my remarks focus on Aquinas's discussion of charity in the *Summa Theologiae* (II-II). The concept of charity presented there is most certainly the understanding that was carried forward, modified, or abandoned by later thinkers.

"Charity" is a translation of the Latin *caritas* which broadly means "love."[20] *Caritas* is a theological virtue for two reasons. First, because as Aquinas notes citing Augustine, " 'by charity I mean the movement of the soul towards the enjoyment of God for His own sake.' "[21] We may love self or neighbor, but the love that is charity ultimately issues in the love of God. Second, *caritas* is a theological virtue in Aquinas because it is an inclination *added to* our natural will. Presumably then, if left to nature alone, we would not have an inclination to charity. This in turn raises the interesting question of just how different charity could be from what nature would presumably have given us, namely, benevolence and beneficence.

For the moment, however, the point to be recognized is that the cardinal virtues must be *infused* with the theological virtues (*ST*, II-II, Q23, A4; Q24, A1–3), for the list of cardinal virtues is not especially Christian. Indeed, these are the same four virtues (prudence, justice, courage, temperance) that seemed to rule the theories of pagan antiquity. Consequently, for the four cardinal virtues to be manifestations of, and consistent with, Christianity, they must be exercised in a context already laid out by the theological virtues. Presumably, then, we could check the difference between an infused and noninfused virtue by comparing the description of the virtue in Aristotle with a description of the same virtue in Aquinas. This is not always easy or even possible to do, since Aquinas is concerned to follow Aristotle as closely as possible and to reconcile reason and faith

[19] The virtue of prudence, however, was technically an *intellectual* virtue, not a moral one. This distinction need not detain us at the moment, for it would only serve to confuse matters further. If interested, see Den Uyl, *The Virtue of Prudence*, ch. 1 and *passim*.

[20] It is worth consulting in this connection the Oxford English Dictionary, which discusses the etymology of the term. In general, it notes that the *Vulgate* (the Latin version of the Bible prepared by St. Jerome in the fourth century) distinguished *dilectio* (love) from *caritas* (charity), but *caritas* was used more often. The English version of the Bible translated the terms this way until the sixteenth century, when "love" was sometimes used where "charity" normally would have been used. By 1881, however, "love" was used for everything, thus eliminating the distinction between *dilectio* and *caritas*.

[21] St. Thomas Aquinas, *Summa Theologiae*, ed. Timothy McDermott (Westminster, MD: Christian Classics, 1989), II-II, Q23, A2. I shall refer to this work hereafter as *ST*; references will be given parenthetically in the text.

rather than separate them. Still, we shall see below how infusion may be a partial explanation of the differences between what Aquinas says about one virtue (liberality) and what Aristotle says about it.

Now charity for Aquinas is an act of self-perfection which is not essentially concerned with the sentiment of benevolence or even our relations towards others. Rather, charity involves perfecting our own capacity to love by directing it towards that which is perfectly lovable (God) and by devoting our time to divine things and habituating our heart to God (*ST*, II-II, Q24, A8). In practice, this means that we begin by "avoiding sin and resisting [our] concupiscences" and then progress to pursuing the good as much as possible. In the end, we seek the union and enjoyment of God which these first two stages make possible, but which cannot be fully realized in this life (*ST*, II-II, Q24, A9). The foregoing represents a progression of self-perfection, with others entering into the process as a component of that perfection, but not as its driving principle. We have charity towards others because we love God (*ST*, II-II, Q25, A1), and Aquinas even tells us that charity requires that we love ourselves more than our neighbor (*ST*, II-II, Q26, A4). Moreover, because our neighbors can be sinners or enemies, charity only requires that we love their human essence, that is, their general capacity for improvement and salvation. As individuals, they may be appropriately the objects of hate (*ST*, II-II, Q25, A6, 8, 9).

From this all too brief summary of the elements of charity, a couple of points are worth our attention. First, charity turns out to be a kind of general openness to the good. The love that is charity is one that disposes us in all our actions and thoughts to seek the good and promote it as much as possible. In this respect, then, charity is loving the good for its own sake and keeping that as a general attitude in all one's endeavors. But charity is not simply attitudinal or dispositional in nature. As a form of love it requires an object. As we noted, that object is God, but that in effect means everything, since God is master and creator of all. Consequently, the charitable person does not approach any situation with an attitude of suspicion or distrust, nor does such a person do so opportunistically, selfishly, or instrumentally. Instead, one enters into any circumstance with the recognition that this situation too is an opportunity to do good. It is this general positive, even optimistic, approach that gets transformed by later thinkers into such things as universal benevolence. What one is therefore impressed with when considering classical charity is its scope. Not only is it not limited to transferring resources, it is not even limited to one's dealings with others. Charity encompasses everything. But what does that mean once the virtue is secularized? We shall return to that question in a moment.

The other point that needs to be made is that charity is not a *means* to self-perfection but a constituent of it. Consequently, one is not charitable so that one may become self-perfected, but rather charitable conduct is the very expression of one's self-perfection. More importantly, it is self-perfection that defines the context for the classical conception of charity (and indeed the classical conception of all virtues) in the first place. This is because virtue in general is the disposition to perfect the powers of the agent as those powers relate to their appropriate objects or ends, e.g., reason and knowledge (*ST*, II-II, Q55, A2). Man's end for Aquinas was God, for Aristotle happiness or *eudaimonia*. These ends served as standards of success, and defined for the classical world (both pagan and Christian) the most important and foundational concern of ethics, namely, what is the good and how should one achieve it? This is an approach quite different from that of the modern period, where the central question of ethics concerns what duties one may have towards others.[22]

In a very real sense, the ethics of antiquity is characterized by self-realization, and this in turn is due to the teleological metaphysics that stood behind it. In contrast, modernity abandoned teleology, and consequently the question of achievement was replaced by the issue of adherence to duty, understood either in terms of deontic rules or in terms of maximizing some form of social utility. In either case, the agent was asked to constrain self-interest in response to some pressing moral principle which was almost always social in nature. So-called "duties to self," if they existed at all, were relegated to the back burner in modern ethics.

Because of the central idea that the good is brought into being by the achievements of the self, it might be said that the classical model of ethics was "supply-sided." The more modern approach — whereby ethics is viewed as fulfilling certain duties towards others — might be termed "demand-sided." There were, of course, elements of demand-sidedness in classical ethics, just as one can find some elements of supply-sidedness in modern ethics. But as archetypes and designators of the central focus of approaches to ethics, these labels will serve us nicely.

In a significant sense, classical virtue ethics is *inherently* supply-sided, since it places the bulk of its attention on the agent's own character, defines moral goodness in terms of the agent's nature, and expects that goodness to be the direct product of the agent's own actions. Moreover, the "beneficiary" of the conduct is the agent himself. The exception to this

---

[22] For a further discussion of this distinction between ancient and modern ethics, see Douglas Den Uyl and Lee C. Rice, "Spinoza and Hume on Individuals," *Reason Papers*, no. 15 (Summer 1990). In the meantime, one of the best contemporary statements about "love" (and thereby "charity") in the classical sense is given by David L. Norton in *Democracy and Moral Development* (Berkeley: University of California Press, 1991), p. 40:

> [L]ove is not exclusively or primarily interpersonal; it is first of all the right relationship of each person with himself or herself. The self to which love is in the first instance directed is the ideal self that is aspired to and by which random change is transformed into the directed development we term growth. When the ideal of the individual is rightly chosen, it realizes objective values that subsisted within the individual as innate potentialities, thereby achieving in the individual the self-identity that is termed "integrity" and that constitutes the foundation of other virtues.

seems to be, once again, the virtue of justice, which appears to be exclusively other-oriented. The perception that justice is the exception to the supply-sided character of classical virtue is, in fact, a misperception. One need only recall Plato's definition of justice as "having one's soul in proper order," and Aristotle's description of justice in Book V of the *Nicomachean Ethics* (1129a6; hereafter *NE*) as being a state of character, to realize that justice, like the other virtues of antiquity, is still within the self-perfective context.[23] The *object* of justice may, of course, be other-oriented, but not its ground or justification.

Christianity, however, may have brought some ambivalence into the picture by its *infusion* of theology into ethics. Aquinas, for example, when discussing the virtue of liberality claims it is closer to justice than charity (*ST*, II-II, Q117, A5).[24] Although liberality is not a *species* of justice, because it does not involve something that is owed to another (thereby indicating Aquinas's commitment to the distinction between justice and charity), liberality is, nonetheless, closest to justice because of its interpersonal nature and its concern with material things (i.e., money). It is only like charity in its "particular regard for the recipient." Oddly enough, when "beneficient" and "merciful" giving is directed to a particular individual (and is *not* concerned with money) it fits under the rubric of charity for Aquinas. In contrast to contemporary understanding, charity is thus the "perfect" duty (i.e., one where the recipient of the duty is specified) and liberality the "imperfect" duty. Yet Aristotle mentions justice only once during his discussion of liberality (*NE*, IV, 1120a20) and then only in a way that would separate it entirely from liberality. There is no problem for Aristotle in deciding whether liberality is a species of justice or charity, as there is in Aquinas. This is not just because there is no exact equivalent for charity in Aristotle's list of virtues (elements of friendship and magnanimity are closest), but because those virtues are not infused with anything outside themselves.

If God's love for us is the paradigmatic form of charity, then our own charity will be more perfect the more it imitates God's. Since God's love extends to everyone, our own charity must also. But this means that the interpersonal realm is now dominated by *two* significant virtues: justice and charity. Which one governs which minor virtue becomes increasingly difficult to determine in interpersonal cases, as we just saw. This is so evident that at least one commentator has claimed that Aquinas explicitly

---

[23] Aquinas notes that justice is exclusively concerned with others (*ST*, II-II, Q58, A2), and Aristotle suggests something similar (*NE*, V, ch. 11). But my point is not to suggest that supply-sided virtues cannot have others as their object, but only that their ultimate justification is grounded in the person's own good or character development, and that that is the focus of classical ethics, but not modern.

[24] But the Dominican fathers believe this has roots in some Roman authors (e.g., Cicero) whom Aquinas is looking to in *ST*, II-II, Q117, A5, when he says that "liberality is listed by some authors as a part of justice."

"argued against the separation of charity and justice."[25] In one sense, of course, that claim is true — none of the virtues are *separated* from charity, since all are infused with it. The basic distinction in Aquinas, however, is the one I have already elaborated in Section I, namely, that justice deals with what is owed to another while charity does not. The problem of the distinction between justice and charity arises for the modern mind because Christian charity makes such things as almsgiving obligatory (*ST*, II-II, Q32, A5).[26] But it is critically important to understand that we have this obligation for Aquinas not because we owe it to the other, as in justice, but because we owe it to ourselves; that is, such actions are a sign of our self-perfection (i.e., of our love of God).[27] It is from mercy that we give alms, and not out of a sense of justice (*ST*, II-II, Q32, A1).[28] The self-perfectionist or teleological character found in Aristotle is still dominant in this model, but the infusion of Christian charity has been more insistent about our obligations to others, especially the needy.

Suppose now that we de-theologize the doctrine and remove God from the picture. Only two of the three possible ultimate objects of charity would remain: self or others. As long as God was present, it could be argued that self and others were nicely balanced, because our obligations to both had to be understood through God. And although teleological metaphysics (ethics) gave the self precedence over others, the infusion of

---

[25] Edward Andrew, *Shylock's Rights* (Toronto: University of Toronto Press, 1987), pp. 7–9.

[26] I am not, however, saying that the mere fact that something is obligatory renders it a matter of justice, but rather that when something is conceived of as obligatory outside of the self-perfective framework and within the strictly social or modern framework, the problem of the conflation of justice and charity would be likely to arise. It is also worth noting that this article in Aquinas is also cited by Andrew along with Q58, A12 and Q66, A7–8. How he misinterprets Q32, A5 is explained above in the text. The other citations also do not support his contention that Aquinas does not want to separate justice from charity, assuming again that "separate" means something close to "distinguish" (for if it did not, Andrew's point would be trivial).

[27] One should not now assume that therefore others are simply instrumental to one's own self-perfection. Giving alms for "God's sake" is another way of saying that one's love of God causes one to recognize the love of others *for their own sake*. Aquinas would argue that it is in the absence of that sort of love that we treat others as instruments.

[28] Elsewhere (*ST*, II-II, Q66, A7–8, noted by Andrew and cited in n. 26 above) Aquinas does seem to say that those in need have a "right" to the surplus of others and that this has something to do with justice. Moreover, he says (*ST*, II-II, Q58, A2) that justice is exclusively other-oriented and (*ST*, II-II, Q58, A12) that justice is the supreme moral virtue. But this should not be interpreted to mean that justice and charity collapse into one another. In the first place, charity as a theoretical virtue is obviously the broader notion. Secondly, we have already seen at least one case where they are distinguished, and we have observed the manner in which their distinction was the basis for the problem of categorization. Finally, as I have already noted, the fact that something is the object of a virtue does not necessarily make it the ground of the virtue. So even if others were the exclusive object of justice, it would not necessarily be the case that justice must be understood exclusively in terms of others. That would be like saying we must understand courage solely in terms of risky circumstances, without reference to the agent. It would still not be accurate, then, to say that for Aquinas one owes the other goods as a matter of justice, although other Christian thinkers do hold that position.

charity was thought to keep that precedence from lapsing into an egoism. But if we remove teleology as well, the self would lose its standard of perfectibility. This would be especially true if the self were conceived as a bundle of passions without a *summum bonum*. For now there could be no end to serve as a standard of perfection by which to measure one's achievements, leaving the satisfaction of desires to constitute the good for the self. Yet the satisfaction of desire is something one pursues anyway. Consequently, our relations with others would have to come to claim the central focus of normative theory and become the object of charity (since God and self no longer have any claim). This line of reasoning should have brought to mind a particular individual, namely the father of all modern social and normative theorizing—Thomas Hobbes.

Hobbes is quite explicit about the object of charity being others:[29]

> Moreover, that moral virtue, that we can truly measure by civil laws, which is different in different states, is justice and equity; that moral virtue which we measure purely by natural laws is only charity. Furthermore, all moral virtue is contained in these two. . . . Nor in truth, should one demand that the courage and prudence of the private man, if useful only to himself, be praised or held as a virtue by states or by any other men whatsoever to whom these same are not useful. So, condensing this whole teaching on manners and dispositions into the fewest words, I say that good dispositions are those which are suitable for entering into civil society; and good manners (that is, moral virtues) are those whereby what was entered upon can be best preserved. For all the virtues are contained in justice and charity. (*De Homine*, ch. 13, sec. 9)

> It is also a law of nature, That every man do help and endeavour to accommodate each other, as far as may be without danger of their persons, and loss of their means, to maintain and defend themselves. For seeing the causes of war and desolation proceed from those passions, by which we strive to accommodate ourselves, and to leave others as far as we can behind us: it followeth that that passion by which we strive mutually to accommodate each other, must be the cause of peace. And this passion is . . . charity. (*Elements of Law*, pt. 1, ch. 16, sec. 8)

Notice that the purpose of charity is now social cooperation. It is still broader and prior to justice, for it represents the sort of attitude needed to escape the state of nature or solve the Prisoner's Dilemma, namely, good will towards others and a willingness to cooperate. Justice, in contrast, is adherence to the rules of order established by the sovereign for

---

[29] Both of the following quotes are drawn from Thomas Hobbes, *English Works*, 11 vols., ed. W. Molesworth (Evanston, IL: Adlers Foreign Bks., 1966).

the maintenance of the sought-after peace and security. In neither case is what is "useful only to [one]self" to be counted for anything. The self-perfectionist ethics has been traded for an ethics of social cooperation. Altruism in the *normative* sense has now been placed at the center of modern ethics, although it has been removed by Hobbes as a *descriptive* category of human action. In any case, for Hobbes as for Aquinas, the term "charity" is still broader than and logically prior to "justice." But if justice is what the sovereign commands, then the two can and should be merged in practice. Consider:

> And whereas many men, by accident unevitable, become unable to maintain themselves by their labour; they ought not to be left to the Charity of private persons; but to be provided for, (as far-forth as the necessities of Nature require), by the Lawes of the Commonwealth. For as it is Uncharitableness in any man, to neglect the impotent; so it is in the Sovereign of a Commonwealth, to expose them to the hazard of such uncertain Charity.[30]

If one wishes, however, to see justice and charity collapsed together in a thoroughly demand-sided approach to ethics, one must look elsewhere.

It may seem surprising, but a most explicit reduction of charity to justice, and a narrowing of charity to the question of aiding the poor, is contained in the following passage from John Locke:[31]

> But we know God hath not left one Man so to the Mercy of another, that he may starve him if he please: God the Lord and Father of all, has given no one of his Children such a Property, in his peculiar Portion of the things of this world, but that he has given his needy Brother a Right to the Surplusage of his Goods; so that it cannot justly be denied him, when his pressing Wants call for it. And therefore no Man could ever have a just Power over the Life of another, by Right of property in Land or Possessions; since 'twould always be a Sin in any Man of Estate, to let his Brother perish for want of affording him Relief out of his Plenty. As *Justice* gives every Man a Title to the product of his honest Industry, and the fair Acquisitions of his Ancestors descended to him; so *Charity* gives every Man a Title to so much out of another's Plenty, as will keep him from extream want,

---

[30] Thomas Hobbes, *Leviathan*, ed. Richard Tuck (Cambridge: Cambridge University Press, 1991), ch. 30.

[31] John Locke, *Two Treatises of Government*, ed. Peter Laslett (Cambridge: Cambridge University Press, 1988), Book 1, ch. 4, sec. 42. It is not my intention to imply that Locke was the first to look at matters in the way described below. Pascal, for example, favorably cites St. Gregory (*Provincial Letters*, 12): "When we give the poor what is necessary to them, we are not so much bestowing on them what is our property as rendering to them what is their own; and it may be said to be an act of justice rather than a work of mercy."

where he has no means to subsist otherwise; and a Man can no more justly make use of another's necessity, to force him to become his Vassal, by with-holding that Relief, God requires him to afford to the wants of his Brother, than he that has more strength can seize upon a weaker, master him to his Obedience, and with a Dagger at his Throat, offer him Death or Slavery.

Notice that not only can those in need lay title to the "surplusage" of others, but those others cannot *justly* refuse. Notice also that the perspective here is from the standpoint of those in need rather than the person supplying the benefit. In other words, nothing is said about the perfective qualities of such actions with respect to the benefactor.

We have seen over the course of this historical sketch that the context for understanding the virtue of charity has been dramatically altered. We have also seen that the exact relationship between justice and charity has been problematic for some time. By the same token, our account has made it clear that charity and altruism (the moral primacy of others) are not necessarily bedfellows, and that if one looks for that partnership, one is more likely to find it in the modern than the premodern or classical world.

The problematic nature of the relationship between justice and charity is not, as Edward Andrew has argued, a reason to claim that early modern liberalism sought to separate justice from charity in order to remove the barriers to commercialization.[32] If anything, the matter almost seems the reverse. Modern liberals are keen on making some sort of charity a right, if for no other reason than to avoid the whimsy and uncertainty of leaving it to individual choice.

It may nevertheless be correct to suppose that liberalism essentially calls for distinguishing, even separating, justice from charity (now understood in the narrow sense of aiding the poor). It may do so not, as neo-Marxists might suggest, to protect selfishness and allow one to avoid charitable conduct, but rather because liberalism conceives of itself as an inherently classless system unable to institutionally recognize certain members of society as the class from which charity should flow and others as its perpetual recipients.[33] The best it can do is speak in terms of rich and poor, but these are fairly amorphous and (for any individual) un-

---

[32] See Edward Andrew, *Shylock's Rights*, p. 5. Later in chapter two (p. 58) Andrew cites the same passage from Locke that I do above. Nevertheless, he refuses to believe it, asserting instead that his thesis about early liberals separating justice and charity must be correct so we should not read this in terms of what it says but in terms of something else. No further textual evidence, however, is provided, and from my point of view it is because Andrew has at least partially misconstrued the problem that he cannot read the texts correctly.

[33] Recall that early liberals such as Smith saw commercial societies *not* as a means of entrenching a wealthy class, but of closing the gap between rich and poor that older systems had solidified. The rise of the *middle* class was thought to be the great product of liberal orders.

stable categories compared to pre-liberal class systems with defined, multigenerational hierarchical orders. As we saw from Smith in Section I, it was part of the promise of liberalism to remove the system of charity which depended upon alms from the clergy or aristocracy. Those who then came to occupy the ranks of the rich and poor would have no particular occupation or class association, because various individuals of differing occupations and social status would cycle through these ranks. Consequently, no one under liberalism would be identifiably born into or inherit the role of almsgiver or receiver. Another way of putting this point is to suggest that the rise of commercialism and the middle class transformed charity from a "perfect" to an "imperfect" virtue.

Critics of liberalism charge that liberalism has no place for charity. This would seem to mean that if charity is not a right, people are free not to be charitable. And this in turn is interpreted to imply that liberalism does not care about charity. Perhaps. But we have seen that *thinkers* who are liberal certainly care. These same thinkers, however, did not believe it was the role of the state to manage the entire moral landscape. Indeed, the state was only really fit to manage one virtue — justice. But therein lies our opening problem: either everything that matters gets reduced to justice (e.g., formulated in terms of rights) or liberalism seems indifferent to virtues distinct from justice. Since the *cultural* inheritance of liberalism is predominantly Christian, and Christianity does not permit indifference about aid to the poor, liberalism would appear indifferent if it failed to institutionalize some right to charity. Yet doing that may run counter to other features inherent in liberalism.

The problem just stated can be characterized in another way: liberalism has no systematic procedure for determining whether conduct is virtuous or not. This is because liberalism was founded on the idea that the state is concerned with outward conduct rather than with inner states of being. But if that is so, liberalism may permit confusing the appearance of virtue with its real expression. The various aspects of this problem were first noticed by Bernard Mandeville.

III. The Mandevillian Problem of Charity

To appreciate Mandeville's discussion of the appearance/reality problem as it applies to the virtue of charity, we must first understand something of how Mandeville conceived of charity. He defines charity in the following way:

> Charity is that Virtue by which part of the sincere Love we have for our selves is transferr'd pure and unmix'd to others, not tied to us by the Bonds of Friendship or Consanguinity, and even meer Strangers, whom we have no obligation to, nor hope or expect any thing

from. If we lessen any ways the Rigour of this Definition, part of the
Virtue must be lost.[34]

With regard to our historical sketch of the last section, this definition still
shares many of the characteristics of the classical view: it is broad in
scope, supply-sided in nature, and does not reduce charity to the giving
of alms. It also clearly supposes that charity is freely given and directed
towards those "whom we have no obligation to." Yet although this definition provides a context for our discussion, it is not its components that
concern us, but the ways in which its "rigours" might be lessened.

Charity manifested itself in three distinct aspects for Mandeville: (1)
when we interpret the actions of others in the best possible light ("and
if a Man sleeps at Church . . . we ought to think he shuts his Eyes to increase his Attention"); (2) when we "bestow our Time and Labour for
nothing" on the behalf of others; and finally (3) when we give away what
we value ourselves, "being contented rather to have and enjoy less, than
not relieve those who want" (p. 254). Most of Mandeville's essay is spent
on the third manifestation of charity, but the particular "Mandevillian"
problem that concerns us is applicable to all three. Now the basis for the
Mandevillian problem of charity is brought to light directly after the three
aspects of charity are identified:

> This Virtue is often counterfeited by a Passion of ours, call'd *Pity* or
> *Compassion*, which consists in a Fellow-feeling and Condolence for
> the Misfortunes and Calamities of others: all Mankind are more or
> less affected with it; but the weakest Minds generally the most. It is
> raised in us, when the Sufferings and Misery of other creatures make
> so forcible an Impression upon us, as to make us uneasy. . . . [A]nd
> the nearer and more violently the Object of Compassion strikes those
> Senses, the greater Disturbance it causes in us, often to such a De-
> gree as to occasion great Pain and Anxiety. (pp. 254–55)

Following this description of the confusion of pity or compassion with
charity, Mandeville gives a particularly gruesome account of an infant being devoured by a swine as one looks on helplessly. He notes in this connection that "there would be no need of Virtue or Self-Denial to be moved
at such a Scene; and not only a Man of Humanity, of good Morals and
Commiseration, but likewise an Highwayman, an House-Breaker, or a
Murderer could feel Anxieties on such an Occasion" (p. 256). The passion
or sentiment of pity or compassion, then, is nearly universal in scope and

[34] Bernard Mandeville, "An Essay on Charity and Charity-Schools," in *The Fable of the
Bees* (Indianapolis: Liberty Classics, 1988), p. 253. All references to Mandeville will be to this
edition. Hereafter, page numbers will be given in the text.

capable of great power. These sentiments are not, however, the end result of sophisticated moral education or habituation.

The essence of the Mandevillian problem can now be stated quite simply: *Acting to relieve or satisfy the sentiment, desire, or passion of pity or compassion is no different in principle from the relief of any other sentiment, desire,
or passion.* There is no virtue here. Easing the anxiety one feels in the face
of a pitiable circumstance is no different from easing the anxiety one feels
in the face of a good one wishes to possess, or a sexual opportunity one
wishes to exploit. Remember Mandeville's definition stated that we must
transfer "sincere Love" "unmix'd" to others. The endeavor to relieve the
anxieties accompanying compassion is, on its face, more like self-gratification than pure unmixed love. But this problem is further heightened by
a host of vanities that attend pity or compassion:

> As Pity is often by our selves and in our own Cases mistaken for
> Charity, so it assumes that Shape, and borrows the very Name of it;
> a Beggar asks you to exert that Virtue for Jesus Christ's sake, but all
> the while his great Design is to raise your Pity. . . . But he trusts not
> to one Passion only, he flatters your Pride with Titles and Names of
> Honour and Distinction; your Avarice he sooths with often repeat-
> ing to you the Smallness of the Gift he sues for, and conditional
> Promises of future Returns with an Interest extravagant beyond the
> Statute of Usury tho' out of reach of it. . . . For when Pity seizes us,
> if we can but imagine that we contribute to the Relief of him we have
> Compassion with, and are Instrumental to the lessening of his Sor-
> rows, it eases us, and therefore pitiful People often give an Alms
> when they really feel that they would rather not. (pp. 257–58)

The Mandevillian problem of charity, therefore, poses the problem of dis-
cerning whether we are acting out of a sense of moral worth for its own
sake (the virtue of charity) or just seeking to relieve another discomfort
(compassion) we experience. And while it may be true that passions such
as pity and compassion are social in nature and therefore that "there are
not many Occasions on which we ought to conquer or curb [them]" (p.
260), this alone does not transform compassion into charity. Further, it is
clear that charity is often *apparently* present but actually absent altogether.
For as Mandeville points out, "Pride and Vanity have built more Hospi-
tals than all the Virtues together" (p. 261). It is therefore easy to *look* charitable and also to confuse our own feelings of compassion and the
conduct they evoke with the virtue of charity itself.

It is tempting at this point to start accusing Mandeville of what he was
accused of in his own day and beyond—namely, rigorism (the view that
virtue is inseparable from self-denial). Mandeville believes that people are
moved by self-interest and yet holds a theory of virtue which entirely excludes the presence of self-interest. It is then easy to mock the virtues and

show their absence from everyday life, and to claim that those who preach them are being hypocritical. But, so the argument goes, we need not accept such a rigoristic conception of virtue. Yet one must not be too quick here, for the Mandevillian problem is precisely the one Kant employed to reject the whole course of sentimentalist ethics from Hobbes through Hume to Smith. No matter how one twists and turns and otherwise obfuscates the issue, there is no way, according to Kant,[35] to transform passion or sentiment into principle. Morally speaking, Mandeville is right: one no more acts out of principle in the relief of the anxiety of compassion than in the relief of sexual lust, and conduct must be principled for it to qualify as moral or virtuous.

In this respect, it is not simply the *distance* between virtue and practice that makes Mandeville's problem of the appearance versus the reality of virtue worthy of consideration, but the problematic character of virtue itself. For a typical sort of response would be to suggest that as long as the "good" gets done, what difference does the motive make? In other words, as long as the hospital gets built, what does it matter that the chief donors were moved by pride and vanity? In many respects this is the utilitarian response to the Kantian challenge—to focus on effects. But this response only points to the dichotomous nature of modern ethics (between deontologists and utilitarians) and not to the nature of virtue. Indeed, the very conflict over effects versus motives reflects the abandonment of classical virtue, which involved both.

Mandeville's point, then, is that the virtue of charity (like any other virtue) requires something well beyond an expression of concern for the plight of the poor. But suppose, in any case, we wanted a system to assuage our feelings of compassion and pity in the efficient manner in which many of our other desires are relieved. What would such a system look like? First, we would expect such a system to maximize the relief in the least costly way to us personally. Second, if we could relieve our desire in this case without much interference with the pursuit of other desires, then we could increase the efficiency of relief. And finally, if we could feel like we have done a great deal with little effort, the very confusion between compassion and charity mentioned by Mandeville can go on unmasked.

We do have a system that meets these criteria quite well; it is the modern welfare state. Unlike the less fortunate Mandeville, who had to face

---

[35] Cf., e.g., Kant, *Foundations of the Metaphysics of Morals*, sec. I. Kant shares with the classical moral tradition a recognition of the importance of principle and a rejection of social utility as the foundation of ethics. Nevertheless, Kant's formalism, rule orientation, and impersonalism are antithetical to the classical virtue of charity as I have described it here. Moreover, attempts to turn Kant into a virtue ethicist are unconvincing (see Den Uyl, *The Virtue of Prudence*, ch. 5). Nevertheless, the second formulation of the Categorical Imperative does share something of the basic spirit of classical charity. I thank Thomas Hill for showing me this.

beggars daily, we can effectively relieve our consciences by mail. Through the system of paying taxes to support welfare programs, we may never actually confront the spectacle of a person in need. They are swept from our streets and institutionalized out of sight. One simply mails in one's "contribution" in the form of taxes[36] without much interference with the pursuit of one's other projects or desires. Indeed, one can clamor for more relief on a regular basis through political action and thus demonstrate one's compassion even further. When those who might otherwise qualify for welfare *do* confront us — and this is increasingly the case on the streets of large cities — we regard this as a *failure* of the system and something to be corrected. The welfare state, in other words, does not just provide the needy with benefits; it also provides a comfortable and convenient way to relieve one's conscience or satisfy one's duty to the poor.

It is not my view that compassion should be relieved privately rather than publicly because private systems would somehow better accord with people's interests. I do not think the welfare state is a plot foisted on the freedom-loving masses by an elite group of maniacal socialists. We have welfare states because people want them; we want them so that in a relatively easy and convenient way, we can do our part for the poor at little cost to ourselves. Provided we never do what Mandeville did and question the equation of acting out of compassion with charity, we can (in a manner that seems less possible in a system where all charity is private) contribute to the betterment of the poor without having to make such betterment an actual part of our personal projects. Compassion may be relieved under any system, but in the welfare state, where "charity" is impersonal, institutional, and professional, the only required inconvenience to us personally is the tax rate — and that is supposed to be, in the name of justice, graduated. Consequently, the welfare state, in which everyone has a right to welfare if need be, makes it convenient to trade on the confusion between compassion and charity. A private system, in contrast, would tend to make charity much more a matter of personal responsibility.[37] But then making something a matter of personal responsibility may be the first step one takes to avoid the confusion between compassion and charity and to move from sentiment to virtue. For the welfare state appeals to one's compassion, the private system to one's obligations.

[36] This is not to suggest that taxes cannot be onerous, but the degree of the burden is a separate issue from the replacement of charity as a virtue with charity as a commodity.

[37] This is not to say individuals in this system might not also confuse compassion and charity. A critic might be more likely to respond that the private system allows "charitable" deeds to be done more from motives of "pride" and "vanity" than a public system which, in a sense, removes motives altogether. But part of the issue here is whether having to occasionally appeal to those vices is worse than systematically abandoning the possibility of charity being a question of personal responsibility.

IV. The Right to Welfare and the Virtue of Charity

Among the theses I have sought to support is the idea that in a society of moral equals, the virtue of charity most accords with that system which does not sanction it with coercive force. As we have seen, we can abandon the assumption that we are all equal, which might allow the provision of welfare by the state on "paternalistic" grounds, or we can abandon classical virtue altogether. The first alternative seems unacceptable to the modern mind, while the second runs contrary to what amounts to an operating assumption of this essay, namely, that classical virtue is a viable candidate in moral discourse.

In addition, one of my motivations has been to contrast the self-perfective framework of classical virtue with more modern approaches. It could not, of course, be my purpose here to show the superiority of the classical conception over its competitors, for that is a project that extends well beyond the confines of this essay.[38] But modern discussions of welfare seem to take for granted that the moral worth of the right to welfare can be justified independently of any mention of the virtue of charity. It is necessary therefore that we examine some of the broad parameters of defenses of the right to welfare, if for no other reason than to identify just how absent the virtue of charity is from these discussions.

Norman Barry has stated that "liberals and welfare philosophers can agree surely that the existence of deprivation does constitute a prima facie reason for action."[39] While this statement may be true, it is unfortunately the principles used to explain why deprivation is a "prima facie reason for action" that end up making all the difference in this debate. The Mandevillian perspective, for example, would hold that the "prima facie reason" is grounded in relieving our anxiety in the face of suffering. But the problem with this sort of account is that putting it into practice may provide perverse incentives to free-ride on the provision of welfare by others and to strategically exploit the system, either by exaggerating one's own need for welfare, or by advancing programs for one's own benefit that others will have to pay for. In addition, in democratic systems welfare programs become "commodified," that is, traded like other goods or services in exchange for political concessions and like benefits through a process of logrolling and interest-group competition.[40] This tends to

---

[38] Some attempt to begin such a defense is contained in my two books: *Liberty and Nature* (with Douglas Rasmussen) (La Salle: Open Court, 1991), and *The Virtue of Prudence*.

[39] Norman Barry, "The Philosophy of the Welfare State," *Critical Review*, vol. 4, no. 4 (Fall 1990), p. 551.

[40] See Alan Wolfe, *Whose Keeper?* (Berkeley: University of California Press, 1989), pp. 154ff. See also Richard Wagner, *To Promote the General Welfare* (San Francisco: Pacific Research Institute, 1989), ch. 8, pp. 159ff. Wagner discusses (pp. 164ff.) the "Samaritan's dilemma" where the provision of welfare produces the moral hazard of the demand for more welfare. I do not wish to trade on this as part of a criticism of welfare liberalism, and as I state in the next paragraph, I believe defenders of welfare are also concerned to avoid such hazards. But

make welfare less a moral matter of the relief of suffering and more a political mechanism for catering to middle-class desires for security.

Most moral arguments, however, are made with a sincere interest in relieving suffering and would be unlikely to condone the perverse incentives just mentioned. Instead, these arguments make an appeal to the idea that welfare is in some way morally obligatory. We have already seen that the notion of an obligation can have ambiguous political implications. It may be, for example, that one can have the obligation without it being permissible for the state to sanction that obligation with coercive force. This possibility would make welfare consistent with classical laissez-faire liberalism.[41] Yet I have also been trying to indicate that at a deeper level, the very character of the obligation can have an effect on one's understanding of the nature of charity. Is the "prima facie" reason, in other words, a reason because suffering provides the occasion on which others can make certain claims upon us, or is the "prima facie" reason of the sort where the suffering represents the object of a self-perfecting act?

We are, of course, tempted to avoid such dichotomous choices by answering, "Something of both"; but as we have already seen to some extent, and will see more completely below, the division is basic. If we examine the arguments for some kind of right to welfare, we shall see that they are all demand-sided—that is, of the first sort. Furthermore, I suspect that the second type of argument (the self-perfecting one) is ignored because it is unlikely one *could* generate a right to welfare out of it. The best one could do towards giving those in need an entitlement would be to do what antiquity did, namely, suppose a basic inequality and then claim a paternalistic responsibility on the part of superiors and an inevitable dependency on the part of inferiors.[42]

But leaving aside antiquity for the moment, defenses of the right to welfare tend to fall into three main types: reciprocity arguments, agency arguments, and (for lack of a better name) its-really-not-your-property-after-all arguments (henceforth "RNY" for "really not yours"). Of course, some arguments combine elements of each of these basic categories,[43]

---

the system of private charity would be more likely to avoid this problem, although it might be charged with undersupplying the benefit (see below). Wagner also discusses this last problem in economic terms (p. 172) and notes that it is not all that clear that welfare is a public good undersupplied by the market.

[41] But in a sense my argument of the first section was that this would no longer be a welfare state but, if you will, a *charity* state.

[42] Leibniz is one of the few moderns who understood this. His concept of justice is based on a basic inequality that has roots in the classical order. Its connection to charity was that he defined justice as "*caritas sapientis*" (charity of the wise). See Den Uyl, "The Aristocratic Element in Leibniz's Political Thought," *Journal of the History of Philosophy*, vol. 15, no. 3 (July 1977).

[43] Loren Lomasky's argument, for example, seems to be a combination of the agency and the RNY arguments. See Loren Lomasky, *Persons, Rights, and the Moral Community* (Oxford: Oxford University Press, 1987), especially pp. 125–28.

while others do not seem to fit neatly into any.[44] And as with any effort to categorize, oversimplification is inevitable. Nevertheless, my reading of the literature does suggest these as the main types of defenses.

To take the last first, the RNY arguments essentially regard all property as conventional, and thus no one has any absolute claim to his possessions or resources.[45] Sometimes people are regarded as trustees of the resources of society,[46] which would make it a relatively easy matter to transfer those resources if the trustees were not using them wisely, or if society had more pressing needs elsewhere. By themselves these arguments can only stand as negative defenses of the right to welfare. In other words, they might be marshaled to defeat arguments against welfare which depend on an absolute natural right to private property. Beyond this, they can only grease the wheel of more positive arguments for welfare, since the notion that property is conventional does not of itself make the case for transferring it.

We can put all contractarian arguments in the RNY category, because property rights for contractarians are either all, or for the most part, the product of the social contract. So if there were a contractarian case for the right to welfare[47] then the agreed-upon contractual rules would include the legitimacy of redistribution, since that would be nothing other than living up to the bargain struck by the contractors. Yet it is for this very reason that contractarianism can be rejected, for purposes of this essay, as being necessarily incompatible with an explanation derived from the virtue of charity. The redistribution that occurs takes place because of the terms of the agreement, so the sanctions involved are there to enforce that agreement. In this respect, then, contractarian redistribution is all a matter of justice, not charity, since keeping or enforcing agreements are matters of justice. Of course, contractarians may individually care about "charity" and make agreements with each other such that it has a large place in their social system. This may give charity some practical leverage, but it does not give it any theoretical footing; for the final appeal of the argument is not to the virtue of charity itself, but to the terms or process of the agreement. Charity comes out looking like one among a num-

---

[44] An example here might be Baruch Brody in "Redistribution Without Egalitarianism," *Social Philosophy & Policy*, vol. 1, no. 1 (Autumn 1983), where "redistribution programs . . . are forms of compensation for the violation of rights" (p. 86). This view, however, would be closest to a type of reciprocity argument.

[45] Gerald F. Gaus correctly notes that this is the Rousseauian perspective on political philosophy, where property cannot be antecedent to political society but is itself the product of convention, law, and politics. See Gerald F. Gaus, "A Contractual Justification of Redistributive Capitalism," in *Markets and Justice*, ed. John W. Chapman (New York: NYU Press, 1989), p. 90.

[46] This seems to be the view of Jeremy Waldron in "Welfare and the Images of Charity" (see n. 10 above).

[47] And of course there are contractarian cases. See, for example, Gaus, "A Contractual Justification of Redistributive Capitalism"; and Christopher W. Morris, "A Hobbesian Welfare State?" *Dialogue*, vol. 4, no. 27 (Winter 1988), pp. 653–73.

ber of possible preferences held by the contractors. It is, in other words, instrumental to the terms of the agreement and not itself the moral basis for the defense of welfare.

The essence of agency arguments is perhaps best and most succinctly summed up by Loren Lomasky:

> Individuals have reason to value the maintenance of a regime of rights because they value their own ability to pursue projects. Should that ability be placed in jeopardy by a system of rights such that one can *either* continue to respect others' rights *or* be able to pursue projects *but not both*, then one would no longer have a rational stake in the moral community established by that system of rights. (*Persons, Rights, and the Moral Community*, p. 127)

When individuals are put in the position of having to either respect rights or pursue projects, they have reached the point where they can no longer effectively function as agents in the community; for the central feature of agency — pursuit of personal projects within a human community — is no longer available. It is this aspect of the argument that seems common to all agency positions, namely, that (potential) loss of agency calls for rectification to bring the individual back to the level where agency is again functional. Differences would then be over what does or does not threaten agency and over the various means that might be employed to recover it.

Lomasky himself, like Locke, goes on to argue that the agent in these dire circumstances has a residual claim to the surplus property of others. We do not have an absolute claim to our "surplus," because it is possible for each of us to fall prey to agency-removing circumstances. When that happens, we too would not value any system of rights that failed to restore our agency. Consequently, the only system that would be valued would be one in which individuals did not have absolute entitlement to their surplus property, even when that property was legitimately obtained. "Surplus" here means something like "that which goes beyond what is necessary to maintain agency." Lomasky seems to interpret what is necessary for agency in fairly minimalist terms, so that the right in question entitles one to sufficient but not extensive or necessarily continuous aid. However, the questions of what constitutes a surplus, when agency has been restored, and what is necessary to maintain agency would all seem open to interpretation and dispute.

Agency arguments are structured in terms of the agent in need and not the one giving the aid. In this respect they all trail off into general abstract conclusions about how "someone" must provide the benefit "owed" to the recipient. This may seem analogous to all rights arguments, where some indefinite "others" are bound to respect the right in question. Yet unlike, for example, the right to negative liberty, which each and every individual is bound to (and can) respect at all times, the right to welfare (or the restoration of agency) could not be taken this way without thereby thrusting the recipient(s) into riches. Instead, the right seems to be understood to mean that anyone *may* be called to contribute and that all should be prepared to meet the obligation, but that only so much will be demanded as is necessary for the restoration of agency. Nevertheless, like the negative right to liberty, the right to welfare based on an agency approach considers nonrecipients only to the extent that they may be in a position to respect the right. Otherwise, the entire focus is on the claimant, making these sorts of arguments thoroughly demand-sided.

In Lomasky's case, for example, the argument at best establishes that the agent in need no longer has reason to value the system that does not restore his or her agency, not that perhaps hundreds of millions of others have a reason to disvalue that same system. One can respond to this either with some sort of contractarian argument ("No one would agree to such a system . . .") about which I have already had my say, or one can suppose that agency is the *sine qua non* of morality, such that failure to rescue the (presumably) involuntary departure from it on the part of some is tantamount to rejecting morality altogether.[48] This latter alternative still suffers, however, from what might be called the "problem of engagement"; that is, it fails to provide a direct *personal* reason for taking the action. Even if we grant, for the sake of argument only, that the indirect impersonal case has been made—where the individual's own membership in the class of agents commits that individual in some way and on "pain" of inconsistency to a concern about the agency status of others— what does the argument say to each person individually about the action and his own projects?

Notice that if our appeal is to the virtue of charity, instead of the right to welfare, the problem of engagement is immediately met, for the focus then is on the one(s) who will provide the benefit, not the recipient. Yet unlike the agency argument, which ignores the provider altogether, this focus does not preclude the person in need from being a part of the nature of the virtue of charity, and not just abstractly. Indiscriminate or impersonal giving would be unconcerned with those specifics (e.g., how

[48] A better argument, and one more consistent with other things that at least Lomasky says in his book, is to say that agency is a necessary condition of human communities. To let anyone's agency lapse without taking action is equivalent to a lack of commitment to a necessary condition for a human community which, in quasi-Hobbesian terms, puts one in a state of nature with respect to the community. So one's property can be taken either because one is an enemy of the community or because as a member one is committed to doing what is necessary to maintain the conditions of community. So far as I know Lomasky does not make this argument, but this argument may represent his own view, since his approach often seems to me to be at least partially contractarian. Incidentally, this is an argument I would accept, though not as a foundational argument, but rather as one that has force within a self-perfective context. It would not, in my view, imply a *right* to welfare, although it might at least partially establish an obligation to aid. For further information on my own position, see Douglas Rasmussen and Douglas Den Uyl, *Liberty and Nature*, pp. 144–51.

much, how long, to whom, why) necessary for making charity an integral part of one's own projects. Doing so becomes increasingly difficult the more the projects are impersonally conceived and universally required.

It is worth noting at this point that there is nothing especially self-perfecting about aiding those in need,[49] except perhaps for those positive feelings that naturally result from our propensity for benevolence. Yet as part of a more broadly conceived charity such actions may indeed be perfective. For as premodern philosophers seem to have seen more correctly, the general outlook of cooperation, good will, or moral optimism is what is self-perfecting—the particular manifestations (such as giving aid to those in need) are but the sign of moral accomplishment. Consequently, we can say that the failure to render appropriate aid signifies one's moral defectiveness, but that the giving of aid is not itself necessarily a sign of one's self-perfection or possession of the virtue of charity. If, on the other hand, the concept of charity is narrowed to the act of giving aid to those in need, is it really surprising that the recipient is the object of analysis and the provider entirely ignored? After all, under this way of looking at things, what more is there to say to the donor about the act of transferring resources to those with less, except that one will "feel good" afterwards?[50]

It may still be possible, however, to get a less one-sided perspective on welfare out of reciprocity arguments. In general, reciprocity arguments take the form of returning "good for good" (or "evil for evil"). This would suggest that both the benefactor and recipient would be given at least equal consideration.[51] Indeed, it is precisely because one may play either role that reciprocity arguments do not seem as demand-sided as agency arguments might be. As Lawrence Becker has noted in his book *Reciprocity*, if a system of reciprocity cycles correctly, the benefits should tend to equal out without too much domination or exploitation.[52] This continues

---

[49] At least in the absence of a theology which promises eternal rewards for such conduct, there is nothing especially self-perfecting about the mere act of aiding those in need.

[50] Indeed, the appeal to "good feelings" is just the Mandevillian problem all over again.

[51] A classic example of a reciprocity argument outside a teleological ethical context is Kant's famous position in the *Foundations* that we all have a duty to aid others because we would will such aid for ourselves. One problem here, though, is that if we specify "will" in any concrete way, the argument may take on a contractarian character. Kant himself, of course, was making the case that we would somehow contradict ourselves if we did not will for others what we will for ourselves. Consistency therefore is the main ingredient in reciprocal willing for Kant; but as is well known, this tends to give more formal than substantive results. Contemporary thinkers, such as Alan Gewirth, who use the same sort of strategy, try to obviate the formalism by referring to what is implied by the *actions* of agents rather than their "wills." But then these arguments look less and less like reciprocity arguments and more like agency arguments. And like the agency approach just discussed, these arguments tend to regard persons impersonally and thus suffer from the problem of engagement.

[52] Lawrence Becker, *Reciprocity*, p. 133 (see n. 14 above). Subsequent page references in the text refer to this book.

to make it look as though both benefactors and recipients are given equal consideration and as though the middle ground between the right to welfare and the virtue of charity has finally been discovered.

Yet we have it on the same authority that

> [r]eciprocity is a *recipient's* virtue. It is the way people ought to be disposed to *respond* to others. It says nothing about how people ought to behave, or feel, when they *give* a gift. (p. 93; emphasis in original)

This clearly indicates that the focus of reciprocity arguments is again not on the benefactor, but on the recipient. But why should this be the case? After all, if reciprocity is truly reciprocal, it would seem that the conduct of the benefactor is of equal concern to that of the recipient.[53] In Becker's case, however, the recipient is the focus of the theory because virtue is itself justified in terms of increasing aggregate goal satisfaction (pp. 87 and 125). So although the argument is conducted in terms of dispositions necessary for flourishing as a moral agent (e.g., pp. 74–75), the final justification of that flourishing is social rather than self-perfective. This is demonstrated at the critical juncture where the most controversial of Becker's maxims of reciprocity is being defended: to wit, reciprocation should be made for any good received, not just those we seek or accept. The other maxims (p. 74) are quite compatible with the more ordinary notion that reciprocal arrangements are voluntary and that one is not obligated to reciprocate for positive externalities that one has not sought or accepted.

We get locked into the stronger claim, however, by the argument that certain social goods will not be as forthcoming if we do not make the disposition to reciprocate for every good received obligatory. Aggregate goal satisfaction, in other words, will be diminished without this obligation (p. 125). Apart from any empirical doubts one may have, this claim immediately makes the virtue in question instrumental in a way that the self-perfective qualities of classical virtue were not. The flourishing moral agency that seems to be the focus of the theory is itself secondary to a social good (*aggregate* goal satisfaction) that serves as its measure or standard. Classical virtue, in contrast, was exercised for its own sake, which means that its self-perfecting qualities were realized through the very performance of the virtue itself. Social benefits were expected, and were sometimes even the object of the virtue, but they were not its ground or measure.

It is important to realize that Becker's own argument is not about char-

---

[53] In saying this, I am temporarily ignoring a possibility that may lie unstated in the background of Becker's argument and perhaps all reciprocity arguments, namely, that there are *only* recipients. In other words, benefactors are nothing but recipients paying off their debts. In the end (see below) this is the conclusion I finally arrive at about these sorts of arguments.

ity, welfare, or many of the other themes we have been talking about. These topics are left largely undiscussed in his book. But reciprocity is given fundamental status by Becker and is rivaled only by justice as a basic virtue (pp. 149–50). Consequently, accepting the maxim mentioned above is likely to have important welfare implications. This is because we all are most certainly the beneficiaries of positive externalities we do not seek, and with something as vague and impersonal as aggregate goal satisfaction as our standard, each of our lives could be perpetually mortgaged to whatever someone's conception of our obligation to reciprocate might be.[54] In practice at least, that is likely to translate into entitlement or rights claims by recipients. The benefit of focusing primarily on the morality of the benefactor, as the virtue of charity does, is that individuals can vary both the degree and object of their charity to better fit the pursuit of their own projects. This seems to accord more directly with the pluralism assumed and encouraged by classical liberalism.

It has not been my claim here that the reciprocity or agency arguments may not be compelling in some practical sense. No doubt social goods are more likely to be produced under a strong ethic of reciprocity and we should not fail to be moved in the face of a possible loss of agency. But apart from any doubts we may have about these arguments establishing a positive *right* to welfare, the arguments clearly say nothing about the moral context in which traditional virtues such as charity arose. It is likely, though, that we knew all that going in. What we may have established even more clearly here is the nonaltruistic and noncommunitarian character of virtue within the self-perfective framework. Virtue theories, under the rubric of self-perfection, tend to appeal to self-initiated and proactive sorts of arguments. Reciprocity, then, would be more compatible with a virtue like charity if it could include self-initiated action. Apart from the question of whether self-initiation is precluded from reciprocity on definitional grounds (since reciprocity is always *responsive*), Becker's controversial maxim virtually wipes out self-initiated nonresponsive action. In other words, the right to welfare is destructive of the virtue of charity because it alters the character of virtue from its classically proactive posture into a reactive one.

[54] I find it strange that a sustained argument on reciprocity exists anyway. As Adam Smith points out, it is virtually a natural sentiment. If there is virtue in it, it would come from transforming the sentiment into a "moral sentiment," but that has less to do with reciprocity than it does with the other features of a moral outlook for Smith, such as impartiality. But other than Becker's maxim 7 ("returns should be made for goods received, not merely for goods accepted"), and insofar as we are no longer speaking of simply natural inclinations, the rest of the maxims would have been captured under the traditional virtue of charity or the pagan virtue of magnanimity. This is also a way in which the discussion would be less likely to get confused with justice. I am by no means suggesting that Becker's project is a failure. Indeed, the discussion is often brilliant and always sensitive, and since I have forced the argument in a direction Becker himself does not take, I should be circumspect about criticism. Becker's discussion is, as far as I know, the only position that gives a central and fundamental place to reciprocity.

V. CONCLUSION

My argument in this essay has *not* been that the right to welfare is destructive of the virtue of charity because the virtue of charity cannot exist if the state provides any form of welfare. Even if "bad welfare" drove out the "good," it is unlikely that a modicum of state support to the truly needy would in practice threaten the virtue of charity, although some empirical evidence suggests that more extensive aid may do so.[55] That some welfare is a legitimate function of the state is a basic tenet of classical liberalism (as opposed to libertarianism). Instead, my argument was about the theoretical threat to the virtue of charity posed by the right to welfare. Perhaps "threat" is too mild a term; for while the virtue of charity may still be alive among private individuals, it is moribund among theoreticians. If charity is mentioned at all, it is simply as a synonym for "welfare," or it is mentioned critically as part of a larger effort to guarantee the final triumph of the welfare state, namely, the obliteration of the distinction between charity and justice.

While there are clearly many parameters to this debate and many facets of it to consider, I might conclude by suggesting that the debate nonetheless seems to me to be another version of a more common discussion in our era over public activities versus private ones. The virtue of charity is essentially private, while the right to welfare is essentially public. Classical liberalism and libertarianism put their trust in private approaches, whereas the "new" liberalism and socialism seek more public or socialized measures. It is therefore no accident that as our culture continually sheds its classical-liberal heritage in politics, it comes to focus less upon an ethics supportive of private measures. I have suggested both that charity is being forgotten and that it might be worth our further attention. Perhaps more importantly, I have suggested that certain theoretical foundations that predate liberalism itself may be necessary to resurrect charity. It is, after all, in an evolved state of liberalism that this discussion is being conducted. If charity has gotten lost as liberalism has evolved, then perhaps we need to look carefully at where it was lost, the reasons for its departure, and what might be done to reestablish its importance in liberal orders. We may even discover that virtue is best served when classical ethics is allied with classical liberalism.

Philosophy, Bellarmine College

---

[55] See Wolfe, *Whose Keeper?*, pp. 89–94 and 168–77. Wolfe himself, however, regards the evidence as mixed. In addition, one could make the case that our current bankrupt and ineffective system of welfare — where the numbers of poor keep increasing despite no real lessening of welfare expenditures — can have the effect of *encouraging* the virtue of charity. More and more people are realizing that the state is so inept at actually relieving suffering that, if individuals do not help on a private basis, no relief will be forthcoming! In such a case we have an uneasy tension between the welfare paradigm and the charity paradigm as they both try to exist together.

ALTRUISM AND THE ARGUMENT FROM OFFSETTING TRANSFERS*

By Tyler Cowen

I. Introduction

Individuals frequently give gifts or make transfers to others for altruistic reasons. Parents devote time to raising their children, spouses make sacrifices on each other's behalf, and friends do favors for friends. We are also linked to many people indirectly because we care for someone who cares for them.

I wish to examine the implications of altruistic feelings for both social policy and rational choice theory. Many economists have argued that the presence of altruistic transfers across individuals influences the outcome of social and economic policies in powerful ways. Specifically, some models imply that governments are unable to redistribute wealth from one individual to another. In these models (explained in greater detail below), governmental attempts to redistribute wealth are offset by changes in private transfers, which restore the initial distribution of wealth.

Derek Parfit and I refer to this result as The Argument from Offsetting Transfers; in this piece I will simply refer to the Argument.[1] If the Argument is correct, consequences for social policy follow. Policies which attempt to redistribute wealth across individuals would be either superfluous or a matter of indifference. Government deficits would not burden future generations, for instance, to cite one common application of the Argument.[2]

Social policy is not the only reason why we might be interested in the Argument. By examining the Argument, we can better understand the operational implications of different kinds of altruism. I consider direct altruism, indirect altruism through chains of caring, altruism in light of collective-action dilemmas, precommitment altruism, paternalistic altruism, and one-sided versus mutual altruism (these are defined below); each type of altruism has different effects upon the distribution of wealth.

* The author wishes to thank Penelope Brook, Kevin Grier, Greg Kavka, Daniel Klein, Randall Kroszner, Carrie Meyer, David Schmidtz, Daniel Sutter, and Alex Tabarrok for useful comments and discussions.

[1] See Tyler Cowen and Derek Parfit, "Against the Social Discount Rate," in *Philosophy, Politics, and Society, Volume 6: Justice Between Age Groups and Generations*, ed. James S. Fishkin and Peter Laslett (New Haven: Yale University Press, forthcoming).

[2] See Robert J. Barro, "Are Government Bonds Net Wealth?" *Journal of Political Economy*, vol. 74 (1974), pp. 1095–1117.

I argue that the presence of altruistic feelings does not imply that the Argument is true. This differs from arguing that altruistic feelings are weak or nonexistent. I consider why a given level of altruism often does not translate into concrete results for beneficiaries.

The Argument

The Argument is based upon simple and intuitive concepts. To consider a concrete example, suppose that Mr. Charity gives $100 to Mr. Poor each year. The government then decides to tax Mr. Charity by $50 each year and send this $50 to Mr. Poor. The Argument claims that Mr. Charity will reduce his transfer to Mr. Poor by $50 to maintain the same net transfer of $100.

A policy to tax Mr. Poor by $50 and give this $50 to Mr. Charity will be offset also. Mr. Charity will simply increase his gift to $150 to maintain the same net transfer of $100. If Mr. Charity wished to give $100 to begin with, he can maintain the same net transfer by increasing his gross transfer.

Consider also a multi-person example. Mr. Charity might give $50 to Mr. Poor and $50 to Mr. Destitute. If the government now taxes $10 from Mr. Poor and sends this money to Mr. Destitute, Mr. Charity can offset this government policy by changing the size of his transfers. Mr. Charity will now give $60 to Mr. Poor and $40 to Mr. Destitute. The final net result is still $50 for Mr. Poor and $50 for Mr. Destitute. Note also that Mr. Destitute will not find it worthwhile to lobby for this tax.

Such examples, and the Argument in general, originate from the work of Gary Becker on the economics of the family. Becker stated an early version of the Argument, which he termed the "Rotten Kid Theorem." The Rotten Kid Theorem states that even selfish children act to maximize the income of the entire family. Such children, for instance, will not try to seize resources for themselves at the expense of siblings. Just as Mr. Destitute does not bother to lobby for the tax, children in a family do not steal from each other.[3]

The Rotten Kid Theorem requires a family head who makes altruistic gifts to each of his or her children. Children who attempt to seize resources from their siblings will find their gifts reduced and the gifts of the exploited sibling increased. The family head does not punish the siblings out of retributive motives, but simply restores the initial distribution of income. Plunder among siblings proves counterproductive, and each sibling prefers to maximize total family income, so as to receive the maximum gift. Becker notes: "Each beneficiary, no matter how selfish,

---

[3] See Gary S. Becker, "A Theory of Social Interactions," *Journal of Political Economy*, vol. 82 (November/December 1974), pp. 1063–94, and *A Treatise on the Family* (Cambridge: Harvard University Press, 1981).

maximizes the family income of his benefactor and thereby internalizes all effects of his actions on other beneficiaries."[4]

The Argument can be applied to show that issues like social-security programs, the provision of public goods and charitable contributions, and the choice of social discount rate are not issues of practical importance.[5] The underlying logic is the same in each case. Governmental attempts to change the distribution of resources are offset by changes in private transfers. The private sector selects an optimum which is immune to government attempts to affect outcomes. These arguments are examples of what Albert Hirschman has recently labeled the "Futility Thesis" critique of redistribution.[6]

Robert Barro, in his analysis of government budget deficits, provides the most frequently debated application of the Argument. Barro argues that it does not matter if we finance a given amount of spending by taxes (which current individuals must pay) or deficits (which our descendants must finance through future taxes). If generations are linked by a series of altruistic transfers, attempts to redistribute wealth across generations through fiscal policy will be offset by the actions of private-sector agents. This result was subsequently termed the debt-neutrality or "Ricardian equivalence" theorem.[7]

The mechanics of this example are easy to explain. Assume that a father is altruistic and plans to devote $200,000 (in present value) to his son's upbringing and education. The government now undertakes some policy designed to redistribute $10,000 from each member of the son's generation to each member of the father's generation (e.g., taxes are cut and the deficit is increased). That is, the father pays $10,000 less in taxes and the son will be burdened with a future tax increase with a present value of $10,000.

The father can offset the results of this policy by increasing his transfer to his son by $10,000. If $200,000 was the preferred transfer, the father can still achieve this result by a change in the gross bequest (to $210,000) to maintain the same net transfer of $200,000. Similarly, if the govern-

---

[4] See Becker, *A Treatise on the Family*, p. 183. Parents (and children) may be suspicious of the theorem already.

[5] The application of the Argument to discount rates is criticized by Cowen and Parfit, "Against the Social Discount Rate." On the other applications, see B. Douglas Bernheim, "On the Voluntary and Involuntary Provision of Public Goods," *American Economic Review*, vol. 76 (September 1986), pp. 789–93; and Peter D. Warr and Brian G. Wright, "The Isolation Paradox and the Discount Rate for Benefit-Cost Analysis," *Quarterly Journal of Economics*, vol. 95 (February 1981), pp. 129–45.

[6] See Albert O. Hirschman, *The Rhetoric of Reaction* (Cambridge: Harvard University Press, 1991).

[7] See Robert J. Barro, "Are Government Bonds Net Wealth?" An early version of the theorem has been attributed to classical economist David Ricardo. Many deficits, of course, are paid off within the lifetimes of those who incur them. In this case, deficits and taxes are equivalent even in the absence of offsetting transfers. An increase in the deficit simply induces more saving to pay future taxes.

ment attempts to redistribute $10,000 of resources from father to son (e.g., budget deficits decrease), the father will decrease his bequest by $10,000 to achieve his preferred allocation. This reasoning can be applied to each father-son relationship affected by the policy.

The debt-neutrality theorem (and the Argument in general) can be stated also across *many* generations (or individuals) when each individual is connected to the previous generation by altruistically motivated bequests. A parent may not care about future grandchildren, but the theorem goes through as stated if parents care about their children. In effect, parents care about their grandchildren indirectly because they care about someone (their children) who cares about these individuals. If my grandchildren are taxed, I know that my children will increase their gifts and bequests to their children, so I will in turn increase gifts and bequests to my children. The family is modeled as an ongoing dynasty which behaves like an infinitely long-lived individual (more on this below).

Qualifications

The Argument is open to objection on a number of practical grounds. Many individuals, for instance, are selfish or do not have either offspring or living parents. In the case of these individuals, governmental attempts to redistribute resources will be effective because the appropriate offsetting transfers cannot be made.

In other cases, the governmental redistribution of wealth is so large relative to the initial transfer that no offsetting transfers are possible. In effect, individuals are driven to "corner solutions" at which the altruistic gift motive is no longer operative. Assume that John gives $100 worth of gifts to Sally, and the government then transfers $200 from John to Sally. John cannot contract his gift by more than $100; in effect, he is driven to the "corner" of a zero gift. John can offset $100 of the government's transfer, but not the entire $200 transfer.

In addition, gifts and transfers are not always motivated by altruism. Bernheim, Shleifer, and Summers (1985), for instance, argue that gifts and bequests are frequently motivated by the desire to control one's children, rather than by the desire to help them. In this case, private gifts and resource transfers through the government are not perfect substitutes because the latter cannot be used for purposes of control.[8]

Gifts may also be motivated by the joy of giving rather than simply the well-being of the recipient. Some parents might prefer to give their

---

[8] See B. Douglas Bernheim, Andrei Shleifer, and Lawrence H. Summers, "The Strategic Bequest Motive," *Journal of Political Economy*, vol. 93 (December 1985), pp. 1045–76. These authors even present econometric evidence which demonstrates correlations between expected size of bequests and the number of letters written to parents, visits to nursing homes, etc. I have recently seen a bumper sticker which read "Get Even — Live Long Enough to Be A Burden to Your Children."

daughter $20,000 for a college education rather than see their daughter win the lottery. In the former case, the parents can brag to the neighbors about how much money they have spent. To the extent that such motivations are present, the Argument does not apply.[9]

While such objections are clearly relevant to the truth of the Argument, they are not the focus of my attention. Even if the debt-neutrality theorem does not hold for childless individuals, for instance, the result might remain important for those of us who have children. Similarly, the possibility of corner solutions implies that large redistributions of wealth are possible, but it might still follow that smaller attempts at redistribution are impossible. I wish to examine whether the Argument is in principle correct in those cases when it possesses potential empirical relevance.

The arguments I present should not be taken as a criticism of Robert Barro or others associated with the Argument. Barro, for instance, emphasizes that the Argument is not always descriptively true. In many cases, the purpose of the Argument is to force us to account explicitly for why transfers of wealth do matter. My inquiry proceeds in this constructive spirit.[10]

II. Evidence

Many economists and most philosophers find the Argument hard to believe, although they often cannot put their finger upon the source of their disbelief. Yet, there is some empirical evidence in favor of the Argument, especially in the form of the debt-neutrality theorem. Despite what we read in the popular press, economists have not succeeded in finding hard statistical evidence that government budget deficits affect the real economy. Barro's argument offers one potential reason why we do not find significant results here. Similarly, the evidence is not overwhelming that social-security programs have altered the intergenerational distribution of wealth significantly.[11]

More generally, the empirical generalization known as Pareto's Law indicates that the distribution of wealth is relatively invariant across societies with quite different economic policies. Perhaps various institutional attempts to change the distribution of wealth are offset by changes in private transfers. While the Argument is certainly not the only explanation for these results, it is one possible factor in explaining some otherwise puzzling features of the data.

The Argument, however, is strongly inconsistent with many of our common-sense beliefs. Bernheim and Bagwell (in their article "Is Every-

[9] See James Andreoni, "Giving With Impure Altruism: Applications to Charity and Ricardian Equivalence," *Journal of Political Economy*, vol. 97 (1989), pp. 1447–58.

[10] See Robert J. Barro, "A Ricardian Approach to Budget Deficits," *Journal of Economic Perspectives*, vol. 3 (Spring 1989), p. 52.

[11] See, for instance, *ibid.* for a survey of the evidence, pro and con.

thing Neutral?") show that the Argument is vulnerable to a potential *reductio ad absurdum*. We can extend the reasoning behind the debt-neutrality theorem to show the neutrality of almost any policy a government or private-sector agent might undertake, including not just redistributions but also taxes, subsidies, and changes in relative prices. Changes in private transfers can offset a wide scope of policies.[12]

The *reductio* starts by noting that we are linked not just to our immediate heirs and their descendants, but to every member in society. Different families are linked by marriages and common relations. We have close friends who are in turn linked to others. Indirect links connect nearly all members of society; these indirect links imply the curious result that all government policies are neutral.

The logic of the *reductio* can be illuminated by first examining the single-person case and then extrapolating to many individuals. Consider the degenerate case of one individual who is the sole taxpayer and the sole recipient of government services. A tax upon income will not influence labor supply, or anything else, in this world. Our Robinson Crusoe knows that any resources "taxed" from him are returned to him through the government. In fact, Crusoe *is* the government. The tax has no effects.

Now consider a two-person world where Crusoe is the government and Friday is taxed. Crusoe makes altruistic gifts to Friday. The income tax has no effect on Friday's behavior. The resources received by Crusoe are refunded to Friday, and relative prices do not change. Assume that Crusoe originally gave $100 to Friday and now also collects $500 through the tax. Crusoe will maximize utility by increasing his gift to $600, which ensures that Friday pays no net tax. This reasoning can be extended to the *n*-person case. The taxed persons will eventually receive the funds which they pay for the tax.[13]

The Argument implies that taxes do not affect relative prices and are thus neutral. We can construct a similar argument for subsidies or any change in relative prices. Changes in relative prices can be represented or decomposed in terms of a tax upon one individual and a subsidy for another.

If changes in relative prices do not matter, not only are changes in government policy neutral, but so are private market prices. The presence of a monopoly, for instance, would have no effects upon either the allocation of resources or the distribution of wealth. Monopolies raise prices, but this increase in prices would be rebated eventually to consumers in

---

[12] See B. Douglas Bernheim and Kyle Bagwell, "Is Everything Neutral?" *Journal of Political Economy*, vol. 96 (April 1988), pp. 308–38.

[13] Many changes in transfers are required for this result, but the Argument allows for, and indeed requires, the possibility of longer altruistic linkages. If we deny the relevance of longer linkages (I examine this issue below), we can avoid these conclusions, but then we must also reject many of the more modest applications of the Argument.

the form of increased gifts and transfers. The increase in prices does not even occasion a substitution effect, as changes in gross revenue and expenditures are offset exactly by changes in transfers. Those who profit from the monopoly will increase their transfers to those who do not.[14]

The Argument implies that as long as we do not push individuals to corner solutions, we could abolish market exchange for a sufficiently small subset of the economy and achieve the same allocation of resources by direct transfers. At the margin, relative prices do not matter. If apparent changes in relative prices do not change the real relative prices which individuals face, however, rational choice theory and economics as we know it cannot survive.[15]

Yet another *reductio ad absurdum* can be applied to the Argument. Consider the earlier point that very large redistributions of wealth cannot be reversed (because of corner solutions), but relatively small ones can be. If I win ten million dollars in a lottery, other individuals cannot decrease their gifts to me by ten million dollars; the gifts are not this large to begin with. In contrast, if I lose five dollars purchasing losing lottery tickets, this loss can be reversed by offsetting transfers. Knowing this, I will have an infinite demand to play the lottery. In a world where the Argument holds, I can only win playing the lottery and can never lose; losses are offset but gains cannot be. The demand for fairly priced lottery tickets will be unbounded.

Most of us believe that relative prices matter, government policies are not neutral, and the demands to purchase lottery tickets are bounded. Similarly, family members fight. Private firms which give Christmas bonuses to their employees do not automatically eliminate harmful rivalries within the firm, as the Rotten Kid Theorem would suggest.

For these reasons we should be suspicious of the realism of the Argument. But simply criticizing the Argument on the grounds that it is unrealistic is an endeavor of limited interest. I now proceed to consider why the Argument does not hold and what this might teach us about altruism.

III. ALTRUISTIC LINKAGES: TOO MANY OR TOO FEW?

The nature of altruistic linkages might invalidate the Argument. I first consider whether lengthening the chain of altruistic linkages makes the Argument less likely to hold because of uncertainty. Secondly, I examine

---

[14] Those familiar with Hicksian consumption theory might wonder why consumers do not simply receive a compensating transfer of income to maintain their well-being, but still face the new set of relative prices. This form of offsetting transfer, however, would not reverse changes in producer surplus and thus in the welfare of producers, who would face a new set of relative prices. The transfers which restore the initial position of both consumers and producers completely reverse the initial apparent change in prices.

[15] Ironically, the father of the Rotten Kid Theorem, Gary Becker, is best known for his attempt to explain human behavior universally in terms of changing relative prices.

whether the presence of multiple altruistic chains among individuals invalidates the Argument because of free-rider problems.

Lengthy altruistic chains

If the Argument is to hold for chains of more than one link, individuals must believe in specific behavioral hypotheses about how other individuals will react to changes in the distribution of wealth. For the Argument to work, it must be common knowledge that individuals reason using a principle which game theorists call "backwards induction." Assume we have four generations, each of which cares directly about its immediate descendants only. A government policy, say a decrease in environmental protection, now transfers resources to the current (first) generation at the eventual expense of the last (fourth) generation.

Members of the first generation will change their transfers to the second generation only if they reason by first considering the last period of the sequence and then working backwards. Members of the first generation must realize that members of the third will see that their children, the fourth generation, will be especially poor (because of the policy). Members of the third generation will therefore give especially large gifts to members of the fourth. This will decrease the well-being of the third generation. Knowing this will happen, members of the second generation are prompted to make an especially large gift to their children, the third generation. Members of the first generation realize that members of the second will be placed in this position, and they compensate by making an especially large transfer to members of the second generation at the beginning of the sequence.

This reasoning resembles the argument used to establish noncooperation as the unique equilibrium outcome in a finite-horizon prisoner's dilemma game. Individuals reason that cooperation will not be forthcoming in the last period of the game and then set strategies for the next-to-last period. This reasoning proceeds sequentially from the end of the game until the beginning, when noncooperation is established as the equilibrium for all periods of the game, including the first period.[16]

It is now well-known that reasoning from backwards induction is inappropriate when there is uncertainty about what will happen in future periods of the sequence.[17] Assume, for instance, that the first generation is uncertain about the behavior of the third generation. Perhaps the mem-

---

[16] The structures behind the multi-link Argument and the prisoner's dilemma are not identical, however. In the Argument, one attempts to establish the correct course of action given expectations about the future, but one is not playing against an opponent. Furthermore, the Argument requires that a sequence of separate individuals reason according to backwards induction.

[17] See, for instance, Robert Axelrod, *The Evolution of Cooperation* (New York: Basic Books, 1984).

bers of the third generation will be purely selfish, or will simply not realize that they should increase their gifts to generation four. Furthermore, members of generation one know or at least suspect that members of generation two will share these doubts about members of generation three.

If members of preceding generations know there is some chance that members of generation three will not make the correct offsetting bequest, they will decrease their offsetting transfers accordingly. The members of generation one care directly about generation two only, and if the members of generation two are not required to bail out generation three, the members of generation one will feel no additional obligation to generation two.

Once the chain is several links long, uncertainty may be so great as to preempt offsetting transfers from the current generation. The members of generation one must not only try to forecast the rationality and altruism of succeeding generations, but also try to forecast how each generation will forecast the rationality and altruism of its successors. The computational complexity of this task may induce people simply to plan a fixed gift to their children and keep this gift constant in the absence of drastic changes.[18]

Uncertainty about how others will behave is also present in atemporal versions of the Argument. If a tax is levied on current individuals connected by altruistic transfers, for instance, there exists a neutralizing reallocation which can be achieved by offsetting transfers. This neutralizing reallocation can be achieved, however, only if all individuals coordinate upon the same sequence of offsetting transfers.

An additional difficulty exists in the atemporal case because we have no obvious cue as to who should move first and change transfers. The coordination problem may be simpler in the intergenerational case, when the order in which transfers change is specified by the order in which we are born.[19]

Completely effective altruism involves enormous informational requirements on the part of benefactors. Benefactors must know both the reactions and expectations of all individuals in the altruistic chain. This form of altruism likely fails for the same reason that rational economic calculation under socialism is impossible: the informational requirements for solving the problem cannot be contained in a single mind or committee of minds.[20]

---

[18] Similarly, consider religious tithing, which is usually based around a fixed percentage of one's income, and not the contributions of other church members.

[19] This is not true, however, to the extent that different generations live and offer gifts at the same time. Who should be the first to buy the children additional Christmas presents, Mother or Grandmother?

[20] John C. Calhoun stresses the limits which imperfect information places upon altruistic behavior; see Alexander Tabarrok and Tyler Cowen, "The Public Choice Theory of John C. Calhoun," forthcoming in *Journal of Institutional and Theoretical Economics*. Hayek's distinction between the extended order and traditional society also stresses the role of markets in

Different kinds of uncertainty, however, have contrasting effects on the Argument. Uncertainty about how other individuals in the chain will behave tends to invalidate the Argument. In contrast, uncertainty about the magnitude of the burdens which other individuals must bear (i.e., the future well-being of such individuals) can amplify the strength of the Argument. In the case of national debt, for instance, current benefactors may not know exactly how much their descendants will pay in taxes.[21]

Uncertainty about the well-being of others strengthens the Argument under the plausible assumption that people take into account the risk-aversion of their descendants. Compare, for instance, the following two cases: future generations bear a certain burden of $5,000, or future generations face a 50-percent chance of a zero burden and a 50-percent chance of a $10,000 burden. The latter case will induce a greater offsetting transfer. In effect, altruists will wish to grant insurance to their risk-averse descendants. Uncertainty about future burdens, far from vitiating the Argument, actually increases the offsetting transfer.[22]

Collective-action problems and altruism

So far, I have assumed that each individual is connected to the rest of society by only one link in an altruistic chain. The examples of sequential overlapping generations presented above portray this assumption clearly. In reality, each individual is connected to others by many links; e.g., John may receive transfers from both Sally and Thomas. I refer to this case as "multiple links."

Consider interlocking family structures as a case of multiple links. Generation one consists of two families, the Smiths and the Browns. In generation two, John Smith marries Sally Brown. This marriage links the new Smith-Brown family to the previous generation through two different families.

The government now undertakes a policy which transfers resources from generation two (John and Sally) to their parents. To what extent should the appropriate offsetting transfers come from the Smith family and to what extent should they come from the Brown family? Here we have a collective-action problem. Even though both the Smith and the

---

substituting for the informational limitations of altruism. See Friedrich A. Hayek, *The Fatal Conceit* (Chicago: University of Chicago Press, 1989).

[21] New Zealand author Janet Frame, in her novel *Living in the Maniototo* (New York: George Braziller, 1979), pp. 41–42, presents the character of Lance Halleton, who slept with two pocket calculators under his pillow so he could reckon accurately the national debt. Lance was extremely concerned with how high the debt was and who would pay it off. Appropriately, New Zealand has an astronomically high per-capita debt.

[22] This is demonstrated formally by Robert J. Barro, "Are Government Bonds Net Wealth?"

Brown parents are altruists, they would rather see the other family make the altruistic transfers.[23]

The Smith and Brown elders might get together and write a contract specifying the appropriate offsetting transfers. The Argument, however, does not require such contracts and would be extremely limited in application if it did. Nor can we argue that each family will increase its contributions to the extent it benefits from the new policy. Consider the limiting case when the Smith family reaps all the benefits from the government policy. The Smith family now has a higher income, but it will not feel compelled to contribute the entire offsetting transfer. It will still attempt to free-ride upon the marginal propensity of the Brown family to contribute. Changes in income may affect propensities to contribute through the mechanism of income effects, but they do not remove the free-rider problem. The free-rider problem may be (partially) soluble across transfers of a single link. When offsetting transfers must go through many links, however, the collective-action problem increases greatly in complexity.

In the case of offsetting transfers, the number of individuals who must adjust their gifts becomes large very quickly once we consider chains of several links in length. Assume first a chain of only one link—who might be tempted to look out for my interests? Perhaps I could count upon my fiancée, my parents, my sister, my grandmother, and five or six close friends. Even if my family acts as a single unit (not the case, I assure you) we have at least nine potential free-riders. If we count moderately good friends, the number exceeds twenty.

Now, how many individuals are two steps removed from me? That is, how many individuals care about someone who cares for me? If we assume that my benefactors are as popular as I am, a modest estimate is eighty-one (nine times nine) and a liberal estimate is four hundred (twenty times twenty). If we consider chains of three links or more, the numbers climb to the range of 729 to 8,000. I have heard anecdotally (from Lawrence Summers) that a chain of five links will connect me to every person in the United States (and to many persons abroad).[24]

Coordination and free-rider problems grow exponentially as the number of links increases. Free-rider and coordination problems may not be serious enough to stop gifts of one link from one individual to another. Yet, these same problems may be insurmountable when we need to make offsetting transfers of more than one link in length.

Under one view, the Argument holds regardless of how long and complicated the chain is. Individuals adjust their gifts sequentially, starting closest to where the initial redistribution occurs. If I lose resources, for in-

[23] On the collective-action problem of altruism, see Gregory N. Kavka, "Two Solutions to the Paradox of Revolution," *Midwest Studies in Philosophy*, vol. 7 (1982), pp. 455–72.

[24] Overlapping friendships would reduce these numbers. Some of my friends have the same friends, who should not be counted twice.

stance, my family may start by compensating me. Then, my family's friends compensate them, and so on through the different links of the altruistic chain.

Sequential adjustment, however, takes time. If a total of four thousand offsetting transfers are required to restore the initial distribution of wealth, the Argument may not hold. First, completion of these transfers may take a very long time. Second, by the time a large number of transfers are completed, conditions will have changed and yet further transfers will be required. Changes in transfers may always be behind the data, trying to rectify redistributions initiated many years ago. Once adjustment is temporal, we have no guarantee that convergence will occur.

Another possibility is that all four thousand offsetting transfers occur at once. But this outcome is unlikely. Individuals in the chain three links away from me are unlikely to have information about my well-being; as a result, they will not increase their transfers to the friends of my friends. Even if individuals three links away have information about my well-being, they may be unwilling to move first. If these individuals are uncertain about how others will behave, they will not adjust their gifts until they observe a decline in the well-being of individuals they care about directly. But then we are back to the case of sequential adjustment.

The collective-action problem implies the ironic conclusion that altruism is ineffective precisely because we have so much of it. If fewer individuals had altruistic dispositions, we might find less free-riding. The relevant chains and links across different individuals would be clearer, and offsetting transfers might be more effective. I am not advocating less altruism, because we would also find more predatory behavior. But those altruistic preferences which would remain might also be more effective.

IV. Goods Which Cannot Be Redistributed

The Argument assumes that all distributions and redistributions occur through a common medium. The debt-neutrality theorem is a clear example of this assumption. A government redistributes monetary wealth, and individuals respond by changing their monetary gifts and bequests. The medium of redistribution is usually represented as money, but could be any other good or service which can be transferred from one individual to another.

Some goods, however, are costly or impossible to redistribute by their very nature. The Argument may fail to hold if not all goods and services can be transferred from one individual to another.[25]

---

[25] This point is made most clearly by Theodore C. Bergstrom, "A Fresh Look at the Rotten Kid Theorem — and Other Household Mysteries," *Journal of Political Economy*, vol. 97 (1989), pp. 1138–59. Daniel B. Klein, "The Microfoundations of Rules versus Discretion," *Constitutional Political Economy*, Fall 1990, pp. 1–19, demonstrates the relation between the Rotten Kid Theorem and the literature on time consistency.

Consider the Rotten Kid Theorem again, and assume that we have two goods in a family, money and education. Money can be transferred at zero cost, but education cannot be. Education is not completely nontransferable; we can give books from one individual to another, or we can give money to individuals to help them buy education. More generally, substitutes for direct education can be transferred. Nonetheless, reallocations of knowledge cannot be achieved in the same fashion as reallocations of money.

Assume the presence of a benevolent family head, Martha, and two children, Tommy and Franky. Martha gives financial support (and love) to her two children, but she cannot give them many kinds of education. She reads to her children at night, but cannot provide full tutoring services.

Both Tommy and Franky are in contention for a spot in the honors class at school. This spot would be more valuable to Franky, who has more academic talent than Tommy. Knowing this, Martha prefers that Franky be awarded the spot. At school, however, Tommy steals the spot from Franky by cheating on an exam. Tommy is a rotten kid.

Martha cannot offset Tommy's rotten behavior. Ideally, she would prefer to take Tommy's marginal increase in education and transfer this education to the more deserving Franky. But this offsetting transfer is impossible because education cannot be taken from one individual and given to another. Martha might transfer some substitutes from Tommy to Franky; she might, for instance, now spend more time reading to Franky at night and less time reading to Tommy. But these transfers are imperfect substitutes for the reallocation that Martha wishes to achieve.

A transfer of money will not offset Tommy's rotten behavior either. Franky is needier and more deserving with respect to education, but is not necessarily needier with respect to money. Martha may transfer some additional money to Franky because money can serve as a partial substitute for education. But again, she cannot neutralize Tommy's cheating completely.[26]

We can introduce various considerations external to the Argument to show that Martha might take resources away from Tommy. Perhaps she punishes Tommy to prevent such behavior from recurring. Or perhaps she punishes Tommy out of her sense of fairness, or simply out of spite. But neither of these transfers restores the initial equilibrium, as the Argument requires.[27]

---

[26] In fact, the Argument may imply that Martha will give *additional* money to Tommy. Assume plausibly that the marginal utilities of education and money interact. A better educated individual receives more pleasure from money than an ignorant individual; Martha will now give more money to Tommy, the rotten kid.

[27] Similarly, if Martha can precommit to punishing Tommy with sufficient severity, Tommy will not cheat on the test in the first place. But this does not rescue the Argument, which requires that redistributions which actually occur can be offset.

The Argument need not hold when the number of goods in society is greater than the number of policy instruments available to altruistic benefactors. When benefactors cannot control the allocation of a good whose distribution changes, offsetting transfers are not possible.

Money and affection are two goods which altruistic benefactors can conceivably control. Yet, many goods (including health, self-esteem, and knowledge) are not easily controlled or reallocated by our benefactors. For these goods the Argument does not apply. Changes in their allocation which are induced by government policy will not be offset completely by changes in private transfers. When analyzing the effects of altruism, we must consider not only what an individual cares about, but what an individual can control. Under different assumptions about control, the effects of caring are quite different.

Precommitment

The above discussion of the Rotten Kid Theorem directs our attention to another factor which limits the effectiveness of altruistic preferences. A true altruist may sometimes precommit to not helping the individual he or she cares about. When such precommitments are present, offsetting transfers will not always occur; I call this "precommitment altruism."

Beneficial examples of precommitment altruism are common. Parents may precommit to not supporting an idle son, for instance. The parents do care about their son and would prefer to support him rather than see him starve. But a precommitment to let the son starve may be in the son's (and parents') best interests. The son is then required to hold down a steady job and support himself. Knowing this, the parents will engage in various strategies to prevent themselves from making transfers to their son if he does not work. Similar examples are common in altruistic relationships.[28]

The presence of precommitments not to help may invalidate the Argument. If the son experiences a decline in wealth, the parents cannot always tell if the son's laziness is at fault, or if the son is simply the victim of bad luck. In the presence of a precommitment not to help, the parents will not make an offsetting transfer.

If an offsetting transfer is made in a borderline or ambiguous case, the son's laziness will be encouraged, to everyone's detriment. As a result, offsetting transfers will not always occur even when the son is simply the victim of bad luck. Even those individuals close to the son cannot distinguish perfectly between self-inflicted misfortune and bad luck.

---

[28] The desirability of precommitment requires that not all goods can be redistributed by the benefactor. In the case of the idle son, leisure is the additional good which cannot be transferred. See Assar Lindbeck and Jorges W. Weibull, "Altruism and Time Consistency: The Economics of Fait Accompli," *Journal of Political Economy*, vol. 85 (December 1988), pp. 1165–82.

V. Two-Way Altruism and the Hall of Mirrors

The models used to establish the Argument generally assume that altruism operates in only one direction. John cares about the well-being of Sally, but not vice versa. The results may change if John cares about Sally *and* Sally cares about John. I distinguish between one-way and two-way altruism.

Two-way altruism creates theoretical problems that do not arise with one-way altruism, such as the "Hall of Mirrors" problem. Attempts to resolve the Hall of Mirrors problem require us to reconsider how altruism should be modeled. This in turn, has implications for the Argument. Before returning to the Argument, I first digress and consider different ways of modeling altruistic feelings.

Modeling altruism

When modeling altruism, we face the choice of which objects to place in the domain of the altruists' utility functions. The first possibility, adopted by Barro, Becker, and others, is to place the utility or welfare of one individual in the utility function of another. In this case, the utility function reads:

$$(1) \quad U1 = F\ (C1,\ U2)$$

Under this function, an individual cares about his own level of consumption (C1) and the utility enjoyed by individual two (U2). I refer to this method as "utility evaluation."

A second alternative is to place the consumption bundle of individual two in individual one's utility function. The utility function now reads:

$$(2) \quad U1 = G\ (C1,\ C2)$$

Entering the utility function are the consumption bundle which an individual receives for himself (C1) and the consumption bundle received by the other (C2). I refer to this as "goods evaluation."

These two methods of modeling altruism differ in their implications when we consider two-way altruism. When altruism is two-way, utility evaluation leads to the "Hall of Mirrors" or "benevolence loop" problem.[29] If the utility of individual one depends upon the utility of individual two, and vice versa, these utilities may bounce back and forth and "reflect" each other. John experiences a slight increase in happiness, per-

---

[29] Miles S. Kimball, "Making Sense of Two-Sided Altruism," *Journal of Monetary Economics*, vol. 20 (September 1987), pp. 301–26, uses the phrase "Hall of Mirrors." David Estlund, "Mutual Benevolence and the Theory of Happiness," *Journal of Philosophy*, vol. 87 (April 1990), pp. 187–204, refers to "benevolence loops."

haps because he has just seen a pleasing butterfly. Sally then becomes happier because she knows that John is happier. John is now made even happier, because he knows that Sally is happier, and so on. In similar fashion, John and Sally can also drag each other down into depression.

In some cases, benevolence loops will converge to a finite level of utility for both individuals. But with some utility functions, John and Sally skyrocket to bliss when John spots the butterfly. In this case, the butterfly serves as a perpetual-happiness machine. I see the perpetual-happiness machine as an implausible outcome which a good theory of altruism should rule out.[30]

Miles S. Kimball calculates mathematically which utility functions will lead to convergence. If we restrict utility functions to converging solutions, the Hall of Mirrors problem is less serious. Mathematical restrictions alone, however, are not an adequate solution to the Hall of Mirrors problem.[31]

First, the required restrictions, although plausible, do not appear universal. What happens if individuals do not have utility functions which produce convergence? Under fairly general assumptions, Kimball demonstrates that utility is bounded if the product of Sally's concern for John's total utility (expressed as a weight in proportion to Sally's concern about her own utility) and John's concern for Sally's total utility (expressed in analogous fashion) is less than or equal to the fraction one-half. "Fifty-percent" altruism on both sides, for instance, would lead to a stable solution (0.5 times 0.5 is less than 0.5), although "80-percent" altruism on both sides would not (0.8 times 0.8 is greater than 0.5).[32]

While 50-percent altruism or less on both sides may be more often the rule than the exception, there is nothing to prevent stronger degrees of altruism. It is not unheard of for one individual to give his or her life for another. Yet it is difficult to believe that these individuals are capable of producing a perpetual-happiness machine. The postulation of mathematical restrictions is not a sufficient solution to the Hall of Mirrors problem.

Even when utility converges, we should still be uncomfortable with the implications of the Hall of Mirrors problem. Even if John and Sally do not possess a perpetual-happiness machine in the butterfly, we are double-

---

[30] However, perhaps romantic love is precisely such a perpetual-happiness machine and should be included as a possible case in a theory of altruism.

[31] For the relevant mathematical calculations, see Kimball, "Making Sense of Two-Sided Altruism."

[32] We cannot rely upon the postulate of diminishing marginal utility to promote convergence. The value of additional goods diminishes at the margin, but the value of extra utility need not. The diminishing marginal utility of utility is a meaningful concept for an altruist only if the altruist's concern for the other's utility is inversely related to how happy the other individual is. I may weight your utility as 50 percent of mine if you are miserable, but 20 percent of mine if you are very happy. This kind of weighting promotes convergence, but this does not follow necessarily from the postulate of diminishing marginal utility. Diminishing marginal utility in the traditional sense means only that I attach less importance to subsequent units of wealth that you receive.

counting by allowing utility reflection. When John spots the butterfly, he receives an initial spurt in utility, which gives Sally a spurt of utility, and so on for an infinite number of (converging) reflections. Why should the mathematical utilities produced by each of these reflections represent a real increase in well-being? Are we not double-counting when we consider the eighty-seventh reflection of utility, even when convergence to a finite sum is assured?

Escaping the Hall of Mirrors

We can approach interpersonal dilemmas in rational choice theory by seeing if we can find an intrapersonal analogy for developing our intuitions. At least two different intrapersonal analogies are available for the Hall of Mirrors problem. First, consider John's intertemporal Hall of Mirrors. John derives pleasure from the thought or expectation that his future self will be happy. Similarly, John's future self will derive pleasure from knowing that his earlier self was happy. John's earlier self achieves the benefits of utility reflection because he anticipates the pleasure that his later self will receive, etc.

We can also formulate an atemporal, intrapersonal version of the Hall of Mirrors problem. Consider James, who takes pride in being happy. Should we say that James's utility enters his utility function? Under this approach, a Hall of Mirrors problem results if James sees a pleasing butterfly. The sight of the butterfly increases James's utility, which leads him to be happy for being happy, which in turn makes him happier, etc. If James is sufficiently smug in preferring his own happiness, he may possess a perpetual-happiness machine in the butterfly.

At this point, the reader may suspect that something funny is going on in the Hall of Mirrors problem. Surely it is odd to allow James's utility to enter his utility function. We are double-counting when we use this modeling technique. These intrapersonal analogies focus our attention upon the modeling technique, rather than the issue of altruism. The paradoxes do not arise under the alternative modeling technique which I refer to as "goods evaluation."

The case for goods evaluation

Goods evaluation implies that John's consumption of concrete goods, rather than John's utility, enters Sally's utility function. John's observance of the butterfly is consumption of a good which enters his utility function and Sally's utility function. Sally's utility does not enter John's utility function positively, although Sally's observance of the butterfly does enter John's function positively. Each individual values the other individual's observance of the butterfly, but no reflection occurs. Utility double-counting is avoided, and there is no danger of a perpetual-happiness machine. Altruistic feelings are counted only once.

One might object that the goods-evaluation approach incorrectly specifies the objects of valuation. According to this objection, when John has altruistic feelings for Sally, he does not care about her consumption of particular goods per se, he cares about her well-being. Therefore, it is her well-being, and not her consumption of particular goods and services, that should enter his utility function.

But this argument confuses two different ways of representing what John really cares about. With goods evaluation, what John really cares about is represented by how goods contribute to utility. Assume, for instance, that John enjoys eating cheese and that cheese enters his utility function positively. That John cares about the enjoyment of eating cheese and not cheese per se is represented by the postulate that John prefers more utility to less utility. Writing down a utility function which represents cheese as a source of utility (rather than "the utility of eating cheese" as a source of utility) does not imply that cheese is an end in itself. The postulate that more utility is preferred to less represents utility as the ultimate end of consumption.

Entering "the utility of eating cheese" in the utility function, rather than entering cheese itself, is simply the result of confusion. We have already accounted for the desirable nature of utility; the variables in the utility function represent sources of utility, not ultimate statements about what an individual "really cares about."[33]

The contradiction in the above argument about "what an individual really cares about" becomes more apparent if we take this argument to its logical conclusion. Presumably we should assume that Sally has no preferences for goods per se, but has only preferences for having her preferences satisfied. In this case, only Sally's level of utility should be allowed to enter her utility function. But then Sally's utility is undetermined, like the smile of Lewis Carroll's Cheshire cat.

The implications of goods evaluation

The superiority of goods evaluation over utility evaluation has consequences for the Argument. If we use utility evaluation, Barro's argument about successive intergenerational linkages goes through as stated. I care indirectly about the utilities of my distant descendants, because these utilities enter the utility function of my less distant descendants, etc.

---

[33] The economic theory of revealed preference requires that preferences be defined across observable entities and thus requires goods evaluation. The theory of revealed preference, however, is itself open to question and does not furnish a decisive argument in favor of goods evaluation.

If we use goods evaluation, however, the indirect links across individuals may be broken. Goods evaluation allows a benefactor to care about only parts of a beneficiary's consumption and not the beneficiary's entire utility stream. This distinction may affect the operation of interpersonal linkages.

Consider a model based upon goods evaluation in which Mary is altruistic and her son's consumption of goods enters her utility function. Her son (George) cares about the natives of Bangladesh, and Bangladeshi consumption of goods enters George's utility function.

Under goods evaluation (in contrast with utility evaluation), these relations do not necessarily imply a linkage between Mary and the Bangladeshis. Mary cares about George's consumption, but she does not care about George's consumption unconditionally. She cares that George receives $200,000 worth of consumption opportunities in addition to his lifetime wages, but she will not compensate George if he gives this money away to strangers. That is, what Mary cares about is that George has $200,000 to spend or invest as he sees fit. "George receiving $200,000 worth of opportunity," rather than George's utility, is the good which enters her utility function.

The absence of a link between Mary and the Bangladeshis can be illustrated by the following case. Assume that Mary gives George $200,000 worth of opportunity through a gift or bequest. George cares about the fate of Bangladesh, but Mary does not. The government now decreases foreign aid to Bangladesh and decreases Mary's taxes. Mary is wealthier, but suffering in Bangladesh increases, which causes George to give away one hundred dollars of his bequest. Mary, however, does not feel compelled to increase George's bequest by one hundred dollars. She has already given George access to the consumption bundle that she wished to provide him. George's unwillingness to spend this money on his own self-interest (narrowly defined) will not prompt additional transfers.

Goods evaluation allows for distinctions between different kinds of altruism, whereas utility evaluation does not. Under utility evaluation, Mary is concerned with restoring George's utility level after the cyclone in Bangladesh hits. In contrast, goods evaluation focuses upon the opportunities that George receives. Mary is concerned primarily with George's opportunity set. Mary has already provided George with the appropriate opportunity set and does not adjust her gifts in response to George's charitable donation. Similarly, Mary may not increase her gift if George loses the money gambling.

Benefactor preferences about how their gifts are used can be called paternalistic altruism. A benefactor cares about a beneficiary, but the benefactor also makes independent judgments about how the beneficiary should spend his or her money. These independent judgments can break altruistic chains across individuals.

Our intuitions support the conclusion that effective altruistic chains are usually not very lengthy. We observe charity telethons for those who are handicapped, but we do not observe charity telethons for those who have contributed to the handicapped. Paternalistic altruism explains the difference between these two cases. We do not feel a need to compensate individuals when they spend their money as they see fit.

One might argue that paternalistic altruism is not true altruism, but I regard this argument as semantic rather than substantive. Consider parents who care for their daughter, but care only for their daughter's self-regarding preferences. In this sense, the parents are paternalistic. They value the outcome which coincides with their daughter's self-interest, narrowly defined, rather than the outcome that their daughter prefers. If a daughter incurs great sacrifices to accommodate her spouse, her parents may find this distressing, even if the daughter makes such sacrifices willingly. Altruistic parents would still prefer that their daughter did not make these sacrifices. These parents would rather see the daughter serve her self-interest. In this sense the parents are paternalistic. But I would still call these parents altruistic.

The use of goods evaluation does not rule out the Argument. Our preferences about the goods consumed by those we care about need not be characterized by paternalistic altruism, for instance; in this case, the Argument may still hold. But goods evaluation avoids the conclusion that the Argument necessarily holds. Similarly, goods evaluation avoids the Hall of Mirrors paradox. For these reasons, goods evaluation is a promising approach to thinking about altruism.

VI. CONCLUDING REMARKS

The Argument from Offsetting Transfers teaches us that altruism is complex and multifaceted. Operationally meaningful distinctions exist among direct altruism, indirect altruism through chains of caring, multi-link altruism, precommitment altruism, one-way versus two-way altruism, goods evaluation versus utility evaluation, and paternalistic altruism. The kind of altruism which exists will influence the effects of this altruism upon the distribution of wealth. We should not analyze altruism in purely general terms without considering these (and other) distinctions.

The distinctions I consider suggest that altruism is a relatively weak force in determining the distribution of wealth. I am not arguing that altruistic feelings are weak or rare, but rather that these feelings frequently have little influence. We have altruistic preferences for a particular distribution of wealth. But when matched against government policy or the forces of nature, altruism is a relatively weak opponent, even when altruism is strong in intensity. Even relatively simple redistributions of wealth cannot be offset automatically by changes in private-sector transfers.

We might consider the ineffectiveness of altruism either good news or bad news. If we think that government-engineered wealth redistributions are desirable, but that private-sector altruism is weak or rare, we may consider the ineffectiveness of offsetting transfers desirable. Ineffective private-sector preferences about the distribution of wealth would give government considerable license to implement a superior outcome.

In contrast, we may believe that the altruistic preferences of the private sector are a better guide to the distribution of wealth than government policies. Government, for instance, might be less altruistic than the private sector. In this case, we may regret the relative ineffectiveness of private offsetting transfers. Governments then have the license to change the distribution of wealth for the worse, and the private sector cannot undo these effects.

In either case, however, analysis of the Argument illustrates the common gap between intentions and results. The presence of benevolent feelings does not remove this gap and may even worsen it. The results which our altruistic tendencies prompt us to implement, whether through government or through offsetting private transfers, are not always the results we get.

Economics, George Mason University

INDEX